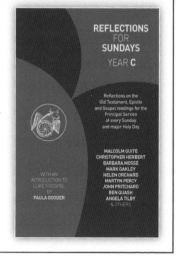

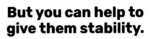

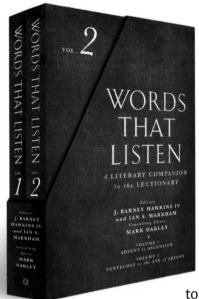

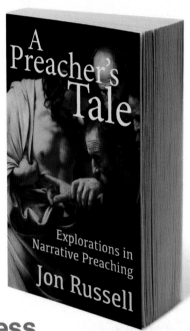

10 CHURCH TIMES
reasons to subscribe

1. Informed, independent and fair reporting

2. Lively debate on current affairs

3. Not one, not two, not three, but FOUR cartoonists

4. In-depth exploration of life with a faith perspective

5. Biblical insights to deepen your faith

6. Interviews with key figures in the church and public life

7. The most comprehensive weekly review of Christian books anywhere

8. Professional support for all who work in the church – and an extensive jobs board

9. 150 years of news and comment in the Church Times digital archive

10. A place where your views are heard

In print
Online
App
Podcast

www.churchtimes.co.uk

The Canterbury Preacher's Companion 2019

This book is also available on Kindle

The
Canterbury Preacher's
Companion 2019

Sermons for Sundays, Holy Days,
Festivals and Special Occasions
Year C

Edited by Roger Spiller

CANTERBURY
PRESS
Norwich

© The Contributors, 2018

First published in 2018 by the Canterbury Press Norwich
Editorial office,
3rd Floor, Invicta House
108–114 Golden Lane,
London ECIY OTG, UK
www.canterburypress.co.uk

Canterbury Press is an imprint of Hymns Ancient & Modern Ltd
(a registered charity)

Hymns Ancient & Modern® is a registered trademark of
Hymns Ancient & Modern Ltd
13A Hellesdon Park Road, Norwich,
Norfolk NR6 5DR, UK

British Library Cataloguing in Publication data

A catalogue record for this book is available
from the British Library

978 1 78622 082 0

Typeset by Manila Typesetting Company

Printed and bound by CPI Group (UK) Ltd, Croydon, CRO 4YY

Contents

ix

Preface

It is a privilege and delight to have the opportunity to take over from the late Michael Counsell in editing *The Canterbury Preacher's Companion*. I will not emulate him and write all the sermons myself, but will draw on other preachers who offer different styles, traditions and specialisms.

Preaching has been a major influence on my life from my early years and I have been fortunate to have encountered fine preachers. The most influential was Canon Bryan Green, once Rector of Birmingham, a huge personality, brilliant debater with indefatigable energy, who was widely known through television and press, books and articles. He had a lively wit and enjoyed controversy. Bryan was also an international evangelist, who travelled extensively, particularly in North America, with a typically punishing itinerary. He began as a definite evangelical but was open to liberal, catholic and charismatic influences, always with an evangelistic gospel that faced all the difficulties while rooted in the offer of a personal relationship with Jesus Christ. It was Bryan who, with his friend Donald (later Archbishop) Coggan, founded the College of Preachers.

After seven years gaining experience in industry in Birmingham, I went to Durham University where C. K. Barrett was the illustrious New Testament scholar. He taught me that we must follow the biblical text where it leads and not try to force it into a predetermined theological perspective. Barrett was also an inspired preacher, who spent his Sundays taking services in small mining churches around Durham. I served as a curate at Bradford Cathedral whose Provost (Dean) Alan Cooper was brought to faith by Bryan. At the Cathedral I got to know Frank Sargeant, later Bishop of Stockport and Lambeth, who demonstrated the importance of adult education, which in the preaching context aspires to equip preachers to enable our hearers to be active learners in the preaching event. It was Frank, I was to learn more recently, who proposed me as a

Fellow of the College of Preachers in 1996. That has resulted in some of the most rewarding and exciting days leading workshops and seminars across the country. After further studies at Cambridge and a hugely formative semester at the Ecumenical Institute at Bossey outside Geneva, I served as a minister at Stratford upon Avon and then Chilvers Coton, Nuneaton. I was involved in theological education for seven years as Principal of the Church of England's national pre-theological course, Aston, and then became Director of Ministry and DDO for Coventry Diocese. A few years ago I became Vice Chair of the College of Preachers and, during a challenging period for the College, we secured a partnership with Hymns A and M that will enable us together to provide a full range of resources for preaching: *The Preacher*, workshops, festivals of preaching and books on preaching.

I remain committed to making preaching an eventful encounter, able to show its capacity to address contemporary issues and excite people with the gospel. Preaching creates my own learning study programme and drives me to revisit and rethink the message of the Bible. Preaching has kept my faith alive and fresh and fed my own relationship with God in Christ. I believe that God has chosen the folly of preaching to bring his wayward people back to himself.

I hope the sermons will serve that great purpose. This has been a hectic initiation into the business of editing, not to speak of the mysteries of the lectionary, but I would like to acknowledge the contribution of my long-suffering wife Penny who has tolerated my lengthy periods of withdrawal, discharged me from household duties, and been an unfailing encourager and perceptive and wise conversation partner. The mistakes, as they say, are mine.

Roger Spiller

Eventful Preaching

The expectation on preachers has grown recently in the aftermath of 'that sermon'. It was unimaginable that a sermon, especially one given in the decorous setting of a royal wedding, could 'blow the place apart', 'steal the show', and be the main talking point in the press and on television. True, the preacher was a charismatic figure, but it wasn't just the delivery that was recognized to be the source of its power. 'Delivery and content were woven together,' as the *Church Times* editorial expressed it. 'A powerful and influential congregation . . . was assumed to collude with a world vision that put God's love at the heart of everything.' The preaching wistfully invited all who heard it to imagine, entertain and feel the compulsion of God's alternative world view. Even the seasoned political journalist Nick Robinson reported that 'the earth is still moving from that sermon'.

For preachers this should inspire us to take stock of our own preaching and to 'raise our game', so that our own discernment, preparation and delivery, 'in the power of the Spirit', can enable our hearers to entertain and inhabit that glorious alternative gospel lifestyle. I try, in the comments that follow, to set out some of the immediate issues we might consider, both in the preparatory stage of discerning the word, and then in communicating it in the preaching.

Discerning the word

Why do we need to 'discern the word'? Don't we, instead, need to reach for our Bible, look up the set passage and, with the aid of commentaries, find a theme, breathe a sigh of relief and begin to compile a sermon? The objection to that is that preaching is the opportunity we create for God to speak, to have his say, and to address his confused and tormented people. For this reason, the New Testament sometimes calls preaching 'the word of God', no less than Scripture. Preaching, then, has to be more than retrieving a message from some ancient texts. It is intended to be a concrete, personal, particular, time-bound, eventful address that generates a human–divine encounter. If preaching is merely descriptive or informative, rather than an encounter, it lacks the efficacy to bring about change and transformation. It has, then, first to captivate the preacher with its newness, and to be received as fresh bread, a new word from God.

Preaching is always more than a few thoughts on a Bible passage, more than teaching (although some information may be needed to support the preaching), and more than a set piece, a crafted script awaiting delivery. Busy preachers look at texts, hoping to find something they can say, to get them off the hermeneutical hook, and ensure they're not exposed when they stand up to preach. But finding something to say is not the same as having something you simply have to say. Preachers like Bishop Curry convey authenticity and conviction because they have become captive to a person whose grace and love has simply to be declared.

If we are to discern the word of God, we have to attend to three 'sources': *gospel*, *Bible* and *context*. These are the three interconnected sources through which we try to discern the word to preach. Without Scripture our message risks becoming free-floating; without gospel, our message would be dense and unclear; and without context, our message would lack immediacy and particularity. If preaching is to be eventful, we have to answer to all three potential conduits of God's word. It's rightly said that preachers do well to spend as much time exegeting their context, the culture and background of their hearers, as they do on Scripture. But the preparation is only concluded when, in the prolonged interaction between gospel, Bible and context, we discern a clear, fresh, thrilling word that we feel emboldened to try to proclaim.

Gospel

'Biblical preaching preaches the Gospel and uses the Bible, it does not preach the Bible and use the Gospel,' so said the theologian P. T. Forsyth.[1] This is surely faithful to the New Testament, where the subject of preaching is always 'the kingdom' or 'Jesus'. The earliest Christian preachers didn't preach on texts, they preached Christ. Lectionary-based sermons that seek to explain and analyse whole chunks of texts, moving from line to line, trying to recover ancient meanings, can suffocate the summons of the gospel. The Bible, or, more accurately, the way we use the Bible, can get in the way of the gospel. The gospel is good news, and if it is news, it is new, fresh, contemporary and concrete. The gospel has a formal content without being a mere formula; its subject is Jesus Christ and his kingdom; but it's not simply a message, not even a message from God, however stupendous that must be. The gospel is God in Christ's direct encounter with human beings and their experiences. No one could doubt the theme of Curry's sermon. We heard the refrain again and again, and, moreover, we felt its force, its relational and transformative intent. Even avowed unbelievers acknowledged that they had been inextricably drawn to contemplate a world transfigured by grace and love.

Bible

If the gospel brings focus, the Bible brings depth. There are those of whom it is said they never let the Bible get in the way of the gospel! But without the rich grain of Scripture, the gospel can sound formulaic and generalized. Without engagement with the Bible we can sit light to the diverse contexts offered in Scripture. These give us new and varied perspectives by which we can discover the way the gospel addresses diverse human conditions and experiences, and creates new genres and images to express it. Without the panoramic perspective of the Bible, we are unable to place ourselves within the overarching story of God's relationship with his people down the centuries.

Mark Twain's comment deserves to be recalled every time we read the passage of Scripture for preaching: 'It ain't those parts of the Bible that I can't understand that bother me, it's the parts that I do understand.' The parts we can't understand force us to mine and dig and struggle with a text that won't give up its meaning without a struggle, but the effort will be rewarded when new treasure is discovered and we are reeling with excitement and inspiration. Besides, the Bible is a strange book, whose obscure and hard texts serve to show the strangeness of God.

The Bible offers a wide range of approaches for the preacher to take. The Bible is a *resource*, for construing what Old Testament scholar Walter Brueggemann regards as an artistic, poetic and truthful alternative description to the prevailing fixed, fated, dominant world view. The biblical language offers poetic language to enable us to inhabit imaginatively the world of God's promises.

The Bible is a *story*, the classic, master-story of the human history of God, and it invites us to find our place in God's story.

But conversely, the Bible's story illuminates and offers paradigms by which the preacher can help to interpret the little stories of our human lives in the light of Christ and the ultimate purposes of God.

The Bible is also a *witness*, a compilation of witnesses who over vast timescales and diverse geographical areas attest the activities they attribute to the action and agency of God where that was particularly transparent and immediate.

The Bible is a *literary genre*, including story, poetry, history, lament, argument, letters, love songs. It serves to remind the preacher that form is intrinsic to the content of preaching. It must be consonant with the message of the gospel and, by the variety of its shapes and forms, ensure that preaching exemplifies the surprise of the gospel.

If the gospel is the subject of preaching, it will be evident that there is no need to start with the Bible. Starting with issues, experiences, questions that are preoccupying our hearers can show that the gospel interacts with and transforms the realities of our existing lives. On the other hand, if the gospel is scaled down to meeting human needs without effecting transformation it loses faith with the thrust of Scripture. By contrast, starting from the Bible relocates us from our own self-preoccupations into the radical, alternative world of the gospel, helped by the poetic, imaginative and narrative content of Scripture. Preaching that starts from a Bible passage will be sure to raise the questions, issues and problems that might be provoked by the hearers, but in competing for attention it must also attempt to indicate why this text matters, and what the congregation will miss if they neglect to hear what is being said. The preaching is emphatically not a Bible study, nor a teaching session. It is the good news of the gospel enriched by the imagery, arguments and narrative of Scripture.

Context

The preaching we find in the New Testament is always situational. The language of the gospel is shaped by the questions, experiences and wider events with which the audience is consumed. Context, then, denotes hearers, congregation and the wider cultural life, both local and global, in which our hearers live and have their being. What is the good news that I must bring to them *today*? What, if anything, is different about *today*? When in parish ministry and struggling to prepare a sermon, I learnt that it was often better to spend the time making one or two home visits. It made me think about the language, the ideas, the concerns, the stage of faith development of the people. I often found that by the time I returned I had discerned the gospel. It is people who give us our sermons.

Conclusion

The process of discernment is an exercise not in finding something to say but in discerning what needs to be said and what God may be wishing us to say to a particular people. There must, of course, be space for prayer, listening and reflection. You may well be asking how hard-pressed lay or clerical preachers have time for extended preparation, especially when they have a line-up of sermons to deliver as long as planes waiting to take off after a long delay. I found it beneficial, when in parish ministry and preaching very regularly, to read through all the biblical readings for all the preaching sessions I knew I would be expected to deliver, making notes on, or mind mapping, each of the sets of readings on a separate page for each sermon, with brief initial thoughts. Sometimes, too, convening a meeting with other preachers to read forthcoming lectionary readings began the long chain of discernment. Like a large stone gathering moss, the initial effort triggered the mind to find, connect, recall ideas and experiences that might be germane to the preaching process.

Paul Scott Wilson, the leading American homilitician, has commented that sermons that are prepared at the last minute are, at best, likely to be informational, while sermons that were started in good time are more likely to be transformational. Sermons, like seeds, take time to germinate and early planting often produces better results.

Preaching as performance

Sermons are black notes on a page; sermons don't preach – it's the preacher who preaches. The preacher is part of the message he or she declares. Are we there to describe a past event or to perform a script so that it becomes a new event? Reviewing a performance of Simon Rattle's Mahler Second Symphony some years ago, the reviewer said that last night 'we didn't have a performance of the *Resurrection Symphony*; the resurrection itself happened last night at Symphony Hall'. Yes, it did for me also. Preaching, too, is performance. 'We do not merely preach the kingdom, but through the preaching we bring it about,' said Norman Perrin.

We preachers don't need the athletic spins and turns of the American, Michael Curry. But neither do we need to keep our bodies and face muscles as still as if we were rehearsing for the part of a dead body in a murder mystery. When we have good news to tell, about an engagement, a new job, the birth of a child, some achievement, we don't need to read it out of a script we prepared earlier. I'm sometimes suspicious when the preacher doesn't have notes or a script. But I'm more disturbed if the preacher cannot voice a couple of sentences without needing to check their script. In any case, it's perfectly possible to train ourselves to follow a script without losing eye contact. Politicians know the value of persistent eye contact and space out a few large-print sentences to a page and learn to turn (small) pages unobtrusively. It may be that if sentences are too long or intricate to be remembered, they are also too long to be preached.

Preachers, by the quality of their embodiment, their at-one-ness with the message they bring, convey the authenticity, trustworthiness and credibility vital for eventful preaching. Theatrics don't suit all people. We have only to be comfortable in our own skin to be authentic, but, like Michael Curry, captive to the message we're dying to relate. A finely crafted sermon may be self-defeating, undeliverable. It may only reach our heads and leave our hearts unmoved. It may be so perfect that our only response can be admiration, but it won't have room for us. John Constable said he painted trees always with spaces for the birds to fly through. Preaching, too, must have spaces, gaps the size of an Emmental cheese, so that our hearers can engage in the event. And if that makes preachers feel vulnerable, that, too, embodies the fearsome vocation that we've been called to discharge.

Introduction

Most of the sermons in this compilation have been written for this publication but some have been reprinted from *The Preacher*. I have tried to contact all those whose sermons are included, but offer my apologies if any have slipped under the radar. Sermons are written to be spoken, even though we do not expect they will be used as they are. To avoid interrupting the oral flow, all but essential references have been omitted. Most smaller quotations will be indicated by quotation marks but will not be acknowledged by name, and doubtless some filching of phrases will not be attributed, supposing their source is known.

Preaching is more than a sermon. It is an embodied, living communication that brings black marks on a page to life. Printed sermons cannot, of course, replicate this, but when we feel dry or uncertain about a Scripture passage, a written sermon can be a provocateur, or conversational partner to stimulate our own sermon preparation. Preaching is also a representative activity by which the Church is speaking on our behalf, and so attending to other preaching voices can add to the representative character of preaching as well as warning us off any idiosyncratic interpretations of biblical texts.

The hymns suggested for each of the sermons can all be sourced from Google and are mostly found in half a dozen of the most-used hymn books. Some trouble has been taken to choose hymns that really do connect with and reinforce the message of the sermon. Sifting through hymns, I have been surprised by the abundance of new hymns free of the cloying and stylized language of some older hymns and which have a freshness and directness that can speak to our more sceptical generation.

Contributors

The Revd Ally Barrett is Tutor of the Westcott House Foundation in Cambridge. As Pastoral Tutor to the college, she was external tutor for All Age Worship. She was a priest in a parish in the Ely Diocese.

The Rt Revd Michael Baughen, former Bishop of Chester, is a musician and hymn writer and compiler of *Mission Praise* (Marshall Pickering).

The Revd Darren Blaney has been a Baptist pastor for 25 years and currently serves in Herne Bay.

The Revd Dr Kate Bruce is an RAF chaplain and Visiting Fellow of St John's College, Durham. She is the author of *Igniting the Heart* (SCM Press) on preaching and imagination.

The Revd David Bunyan was a minister in the Scottish Episcopal Church in the west of the Edinburgh Diocese. He is now retired.

The Revd Canon Dr Christopher Burkett is Director of Ministry for Chester Diocese; he is editor of *The Preacher* and a sociologist.

The Rt Revd Stephen Cottrell, Bishop of Chelmsford, is President of the College of Preachers and a writer.

The Revd Dr Megan Daffern is Chaplain at Jesus College, Oxford, and a lecturer in the Faculty of Theology and Religion, University of Oxford. She combines pastoral and academic work in her ministry, and is passionate about communicating the Bible to a wide audience. She is married to Adrian, Vicar of Great St Mary's, the University Church, Cambridge.

Anne Davidson Lund, is a Reader in the benefice of three Anglican parishes in rural Cheshire.

The Revd Dr Susan Durber is Minister of Taunton United Reformed Church and Moderator of the Faith and Order Commission of the World Council of Churches. She speaks and publishes about preaching, including *Preaching Like a Woman* (SPCK, 2007).

The Rt Revd Dr Christopher Herbert, former Bishop of St Albans and currently a Trustee of the Royal Hospital for Neuro-disability, Putney, is a lecturer for the Arts Society and Visiting Professor of Christian Ethics in the University of Surrey.

Canon Robert Hill, a priest in the Roman Catholic Archdiocese of Glasgow, is Honorary Teaching Fellow of the University of Glasgow and occasional presenter of 'Thought for the Day' on BBC Radio Scotland.

The Revd Ann Jack is a retired United Reformed Church minister and former contributer to *The Preacher.*

Paul Johns, a Methodist local preacher, is also a former Director of the College of Preachers, currently working on community developments in Srebrenica, Bosnia.

The Revd Dr Victoria Johnson is a residentiary canon at Ely Cathedral and a tutor for the College of Preachers. She studied homiletics at Yale Divinity School and teaches preaching to those training for ministry.

Diana Jones is a Reader in her Anglican home parish in Nottinghamshire. Her MTh focused on fist-person preaching. She mentors trainee Readers in the diocese and works as a tutor for the College of Preachers.

The Revd Dr Wendy Kilworth-Mason, is a Methodist presbyter and a former theological tutor and mission partner with an interest in preaching the Old Testament.

The Revd Dr Bandy Long is Professor Emeritus of Preaching in the USA and author of books on preaching and pastoral care.

Duncan Macpherson is a Roman Catholic Permanent Deacon in the Diocese of Westminster. He taught in the theology department at St Mary's University, Twickenham, for more than 35 years. He holds a Doctor of Ministry degree in preaching from the Aquinas Institute in St Louis Missouri. He has written several books on preaching, and is a tutor of the College of Preachers and features editor of *The Preacher*.

The Revd Canon Michael McAdam, now retired, was a school chaplain, Chaplain to the Bishop of London and served in parish ministry.

The Rt Revd Dr Gordon Mursell, former Dean of Birmingham, and then Bishop of Stafford until he retired, is the author of *English Spirituality* (2001) and other books.

Anne Peat, an Anglican Reader for 32 years, and a Methodist local preacher, served in three parishes in the St Alban's Diocese. She is a former teacher and was a finalist in *The Times* Preacher of the Year Award in 1996.

The Revd Dr John Pridmore was Vicar of Hackney until his retirement. He was also a regular columnist with the *Church Times* and a lecturer at Ridley Hall, Cambridge. One of his specialisms was the place of children in the Church.

The Very Revd Michael Sadgrove retired as Dean of Durham in 2015. He has been a parish priest and theological educator, and served in Coventry and Sheffield Cathedrals before going to Durham. He lives in Northumberland.

The Revd Canon Roger Spiller, is Chair of Trustees of the College of Preachers and convenor of tutors. He was Director of Ministry for Coventry Diocese and a theological educator. He is Chair of the UK Bossy (Ecumenical Institute), Geneva.

The Revd Barbara Steele-Perkins is a priest and part-time priest-in-charge in Grayswood, Surrey. She was originally a primary school teacher, and has also been involved in training people for ordained and lay ministry.

Fr Terry Tastard is a priest in the Diocese of Westminster, with a parish in North London. He is a contributor to *The Preacher*.

The Revd Brett Ward is a parish priest in Eltham, in the Anglican Diocese of Southwark. He holds an MTh in preaching from the College of Preachers and is a sermon commissioner for *The Preacher*.

The Revd Catherine Williams is an Anglican priest working as a National Adviser for Selection for the Ministry Division of the Archbishops' Council. She is licensed to the Bishop of Gloucester as a public preacher.

The Revd Dr Stephen Wright is Vice-Principal and Academic Director, Spurgeon's College, London. He is a former Director of the College of Preachers and the author of a number of books on preaching

YEAR C, the Year of Luke

(Year C begins on Advent Sunday in 2018, 2021, 2024, etc.)

Advent

First Sunday of Advent   2 December
Principal Service   **Living into the Future**
Jer. 33.14–16; Ps. 25.1–9; 1 Thess. 3.9–end; **Luke 21.25–36**

Christmas can't come too soon for some people. The decorations
come out and the bling and lighted Father Christmases, snowmen
and Christmas tree lights are displayed. And hearty Christmas carols are played in large shops. But for Christians it's the season of
Advent, right up to Christmas Eve. And there can be no better way
of entering into the marvel of Christ's coming and living with God's
promises for our future than a prayerful, purposeful Advent.

Future orientation

It's often been observed that one of the characteristics of men and
women today is that we live for the future, project ourselves into
a future that does not yet exist. We're affected by the realization
that we're outgrowing our present condition and being thrust into
a new era. Our political structures no longer seem adequate, the
post-war consensus is collapsing, new threats to the ecology of the
planet are facing us, and millions of our fellow humans are victims
of corruption, abuse, violence, barbarism and homelessness. We are
inevitably living into the future and no longer just in the memory of
the past. It will not then come as quite such a surprise when Advent
keeps our eyes focused on the future, God's ultimate future.

A disturbing text

We were confronted by a bizarre, disturbing Gospel reading this
morning, reminiscent of a description of a Hollywood horror movie
film set. It's a genre known as apocalyptic, a kind of lifting of the
veil into a strange future. It gives us a glimpse of cataclysmic events
determined by supernatural forces interspersed with practical,
mundane advice, such as routes of escape when disaster strikes. It's

2

a pastiche of Old Testament prophecies, reminiscences of the siege of Jerusalem 600 years before Christ, and possibly also echoes the destruction of Jerusalem in AD 70. In the same vein, we have the promise of the return of the Son of Man in a cloud of glory.

That dramatic, interventionist, other-worldly perspective sits alongside the much more usual gradualist, this-worldly, developmental way in which God's kingdom normally operates. It's a bit like the tension between elective surgery that has been planned by us and emergency surgery that is sudden and dramatic and overtakes us when we least expect it. This strange text is telling us that the world will not be left alone to run its course; the kingdom will be realized, and its king will reign. We live between God's promise and its fulfilment. Or rather, we live from the fulfilment of God's former promise in confidence of the fulfilment of the promise made to us in today's Gospel reading.

Isn't it more reliable to extrapolate from the present that we know into a new future than to imagine a new future when everything contradicts it? The past may seem a more reliable basis than the future. But is it really safe to rely on extrapolations and computer modelling from the past? Are the predictions of the bank rate, inflation level, GDP, the future growth rate, reliable?

Charles Smith, once president of an international firm of management consultants, says change is limited by people's current beliefs about what is possible ... changing people's beliefs about the future can produce extraordinary improvements in their performance. He calls this the 'Merlin Factor' after the legendary magician, who was able to construct the present because he came from the future, he lived 'backwards in time', inspired by a future far beyond what the current scene might suggest.

Truthworthy promises?

Jeremiah was writing in the midst of the carnage and destruction of Jerusalem and the occupation of the country of Judaea. The city looked like a forest all of whose trees had been cut down and removed by overenthusiastic loggers. Nothing was left except a nation of stumps. And into this devastation Jeremiah tells us that a branch, a 'righteous Branch will spring up for David'. It must have seemed like clutching at straws.

Shortly we will be celebrating the fulfilment of that promise, that a mere branch has become Jesus the Lord and King. 'Jewish history is filled with miraculous deliverances' – so wrote the historian Simon Sebag Montefiore. As a historian, he's supposed to explain them but all he can do is stand back amazed and acknowledge their true source. 'The promises of God', says Karl Barth, 'are surrounded by the things that contradict them.' We're promised life in a culture of death, light in a world of darkness, hope in a sea of despair. We can't prove the promises of God, but if you live them then you'll find they're true.

Living backwards

We're often told in Advent to wait; to wait for the return of Jesus. But I'm not sure that we are expected simply to go on waiting, certainly not passively, as if life is on hold. Our text suggests it is not so much waiting as a 'spiritual wakefulness' that we need to nurture. It's living in the future of God's promises. We can be captive to the past, even by the doubtful idea that everything has to follow some predetermined divine plan. This can impede us from living in the daring newness of God's future; the God who is always going on ahead of us.

So Advent calls us to live life backwards, from the future God, the God of resurrection who promises to 'make all things new'. And so we lift up our heads and think of God's promise, because we know the One who is coming is the One in whom we already place our trust. What a way to begin the Church's New Year!

Roger Spiller

Hymn suggestions

Sing my song backwards, from end to beginning; Standing on the promises; When all thy mercies, O My God; Lord for the years, your love had kept and guided.

First Sunday of Advent   2 December
Second Service   **The Grapes of Wrath**
Ps. 9 [*or* 9.1–8]; Joel 3.9–end; **Rev. 14.13—15.4**

Forget about Christmas trees, baubles and *The Snowman* played in a thousand shops while we are at worship this morning. This is more the grim world of John Steinbeck's dust bowl. Prepare to be startled, even shocked. Here is Advent in all its seriousness and with the blood flowing freely: death, judgement and hell, laid out for us in two magnificent but perplexing readings.

The book of Revelation is better called the Apocalypse. It means the unveiling of what is hidden, kept under wraps until the time is right. It is a familiar genre in the Scripture. In each case what is 'unveiled' is secret knowledge about the future. But not just any future. Apocalypse concerns the specific future of the people of God: Israel in the Old Testament, the Christian Church in the New. Ask yourself when the future matters most to us. The answer may be, when it is uncertain, when we have reason to be afraid of it. Apocalypse comes into its own when life is frightening and fragile, threatened by nuclear holocaust, global warming, terrorism, or, more personally, terminal illness, death, bereavement. At times like these we want to know whether we shall survive, still be here tomorrow. To the apocalyptic writers, the threat that promised to overwhelm their communities was persecution. These books are meant to open up a future that puts a question against pain, suffering and mortality. By affirming that it lay in God's hands, it aimed to bring strength and hope to the persecuted and afraid.

Judgement

With that background, what do we make of this tough text? We can at least understand why it has been chosen for Advent Sunday. This season is meant to turn our minds towards the future that is coming upon the world, what theologians call eschatology. Today we begin this Advent journey by considering the grand sweep of the eternal purpose for the cosmos, for our world, for humankind and for ourselves personally. This passage faces us with the unwelcome but inescapable fact of divine judgement. I spoke earlier about crisis. It literally means 'judgement', which is, when we think about it, what every crisis presents us with: a judgement on how we shall respond, what our motives will be, whether the easy speeches about loyalty, goodness, obedience and trust that we make in good times will still be on our lips when things become almost unendurably hard.

The image of judgement is the ripened harvest. It is reaped by the Son of Man with a golden crown and a sharp sickle in his hand. The picture is borrowed from our Old Testament lesson in Joel. The wicked of the earth are always a preoccupation of apocalyptic where they are contrasted to the remnant of the righteous few. The bloodbath that occurs when the terrible sickle is wielded is likened to the harvested grapes that are thrown into the great winepress of the wrath of God. There comes a day when evil is openly named for what it is, when, in the imagery of our passage, the Warrior gathers

5

the nations to claim his victory and a river of blood spreads its crimson stain across the land. You can see how this image would comfort those undergoing fierce persecution. Those with no hope whatsoever in this world could only throw themselves on the mercy of God to intervene spectacularly, wind up history, banish wickedness to its place and redeem the faithful. The redeemed could then look forward to resurrection and immortality, singing Moses' song of liberated slaves that we heard at the end of the reading from Revelation.

The essence of judgement

But there is another dimension enfolded in this Christian apocalypse; we could miss it if we did not look for it. 'The wine-press was trodden outside the city,' says the seer. We know from the New Testament that the shedding of blood 'without a city wall' carries a deep significance. For blood that is shed in that place proves to be not only judgement upon evil but also the redemption of the world. The cross turns out to be the work of Love where love conquers all things. At the end of Revelation, the river of blood that issues from the place of the skull is transformed into a river of the water of life that flows from the throne of God and of the Lamb. The essence of judgement is revealed. When 'the wounded surgeon plies the steel', the sickle that cuts into our flesh and bone hurts. It exposes all that needs to be cut out if the body is to live, for the pain of judgement purifies us from the cancerous corruption that threatens to destroy us. But it saves us from ourselves.

Discipline

If we are serious about Advent, this purifying of aspiration and motive is a good task to set ourselves: not as an effort or a work but as a God-given discipline or ascesis. It will prise us open more and more to God's generous, forgiving grace. It will help us to see clearly, mend our broken spirits, strengthen us to become holy and wise once more. Love was, love is always, his meaning. I am not going to tell you in Advent 2018 that this theme of judgement no longer matters. It does, as anyone who knows the fallibility and corruption latent in the human heart knows well. So at the core of our Advent longing, before we get to the manger of Bethlehem, must be the realization that God must act in judgement to root out evil and vindicate whatever is true and honourable and just and pure.

'In wrath remember mercy.' Whatever we read in the law and the prophets, in wisdom and apocalyptic, is summed up simply in this:

'thy kingdom come, thy will be done on earth as it is in heaven'. That is the clue to the heart-work we must do in Advent, Love's work that God does in us at every moment. Don't linger on the intoxicating images of Revelation. Simply pray the Lord's Prayer each day. And add this: 'Amen. Come Lord Jesus!'

Michael Sadgrove

Hymn suggestions

Come and see the shining hope that Christ's apostles saw; There is a fountain filled with blood; River, wash over me; Great and wonderful are your deeds.

Second Sunday of Advent   9 December
Principal Service   The Intrusive Word
Bar. 5, *or* Mal. 3.1–4; *Canticle*: Benedictus; Phil. 1.3–11; **Luke 3.1–6**

God speaks

If in Advent we enter into the hope that lies before us, we do so because of our confidence in the God who has already addressed us. He has spoken to us definitively in the person of Jesus Christ. Yet this was heralded by the coming of God's word. 'The word of the Lord came.' Those words announce God's timely interventions across the long and tortuous history of his chosen people Israel. And they do so now this morning on the lips of John the Baptist. So let us explore the fact of God speaking, and leave to next Sunday the contents of John's message.

Sceptics tell us that we're alone, there's nothing beyond us, no 'outsideness', no one but ourselves; religion is a human enterprise designed to construct some meaning to project on to made-up gods as a coping strategy in the face of the nightmare of our cosmic aloneness.

The coming of the Word

'The Word of God came.' That is what stands in the way of and defies the claim that we are left to ourselves. The Word of God is too audacious, too intrusive, too disruptive to be the product of human invention. It overpowers those to whom it comes and when

7

they discharge the Word they are vilified, abused and mocked. John is in the wilderness, in the middle of nowhere, remote from power politics, but the lonely place where God's word was best able to be heard. The Word brings judgement and promise, and turns prose-speakers into prophets, giving them daring, boundary-shattering, imaginative speech that transports its hearers to the alternative kingdom that God is bringing to birth.

The Word addresses our timebound history

We may have been surprised by the lengthy introduction to today's Gospel. No less than seven political and religious leaders are named, and the setting begins in the Roman Empire itself and nar-rows down to Judaea, then to Galilee, and finally to a godforsaken corner of the Jordan wilderness. Religion is a private matter, we're told, best kept to ourselves; it's private opinion and has no place in the public world. But our reading fiercely contests this. The Word of God *is* public truth. The illustrious prophetic forebears of John, notably Moses, Elijah, Samuel, Isaiah, Jeremiah and Ezekiel, were the guardians of the nation's conscience and the uncompromising advisers and power brokers to the nation. Tiberius Caesar, Pilate, Herod, Philip and others were the unwitting bit players in the great drama that God enacted on the world's stage. The Word of God must engage in the cultural and intellectual marketplaces of our world, because God's Word is the only invincible truth there is. For by this Word the heavens were made, and through it God is calling into being his new creation.

God speaks, yes, to be sure, but God can hardly be said to be talkative, or loquacious. Until John's appearance the prophetic voice had been silent for several centuries. God's people had to make do with lawyers and wisdom teachers. And when John appeared, unex-pected, out of nowhere, he rekindled the prophetic ministry, briefly for the last time, and heralded a new dispensation. No longer would the word of God come exclusively through the mouths of prophets. 'In these last days he (God) has spoken to us by a Son,' says the letter to the Hebrews. The Word of God is no longer confined to speech. It's enfleshed, brought down to earth, God's living, incarnate Word. And the Church becomes the guardian of the memory of Jesus. And through the Spirit now poured out on all people, we have the con-tinuity of Jesus' presence with us. So now the prophetic vocation is universalized, democratized if you will, extended to all believers. So where do we find the Word of God addressing us today?

8

'The Word of God that came to John' was fresh, new, contextual, time-limited. Preachers wouldn't be wise to address you today, as John did, as a 'brood of vipers'! But John was also subject to the written word of God as given to his predecessor Isaiah. That word was, and must remain, the reference point for all our thinking and speaking of God. It's our only source for the life of Jesus, for the great story of our salvation, and it's the word whose purpose is to point and bring us to Jesus, God's incarnate Word.

Bringers of God's word today

How does God bring his word to us today? How can the ancient, strange text of the Bible become the immediate, intrusive word of God? How can this text be explained, interpreted and understood for today? God provides the preaching vocation for this purpose. Hence the New Testament calls preaching the 'word of God'. We ministers wouldn't feel comfortable making any such claim for our sermons. Ours is more of a hope and prayer than a claim or promise: 'May I speak in the name of . . .' But we should all take seriously the fact that God has chosen the foolishness of preaching to speak to us afresh. One confessional put it: 'The Preaching of the Word of God is the Word of God.'[2]

'The Word of God came to John.' May it come to us. May it come through the preaching. May it come through the visual word of the Eucharist. And may it come also through our words and witness.

Roger Spiller

Hymn suggestions

Thanks to God whose word was spoken; Jesus, restore to us again the gospel of your holy name; Come, living God when least expected; Advent candles tell their story.

Second Sunday of Advent   9 December
Second Service   **A Herald Voice**
Ps. 75 [76]; Isa. 40.1–11; **Luke 1.1–25**

Just imagine how frustrated Zechariah must have been when he lost his voice. He would have been unable to tell anyone the amazing news that he and Elizabeth, old as they were, would soon welcome a son into the world. He must have been bursting with joy and gladness as the angel had told him he would be. For this child was to be great in the sight of the Lord and make people ready to meet their God. But he was unable, for a time, to proclaim this wonderful message to anyone. His voice had been taken away. He had been silenced because he doubted the power of God. His lips were unable to express the joy in his heart. The people were waiting for Zechariah to come out of the sanctuary and speak, but when he appeared he was silent.

When Zechariah is given his voice back he immediately sings praises to God. He cannot contain the message that God has given him; he has to share this good news. He erupts with thanksgiving and the words tumble from his lips. Through God's good grace he has become a herald and a messenger.

Speaking creation into being

All of our readings touch on this theme. In our psalm, people tell of God's wondrous deeds. If they are to boast, they are to boast only in the Lord. They are to use their voice to glorify God. In the book of the prophet Isaiah we hear those words that also reach forward to the child Zechariah will name John, with the first words he speaks after his temporary silence. This child John will himself embody the voice that cries out in anticipation of the one who is to come. Through his words and his very being, John will testify to the light that is coming into the world, the Word made flesh.

A voice cries out: in the wilderness, prepare the way of the Lord! The word which the Lord has spoken will herald a new creation, valleys shall be lifted up and mountains and hills will be made low. Just as God created the world through speech, his mighty Word is about to leap down from heaven to make all things new. This good news is to be spoken and sung, it is to be shouted from rooftops, sung by the choir, chanted by monks, whispered in corridors. The story is told from people to people and rung from the bells of church, chapel and steeple.

Go forth and tell

Two thousand years later, in a world that has largely forgotten this story and is sometimes impervious to good news, the Church is called again and again to be a herald of this message and to lift up our voice with strength. The Christian Church stands here today because this message has been passed on, and people who have experienced the living God in their lives have found their voice and spoken of his wondrous deeds. St Luke sets out this vision at the very beginning of his Gospel. He wants to share the truth about Christ; he is a messenger of the good news, an evangelist, and we are called to be the same.

We perhaps take our voices for granted and might reflect on what stops us from proclaiming the good news we have been given in Jesus Christ. What stops us from speaking up for the kingdom of God, which is justice, mercy and peace? What is preventing us from being people who speak, or sing, or tell, or teach of God's wondrous deeds and share the faith that is within us?

We are all called to be heralds – to get up metaphorically to a high mountain and proclaim that God does indeed reign. We are to move from the sanctuary as people ready and willing to be messengers and evangelists, that is, those who tell the good news and live it out in our lives that others may see and hear and know that the Lord is near.

There is a lovely prayer that is often used by choristers after they have sung during worship:

Bless, O Lord, us Thy servants who minister in Thy temple;
Grant that what we sing with our lips we may believe in our hearts,
and what we believe in our hearts we may show forth in our lives.

It reminds us that our worship is the place from which we are sent into the world to live out, through thought and deed and word, the truth that we have found in Jesus Christ, telling those who have not yet heard the good news that is for all people.

Victoria Johnson

Hymn suggestions

Hark a herald voice is calling; Hark the glad sound!; Hills of the north rejoice. Go forth and tell, O Church of God awake!

Third Sunday of Advent   16 December
Principal Service   **Time for Savage Pruning**
Zeph. 3.14–end; Isa. 12.2–end, *or* Ps. 146.4–end; Phil. 4.4–7;
Luke 3.7–18

'You brood of vipers! Who warned you to flee from the wrath to come?' – That's no way to address a congregation, however tempting it might be for the preacher to do so from time to time. And, after all, these are people who are serious enough to come for baptism. But John the Baptist wasn't on a charm offensive. A strange, angular, enigmatic figure. A Bob Geldof in a leotard, perhaps. An awkward, uncomfortable presence. There he was, crunching his way through locusts, as if on a Celebrity bushtucker trial. Trained by his austere desert experience to pierce straight through to the heart of an issue and tell it as it is. John is on the edge of society, and things always look clearer from the margins, which is why the desert has often been the breeding ground of prophets.

When John opened his big mouth, the voice of the prophets before him had been silent for several hundred years. Lawyers, not prophets, were in the ascendant, and the legalism that ensued meant that people didn't get too serious, singleminded and passionate about their faith. But now this disturbing Elijah-like figure appears, speaks the harsh, abrasive, lacerating word of crisis to a people whose faith had become routine and who saw baptism as a precautionary insurance policy.

Defusing a sharp assault

The hearers had the predictable strategies for defending themselves against this fierce personal onslaught. 'We have Abraham, as our ancestor.' 'I come from a religious family.' 'My uncle was a church-warden.' 'I was brought up on the Bible.' There's still the view that religion is transmitted by descent, or by proxy, but, as Corrie Ten Boom said, 'God has no grandchildren.'

Of course the people expected judgement, but not for them. They thought they were the exception. They thought they would side-step it so that the Roman occupiers would be first in line for God's wrath. There are always scapegoats that can be found to take the heat off ourselves. But, as John makes clear, judgement starts with the house of God, with the people who think of themselves as the 'insiders'. And that judgement can only be averted through a dramatic national and personal repentance. So John embarks upon a moral crusade. No one escapes the lash of his tongue, his fierce religious indignation. He exposes hypocrisy and double standards. So successfully did he create a mood of utter desperation that people in their occupational groups were crying out, 'What, then, should we do?'

National and personal change

There's a need from time to time for a nation to be brought to its knees – to take stock of its moral and spiritual degeneration, its loss of civility, tolerance, respect, the violence of its public discourse and the spirit in which disagreements and divisions are managed. That time may be now. But we today, who are within earshot of the voice from the desert, must first respond.

And what exactly is it that we are required to do? 'Even now the axe is lying at the root of the tree.' John is calling for some savage pruning of the sort we should perhaps now be beginning to apply to our garden shrubs in order to make way for new growth and fruit. And the pruning has to be particular and concrete and unsettlingly personal. Food, clothing, wages, job satisfaction. General and vague intentions provide cover for deceiving ourselves that we can escape from John's challenge. No, faith has to be worked out in every minute particular. I don't know quite why it's so important to my wife that I should leave no used clothes lying about. But it means far more to her than I can imagine, so it makes sense to attend to it. But then, in this most materialist of faith, it's always the concrete and particular choices of everyday life that test the seriousness of our faith anew.

We won't hear much, if anything, from Jesus about repentance, but that doesn't mean it's not implicit in his ministry. John will always be coming round to disturb and confront us. Doesn't it make sense for us to take John's annual visitation to heart, so that we're prepared with clear eyes to recognize and receive Jesus when he comes to us at Christmas? The waiting's nearly over, the Coming One is close, there's just time for some hard pruning to make space in the cramped quarters of our lives for his coming.

Roger Spiller

Hymn suggestions

On Jordan's bank the Baptist's cry; Sing we of the kingdom, giving thanks to God; We shall stay awake and pray at all times; We have scorned the truth you gave us.

Third Sunday of Advent   16 December
Second Service   Rejoice, Rejoice, and again I Say, Rejoice
Ps. 50.1–6 [62]; **Isa. 35**; Luke 1.57–66 [67–end]

Gaudete – rejoice, as the darkness is beaten. Mention Steeleye Span, the British folk-rock band formed in 1969, and people start to guess your age! But, along with Fairport Convention, they were among the best known acts of the British folk revival and were among the most commercially successful, thanks to their hit singles 'Gaudete' and 'All Around My Hat.' Gaudete means 'rejoice' in Latin, and the song was originally a sacred Christmas carol, composed in the sixteenth century. The single, released in 1973, was one of only three top-50 British hits ever sung in Latin.

This Third Sunday in Advent is known as Gaudete Sunday, as it looks forward again to the joyful celebration of Jesus' birthday. It also reminds us of the joyful anticipation Christians have of the Second Coming of Christ – think, no more Christmas shopping ever – but our joy is tempered with the fact that this return will also bring judgement to all. Those of us who count down the Sundays to Christmas with an Advent candle ring will also be aware of the significant symbolism of this Sunday, for today, when the third of our five candles is lit, the light is then greater than the darkness – with light, new things are possible, little grows in the dark.

Rejoice when there is life in the desert places

We know that plants need light and water to grow, and although deserts have plenty of sunshine, they lack water. I once spent a couple of weeks in Boulder City, Nevada, and the desert there is a hot cruel place, often lacking in much colour. So it is obvious when there is any water around, for instead of just the rocks and dust, there is suddenly a patch of green and colour. I did not witness it, but I have been told that within a few minutes and for a brief spell following a heavy rain shower the desert comes alive with colour and activity, in much the same way as an oasis sustains life more consistently.

Jesus, whose birth we celebrate at Christmas, came to bring colour to colourless lives, came to bring sustenance and growth to dry lives. As Isaiah puts it:

The wilderness and the dry land shall be glad,
    the desert shall rejoice and blossom;
like the crocus it shall blossom abundantly,
    and rejoice with joy and singing.
The glory of Lebanon shall be given to it,
    the majesty of Carmel and Sharon.

14

They shall see the glory of the Lord,
  the majesty of our God.

Now, the next verses in Isaiah we could equally use as a prayer at this time of frenetic Christmas shopping:

Strengthen the weak hands,
  and make firm the feeble knees.
Say to those who are of a fearful heart,
  'Be strong, do not fear!
Here is your God . . .
  He will come and save you.'

The second Advent means no more Christmas shopping – for ever – especially gratifying for us as Scots! Rejoice when you see what the Christ is doing. Isaiah is looking forward to good times, heavenly times, when suffering is no more. He anticipates a time when the blind can see, the deaf can hear, the lame will dance, and those who cannot speak will shout the Lord's praises with joy. But in our own time, we have to continually remind ourselves that this same God is at work in our world. We have to look beyond the apparently dry, unforgiving places, where human hearts seem hard and hope is often all but gone. For often you don't see small places in the desert, where just a little moisture is trapped, where even some condensation is enough to produce life and growth.

Rejoice, rejoice, Christ is in you

So this time of year should be a time of preparation for our hearts and rejoicing. But note that although it is the time of 'tidings of great joy', it is not the time of greatest joy. For Christians, that comes on Easter morning. This side of the cross we cannot ever forget the joy that we have then, when we greet the resurrected Christ. Like the song says: 'You can't have one without the other!'

We should rejoice as we anticipate this special time of the year – in fact, 'Rejoice! Rejoice!' as the words of that Graham Kendrick chorus remind us. For we really know that Christ, whom we anticipate today, is with us, and by his Spirit is with us and in us, in all we do for him today. As we rejoice, our Jesus rejoices with us! This joy can even transform our Christmas shopping! For we give in love

15

for that special person, in the same way that Jesus continually and abundantly gives to us.

We can pray, as we shop, for weary shoppers to find joy. We can be encouragers for the stressed shop assistants as we shop, for our incarnate God will use us to overcome the darkness if we let him.

David Bunyan

Hymn suggestions

Rejoice, Rejoice, Christ is in you; When the King shall come again; The Kingdom of God is justice and joy; In the cross of Christ I glory.

Fourth Sunday of Advent   23 December
Principal Service   **Jump for Joy!**
Mic. 5.2–5a; *Canticle*: Magnificat, *or* Ps. 80.1–8; Heb. 10.5–10;
Luke 1.39–45 [46–55]

Getting ready

Not long now! Carol services, end of term, shopping, office parties, cards written and sent, gifts bought and wrapped, more shopping, food planned, TV Christmas specials, more shopping – it must be Christmas: almost – but not quite. Teetering on the brink, tension in the air – we're waiting – expectant . . .

Have you planned your Christmas carefully, following traditions laid down over many years? Have you planned your church-going, family visiting, Christmas eating, TV watching, present opening? If so, then this is the time to remind yourself that God is a God of shimmering surprises – who loves to do things differently, laughs at our plans and is a connoisseur of innovation, renewal and risk.

A new way

It's from the little town, that backwater of Bethlehem Ephrathah – the 'fruitful house of bread' – that Micah the prophet says a Saviour will come, who will rescue the besieged people of Israel, bringing a new kind of King, whose leadership will be one of peace, security and strength. It's the kind of rescue Israel dreams about, but will be worked out in a way quite different from her expectations.

The writer to the Hebrews too reminds the young church (and us) that the Saviour comes to do the will of God. It's no longer sacrifices and burnt offerings that will win God's favour. That way of doing things has been swept away – by Jesus, who through his incarnation, death and resurrection makes each of us acceptable and presentable to God. In Jesus, God brings about a new way of relating to him and to one another. We no longer have to seek out God – God comes to find us. It's not what we expect at all.

Mary and Elizabeth

Mary and Elizabeth too encounter God working in surprising and unexpected ways. Elizabeth, unable to have a child, finds herself pregnant in old age. Mary, still a virgin, finds herself pregnant by the Holy Spirit – two seemingly impossible pregnancies. No wonder the women seek each other out for companionship and solidarity. Elizabeth's holy sixth sense already knows the extraordinary news that Mary is carrying the Lord. Her blessing of Mary echoes the words of Gabriel – and earth and heaven – a woman and an angel are united in affirmation of this courageous teenager, chosen by God.

And then that wonderful moment when the baby inside Elizabeth responds to the baby inside Mary – and John jumps for joy at his first meeting with Jesus. Elizabeth is filled with the Holy Spirit and shouts praise to God, and Mary sings her great song of revolution – the Magnificat. The Holy Spirit brings about recognition, boldness, declaration and joy. Already God's kingdom is breaking in and the old order in being overturned. Liberation is possible. Salvation is imminent. God is doing a new thing for the world – through women and children – and it takes everyone by surprise.

I'm inspired by the way Elizabeth walks alongside Mary and helps her to bring Christ to birth. I'm inspired by Elizabeth's quiet commitment and openness to the Holy Spirit's prompting. I'm inspired by Mary's obedience and courage. I'm inspired by the way both women aren't fazed by God's surprises but are open to all possibilities – however risky. This is only the beginning and, as we know, there is much, much more to come – demanding, devastating and extraordinary as God's plan for the world unfolds through these women and their children.

Expectant

And so – though we think we know what's going to happen in the next few days, let's be expectant for God's surprises. Though we know the story so well, let's be startled and awed again by the incredible innovation of God being born among us. Let's not forget that responding to God's self-giving may require courage, obedience, tenacity and suffering, alongside the incredible love, joy and gratitude that bubbles up within us when we encounter Jesus – God for us, and with us and in us.

This week, can you be Elizabeth? Can you walk alongside someone in the next few days? Someone for whom this might be a difficult time? Is there someone you can invite to one of the Christmas services over the next few days? Who do you know who might love to come but needs a friend to accompany them? Can you sense where God is at work within another and affirm and celebrate that? Can you meet here with an open heart and generosity towards strangers, visitors, the curious, and those who don't believe they belong?

And for yourself – are you ready to invite Jesus into the besieged city of your heart again, asking him to bring peace, security and strength? Are you open to his surprising call? Are you ready like Mary, Elizabeth and John to be caught up in the drama of God's love and find yourself turned upside down and inside out as old greets new and heaven kisses earth.

When Elizabeth met Mary, the child in her womb leapt for joy. Wherever you find yourself and whoever you are with in the next few days, get ready to jump for joy with the thrill of meeting Jesus afresh this Christmas.

Catherine Williams

Hymn suggestions

O come, O come, Emmanuel; With Mary let my soul rejoice; Come, thou Redeemer of the earth; Tell out my soul.

Fourth Sunday of Advent   23 December
Second Service   **The Importance of Roots**
Ps. 123 [131]; Isa. 10.33—11.10; **Matt. 1.18–end**

The childhood question 'Why?' is such a wind-up when asked again and again . . . we don't have an answer that will satisfy our 6-year-old questioner! But it speaks of the importance of tracing something back to its source, understanding how it became what it went on to be, thinking about its workings. These can often be hidden from view, but explain a lot about how something came to be as it did. It's the same with people. Sometimes we might be curious as to how a friend or colleague developed some aspect of their character, or their giftedness. Nature or nurture? Where did they get their particular talents from? Did their understanding of life come from a very different background to ours? Was their ability with language or music or maths because they were brought up in a multi-lingual household, or spent a lot of time with a talented grandparent, or had an inspiring teacher at school?

Where from?

That was a big question that people were always asking of Jesus. It's not surprising that Matthew, the most Jewish of the Gospel writers, begins by rooting Jesus firmly within the Jewish tradition. The first 17 verses of his Gospel trace Jesus' genealogy from Abraham, through David, through the seminal crisis in Israelite history, the exile: each stage symbolically worked out as 14 generations. Hebrew is fond of numbers, and some numbers – like 7 – in particular. So Matthew traces Jesus' family tree in cycles of seven, from father Abraham to the Psalmist and famed King David; through the kings to the downfall of Jerusalem; and to the Messiah, the Christ. Matthew wanted to situate Jesus well and truly in the heart of Jewish thought, in the most Jewish line, in the most Jewish style. Genealogies like this are deeply rooted in Hebrew Scripture, right from the very beginning: family trees matter from Genesis onwards. Both Matthew and Jesus knew it mattered where you came from.

An exemplary 'father'?

So we get down this important line to Joseph. The neighbours would either see Joseph as the premature father of his fiancée's unborn child, or the fiancé who has been cheated on by his future wife even before they got married! Neither was exactly going to be a great start for either of them . . . So Matthew is at pains to show Joseph in the bloodline of the righteous. Joseph tries to avoid making a fuss, to let it blow over and let them both go their separate ways, so that there's a minimum of damage, whatever has happened to make her pregnant . . . Matthew shows us deep within his train of thought, and takes us into Joseph's sense of surprise and calling. We see with Joseph the life-changing vision from God that explained that the child was conceived by the Holy Spirit. Joseph is called to be an earthly father to him. The dream ends with quotations and illusions from Isaiah 7 and 8, showing how rooted this all is within Joseph's faith and Jewish foundations. Joseph rises to the challenge, in the most proper way. Jesus would have a father figure who would look after his mother, who would be an example of righteousness, care and compassion – and who was a devout Jew.

Like father, like son: wisdom in wood

Fathers would often pass on their livelihoods to their sons. Joseph passed on his ability to work with wood to Jesus. And there's a lot of wood in the Jewish story, as well as in Jesus' story.

Today's passage from Isaiah describes the forests, the great Lebanon woods, a symbol of the old order of Israel's strength. These are brought down by God, leaving just a discarded stump. From here comes the tiniest little sprig, which will bear fruit. At the end of our Old Testament reading, this shoot is invigorated through the roots of the great old stump, the tree of Jesse, father of King David, and it grows into a landmark and place of muster for the faithful.

This tender shoot is characterized as a person from verse 2. Upon him comes the spirit of the Lord, a spirit of wisdom and understanding, a spirit of counsel and of strength, a spirit of knowledge and fear of the Lord. The Hebrew word for 'counsel' looks very like the word for 'tree'. Is this a coincidence, or something more? Hebrew often involves plays on words, so maybe this coincidence led Isaiah to make a smooth link between the ancient woods of his previous image, and the wisdom of the prophesied new shoot, the ideal, righteous Davidic king.

Connecting with our roots

Isaiah's poetic image of the perfect king, like David of the family tree of Jesse, gives an answer to where the righteousness, the understanding, wisdom and greatness of this ideal sovereign come from. They come *through* the stump of Jesse and they come *from* the spirit of the Lord. It was only natural that Matthew could see the coming Messiah as rooted in such ancient prophesies. Advent 4, the last Sunday before the great celebration of the incarnation, not only reminds us of Joseph's relationship to David, but also shows something important about Jesus' identity. In Jesus, the divine and human meet. Jesus is rooted in both God and in humanity.

What are your true roots?

Megan Daffern

Hymn suggestions

Branch of Jesse's stem, arise!; Behold a branch is growing; To Joseph of Nazareth; The Angel Gabriel from heaven came.

Christmas Eve 24 December
(For a nativity or crib service talk, see p. 367.)
Evening Service (when not a Eucharist) **The Miracle of Christmas Music**
Ps. 85; Zech. 2; **Rev. 1.1–8**

> I looked up and saw a man with a measuring line in his hand. Then I asked, 'Where are you going?' He answered me, 'To measure Jerusalem, to see what is its width and what is its length.' (Zech. 2.1–2)

We human beings love measurement. We measure curtains and rooms and cars . . . but our love of measurement isn't expressed only with a tape measure.

We also, for example, measure music. I'm not referring to the overall length of a piece of music; I'm referring to the distance, the gap, between notes. Those gaps, technically called 'intervals', are hugely important. Let me bring this idea right into the heart of Christmas . . .

Here are three notes: the first note is D above middle C; the second is F sharp above middle C, and the third note is G above middle C. [I'll invite the organist to play those three notes . . .]

. . . and you have already guessed it. Those are the first notes of 'Once in Royal', and for me they signal the beginning of

Christmas. But they do more than that; they also trigger memories of Christmases past. Perhaps you can recall carol singing as a teenager with your friends on a bitterly cold and dark night, the frost crunching under your feet and your breath spiralling like smoke into the air. Or, you may have experienced carols on Christmas Eve in a cathedral where in that vaulting space, with candles flickering in the darkness, those first three notes were sung by a treble with a voice of gold. Or perhaps your experience was in a medieval village church, slipping and sliding your way up the icy path, gradually thawing out in the frosty nave, and waiting for those same three notes to be sung. Or maybe you have listened to the service of Nine Lessons and Carols from King's College, Cambridge; the chapel packed with hundreds and hundreds of people, every seat taken, and you sense an air of expectation and a deep but excited stillness; then from out of the darkness come those three notes and the great and solemn procession of Christmas can begin.

Memories of Christmas

You will have your own memories and I promise not to ask you what they are, but there is something about the combination of the words and music of carols that tugs at the heart. I venture to suggest that carols, like other great hymns, have the capacity to integrate the past and present of our own lives. They have a gentle, healing quality, and just for a moment, as we sing the carols on Christmas Eve, time itself stands still, and if a choir of angels hovered above the roof of this church, and the very air above our heads became liquid with music, we would not be entirely surprised.

Now, why is this? What is it about Christmas that is so wonderful? Well, of course, it's the presents and the fetching and then the decorating of the Christmas tree, and seeing young children's faces glowing with happiness. And it's mince pies, and the lumpy stocking at the foot of the bed, and catching up with family and friends, and eating Christmas dinner together, and watching as the pudding flames blue with brandy. It's all of that, but I think that it goes even deeper.

When we sing the carols, when we see candlelight on the faces of children, when a smile with a friend is reciprocated, when all of that happens it seems to open a window on to another dimension. We glimpse, if only for a second, that our ordinary, humdrum existence might somehow be marked with meaning; we glimpse, again perhaps only for a second, that our lives, as we struggle with illness or sadness or grief, might actually matter to someone infinitely greater than we are; out of the corner of our eye we can see that perhaps eternity really is breaking in to time and time is being lovingly enfolded into eternity.

The miracle of music

But let us push this idea a little further. When you think about it, the act of singing is little short of amazing. All that subtle manoeuvring of the musculature of our larynxes, our throats, our lungs, our mouths, our tongues, our lips, our all-too-fleshy fleshiness can become an instrument that produces sounds that can soar towards heaven. Flesh produces sound; the biology and physics of it are astonishing. And when music is performed well, what a sound it is – we humans have the capacity to create in sound a purity and a grace; and then add to that our capacity for complex and wondrous harmony – is that not in itself a miracle?

And at Christmas those sounds are directed outwards. They are directed away from ourselves and towards 'God'. No other word will do. In its simplicity and depth, that word speaks of infinity, of the vast reaches of the universe, of the particularity and value of each human being, of our own vulnerability, and of the worth and value that God in his love and generous wisdom accords to each single one of us.

It is that God whom we worship this Christmas night, the God who came among us as a child, a mystery beyond the telling of it; a mystery beyond all measurement.

But in the three notes, in music, we sense, we experience, that which is beyond and above all words; by grace and in humility we find ourselves exploring the truth that we have so wonderfully glimpsed, a truth that sustains and courses through all life and that waits with infinite courtesy for us to know him as he truly is.

God in Christ; Emmanuel . . . God with us.

Christopher Herbert

Hymn suggestions

Hark, what a sound, and too divine for hearing; Who can measure heaven and earth; Of the Father's love begotten; O little town of Bethlehem.

Christmas, Epiphany and Candlemas

Christmas Day   25 December
Any of the following sets of readings may be used on the evening of Christmas Eve and on Christmas Day: Set III should be used at some time during the celebration.
Set I   Peace Be with You
Isa. 9.2–7; Ps. 96; Titus 2.11–14; **Luke 2.1–14 [15–20]**

Tonight is the night. The presents are wrapped. The lights are twink-ling on the tree. The turkey is plump in the fridge and the sprouts fill a pan on the stove. Stockings are strung from the mantelpiece. A carrot, a mince pie and a glass of sherry sit ready for Rudolf and Santa. The little ones have been bathed and tucked into bed. Alive with expectation.

Tonight is the night. The donkey has been watered and fed. The stable door is closed and the stars are twinkling through the gap at the top. The breath of the cows is sweet and their flanks are warm and soft to the touch. A bed has been made with cloaks in the piles of hay. A jug of milk, a little bread and some cheese have filled a hole. The girl is as comfortable as can be. Alive with expectation.

Tonight is the night. We have come out in the dark and the quiet to gather together and hear again the old story of a new beginning. Alive with expectation.

Tonight is the night. Once upon a time, in a land far away, a child was born. A child long awaited. A child who would transform the world. A child sent from God. But a child unlike any other. The Son of God. God come into the world. Sheep were needed for temple sacrifices in those days. The men who tended them were rough and ready. They kept to the hills with their flocks. Kept to themselves. They were not welcome in town. But when the angels came, when the messengers from God appeared in the skies over their heads and danced and whirled and sang for joy, they ran. Not because they were afraid. But because they were excited. They raced to Bethlehem, hurtled towards the stable.

Peace promised

Their fathers used to tell them a story. Of a man who lived in the time of the ancient kings. A man called Isaiah who heard God's voice in the darkness. For those were dark times. Unruly hordes of men, armed to the teeth and bent on destruction, waged war in the land. They attacked in the night, plundering and pillaging, killing the vulnerable and carrying off the women. The leaders of the people were uncertain, afraid, defensive and divided among themselves. They had not heard God's voice in a long time. But then, they had not listened. Isaiah listened constantly. And he was far-sighted. He spoke of a time when there would be an end to war and oppression, an end to violence and abuse, an end to fear and divisions between people. He predicted the coming of a child as a beacon of light in the darkness. The child would have many titles; among them, Prince of Peace. Peace. Isaiah longed for peace. He believed that peace was possible. He believed the Prince of Peace would one day bring it about. He offered his prophesy in certain hope. Peace. Not the peace of 'peace and quiet', the absence of noise and discord; nor the peace that is the absence of war, the tense stillness between bouts of conflict; nor even peace of mind, the contentment that all is under our control; but the peace that is a sense of wholeness, completeness, healing and harmony.

Peace tonight?

We can live in peaceful times, in a peaceful place, and yet not be at peace. For peace begins in our own heart. The child born tonight grew into the man, Jesus, who taught those who followed him the way of peace. Jesus, both a man and God, taught us to recognize our relationship with God. God, who is at the heart of all creation, God, who is the spark of all being, is also at the heart of each one of us. When we accept that God lives within us, when we place him at the centre of our life, listen to his prompting, follow his way, we can experience that wholeness, that healing, that peace. When Jesus was born, peace came into the world. An early follower of Jesus, Paul, encouraged everyone to adopt Jesus' way of peace. He knew how hard it was to turn away from our shortcomings, what it takes to bite back a harsh word, to exercise patience, self-control, generosity and kindness. To promote wholeness and harmony.

Peace begins when we accept God, trust in him, embrace the peace he offers us, and ask for his help in nurturing it. Like a newborn baby, peace grows from small beginnings, and it begins with us. Then at peace ourselves, we can speak and act in peace among others, and so work with God to transform the world. Take the gift offered by the child born tonight. Ask the Prince of Peace to make his home in your heart. And resolve to share his peace with others. Alive with expectation. Tonight is the night.

Anne Davidson Lund

Hymn suggestions

It came upon the midnight clear; Put peace into each other's hands; Once in Royal David's city; O come, all ye faithful.

Christmas Day   25 December
Set II   The Shepherds' Good News
Isa. 62.6–end; Ps. 97; Titus 3.4–7; **Luke 2.[1–7] 8–20**

The Christmas season still seems able to create a wistful longing, an expectation for something new, which draws us to church at this time of year. We can put it down to sentiment, nostalgia, escapism. But it's more than that. There's something in all of this that we want. We want things to get better, we want this birth to happen again – in a world that has faced conflict and violence once more, we want something to hope for. But how does the Christmas story connect to our world and meet our hopes?

Rulers or shepherds?

Luke sets the story of the birth of Jesus in history. Caught up into this history are lowly shepherds, in the fields, watching their sheep, and into the dark situation of this world a child is born, a child whose life is destined to change the world's history long after Quirinius and the empire he served is no more.

God's message comes not to the mighty rulers of the world, but to shepherds. They are, and stand for, the poor of the earth, people of ill repute, on the margins of society. Shepherds could expect no respite from their long, remorseless, dangerous and dirty duties. They had no reason to hope that their lives would ever be different from one day to the next in their humdrum existence. But tonight is their night. They are the ones chosen, first to hear the news of a new king's birth. The first to receive God's favour, and the first to celebrate and share the good news with Mary and Joseph.

Love over power

Their story tells us most of what we need to know. It tells us that hope comes from God. It comes from the dark and unexpected corners of the world. It comes because God reaches out to his world with love and promise to lighten the darkness and transfigure places of violence and lovelessness. The Christmas story is full of the unexpected, as is God's way with us.

Here in the story of the shepherds, the angels and a birth, here in the triumph of love over the love of power. Here peace and compassion are part of God's good news for all. Here even in the commercialized, overblown sentimentality of television specials, and must-have presents – in all of this there is something we want. It really depends on whether our lives are shaped by the immediate social and personal landscape or whether they are shaped by the surprising, obscure, hidden activity of God to reach us. St Luke sets out both side by side. There are the power-brokers and policy-makers at work, creating laws, exerting control, extending bureaucracy, causing disruption and hardship. Through their half-baked, though doubtless well-intentioned initiatives, the whole world is on the move, and some like Mary and Joseph will be vulnerable and made homeless.

The choice

We can see the Christmas story as ornamentation of the big picture of our lives and our world. Or we can see the story of Jesus as the key to everything else. We can see Christmas as a season of nostalgia, of carols and candles and firelight and happy children and presents. But that misses the point. Christmas is not a reminder that the world is really quite a nice place. It reminds us that the world is menacing: corruption is widespread, children are murdered and tyrants threaten the world with weapons of mass destruction.

Fantasy or reality

Christmas then is not a dream, a time of escapism. Christmas is the reality that shows up the rest of 'reality'. It's a proclamation that outlasts the emperor's tawdry bureaucratic decree referred to earlier in this chapter in Luke. And it addresses us in all our longing, fear and confusion. 'Glory to God in the highest heaven, and on earth peace among those whom he favours.' As the carol has it: 'The hopes and fears of all the years are met in thee tonight.' Yes, they're met; Christmas is real, God is for us, with us, a gift, given in the fragile, mysterious, breathtaking form of this child, Jesus, who is ready to be born in us. The shepherds heard, as we have heard, but they had to respond, to take action, to seek out the Christ Child. And when we do, we have reason to glorify and praise God, for the new life and hope that are born in us. We become part of the hope of Christmas. The word of the angels is ours to speak and the Christmas story goes on in and from us, and continues to reach out to embrace the whole world.

Roger Spiller

Hymn suggestions

See him lying on a bed of straw; While shepherds watched; O little town of Bethlehem; Hark, the herald angels sing.

Christmas Day   25 December
Set III   **Presents**
Isa. 52.7–10; Ps. 98; Heb. 1.1–4 [5–12]; **John 1.1–14**

Presents which last

I wonder what difference the Christmas presents you receive make to you through the year. Of course, many are simple tokens of affection and regard, which we appreciate but which are not designed to make a lasting difference. I'm grateful for the socks I receive, but I confess when I put them on I forget about them quite quickly. But some presents give us genuine continuing pleasure. It might be something to cheer us or entertain us, like a picture or a CD or a video game – or perhaps a fridge magnet, or mug with a helpful message.

Just occasionally, perhaps, we receive a gift of a different quality altogether, something that touches us on a deeper level. It might be a piece of clothing that we'd never have thought of buying for ourselves, but that makes us feel fresh and new. It might be a book that moves us profoundly. Or it might be a person. How often have we heard, in fiction and real life, the words, 'It was the best Christmas present ever' – when a beloved mother has come out of hospital, or a father has returned from the army, or a son has come out of prison?

Or it might be a newborn baby, who really does change your whole life.

God's lasting present

And one particular newborn baby is the gift God offers to us all tonight. Listen to the truth ringing out again through the familiar words of John's Gospel. The Word of God, God's own creative spark, has taken flesh and come to settle alongside us. The light that is the guide of all people, however dimly we perceive it, has come into the world.

Tonight we have an opportunity to receive this most personal gift of God afresh, as the bread and wine, signs of Jesus' self-giving, are held out to us and we take them with thankful trust, with the songs of the angels in our ears and the wonder of his mysterious birth in our minds.

And what difference will he make?

A transforming present

John wrote, 'To all who received him, who believed in his name, he gave power to become children of God.' Sometimes these words are misunderstood. Sometimes being baptized as a child, or having a single exciting experience of God as an adult, is taken as a kind of insurance policy, a certificate of recognition by God. 'I'm OK, I've been done.' Or, from a different background perhaps, 'I'm OK, I've been born again.' Sadly, it's possible to treat Jesus as someone who will just sign your passport application: someone to be used and then forgotten about. And that is to miss entirely the purpose of the gift.

But, of course, God does not force his gift on us, and nor can we force it on anyone else.

Welcoming Jesus

What does it mean to accept or receive Jesus? Simply to welcome him. True welcome is something we do without preconditions.

When we invite someone to our house, one of the signs of true welcome is that, normally, we leave it to our guest to decide when to leave. If people stay well after our normal bedtime, we may start getting on edge and dropping heavy hints. So we need to hear the implied warning of the Gospel writer: this Jesus is a guest who doesn't want to leave at all, but to become a resident. You can't tell in advance what adjustments to your life this will call for. But we hear also the implied enticement: this is a guest whom you won't want to leave, once you have welcomed him.

Because those who welcome him receive the power to become God's children, to relate to God as he relates to him, to exercise the right kind of human authority in the world as he did.

At Christmas there's always the odd one or two unwanted gifts, and two or three days later you see those bedraggled processions carrying plastic bags down to the charity shop. In John Betjeman's immortal words, 'hideous ties so kindly meant'. Such are the pressures on us in this dark world from one side or another that sometimes, perhaps, we have decided that God's gift of Jesus doesn't need to be kept; he's not for us, though we're happy for other people to have it. That he is too much trouble, maybe, or just can't be fitted into a life already overflowing with things and people. Tragically, perhaps, we've never even stopped to realize what a transformation he can make to everything.

The good news is that God goes on offering him to us, year after year, day after day: whether we have welcomed him for as long as we can remember, or if our welcome has been intermittent, or if perhaps we have never discovered before that God has given us such a priceless present: even if in the past we have shut him out. Jesus is God's gift of his own Word, his own Light, his own Self. Let's not put him on a pile in the corner for getting rid of, as happened to him when he first came. Today he offers himself to us in bread and wine. I pray that we will receive him and know the difference he makes each day, as he gives us power to become the children of God.

Stephen Wright

Hymn suggestions

Christians awake; Thou dids't leave thy throne and thy kingly crown; From heaven you came, helpless babe; O come, all ye faithful.

Christmas Day   25 December
Second Service   Emptying

Morning Ps. 110, 117; Evening Ps. 8; Isa. 65.17–25; **Phil. 2.1–13**, or Luke 2.1–20 (*if it has not been used at the Principal Service of the day*)

The big day in this season of consumption is drawing to a close. It's to be hoped that it's been fulfilling. To be full-filled this Christmas we've filled up on food and drink, filled our fridges and cupboards to bursting point, filled stockings, filled our credit cards and filled our rooms with gifts and presents.

Being filled and full-filled

In this period of social and political turbulence and uncertainty in our national life, Christmas provides a welcome respite from all that challenges and unsettles us. Besides, Jesus enjoyed celebrations and parties and ensured there was sufficient wine at a wedding for it to go with a swing. But for all that, he taught that we don't live just for the food that perishes.

The idea that fulfilment, personal fulfilment, depends upon being filled, filling up, being fully filled, full-filled, is at least questionable. It views our lives as containers that need to be kept filled up, like our petrol tanks. And for that we need to garner and guard all that we can, and keep a close look out for our own interests. Yet we know all too well that as Christmas slips away we can feel let down and disappointed and empty.

Being through emptying

Can the lofty claims of Christmas and God's coming down to earth have anything to say to our condition? Is there an alternative, more lasting ground for hope and fulfilment?

Was there a word that stood out for you from the letter of St Paul? Was there a single word that jarred with the way we kept Christmas? I suggest it might be the word 'emptying', the exact opposite of filling. Jesus 'emptied himself', says St Paul in his letter to the church in Philippi, 'taking the form of a slave, being born in human likeness . . . and became obedient to the point of death – even death

31

on a cross'. Think of it – a festival of filling to mark the One who emptied himself.

Philippi was a city in the Roman Empire where so much of political and civic life was menaced by disputes and feuds and enmities. The interests of individuals and parties and factions seemed to count for more than the interests of the nation as a whole – somewhat reminiscent of our national life at this time, where pursuing our competing interests puts at risk the coherence of the nation as a whole. Paul is calling for a new mindset. 'Let this mind be in you which was in Christ Jesus,' he says. And this mindset involved self-emptying, expending oneself.

Divine self-emptying

Jesus had an equality with God, but he thought of equality not as a filling but as an emptying, not as guarding and snatching at his divine status but as self-renunciation. Jesus didn't treat his position before God as a cause for self-assertion. He treated it as an occasion for renouncing every privilege, divesting himself of every honour, relinquishing every advantage. And, says Paul, 'he took the form of a slave', making himself nothing, so as to share our humanity in all its frailty and finitude, 'accepting death, even death on a cross'. As Charles Wesley's hymn has it, he 'emptied himself of all but love and bled for Adam's helpless race'.

The nature of God is never more fully displayed than in becoming a servant. That's what Jesus was always doing, expending himself, pouring himself out. 'Emptying' is not just what Jesus does. Emptying is the most perfect expression of the eternal love within the Trinity. God is himself a communion of selfless, self-emptying persons. God doesn't lose anything in dispossessing himself. In the Trinity, having and giving are one and the same. St Paul says that it's the mindset that Christ's followers must occupy, but first we have to get used to living on empty.

Emptying

A monk was once visited by a man who wanted to learn about prayer, but instead of listening to the man of prayer the visitor kept talking about all his own ideas. After a while the monk made a pot of tea, and he poured it into the visitor's cup until it was full. Then he went on pouring and pouring, until the tea was all over the saucer and the table and was starting to trickle on to the floor. Eventually, the visitor couldn't restrain himself any longer. 'Don't you see,' he said, 'it's full. You can't get any more in.' 'Exactly,' said the monk. 'Just like you. You're so full of your own ideas there's no room for anything else.'

We're filled, fulfilled, precisely and paradoxically by being emptied, dispossessed. Life with Christ is not a matter of being filled up: with information, rules, goals, good intentions. It's to empty us, to create space, need, hunger, yearning, receptivity. The idea is so countercultural, so much at variance with every instinct for self-survival and self-security, that it would seem absurd and reckless even to try. But it was exemplified in the life and person of Jesus Christ, and for that 'God highly exalted him'. And if this is God's way, filling and fulfilment through emptying and expending, perhaps we can sit lighter to our own interests. If God guards them, then we don't need to do so ourselves. We're not, then, to be containers, but springs, living water springing up to eternal life. That, says Jesus, is the way to life and fulfilment.

Roger Spiller

Hymn suggestions

May the mind of Christ my Saviour; Thou didst leave thy throne and thy kingly power; And can it be; Hark, the herald angels sing.

First Sunday of Christmas   30 December
Principal Service   **Let Children Learn!**
1 Sam. 2.18–20, 26; Ps. 148 [*or* 148.7–end]; Col. 3.12–17;
Luke 2.41–end

Don't we all wish we knew more about the life of Jesus, especially the hidden years, before the three short years of his public ministry? We have portraits of Jesus, by the four Gospel writers, but we don't have anything like a biographical account. That hasn't prevented scholars and novelists from attempting their own reconstruction. But they will always be defeated by the paucity of information we have of Jesus and by the fact that all attempts at biography are sure to tell us more about their authors than they do about the subject about whom they write. But there's a theological reason that tells us that we don't need more details of Jesus' life on earth, much as we wished we had them, and it could be our downfall if we had! It's that the object of Christian faith is a living person accessible to all believers. Trying to construct or immerse ourselves in historical reconstruction of Jesus is like seeking 'the living among the dead'. As St Paul put it in a much discussed phrase, 'We see Christ in the flesh no longer.' And those who tell the story of Jesus do so not to satisfy their curiosity, but to address us afresh and create trust in the living Christ.

St Luke gives us our only story of the boy Jesus before he emerged in public view to begin his ministry. At the age of 12, Jesus had probably reached the age of discrimination, but it's not certain that he was himself bound to go to Jerusalem. That he went suggests his own serious religious intent. He's as close as ever to the palace of Herod, who, according to Matthew, had made efforts to kill him. His religious interest is taken seriously and he is treated as being at a place of worship in his own right, not as being dragged along because his parents needed to be present. He is given the space and independence to pursue his own interests, not expected, as some of us were, to conform to some predetermined child or childish activities. How I hated action songs! I knew where my eyes were and didn't need to point them out while singing 'Two little eyes to look to God'.

Jesus was given the space and freedom to pursue serious religious activity on his own terms. There's no reason to think that Jesus was himself teaching; rather, he was discussing, asking questions more than answering them. But he had access to the religious leaders as though nothing was left to chance where the decisive education of children was concerned. We've sometimes neglected to resource and train the people appointed to lead the worship and learning of children in our churches. And we've failed to inspire successive post-war generations of children to pursue Christian learning.

Professor John Hull, once doyen of schools' Christian education and theologian, created in the church I used to attend a positive learning environment for the young people. He was incredibly respectful of the opinions they expressed and courageous in the demands he made of them. A course on reasons for not believing in God, for example, may seem unusual in a church environment, but, as he argued, where better to rehearse the big religious challenges than where they can be informatively and sensitively discussed. Better that than to send them unprepared and ill equipped into a fiercely sceptical climate outside. Predictably his group grew exponentially.

There's a strong hint that Jesus and his parents stayed in Jerusalem for the full eight-day festival, exceeding what was required of them, and that Jesus was totally absorbed by the theological debate in which he was engaged. Jesus' capacity to be absorbed in religious questions for this length of time indicates that he was being nurtured by his parents at Nazareth. As the firstborn son, Jesus would have been the object of his father's special attention, both for work and for religious education. The decline in Christian religion in our day is attributed by one religious analyst, Callum Brown, to the time in the 1960s when parents largely gave up on reading bedtime stories to their children, especially Bible stories. That tradition, supported by family rituals designed to hold the attention of their children, remains intact within Judaism. 'Tell the story, tell the story,' declares Rabbi Lord Jonathan Sacks.

We know that Jesus was left behind in Jerusalem, and when his parents returned, with a whole day's journey behind them to find him, he uttered words that astonish us. Jesus isn't saying that the Temple is his Father's house but that his vocation is to be present in the Temple. As we are astonished by Jesus' growth into his divine vocation, let us too be inspired to create a space in our church life where our young people can discuss, question and explore their faith, which can lead them to a knowledge of their Father, God.

Roger Spiller

Hymn suggestions

The growing limbs of God the Son; Thou who wast rich beyond all splendour; Each seeking faith is seeking light; Lord, for the years your love has kept and guided.

First Sunday of Christmas 30 December
Second Service **Who Are the Children of God?**
Ps. 132; Isa. 61; **Gal. 3.27—4.7**; *Gospel at Holy Communion*: Luke 2.15–21

'The brotherhood of man and the fatherhood of God' sounds a neat and satisfying way to epitomize our relationships with one another and with God. The idea of the brotherhood of man, or better, men and women in a human family, is a good and unobjectionable notion to believe and still better to practise. The associated assertion that we are children of God is also a reassuring and, still for many people, an unexceptionable idea. But is it true? God is Father of us all, but does it necessarily follow that we are all God's children?

A spiritual not a natural relationship

Let me cite as witness the New Testament scholar and often supposedly radical theologian Bishop John Robinson. He says that 'Though God is the Father of all men (*sic*) not all men are sons of God.' 'This', he said, 'is the consistent view of the Bible.' And it can't be any more explicit than as we find it in our reading from St Paul's letter to the Galatians.

It is the consequence of the fact that God only had one Son who shared his divine nature. If *we* are to be sons and daughters, then it has to be a spiritual relationship and not a natural one. It's not one we tumble into without realizing it. We can't be in a relationship with God without it making a real difference to the way we think, and live.

A changed relationship

The Victorian novelist George Eliot occasionally attended the Shepperton Church of which I was once a vicar. She attended even less frequently when a strident evangelical vicar came to occupy the pulpit. She said of him, dismissively, that he brought a new vocabulary, but not a new experience. In other words, he redescribed things but didn't fundamentally change them. We sometimes conclude that politicians frequently redescribe society, education, health and social provision in reassuring, grandiose terms. But still nothing may have really changed, only the rhetoric. God doesn't go in for idle rhetoric or paper transactions. He promises a real change in our relationships.

By adoption

At the heart of St Paul's gospel is the language of adoption. 'God sent his Son, born of a woman, born under the law, so that we might receive adoption as children.' Before Jesus came, said Paul, we were under a disciplinarian. Well, not the class teacher that prodded and pushed you to work hard at school. Paul is speaking of the law, which was God's stand-in before Christ came. But the law was limited, it could only keep us secure and safe. It couldn't change us. That had to wait until Christ came. Formerly, says Paul, 'you didn't know God'. So, of course, you can hardly be reckoned a child of God if you don't consciously know your divine Father. Jesus came to rescue us from the law, and its slavery, before he could start the adoption process. Paul has given a reason for Jesus being born on earth. It is not merely to deal with our sin. It's to open us to a relationship with God so that we can become his sons and daughters.

St John says the same, but this time using the image of rebirth. 'He gave power to become children of God, who were born, not of blood or of the will of the flesh or of the will of man, but of God.'

The Spirit, God's adoption agent

So what brings about our adoption or rebirth? It is the gift of the Spirit, which is the life of God that can infuse and indwell our lives and give us the power and the right to be God's children. 'All who are led by the Spirit of God are children of God.' And John is in unison with Paul: 'To all who received him (Christ), he gave power to become children of God.' So becoming a son or daughter of God signifies a change that is so big that it can only be described as a rebirth, or as the effect of an adoption process, with all the severing of the old and the transition to the new. And it happens through God's Spirit abiding in us.

How do we know? We know by the way we find ourselves talking to God and the intimacy of the relationship we have with him. This was expressed by Jesus in the word by which he addressed his Father. No one before Jesus, we understand, would have ever dared to use a word of such endearing intimacy of God. But Jesus did, and he taught his followers to do the same. And now St Paul too preserves the word in Aramaic, the language Jesus would have spoken, and says, 'When *we* cry, "Abba! Father!" it is that very Spirit bearing witness with our spirit that we are children of God, and if children, then heirs of God and joint heirs with Christ.' The Spirit declares us his sons and daughters, just as it declared Jesus Son of God at his baptism and at his resurrection. Jesus is God's Son by nature; we can become God's sons and daughters by his Spirit, and heirs of all God's promises. What is more wonderful than that we should hear deep within our hearts the witness of God's Spirit that we are God's children?

Roger Spiller

Hymn suggestions

God the Father, name we treasure; Holy Spirit come, confirm us; Word of God, come down on earth; As water to the thirsty.

Epiphany   6 January
Principal Service   **The Journey We Need to Make**
Isa. 60.1–6; Ps. 72 [*or* 72.10–15]; Eph. 3.1–12; **Matt. 2.1–12**

Christmas feels like it happened a long while ago. Twelfth Night is just behind us, and those who had a crib have probably removed it, along with the wise men. But, before discarding your Christmas cards, notice how numbers stack up for the wise men, say, over the shepherds. Christmas cards of those rather pedestrian, dull, smelly shepherds, watching their flocks, don't sell well, but the wise men, dressed up as if they were going to a Buckingham Palace garden party, remain popular.

It's hard to find a biblical story that has caught the imagination, and stimulated so much research and reflection, as the account of the magi. Along with the crucifixion, it's the most depicted subject by artists, poets, sculptors and musicians. And yet the story of the magi is recounted in just one of the four Gospels, and covers a brief 12 verses.

It's a story, and stories aren't a concession to those who are uncomfortable with argument and evidence. It's that when trying to refer to the ineffable, stories, biblical stories, are primary; they cannot be substituted by propositions or doctrines. We can't express the meaning of the incarnation, God becoming human, except by telling the story and enacting it in heart and mind.

Our traveling companions

It's remarkable, then, that most of what we know of the magi, or wise men, is not found in Matthew. It's the result of speculation and embellishment over many centuries. Were they three, suggested by the three gifts, or four, or even ten? Who were they and where were they from? They're called 'magi', linked to our word 'magic', and magic may have been part of their stock in trade, but were they also astrologers, or Zoroastrian priests? We can't even be sure whether they are viewed favourably or with suspicion by Matthew himself, and by the Church then and now. But at least some decided they were probably wise, men of wisdom, in touch with another reality. And then, by the eleventh century, they were upgraded and called kings, men of wealth and power. And then the modern concern for representation kicked in, and these men became representatives of youth, middle age and old age; representatives of different ancient eastern countries, Babylon, Persia and Iran. And then of course they were given names, not just names but sets of names that people could choose to call them.

Now, we can't make things up as we go along. There's a man in the White House who takes care of that for us. But the story of the magi, like some other biblical stories, allows for reworking, filling out, the story. We know this because it has already happened to the magi story, which reworks several Old Testament stories. Jesus, says Matthew, is a new Moses, greater than Moses, indeed. Just as Moses needed protection from the threat of Pharaoh, to kill him as a baby along with all babies, in Egypt, so Jesus is threatened and will continue to be threatened by King Herod and the whole state apparatus. So Matthew is using his imagination to bring out the relevance of Christ for his readers' lives, and so the story has to be told differently if it's to catch the imagination of a new generation. The story can't be changed, so the magi are Gentiles, not Jews. They are from the East, the land of *Arabian Nights* and spice routes, not gypsies from East London. And if they speak a 'different form of fiction, it's no less truthful for that.

Guides on our own journey

So we're invited to view the sumptuous pictures of the 'Adoring Kings' in our galleries and art books; to read with Yeats and Auden and T. S. Eliot and Evelyn Waugh the embellishments made to help us to make our own journey. And we're to reflect on the night sky, and all of nature, which creates the stage set for our own journey. We're to go to Scripture for directions of travel to find the star and see 'the light that enlightens everyone coming into the world'.

Epiphany means manifesting, shining, showing forth.

We in our household have had our own little epiphany this Christmas. We saw pictures from the scan of the foetus of our first, prospective granddaughter, and rather grotesque they were too. But then we heard the news from the far east corner of the world that what had been hidden was now manifest, the shining face of a new life that reflected God's own glory.

It will require us to make a journey – epiphanies always do. Some of us are reluctant to travel from one parish to another, so there's some work to be done. But, more seriously, there's an inward journey that we all have to make if we're to see and adore the one who waits to be our Saviour and Lord. The journey may be short, as it was for the shepherds, or long and costly for those, like the wise men, encumbered by wealth and worldly wisdom and the accoutrements of power and status. But what matters is our will and devotion to make the journey and to be sure not to pass over God's gracious invitation.

And the purpose of the journey? Why have the magi come on their long journey? 'We have come to pay him homage.' And the first thing they do upon entering the house and seeing Mary and the child is kneel down and pay him homage; giving themselves utterly and completely to Christ. And so may we.

Roger Spiller

Hymn suggestions

O worship the Lord in the beauty of holiness; Arise, shine out, your light has come; Wise men, they came to look for wisdom; Brightest and best are the sons of the morning.

Epiphany   6 January
Second Service   **Exile Undone**
Ps. 98, 100; **Isa. 60.1–9**; John 2.1–11

A puzzle

There's a puzzle about the three kings. The passage from Matthew never refers to them as kings at all, but simply as 'magi'. The only kings mentioned in that passage are King Herod and a new 'King of the Jews'. So, how it is that the wise men became kings?

Déjà vu

Well, it's not at all a mistake, it turns out. In the other two readings we heard there are references to kings – and it seems that the writer of Matthew's Gospel wanted us to hear echoes of those passages as

40

he wrote his story. The prophet Isaiah, writing for a nation enduring great trouble at the time, reassured the people that, one day,
'Nations shall come to your light, and kings to the brightness of
your dawn' – and he promised that these kings would come bringing gold and frankincense. Clever readers of Matthew's Gospel
would have known that the author was thinking of this verse and
invoking this kind of promise. And they would remember Psalm 72
as well, which promises a day when kings will come from Tarshish,
Sheba and Seba and bring gifts and render tribute. The first readers of Matthew's Gospel would have said to themselves, 'There is
something familiar about this story, I've somehow heard it before.'
It's been called a kind of biblical déjà vu, like that moment when
you are watching a film and you suddenly realize what's going on,
when the clues fit together. 'Ah!', they would have said, 'This is the
story I know – this is what I should have seen from the beginning!'

Exile undone

The exile had been the most terrible thing to afflict the people of
God in all their history. Their country had been defeated and colonized. Their most talented young people, like Daniel, had been
taken into captivity. They had become subjects of a foreign king
and humiliated into bowing before the Babylonians. The gold of
Israel had been grabbed by enemies; their most holy place had been
destroyed, and a statue of an idol placed in the holy of holies. But
now, in the gospel story of the magi, the exile is reversed. The 'kings'
from 'the East' bring back the gold, and now *they* pay homage to
the king of Israel. Those who once took Israel captive, desecrated
its Temple and stole its wisdom, now return and bow the knee,
bringing gold – and of course frankincense and myrhh. This is déjà
vu, but also restoration and redemption! The naming of them as
kings is a deliberate way of telling the story of who now really rules.
Those from 'the East' (the East that had previously conquered and
colonized Jerusalem) had now come to Jerusalem seeking wisdom
and to pay homage. And the East finds wisdom *not* where powerful
people might expect to find wisdom (with other powerful people),
but in an ordinary house, away from the palace, in a young child.
So much is turned upside down: the conquerors return to bow the
knee to those they once had conquered; those looking for God find
divinity not in a royal palace but in an ordinary suburban home
in Bethlehem; and the searchers find their 'king' not in a powerful
man but in a helpless child. The gold once stolen from the Temple

is restored. The new King of Israel is found not in the Temple of Solomon, but in an ordinary house among the people. The wise bend the knee to simplicity, and homage is offered to an astonished family.

The feast of Epiphany is the feast where the story of our lives is retold, but in a completely new and upside-down way. The coming of the magi 'undoes' and reverses the terrible story of the exile. The date of Epiphany, 6 January, is also the same date on which the Romans celebrated the triumphs of Augustus – so, in the Roman Empire, Christians deliberately chose to celebrate a very different triumph on that very day, and to parade their allegiance to the child of Bethlehem rather than the pseudo divinity of the mighty Roman Emperor.

My return too

As we bring our 'gold' to the communion table and come to share bread and wine here, we are making a promise to stay faithful to the God who came to meet us in Jesus, to follow the teachings of Jesus and to put him above all other commitments, allegiances and duties. Here we come to pay homage to the king of all kings, lord of my heart, the one I gladly follow.

If I am in any kind of exile, I am called back here. If I am searching for wisdom, here I will find it. If am lost, here I am found. Praise be to our Lord Jesus Christ, amen.

Susan Durber

Hymn suggestions

Arise, shine out, your light has come; How brightly gleams the morning star; O worship the Lord, in the beauty of holiness; Let earth and heaven combine.

Baptism of Christ (Second Sunday of Epiphany)
13 January
Principal Service   **A Bridge to New Life**
Isa. 43.1–7; Ps. 29; Acts 8.14–17; **Luke 3.15–17, 21–22**

'And when Jesus also had been baptized.' How strange those words are. John's baptism, we are told, was 'a baptism of repentance'.

This was an action for those who knew there was something wrong with their relationship with God and other people. Here sins were washed away. One of the reasons the religious leaders hated John so much was that he went about requiring repentance of the Chosen People. Baptism was a rite for Gentiles who wanted to become Jews. They needed uncleanness washing all right; but it wasn't something for good Jews. To them, John's insistence was a scandal. The logic of that criticism is the same for Christians. If Jesus is who we say he is, then the last thing he needs is baptism. If it's for sinners who know their need of forgiveness, it doesn't seem appropriate that Jesus enters that water. Yet all the Gospels agree that enter the water he did. You can see how the Gospel writers struggled with this: Matthew has John arguing with Jesus; Mark makes more of God's word from heaven than the watery event itself; John has it as the thing that convinces John of Jesus' authenticity; and, as we heard, Luke believes it to be the final affirmation to Jesus that his way is God's choosing.

A new age

Perhaps the first clue to the significance of Jesus' baptism lies in what John was actually doing in his insistence on repentance. He was calling the sons and daughters of Abraham to baptism. This was unheard of. John in his actions says that the moment is unique. It's as if John is saying: 'You haven't felt this before, but I'm telling you now that you need God as never before, and the best way of realizing that is to be baptized.' And many responded. God was doing something new – doing something new in Jesus. A new age has begun. Jesus' own baptism marks that.

God with people

If the first clue is about time, the second is about personality. What is this God John talks about like? If those who responded to John had a new awareness of their own need of God, was that need going to be met by the same old religious responses? No; in this different time you should know that God acts in a way you don't even notice. God isn't remote. God isn't aloof. God in the person of Jesus enters your experience. He will go through what you go through. He will be baptized. Mr Graham scared me when I was a junior at secondary school. As long as he was in charge of games, his fearsome shout from the sidelines reduced me to a quivering wreck. I couldn't do a thing right. But when he left – to be a Redcoat at a famous holiday venue – and was replaced by Mr Spinney, everything changed. Mr Spinney used to join in – teaching us by doing things alongside us. I was never shouted at again. My confidence grew – I even represented my school and my county. That's what Jesus is like in his baptism. He involves himself with his people, and that will be the mark of his saving love in all things. And that gives us the courage to live the life of faith.

Made part of a community

The third clue is that our Christian baptism isn't the baptism John offered. Its likeness to what John did is in the fact it is a turning away from something; yes, it is a sign of repentance. But its difference is that it is primarily a turning towards Christ. As Christ stands with us in baptism, so we turn towards his new life and are incorporated into it by our baptism as Christians. We stand the church-side of the cross in a way John could not. By baptism we enter the deathly consequences of sin, and we rise to the resurrection life of the one who conquered that death. Christian baptism always begins in what Christ has done for all. As our text tells us, John 'proclaimed a baptism of repentance'. Christian baptism is that, and more. As Colin Morris declared, it is 'a proclamation to the Church and through the Church to the world that all live, move and have their being in God'. As someone said, it's a bridge, not a roadblock. In baptism we don't reach the end of the road, rather we turn the corner into a new roadway that opens life up in striking ways. Bought, as it were, by the cross, we are made part of Christ's new community. Baptism always speaks of belonging – being part of Christ's people. It always challenges us: are we on Christ's road or not?

Christopher Burkett

Hymn suggestions

When Jesus came to Jordan; My God, accept my heart this day; The kingdom of God is mercy and grace; Word of God, renew your people.

44

Baptism of Christ (Second Sunday of Epiphany)
13 January
Second Service   **You Have Died!**
Ps. 46, 47; Isa. 55.1–11; **Rom. 6.1–11**; *Gospel at Holy Communion*:
Mark 1.4–11

'Are you saved?' There's a hoary old story that a great biblical scholar was approached by a Salvation Army woman. She fired a question to him: 'Sir, are you saved?' Many of us, if we even understood the question, would probably answer, 'I hope so'. But in lightning speed the man retorted: 'My dear, do you mean *sōtheis*, *sesōsmenos* or *sōzomenos*?' 'I have been saved, I am being saved or I will be saved?'

Has anything changed?

If we're from one of the older mainstream churches, we might be embarrassed. 'We don't use this kind of language where we come from.' For other churches, a definite answer identifies who are its real members. But perhaps it's not just embarrassment that makes some of us uneasy with the question. Some churches, often working with new converts, stress conversion as a dramatic turning point. Others, working with lifelong church-goers, put the stress on development, and look to 'slow conversion', a process of change and growth in the Christian life over many years. As the biblical scholar's reply suggests, the work of salvation has a past, present and future dimension. There is need for both conversion and for a more gradual process of development in the Christian life. St Paul would seem unhappy to say 'I was saved on such and such a day', because he was acutely aware that salvation in all its fullness belonged to God's future.

But, then, is our salvation really only a future hope? That nothing has already really changed? It's still a matter of hope in some remote future state. The New Testament language that sets out our new life in Christ is grandiose. But when we look at ourselves and our faith community, we're forced to acknowledge that there's not always much evidence to suggest there's been much change, in either ourselves or in the faith community of which we are part. 'Are we saved?' 'Are we a new creation?' 'Are we living abundantly?' 'I hope so.' Is this tame reply the best that we can say?

A decisive event

'We have died,' says St Paul. Even as a metaphor that makes a decisive and dramatic impact. It declares a life-and-death divide has been crossed, a new state of being irrevocably entered into. But is it merely holding out the promise of a future hope to keep us motivated in the present? Or is it really a declared fact that has decisively, even if not fully, changed us? St Paul has no doubt that something decisive has happened. 'We have died,' he says, and the consequence is that 'we are freed from sin'. If we know ourselves at all, we can hardly think of ourselves as free of sin. But what is sin? Not just guilt, nor the offence of sin. It's also, and primarily, a power – the power of sin. And that power was decisively dealt with through the death of Jesus. As one biblical scholar, Ernst Kasemann, expressed it, 'Christians are set free from sin with a definiteness which death alone can achieve.' In its place, we receive the gift of God's power that does more than galvanize our wills. It determines our new existence. It happens when 'we have been united with him in a death like his'. 'We know', says Paul, speaking with the certainty that befits a past and decisive event, 'that our old self was crucified with him so that the body of sin might be destroyed.' It follows that if we participate in Christ's death we too will 'walk in newness of life' as well as share in his resurrection.

Entering into our inheritance

How can we know? St Paul introduces that most objective, datable, indisputable event: baptism. And what is baptism other than an enacted drowning and rising? It means a real immersion or burying under water, and a rising up out of water. So it represents the death and burial of Jesus. Paul can be read in a way that suggests that by virtue of our baptism we 'were baptized into his death'. It was done to us and for us. It represents and is the means by which we participate in Christ's death and resurrection. In either case, baptism is an effective sign.

We can see how other signs do much more than signify change. They can precipitate it. Our national flag is no more than a piece of dyed cotton. But when it is raised, when it is waved, it takes on a new meaning. It expresses, but it also creates and renews, our sense of shared identity. A kiss expresses our love for another, but it also generates it. So, too, revisiting vows, for those who are married, refreshes the sacrificial love that they publicly and decisively hold before us.

We have been baptized. All there is left for us to do is to discover, and enter into the relationship with Jesus Christ which it has opened to us. Baptism tells us that God's goodwill is always before us, always the initiator, always the Giver. That is the good news of our baptism, and hearing and revisiting it is the means by which God gives us the will to live out the new life, to inhabit a new existence and to exercise our power and freedom from sin and death. I know – I don't hope so – because that's the meaning of my baptism!

Roger Spiller

Hymn suggestions

Source and fount of all creation; My God, accept my heart this day; I am a new creation; Affirm anew, the threefold name.

Third Sunday of Epiphany   20 January
(Week of Prayer for Christian Unity; see page 298)
Principal Service   **The Wedding at Cana: A Narrative Sermon**
Isa. 62.1–5; Ps. 36.5–10; 1 Cor. 12.1–11; **John 2.1–11**

I'm Mary, his mother. Jesus' mother. Should I be proud of him? Well I am. I am. I was yesterday, at that wedding supper, with my oldest sitting by me. I felt so proud of him. But, I tell you, I'm very disturbed by what he did.

I've always liked weddings. There's the procession and the singing and dancing. Then there's the supper, with the groom and bride sitting under that canopy. You should have seen the bride yesterday. She looked gorgeous, all dressed up, with all that glittering gold jewellery. (There's some money in that family.)

But it's not just weddings themselves. It's what they stand for, isn't it? There's so many things going on these days that seem to be undermining family life; undermining the life of God's people. Roman soldiers; foreign ways. I sometimes feel we don't belong in our own land. I feel it's being taken away from us, bit by bit.

A wedding's more than a wedding. It's something for us all to hang on to. Weddings bind us together, families together, God's people together. Weddings make us feel one. As long as we go on arranging for good Jewish boys – like my son – to marry good Jewish girls, we'll keep God's people going. That's the way God protects and preserves his people, isn't it? Isn't it? Well that's what I'd have said if you asked me yesterday.

And what happened yesterday, at the supper? There they were, that young couple under the canopy, sitting in all their finery, waiting, waiting for the moment – the moment when they drink from the cup together. That's the high point, isn't it? They take the cup and they drink God's wine together.

And what happened? The wine ran out! God's wine ran out! There's the bride and groom getting ready to share the covenant cup – and the wine runs out!

Can you think of anything worse? Everyone went silent. I looked at Jesus.

'The wine's run out,' I said.

He didn't answer. He seemed to be the only one in the place who hadn't noticed. He had one of his faraway looks on his face.

I nudged him.

'The wine's run out,' I said.

Then he turned to me. He looked at me very hard and he said something. I'm not going to tell you what he said, because it sounded odd, sounded rude. And if I tell you, you'll misunderstand. It was as though he were talking from another time and place.

All right, I'll tell you.

I said, 'The wine's run out.'

He said, 'What concern is that to you and me? My hour has not yet come.'

Well, I should have thought it was everyone's concern! The whole wedding supper was about to dry up. And there was the bridegroom, under the canopy, the smile wiped off his face, glued to his seat with embarrassment because he'd let his guests down.

Then Jesus seemed to change his mind. Suddenly he seemed to wake up to the seriousness of the situation. I sensed he was going to do something. So I called one of the servants. I said, 'Do as he tells you.'

I don't know exactly what he said to the servant; he'd turned his face away from me. But within five minutes it happened. The water in those great jars, all that water we always use to wash ourselves before we eat, it had all turned into wine! And the best wine too.

48

The wedding supper back to normal? Well everyone started talking, eating, drinking, laughing again. The bride and groom shared their cup. But, back to normal?

I don't think so. You see, I think it was a sign. Peter and the others are wondering the same. I know, because Peter said so afterwards. I don't think the wine running out was just an accident. It's a sign.

And that's what's disturbing me. I lay awake for hours last night thinking about it. I said to myself, 'That wedding nearly dried up – because the wine ran out.' And if Jesus hadn't happened to be there (and I didn't know he was coming) it would have dried up.

And what would that have told us about the wedding, about all our weddings, about God's way of preserving his people? I imagined weddings all round Galilee, all over the country, drying up for lack of wine. And what would that mean? That God no longer wants to preserve his people? God's closing down his vineyard. God's given up on us! O my God!

That's disturbing enough. But who saved the wedding? Who produced the new wine? My son! And what does that mean? What do you make of that? He never said a lot at the supper. He was in one of his faraway moods, as I said. He never said a lot; but it's what he did that's troubling me. His wine took over that wedding.

Is he going to go round Galilee turning up unexpectedly at weddings turning water into wine – new wine, the best wine? Is he going to keep God's vineyard open and save God's people all by himself?

I don't mind telling you, what he did at that wedding has shaken me. From what I hear, it's shaken a lot of people. The bride's mother, my friend Sarah – she invited me to the wedding – said to me afterwards,

'He's a deep one, your Jesus.'

Then she added, 'Mary, d'you really understand him?'

'Does any mother ever?' I asked.

No, I don't understand him. But he's the son God gave me. I'm proud of him – and afraid for him.

Paul Johns

Hymn suggestions

Christ is our light; Jesus, come! For we invite you; As men and women we were made; Songs of thankfulness and praise.

Third Sunday of Epiphany 20 January
Second Service **Is God Speaking?**

Ps. 96; **1 Sam. 3.1–20**; Eph. 4.1–16; *Gospel at Holy Communion*:
John 1.29–42

I used to work with people who claimed to hear voices. They claimed, specifically, to have heard the voice of God calling them to Christian ministry. Which of them was truly hearing the call of God and which of them were hearing only the call formed from their own deep needs and desires? When one person tried to impress the then Archbishop of Cape Town that he was certain that he had heard God's call to be a priest, the Archbishop told him: 'When you next hear God calling you to be a priest, ask him to put it in writing.'

The scope for self-deception is always at work in us, so, as the call of Samuel shows, a rightful scepticism is a healthy first response when someone says they've heard God speak. Besides, although God does speak, he is not a talkative God, not profligate in speech, and, as we heard in the reading from 1 Samuel 3, the word of the Lord was rare in the time of Samuel. And in today's manic climate, the voice of God is also rare.

Might preachers risk being promiscuous in using the language of divine call, telling us that we are all called to this or that task or ministry. Might we do better to leave God to speak and meanwhile encourage patient waiting until it is evident that we have been spoken to? Why did Samuel not recognize the voice of the Lord speaking to him. After all, he grew up from boyhood in the sanctuary and was already 'ministering to the LORD under Eli'. But that didn't equip him to hear God's voice. God's call is never a reward for services rendered, or lifelong faithfulness. His call is always a new departure, a fresh beginning.

Testing a call from God

How then may that call be tried and tested? Samuel is woken by a voice calling his name and he draws the most obvious conclusion that Eli – his guardian – is speaking, and he duly presents himself to him. But Eli sends him straight back to bed. And this happened, not once, not twice, but three times! People who think they hear God's call need not act peremptorily, fearing that they may miss God's summons. When God calls, he persists. So, like some pantomime scene, we see Samuel getting out of bed to visit Eli only to be sent back, again and again, and then finally surrender to the voice that won't take 'no' for an answer.

How is God's call tested? We can't hear God's call to other people, we can only hear it for ourselves, but that call is seldom, if ever, unmediated. Other people enable us to hear it – unbelievers as well as believers can be divine interpreters; they can hear God, as did Eli, even if they refuse to respond for themselves. So it is Eli the renegade under whose custody the divine light is almost extinguished, this man, who finally discerns that the voice to Samuel is from God. And that will be costly for Eli. Some who feel certain, perhaps unhealthily certain, of God's call to Christian ministry can resent the involvement of those appointed by the Church to question and test the reality of their call.

How is God's call tested, one more time? God doesn't waste words to confirm what we're already doing. God's call is to redirect us, to beckon us to a new identity, a fresh task, a life-changing ministry, a vocation that overwhelms us and comes from beyond us. That's why, when we feel called, it isn't a vocation that we simply choose for ourselves. We may seek excitement, but nobody in their right mind would choose to have their lives turned upside down. That's why it's often depicted as a contest of wills. The idiosyncratic and televisual vicar, Peter Owen Jones, describes it as 'overwhelming, almost physical, like waves passing through his body . . .'. 'I have fought it tooth and bloody nail,' he said. 'I can't tell you what it feels like to have lost, only that in losing, you truly find that God and you are found by Him.'

Keep running until you're ambushed

No wonder fight or flight is the response of those who have caught the magnitude of God's call. For, as Samuel was soon to discover, ministry involves grief and heartache, as well as joy. God wasted no time in instructing Samuel to give Eli devastating news. Samuel will again be bearing bad news, this time to God himself as he relays his people's wish to usurp God's reign and ask for a human king instead. Samuel was the bridge between the biggest transition in Israelite history. He was the spokesperson and mediator of God's word, to the whole country, a counsellor to the royal family and the one who found and anointed King David. He was, too, a forerunner of Jesus, as both prophet and priest. It's not the story of a talented leader reaching the top. It's God's call that makes Samuel who he is, God's way of bringing something out of nothing. And he's a model for the way we, too, may hear what we think God may be saying to others, and what he may be saying to us.

Roger Spiller

Hymn suggestions

I the Lord of sea and sky; I heard the voice of Jesus say; Master speak! Thy servant heareth; Lord, speak to me that I may speak.

Fourth Sunday of Epiphany   27 January
Principal Service   **Power in a Small Space**
Neh. 8.1–3, 5–6, 8–10; Ps. 19 [*or* 19.1–6]; 1 Cor. 12.12–31a;
Luke 4.14–21

We owe a great debt to archaeologists, especially those who work in Israel, because they are constantly uncovering materials that help to increase our knowledge of the social context in which Jesus lived.

Take synagogues, for instance. In 2009 an archaeological team from the Israel Antiquities Authority uncovered the remains of a first-century AD synagogue at a place called Migdal on the edge of the Lake of Galilee (we know it as Magdala, the home town of Mary Magdalene). What they discovered was that this particular synagogue originally had stone benches around the walls; it had some mosaics on the floor, and there were frescos on the walls. But they also discovered a large block of stone on which was carved a representation of the Menorah, the seven-branched candlestick in the Jerusalem Temple.

The entire synagogue complex turned out to be about 10 metres by 12 metres, with the synagogue meeting room itself measuring about 8 metres by 7 metres, or about 24 feet by 22 feet, the size of a large living room or a large kitchen-diner. So, it was not massive and certainly nothing like as large as our churches.

The synagogue acted as a community centre and a place for meeting and teaching, as well as for worship. It is worth remembering that in some places, and perhaps this was the case in a poor town like Nazareth, the synagogue might not have been a separate, identifiable building, but would have simply consisted of a large room in someone's house.

So when we try to imagine Jesus going to synagogue on the Sabbath in Nazareth, he might well have been entering a room in a house, capable of holding, at the most, about 30 people.

Worship in the synagogue

The Sabbath worship would have begun with the recitation of the Shema, the opening sentence of which is, 'Hear, O Israel: The LORD is our God, the LORD alone. You shall love the LORD your God with all your heart, and with all your soul, and with all your might.' The readings were from the Torah, the scrolls of the first five books of the Bible, which were kept either in a special cabinet in the synagogue itself or brought to the synagogue by one of the leaders. The Torah scrolls would have been read aloud by a man seated on the so-called Moses chair, as a way of symbolizing the central importance of Moses in giving the Israelites the Law.

The next set of readings, called the *Hephtarah*, was taken from the writings of the prophets and any adult male member of the synagogue could be invited to read them and comment on them.

So, that was the physical setting in the Nazareth synagogue when Jesus was invited to read one of the scrolls. He made his way from the congregation to the front of the room and chose some sentences from the scroll that had been handed to him. Those sentences came from the prophet Isaiah. He declaimed:

> The spirit of the Lord God is upon me, because he has anointed me to bring good news to the poor. He has sent me to proclaim release to the captives, and recovery of sight to the blind, to let the oppressed go free, to proclaim the year of the Lord's favour.

There was then a dramatic pause while Jesus rolled up the scroll (you can almost hear the soft crackling noise the vellum would have made as he did so); he handed the scroll back to the attendant, sat down and, looking at the gathering, said, 'Today this scripture has been fulfilled in your hearing.'

The reaction

You can imagine the sharp intake of breath: people looking at each other trying to gauge what their neighbours were thinking. Among some of the congregation there would have been a sense of shocked excitement, but among others a sense of bursting outrage. This, after all, was a person they knew. In a small town with a population of perhaps 500, they had seen him grow up. They knew his parents; they knew his brothers and sisters. He was not a stranger; he was one of their own, and he, one of their own kith and kin, was claiming to be the fulfilment of Scripture.

The powerful event was crammed into a space no bigger than a large sitting room. It was eyeball-to-eyeball stuff, shoulders jostling against shoulders. No one could be anonymous. Well. Jesus continued his sermon, and it ended in uproar with a lynch mob baying for his destruction.

Now, of course, we have to allow for Luke as a writer heightening the tension. Nevertheless, this is an explosive story. It is a foretaste of what is to come . . . a Messiah whose message of the liberating inrush of God's kingdom would cause joy and dismay in equal measure.

And it began in that small meeting room in Nazareth . . . which is how God frequently seems to work; he reveals who he is, not on the big stage but in small, humdrum places. And that in itself is surely fascinating news – the smallness and insignificance of the Nazareth synagogue was chosen as the venue for a message that continues to challenge and to change the world. A question follows: if that happened in that small synagogue then, what might God have in mind for our own small church now?

Christopher Herbert

Hymn suggestions

God's Spirit is in my heart; O Lord, all the world belongs to you; Put peace into each other's hands; We have a gospel to proclaim.

Fourth Sunday of Epiphany   27 January
Second Service   **Matters of Movements**
Ps. 33 [*or* 33.1–12]; **Num. 9.15–end**; 1 Cor. 7.17–24; *Gospel at Holy Communion*: Mark 1.21–28

Today, Epiphany 4 coincides with Homeless Sunday. And today our first reading is about a homeless community. This passage of Numbers has an equivalent right at the end of Exodus, but this one's far more repetitive. It really hammers home how the Israelites decided when to pull up their tent pegs, and when to pitch camp during their long wandering for 40 years in the wilderness. They had escaped the Egyptians and now had to survive as refugees in tents in the desert.

Being moved on

The homeless on the streets of big cities, with their bundles and plastic bags and cardboard boxes, are most likely to be moved on by the police. Perhaps they have encamped in a doorway and a landowner wants the fire exit clear. Maybe they are spilling out onto the pavements and their possessions are getting in the way of the passers-by going to work. It is an authority figure who tells them to move on, to shift themselves.

But the vast encampments of the Israelites in the wilderness were not moved on by human authority, but divine. In the shape of a miraculous cloud.

Numbers is so called because it begins with a great census of the Israelites on their journeying in the wilderness. All of the tribes of Israel are counted out by Moses and Aaron. They are given a place to camp in relation to their precious treasure chest, the Tabernacle. The Tabernacle was where the tablets of the covenant were kept, and it even had its own tent structure built around it in the centre of the whole camp. This created a great movable Temple, right in the middle of all the different families. It was where they did all the holy rituals following careful rules. Its construction is described in detail in the closing chapters of Exodus. When it was finally fully built, a cloud settled on it by day, and by night that cloud looked like fire. It could always be seen across the whole camp.

This was how the people knew when to move on and when to stay put. When the cloud was settled on the Tabernacle, the people settled in their tents. When it rose up, they lifted their tents and moved on.

Settling down

Our reading from Numbers today makes the point again and again how obedient the Israelites were to this. As long as the cloud was settled on the Tabernacle and its tent, the Israelites stayed put, however long that was. Even if it rose up in the middle of the night, they would rise up and move on too.

For many of us it's not quite so crystal clear. Should we move house, or job, now or later? What about the children's schools, the elderly relatives? It would be much easier if God wrote it in the skies, but we don't often get that in our decision-making. We have to pay attention, keep looking – just as no doubt the Israelites had their watchmen day and night. Put the passage from 1 Corinthians next to this. Sometimes we work out that it's right to stay as we are. That's what Paul is saying to the early Christians in Corinth. This isn't about moving house, but it is about knowing what things we don't need to worry about changing.

'Give me the serenity to accept the things I cannot change . . .'

The popular 'Serenity Prayer', which begins, 'Give me the serenity to accept the things I cannot change . . .', and continues, '. . . courage to change the things I can, and wisdom to know the difference'. There's something of that serenity in Paul's words today, as he repeats the advice not to worry about having to change things, but to let ourselves be content to stay as the people we were when God called us. He has just been talking about marriage and family relationships. Now he focuses on circumcision and slavery. These kinds of things are secondary to salvation, he tells us.

He's not saying that it's good to remain in slavery, but he *is* saying that whatever our circumstances in our day and age, what matters is our relationship with God. Everything else is of much less consequence.

Ready to move

But is it really? Can we say that to the homeless person, the poor, the disenfranchised in our world – it's of no consequence, it doesn't matter? Probably many of the poor or invisible in our society believe everyone else thinks just that – they don't matter.

But that's not how it was to Jesus. The reading from Mark today is the first story of Jesus' ministry. He comes to the synagogue in Capernaum. He teaches persuasively and casts out an evil spirit powerfully. The evil spirit recognizes him as 'Jesus of Nazareth', 'the holy one of God'; and the people see Jesus' authority. His fame spreads throughout Galilee, and by that evening the 'whole city' gathers to him. A wandering preacher and healer, he works in the towns of Galilee. By the end of Mark chapter 1 he cannot go into any town without attracting a crowd, so he stays in the countryside. This doesn't sound like someone who has a comfortable home to go to!

Wherever he was, Jesus attracted crowds. And he was attractive because many people needed that good news. They needed to hear that they *did* matter – that their sicknesses, their demons, their uncleanness mattered, that Jesus wanted to attend to them. He balanced his own spiritual needs and others' needs. And as he did, he was always ready to move to a different place, a different need.

Paul is right: nothing should matter to us as much as our relationship with God. But Paul also knew through Jesus that what matters to God is people. Jesus lived out that message – both his preaching and power revealed God's kingdom – a kingdom where people matter. What should be our next move in life to live out this message?

Megan Daffern

Hymn suggestions

A man there lives in Galilee; Beauty for brokenness; In a world where people walk in darkness; Lord, for tomorrow and its needs I do not pray.

Fifth Sunday before Lent   3 February
(*or* Candlemas; see p. 302.)
Principal Service   It's *How* Not Just *What* You Do
Ezek. 43.27—44.4; Ps. 48; **1 Cor. 13**; Luke 2.22–40

It's one of the richest, most inspiring and endearing pieces of writing, this 'Hymn to Love', written by St Paul. However the word 'love' is used and misused, this passage seems able to bring encouragement to all kinds of people. No wonder, then, it's one of the most quoted passages in the Bible and a favourite reading at weddings and other public celebrations.

We can rejoice when people of all kinds find a passage of Christian Scripture so accessible. Nevertheless, it was first addressed to a fractious church, and its lyrical cadences shouldn't hide the far-reaching challenge that it makes, beginning with the Christian community.

Gifts without love?

The members of the church at Corinth were impressed by the gift of speech, especially ecstatic, unintelligible speech. That led them to infer that such people had a special relationship to God. Today's church members, too, can be self-satisfied by the value and importance of the gifts they contribute. But Paul is clear. Speaking with tongues, or, by implication, exercising other gifts, if not motivated by love, brings no value to the giver.

If dramatic and individualistic gifts like speaking in tongues are worthless without love, surely the same cannot be said for prophecy, discernment, visionary thinking, and the ability to teach and impart biblical knowledge? How much, we tell ourselves, the Christian message is held back by our failure to equip Christians to share their faith confidently and credibly. Can anyone invest in such an enterprise, undertake a diocesan course, take a Religious Studies 'A' level, do a theological degree, without love? But, says Paul, 'I may know everything there is to know, but if I have no love I am nothing.'[3]

What then of faith, the faith that trusts in the stupendous activities of God and is crucial to Christian discipleship? Surely you can't have faith without love? You can't trust in the reality and power of God without loving him, can you? Yes, faith too can grow cold, dutiful, routine, instrumental, without the fire and energy brought to us by love.

But now Paul sets a stiffer challenge: giving away all one's possessions so as to feed others must surely signify love? There may be mixed motives at work – the reward of self-satisfaction, public recognition, tax breaks – but there must surely be love at work powering this self-sacrificial act? Well, says Paul, even that can be bereft of love.

And now, finally, what better proof of the evidence of love could there be than to sacrifice one's own life in the cause of others? But, says Paul, 'If in some great cause I give myself up to the most painful of deaths, but have no love, even this is no credit to me.'

The gifts Paul alludes to are real enough, and not to be discounted, but they are of no value to the giver, and could be of far greater value to the receivers, if given with love.

Not just what you do

I was busily initiating a curate into all the dimensions of ministry, schools, residential homes, churches, hospitals, shops and civic and council offices. My curate was on board, but he would gently drop into his conversation the phrase that became something of a mantra: 'It's not what you do but the love with which you do it that counts.' That phrase of St Teresa of Calcutta (and originally from her namesake, from Avila) began to reorder our perspective over time. Why were we doing what we were doing, and was our 'doing' inspired by and expressing love, or was love being stifled in the breathless pursuit of targets we had set ourselves? The ministry of the curate, Peter, embodied St Teresa's words and, following a tragic road accident, are inscribed on his grave stone.

Added value

Love, then, is the quality that adds supreme value to all that we do and are. It's not natural. It's not natural to subordinate our own ends, our preferences, choices of church, services, hymns, music, church styles and preachers above the unity of the Church. It's not natural to be long-suffering with those who bring us problems. More natural to be touchy, over-sensitive, quick to take offence when we feel we have been unfairly challenged, our efforts haven't been acknowledged, and our views and opinions have not been sought. It's natural to find fault with others, to transfer our disappointments at the decline of the church to the bishop, vicar, older members, occasional church-goers. It's not natural to put the interests of people, the community, before the tasks, goals and projects we have set ourselves, and to value people in and for themselves rather than for what they bring to the party. No, the love that Paul describes is not natural. Its source is God, and it's the gift of his Spirit.

If we're serious about the mission and influence of the Church, St Paul's self-examination may be a good place to start. It's not what you do but the love with which you do it that counts. It's all that counts. With faith and hope, it's the only quality that will abide, and of these love is the greatest. It's love alone that speaks to our condition, love that from the beginning drew people to Christ, and it's the quality of our love alone that will decide the future life and mission of the Church.

Roger Spiller

Hymn suggestions

Love is his word; A new commandment; Filled with the Spirit's power; Love divine, all love's excelling.

Fifth Sunday before Lent   3 February
Second Service   **'Rooted in the Absence of a Place'**
Ps. 34; 1 Chron. 29.6–19; **Acts 7.44–50**; *Gospel at Holy Communion*: John 4.19–29a

The power of place

Christianity has a huge investment in buildings. Church buildings have, for centuries, been the most significant buildings in our communities. For many the entire passage of human life, from baptism to burial, was marked in one particular building. Even in this secular era, buildings of worship still retain enormous physical and spiritual power: unbelievers no less than believers are fascinated by their 'ineffable' space. They embody place, memory and pilgrimage. As landmarks in every community they compel us to define ourselves in relation to the beliefs and experiences they espouse. And for members of historic Christian Churches, it's often argued that sacred buildings are a witness to the God who makes himself accessible and available, not in a general and abstract way but in particular places.

The Temple was one of the three pillars of the Jewish faith. Building the Temple in Jerusalem seemed the obvious thing to do when God's people finally entered Palestine, gave up their nomadic lifestyle and set out to form a nation. As the first king, David was the obvious person to build the Temple, but it fell to his son Solomon to build it, and in doing so he secured the unity of both the northern and southern tribes. The Temple seemed a glorious replacement for the tent where God's presence was believed to be found during the wilderness years. Thereafter the Temple became the touchstone of Israel's faith. The Temple was inviolable, a visible guarantee of God's protection and proof that God would preserve the nation in the face of the hostile nations that surrounded her. At least, that was how people regarded the Temple. Of course, we know they were mistaken and eventually the Temple was razed to the ground.

The limits of place

Our reading from Acts is an extract from a long speech purportedly by Stephen, one of the deacons appointed by the apostles. In it we have one of the most vociferous attacks on the Temple in the New Testament, and, by implication, on the misunderstandings that we can make of our own church buildings. 'The Most High does not dwell in houses made by human hands,' says Stephen. That is to say, the Temple and other buildings set aside as God's house can condition us to confine and control God to a place or territory we call sacred, where special conduct is expected, and blessings and privileges are dispensed. We get a hint of it at the transfiguration when Peter suggested a building programme to preserve and contain the momentary experience. It's why, when we're unsure about the future of the Church, we rush to improve our buildings. The Church becomes identified with a building set aside for the exclusive purpose of worshipping God. We call it the house of God. And this can lead us to imagine that God's power and presence can be scaled down to that shrinking realm we call the sacred. It often appears that we can care more about the church building than we do about God, and easily mistake our duty to God with service to the Church as a building and institution.

People as God's 'place'

Those who built the Temple thought this was a big advance on the tent as God's dwelling place. Well did King David remind his people, in our Old Testament reading, at the outset of building the Temple not to forget that they were 'aliens and transients' before God. But that was easily forgotten in the pursuit of a settled, permanent lifestyle. It was the tent that best reflected the true character of God, the nomadic God, the 'fast God' who occupies spaces and places but who cannot be confined in any of them; who is always ahead of his people. So, St John tells us in the Prologue to his Gospel that Jesus literally 'pitched his tent' among us, that he had no permanent home. And he goes on to make the revolutionary claim that the locus of God's Spirit is no longer the Temple, or any human edifice. It is Jesus, the Christ; he is the one who replaces the Temple. He is God's dwelling place for his time on earth. And after Jesus' ascension, and the giving of the Spirit, St Paul says, 'Do you not know that you are God's temple and that God's Spirit dwells in you? . . . God's temple is holy, and you are that temple.'

That didn't lead, of course, to the abandonment of place. Even St Paul continued to use the Temple, along with other Christians. Church buildings, too, continue to be hosts and agents of mission, propagators of the gospel. They can still make an important contribution, but only when we recognize that it is the living Christian community that is God's temple; that God's living temple has a prior claim over buildings through the love and service we owe to one another. A congregation that is struggling to maintain a high-cost, under-used building can be defeated in its primary vocation to be God's loving, liberated, joyous, outgoing people. Buildings serve to root us in particular places, garner memories and experiences of past encounters with the sacred, and invite fresh pilgrimages. But they can hinder us if we forget that we serve a nomadic God who demands that we are on the move, outgoing, fleet-footed and ultimately rooted not in a place but, as one thinker expressed it, 'rooted in the absence of a place'.[4]

Roger Spiller

Hymn suggestions

O thou not made with hands; Come, build the Church – not heaps of stone; All together in one place; Ye that know the Lord is gracious.

Fourth Sunday before Lent   (Proper 1)   10 February
Principal Service   **Whom Shall I Send?**
Isa. 6.1–8 [9–end]; Ps. 138; 1 Cor. 15.1–11; Luke 5.1–11

The term headhunter usually refers to someone who looks for professionals and executives and invites them to apply for jobs they had never thought of applying for. Believe it or not this happened to Fred. He didn't consider himself particularly good at his job – because he wasn't. He tended to daydream in the office, surfing the net, looking at websites that had nothing to do with his work. He could have gone off on courses to improve his work skills, but he was more interested in going to the pub with his mates. So when a headhunting agency put him in touch with a really plum interesting and overpaid job, he didn't expect to get it. But he did! Maybe it was the fact that his girlfriend was his previous line manager and it was she who wrote the reference – but he got the job: a six-figure salary, a car, foreign travel, and the promise of a lot of job satisfaction. But when Fred got the letter of appointment he hesitated. He knew lots of people more suited for the job than he was, but somehow or other he got over his scruples and took the job.

This emotion of not being the right person to have been chosen was the experience of a personality in all three of the Scripture readings we have just heard.

Send me

Isaiah experienced a vision of the awful holiness of God. He could not describe this experience so he used the language of symbol and mystery: 'I saw the Lord seated on a high throne; his train filled the sanctuary; above him stood seraphs, each one with six wings . . . The foundations of the threshold shook . . . and the Temple was filled with smoke.' And what Isaiah saw made him aware of his own sinfulness: 'What a wretched state I am in! I am lost, for I am a man of unclean lips and I live among a people of unclean lips, and my eyes have looked at the King, the LORD of hosts.' But after the burning coal had touched his lips his sin was taken away and he was able to respond to the call to be God's messenger: 'Whom shall I send? Who will be our messenger? I answered, "Here I am, send me."'

They left everything

In the Gospel, unaided human effort is seen as incapable of bringing in the harvest of fish for which the fishermen are working so laboriously. When the fishermen follow the teaching of Jesus, they cast off their nets and make a great catch. Like Isaiah, Peter recognizes his inadequacy in the presence of divine power and tells Jesus, 'Go away from me, Lord, for I am a sinful man!' And like Isaiah he hears the call to be a messenger: 'Then Jesus said to Simon, "Do not be afraid; from now on you will be catching people." And, like Isaiah, he and the other fishermen respond to the call: 'They left everything and followed him.'

Least of the apostles

Everyone who genuinely hears the call to deliver God's message begins and ends with a sense that they are unworthy of the task. Paul, in Corinthians, lists the people who had the awesome experience of encountering the risen Christ and then adds, 'Last of all . . . he appeared also to me. For I am the least of the apostles, unfit to be called an apostle, because I persecuted the church of God. But by the grace of God I am what I am.'

Send us

Like Fred, like Isaiah, like Peter and the other apostles, including Paul – the one who came last of all, like an unexpected baby to a woman who thought she was past the menopause – each one of us is headhunted for a job by God. Some of us may be called to be lay or ordained ministers in our respective churches, but we are – all of us – by our common baptism, called to be apostles, to announce the message that every heart is longing to hear. Recognizing our own inadequacy, we are able to begin to absorb the wisdom of the teaching that comes from the Christ who comes to meet us as we hear his word this morning. 'I am unfit to be called an apostle . . . But by the grace of God I am what I am.'

Duncan Macpherson

Hymn suggestions

Holy, holy, holy one, Love's eternal Trinity; Will you come and follow me if I but call your name; Go to the world! Go into all the earth; Dear Lord and Father of mankind.

Fourth Sunday before Lent (Proper 1) 10 February
Second Service **Seek Wisdom**
Ps. [1] 2; **Wisd. 6.1–21**, *or* Hos. 1; Col. 3.1–22; *Gospel at Holy Communion*: Matt: 5.13–20

Our society, it's often been said, has knowledge but lacks wisdom. 'Where is the wisdom we have lost in our knowledge?' asked T. S. Eliot in the last century,[5] and still the question reverberates down the years. We know so much about outer space, yet little about our own inner space; we can conquer stubborn diseases, yet we put our nation's health at risk by unproven intensive food production and environmental hazards; we have created a sophisticated global market and yet not counted the cost of our enslavement to the twin gods of production and consumption.

Popular wisdom

Yet, paradoxically, there is a movement in pursuit of wisdom. You see it in these little books displayed at airports and railway stations: 'How to cope with stress?' And then bite-sized books: 'The Wisdom of the Anglo-Saxons', 'The Wisdom of the Desert Fathers', 'The Wisdom of Jesus'. Little books of wisdom so that people can snatch a few random inspirational thoughts as they rush breathlessly from one appointment to another.

Solomonic wisdom

It was a king of Israel, Solomon, who is most associated with wisdom. He prayed to God for it, and his prayer was answered, and his reputation for it brought kings and emissaries to his court from countries far and wide. And it's in keeping with that tradition that there is a genre of wisdom writings in the Old Testament: Proverbs, Job, Ecclesiastes and a few of the psalms. But as you may know, there's a lot more material in the wisdom tradition included in what we call the Apocrypha, which is printed in some Bibles between the Old and New Testaments. One of these is called the Wisdom of Solomon, not attributable to Solomon but in the tradition he established, and written 100 years before the time of Jesus.

Wisdom of Solomon

The Wisdom of Solomon, although not deemed worthy to be included in the canon of Scripture, has been influential on Christianity. It was the source for the notion that love is a pure, universal force that permeates and orders the world. It was the source for the language used by John and Paul in speaking of Jesus as 'word', spirit, radiance, and 'image'. And it speaks of wisdom as a divine intermediary that prepares for St Paul's theme that Christ is the wisdom of God. Christianity has always to express itself through the idiom of cultures different from its own, if it is to spread the gospel, and the book of Wisdom notably draws on and mediates the philosophical tradition of Greek culture alongside Hebrew tradition.

Now to our reading. There is a warning to kings that they need to seek wisdom if they are to discharge their weighty responsibilities. That then leads into a description of wisdom, wisdom personified as a woman, wisdom that is accessible, that rewards those who seek it and that brings us near to God. 'Wisdom is radiant and unfading, and she is easily discerned by those who love her, and is found by those who seek her.'

Wisdom as rallying point

To those who've been put off by religion, the pursuit of wisdom can offer a more acceptable rallying point for discussing the underlying and generative issues that shape our identity and society. It evokes Plato's advice on the training and preconditions for those aspiring to, and those called to appoint, rulers and political leaders. His answer is that it is lovers of wisdom, philosophers, who can look behind the surface, ask fearless questions, be in such rapt love of wisdom that they no longer have any appetite for the temptations and distractions that would otherwise corrupt them.

A way of seeing

What is wisdom for us? It's a way of seeing, which attends to what lies hidden as well as to what lies on the surface, a way of seeing that looks to the future as well as to the past and present. Its source is God. And so it's not found in places where we might expect to find it. It's where the place of the wise is taken by the fool, the place of the strong by the weak and the place of the mature by the child. It's not to be found in the accumulated experience of humankind, even when that is accessed in little pocket books of distilled wisdom.

Wisdom is not, it seems, a logical extrapolation from our present position, acquired through specialist knowledge, through the results of focus groups, commissions, enquiries, conferences, scholarly debate. That may produce knowledge, but it doesn't produce wisdom. Wisdom is a way of seeing; it comes upon us, a mysterious intuition. Clever, sophisticated people have a capacity to miss the obvious that is right in front of their eyes. Those with uncluttered simplicity often see right through to the heart of the matter. And wisdom comes to us through Christ, who is the Wisdom of God.

So, as our Epistle says: 'Let the word of Christ dwell in you richly; teach and admonish one another in all wisdom.'

Roger Spiller

Hymn suggestions

Praise the source of faith and learning; All my hope on God is founded; Disposer Supreme, and Judge of the earth; Put thou thy trust in God.

Third Sunday before Lent (Proper 2) 17 February
Principal Service **Choices, Choices, Choices**
Jer. 17.5–10; Ps. 1; 1 Cor. 15.12–20; Luke 6.17–26

You can't go into a coffee shop these days without being presented with a bewildering array of choices: Latte, Skinny latte, Americano, Cappuccino . . . Life might be easier if they just served Coffee! The promise of choice extends to all arenas of our life. What to wear, what to eat, where to go to school, where to work, live or take our leisure. What holidays do we take? Which utility company do we use? Where do we shop? Which bank do we trust?

Such is the proliferation of choice that a whole industry has grown up to help us navigate the many choices we have to make. We can compare and contrast the market, find out the going rate and get the best deal. But, then again, which comparison website should we choose to begin our research – there are so many to choose from?

Life is not simple in the twenty-first century, and, far from making things easier, too much choice can in fact cause us anxiety and blight our lives with the constant question, 'What if?' Consumer choice is heralded as the way to attain happiness, but is that really true?

Choose life

The prophet Jeremiah presents us with a simple choice – do we trust in God or not? The offer is quite straightforward: if you put all your trust in human powers you will be like a shrub in the desert, desperate for nourishment and shade. If you put your trust in God, you will be like a tree planted by water whose leaves will stay green, bearing fruit to the end of the ages. You could say the choice is a very easy one, do we want to flourish or not? Do we want life or death?

The Psalmist also calls us to consider our choices. If we choose to delight in the law of the Lord, we will be happy; if we choose to ignore the law of the Lord and instead choose the way of wickedness, we will perish. Again, the choice is actually very simple.

In his letter to the Corinthians, St Paul also presents us with a simple choice. Do you believe that Christ was raised from the dead? Or not? This question lies at the very heart of our faith. It provokes us to give a 'yes' or 'no' answer. There cannot be any 'ifs' or 'buts' or 'maybes'. If we answer 'no' then our faith is in vain, the dead cannot be raised and we remain stuck in the mire of our own sins. If we do not choose life in Christ, who has died, who is risen and who will come again, everything begins to unravel. By making this choice, by saying 'no' to God, all future hope is closed down to us. We are people for this life only, and not people who have a vision of the life to come.

In contrast, if we believe that Christ is indeed raised from the dead, if we answer 'yes' to Paul's question, then all manner of possibilities are opened up to us. But we do not have to choose again – God has already chosen us. We are given God's promise for all eternity. Once again, the choice here is relatively easy to make. We choose death, or we choose life in Christ.

Blessings and woes

For those who are in any doubt, we are promised that Jesus is the way, the truth and the life. If we choose him, we choose life in all of its fullness. In him the world is turned upside down, expected human choices are subverted and we are invited to enter into a new way of looking at the world and a new way of navigating life.

If we choose to live by the light of Christ, the poor will inherit the kingdom of God, the hungry will be filled, and those who weep will laugh. They are the ones who will now be called 'happy'. Choosing Christ opens up possibilities for everyone whose lives have been diminished: the downcast, the dejected, the dispossessed. All those who have been denied choice by human powers and dominions will find liberty in the blessings of Christ.

In contrast, those who by the world's standards seem to be blessed with the power to choose whatever they like will find that they will slowly wither on the vine. The rich will be brought low, the well fed will be hungry, and those who laugh will come to mourn and weep.

The choice for us is simple: blessings or woes. To inherit life, and to be like trees planted by streams of water, bearing fruit in its season, we are called to side with those whom Jesus called 'blessed'; through Christ, our allegiance should always lie with them.

If we choose Christ, the other choices we have to make in life will fall into their proper place. Christ will come first, and all other decisions will follow. In him we will find true happiness and perfect freedom. In a world of too many choices, Christ offers us a simple one: believe. Choose life. So let us pray we can all say 'yes' to that.

Victoria Johnson

Hymn suggestions

Blest are the pure in heart; O Happy day that fixed my choice; Be Thou my vision; Be thou my guardian and my guide.

Third Sunday before Lent (Proper 2) 17 February
Second Service **Being Found by God**
Ps. [5] 6; Wisd. 11.21—12.11, *or* Hos. 10.1–8, 12; **Gal. 4.8–20**; *Gospel at Holy Communion*: Matt. 5.21–37.

There are just a few, small moments in the New Testament where we as readers can glimpse the actual working practices of the writers of the texts; these are the moments where their minds, in unconscious but skilful mode, are revealed to us. It's as though we can look through a glass panel and see the clockwork whirring away on the other side. One of those moments is to be found in today's lesson taken from Paul's letter to the young church in Galatia.

Let's be clear, he was not engaged in *writing* the letter himself, he was dictating it; that was his standard method of working. (If you want evidence for this, look no further than the last verses of his letter where he takes over the writing himself: 'See what large letters I make when I am writing in my own hand!')

But let's get back to the main track.

69

Ideas becoming visible

In our Epistle reading we have in front of our eyes an instance where we can see St Paul's thinking processes becoming visible. He is dictating what he wants to say; his secretary takes down the dictation, the quill scratching on the papyrus . . . Paul declaims: 'Now, however, that you have come to know God' . . . and no sooner has the secretary written those words down than Paul corrects and inverts his own thinking. He says, 'or rather to be known by God'.

It is a beautiful moment: theology is being created on the hoof. And what a gorgeous and powerful insight Paul has fashioned for us, even though it has the character of a throwaway line, a kind of afterthought.

Having split the sentence up in my analysis, let me now read the whole sentence to you: 'Now, however, that you have come to know God, or rather to be known by God, how can you turn back again to the weak and beggarly elemental spirits?'

Paul is making it absolutely clear that human beings cannot know God: it is God who takes the initiative and makes himself known to us.

In 1973, a small book was published in English that has been reprinted many, many times since. Its title was *Rule for a New Brother*. The book had originally been written in Dutch for a Roman Catholic monastic community called the Brakkenstein Community of Holy Sacrament Fathers, and it soon quietly made its presence felt among those who read it. Its opening chapter is headed 'Seeking God', and it's very first sentence is this:

> Brother, you want to seek God with all your life, and love him with all your heart. But you would be wrong if you thought you could reach him. Your arms are too short, your eyes are too dim, your heart and understanding too small.
>
> To seek God means first of all to let yourself be found by him.

It is such a simple statement, but that is where its power lies. It mirrors and echoes exactly what St Paul said in his throwaway, afterthought line in his letter to the Galatians.

The opposite of what we might think

Our difficulty is that we find this idea very difficult to grasp. We are much happier believing that we are engaged in a search for God, as though God is somewhere out there and through strenuous spiritual effort we should spend our lives on a quest for him. But it is the exact opposite that is true. God is on a quest for us.

Perhaps we can think of it this way. It is the deep nature of love, isn't it, that the lover searches for the beloved? Think of God as the lover: we, by God's grace, are the beloved. How do we know that God is the lover? Because we have seen in Jesus Christ that God reveals to us who he truly is, what he is truly like, and the heart of his nature is love. More than that, by allowing God to know us we are allowing God to love us.

When Paul was dictating his letter to the young church in Galatia, he knew that he needed to get that message across and, in an inspired split second, he did so: now, however, that you have come to know God, or rather to be known by God, how can you turn back again to the weak and beggarly elemental spirits?

It was an insight that in one tiny phrase turned our thinking about God upside down. So perhaps all that we have to do now, as best we can, is to rest and live in that truth.

Christopher Herbert

Hymn suggestions

Can we by searching find out God?; O God, you search me and you know me; Father who in Jesus found us; Christ triumphant ever reigning.

Second Sunday before Lent 24 February
Principal Service **Even the Winds and Sea Obey Him**
Gen. 2.4b–9, 15–end; Ps. 65; Rev. 4; **Luke 8.22–25**

I have only been to the Holy Land once. Neither did I ever have any great desire to go. I have always thought there are plenty of Calvarys here in England. I also think that the great sites of the Holy Land bear witness to the history of the Church as much as to Christ. This is no bad thing; the Church is Christ's body, and the way we remember him – even in our buildings – is the way we communicate his message and importance to people today. But, consequently, I've never been convinced that visiting those places associated with Christ's ministry on earth would necessarily bring me any nearer to Christ.

But when I did visit, as well as enjoying it much more than I thought, I particularly found myself looking forward to a boat trip on Lake Galilee. This, I surmised, would be an experience hardly changed from the time of Jesus: the same hills in the distance; the same water to travel upon. And I was rewarded more fulsomely than I could have imagined.

We set off in brilliant sunshine, with clear skies and calm waters, but within minutes we were clinging on to the gunwales for dear life! A storm arose from nowhere. Winds pummelled the boat. Waves broke over us. It wasn't so bad that we feared sinking, but we did get a good soaking. It was not the 'still, small calm' of Galilee we were imagining. No one slept in the bows.

But storms don't arise from nowhere. This storm, like the one that battered Jesus' boat and filled the disciples with fear, came from somewhere. Storms are caused by a collision of opposing forces and by pressure rising.

It is Jesus asleep in the storm that is the remarkable thing about this story – and his mastery over it. The disciples are filled with bafflement and wonder.

He gives his beloved slumber

Let us consider the sleep first.

There is an English bishop, who had better remain nameless, who once commented: 'Is there something wrong with me? I've never had a bad night's sleep in my life!'

Well, there may not be anything actually wrong, but this is certainly unusual. Most of us have a bad night's sleep from time to time, and usually it is because storms are rising. Conflict at home or pressure at work make rest impossible.

Jesus asleep in the boat doesn't mean he is immune from these pressures and conflicts. But it does mean he is not overwhelmed by them (though there are, of course, those hours of torment in Gethsemane where he is filled with anguish, and others sleep).

Psalm 127 famously opens with the declaration that 'Unless the LORD builds the house, those who built it labour in vain.' Verse 2 offers the less well-remembered affirmation: 'he gives sleep to his beloved.'

Jesus sleeps because he rests secure in the knowledge of God's love for him and God's purpose for his life. His house is built on solid rock. Storms still come. Conflicts arise. Pressures build. But

God's beloved is the still point of security and rest in the eye of the storm.

But Jesus is also the master of the storm.

He is master of the storm

The winds swell. The waves rise. The boat is tossed to and fro. It begins to fill with water. Still Jesus sleeps. Fearing for their lives, the disciples wake him: 'Master,' they shout, 'we are perishing!'

In the book of Genesis, God's first act in creation is to hover over the deep waters bringing light and order to the dark, formless emptiness beneath. God brings order out of chaos.

Now, Jesus, the Son of God, the one who was 'with God in the beginning' and 'through whom all things were made', brings the same order to the threatening dangers of these waters. He rebukes the wind. He settles the raging waves. There is calm.

But there is something more. He settles the storm, but he unsettles the disciples. As well as saving them, he amazes them. They are amazed he could sleep through a storm. They are even more amazed he can stop one. 'Where is your faith?' he says to them. Which I suppose can mean two things: 'Why didn't you have the faith to stop the storm; why did you wake me?' Or, 'You're with me; why did you think the storm would win? Do you still not know who I am?'

What we see happening in this story is the disciples' understanding of Jesus expanding. They already knew he was a great teacher and a healer. Now they witness something else: the winds and the water obey him (Luke 8.25). This compels them towards the conclusion that is the foundation of Christian faith: Jesus is not just someone who does the work of God, *Jesus is God*.

So, do we have faith? Do we have faith that Jesus is the Son of God? Do we have faith that with Jesus we can be safe, that even when the storms of conflict and pressure assail us we will be secure? Do we have faith that we could be channels of that peace and good order we see in Jesus?

And remember, faith does not mean certainty, but trust. Like the disciples, like Jesus himself in Gethsemane, storms will come and sometimes we will be terribly unsettled, but resting secure in God's presence and in the affirmation of God's love, and wrestling with what this vocation means for us to be those who turn to Jesus to be saved and who turn to the world to offer God's peace to everyone, we trust in the one who calms the storms, even the raging in my heart and mind today.

Stephen Cottrell

Hymn suggestions

Will your anchor hold in the storms of life; Dear Lord and Father of mankind; Jesus, be the centre; Be thou my vision.

Second Sunday before Lent   24 February
Second Service   **Putting the Creation Story to Work**
Ps. 147 [*or* 147.13–end]; **Gen. 1.1—2.3**; Matt. 6.25–end

Let's begin at the beginning, there's no other place to begin. The Bible begins with the story of creation, the starting point. You might be surprised, then, that the first chapter was one of the latest parts of the Bible to be written, some 500–600 years before Christ, though it includes much earlier material that circulated as oral tradition. Why did it appear in written form when it did?

Interpreting the present

When the proverbial sky caves in, when we can't live in the present, because it's been taken away from us, where do we go? The only place we can move to in imagination is in the future or in the past. We can imagine the future in hope for something new to emerge. Or we can look back, to a remote past and ask why things happened as they did and what light from a real or imagined past can shed light on our present. That looking back and imagining our roots in a primordial story of beginnings was what happened when the people of God faced the loss of everything. The year was 587 BC, the only really significant date in Jewish history. Judaea was besieged, Jerusalem was razed to the ground and its key citizens were deported to Babylon. It was then that people asked questions about the past, about beginnings, in the hope that it could be seen where things went wrong, and some sense could be made of the catastrophe that had overtaken them.

Why back to creation?

The creation story in the first chapter of Genesis was written among other literary contributions by a circle of writers called 'P', or 'priestly'. They were active in the post-exilic period between 538 and 450 BC. They had their own theological perspective and traced their version of history right back to the beginning and to a story of beginnings that was congenial to their religious perspective. Its greatness is in its sober reality, focusing on what they believed to have been revealed by God. It's the fruit of reflection by many generations of priests. The whole interest is exclusively on what comes from God, his words, judgements, commands and regulations. It presents history not in terms of persons but of divine regulations on earth. There is a second creation story written by the earliest school of writers in the Old Testament, and viewing creation from a human perspective. That serves as the other side of the picture given in the first story. The authors of our story are emphatically not attempting to describe the way creation takes place. They're explaining the present world to their hearers and affirming that, contrary to all they see, it is still in God's hands.

How does the story address us?

The story tells us that God created and that it is good, and, because it is good, it is a source of joy and beauty. This has sometimes been ignored by an overemphasis on our fallenness, introduced in the second creation story. It's been left to scientists like Brian Cox to entrance us with their awesome, sublime, spiritual accounts of the natural order, where believers have often been content to see creation not for itself but only as the stage setting for the drama of salvation.

It was God's creation and it couldn't answer back to him. But God wouldn't have recognized himself in his creation.[6] His creation was determined and not free, and only what is free is alive and responsive and able to reflect its Creator. If the Creator wanted to see himself in his creation, he must create in his own image, with something of the kind of freedom that he himself enjoyed. Biologists may be right to point out the small genetic differences between humans and other sentient creatures. But this text highlights the wider theological difference between God's creating of human beings and the rest of creation. Try telling people that they are apes minus fur, accidental accumulations of atoms, random genetic mutations. It's not merely that people dislike being described in such terms. It's that the language falls so far short of our conscious experience of reality.

God's creation means, too, that men and women are drawn into God's plan and entrusted with the rule and responsibility of his creation. We are, as the Psalmist daringly expresses it, 'a little less than God'. Our relationship with God and with earth is 'good' and secure as long as we know God as God and the world as God's creation.

A story that interprets our present

Now, it's this story that was designed to provide a diagnostic, or heuristic, account by which the catastrophe of the exile could be understood. How did the finely tuned relationship between God and his vice-regents, the kings and shepherds of Israel, fare against the story of creation? How was the freedom and stewardship entrusted to humankind exercised by God's people? How did the populace use the freedom that was expected to be with God and for his creation, and not as a personal possession? If anything was to be salvaged after the exile, it was along such lines that hopes were reborn. And for us, this story is never more relevant than when the future of the planet is threatened by our exploitative and selfish lifestyle.

David Attenborough chose Handel's setting of Isaiah's hymn of praise to the Creator as one of his Dessert Island disks. Once recently I heard him being asked, 'Do you ever entertain the possibility of God?' 'I sometimes recall looking into a termite mound, and seeing 100 termites, all hard at work, building tracks, carrying items purposefully to and fro, in some highly organized activity, But they can't see me, because they don't have the sensory equipment to do so. I can just imagine that we cannot see God, because we cannot see.' Our natural capacities fail us. The work of science can help us to see the glory of creation, but the word of God can help us to see God.

Roger Spiller

Hymn suggestions

Lord of the boundless curve of space; O Lord of every shining constellation; Oh, the life of the world is a joy and a treasure; The heavens declare thy glory, Lord.

Sunday next before Lent   3 March
Principal Service   **Lifting the Veil**
Ex. 34.29–end; Ps. 99; 2 Cor. 3.12—4.2; **Luke 9.28–36 [37–43a]**

Jesus was transfigured. While he was praying, he shone. Many film-makers have shown Jesus with a perpetual glow or with particularly luminous or unblinking eyes all the time, but this story suggests that it was only rarely, perhaps only once, that Jesus looked any different from the rest of us. He would have sweated as he walked up the mountain in the heat and longed for a drink as he reached the summit. He would have been dusty and tired from the walk.

Most of the time life is ordinary

I find this comforting because for most of the time life feels pretty ordinary. The story of the transfiguration tells me that that's OK, and that God didn't intend us all to be perpetually in a state of religious ecstasy or fervour. And that most of life, even faith, has to be lived down the mountain. I imagine that most of us will know some moments in our lives when suddenly it all makes sense, when we want to shout, 'Alleluia!' But those times are, for most people, rare glimpses.

It's rare, and even dangerous, to see the whole glory of God

There was always a strong tradition in the Bible that very close experience of God was in any case really out of the question. If you did see the face of God, it would probably be the last thing you ever saw. It's out of this tradition that there comes the story that when Moses had met with God on the mountain he came down to the people, and the Bible tells us: 'the skin of his face shone because he had been talking with God'.

The people were afraid even to look on Moses' face because it was shining with the glory of God, so Moses put a veil over his face. We might think this a very strange story indeed, and it's tempting to reduce it to something that sounds as ludicrous as a visit to an over-zealous tanning shop. But I imagine that all of us can remember seeing people who have shone with joy, or something like it – someone in love, a new father fresh with the news, anyone with a new reason to smile and be glad. And sometimes people who are good and lovely, or about whom there is some kind of remarkable serenity and peace, are described as those who 'shine'.

But we also know that no one shines all the time, and that for most of us life has its dull patches, its prosaic ordinariness, its week-a-day feel. Transfiguration would have nothing to transfigure if it were there the whole time. Even Moses, and even Jesus, did not spend all their days shining with holy light.

Beware of claiming to have seen it all

Religious people have a tendency to want to show that their saints shine brighter than the others. Paul tries to persuade the good Christians at Corinth to have confidence in him and to persuade them that the faith he has taught them is much more profound than what they might have learned of Moses. He has a dig at Moses, suggesting that the reason Moses wore a veil over his face was that the glory of God was actually fading! We Christians, he says, have unveiled faces, and we see the glory of God as it is. In Jesus Christ, we have seen the face of God. I wonder whether seeing God is ever as straightforwardly simple as that might imply. We do believe that in Jesus Christ, the love of God has been revealed to us. But that doesn't mean that we now see everything.

Faith must trust that there is always more to see, something 'beyond' . . .

In the story of the transfiguration there is provided a hint, and more than a hint, that this ordinary fleshly reality of the everyday is not the end of it, but that it is a kind of veil – and that there is more to be seen than we have yet known. And it may be, as the ancients believed, that this other reality is after all too much for us to bear all the time, that it is better to live behind the veil, or down the mountain, for most of our days. But to see the ordinary daily life we know as a kind of veil is to develop a longing for the world that lies beyond, as yet unful-filled and unrealized, but always hinted at among us.

Precious moments when the veil is lifted

Those who followed Jesus Christ came to see that in knowing him they had seen God, that the veil had been lifted. And sometimes there are moments when we do see that knowing God through Christ makes life quite different. It transfigures us, for God has shone a light into our hearts. Even the briefest glimpse beyond the veil is enough to transform a life, and to make every day a holy day and any life a holy life. Amen.

Susan Durber

Hymn suggestions

Longing for light, we wait in darkness; Christ is the world's light; Be still, for the presence of the Lord; Jesus, on the mountain peak.

Sunday next before Lent   3 March
Second Service   **Hidden and Found**
Ps. 89.1–18 [*or* 89.5–12]; **Ex. 3.1–6**; John 12.27–36a

Hide and seek is a game that holds its appeal well into middle age. We can still note well-appointed hiding places and recall the thrill of hide and seek from childhood memories. The distinguished psychologist David Winnicott summed up its endless appeal and benefit: 'It is a joy to be hidden and a disaster not to be found.' The dynamics of hide and seek are more than a game. They represent a strategy that we adults resort to at challenging times in our lives, hiding from ourselves, hiding from other people, and hiding from God.

Hiding

We read that 'Moses hid his face, because he was afraid to look at God'. The appearance of an angel in a flame of fire out of a blazing bush led him to encroach unwittingly upon holy ground. When he heard the voice of God, he knew he had to hide his face if he was not to be consumed by the radiance of the divine. So also Elijah hid his face in the mouth of a cave when he encountered God. Hiding from God is the human response of fear and shame. 'Where are you?' asks God of Adam and Eve, in that archetypal drama in the garden of paradise as they tried to hide from their Creator. And people with any sense of the numinous Other have been trying to hide from God, out of fear or shame, down the centuries.

Religion can provide a good hiding place from the excesses of the divine, as it tries to domesticate, routinize and protect us from the wild demands that we might face. A woman I knew tried to stave off the call she heard from God by increasing activities in church. But the call didn't subside, God wouldn't take no for an answer. She simply had to come out of hiding. We are, says Luther, God's enemies before we are his friends, and our enmity and fear of falling into the hands of God can make us fugitives, on the run, from the pursuit of the One who will not give up on us.

Being sought

In the poem *The Hound of Heaven*, the hound following the hare, never ceasing in its running, ever drawing nearer in the chase, resembles God pursuing the fleeing person. For a host of Christians that is the way, and sometimes the poem itself has been the means, through which they have felt cornered by God. John Stott confessed that he was a Christian not because of parental influence, or through his own personal decision, but as a result of being pursued by 'the Hound of Heaven'. C. S. Lewis similarly described that he once thought that the decision was his as to whether to adopt Christianity but admitted there was another party in the affair. As he expressed it:

> The Prodigal Son at least walked home on his own feet. But who can duly adore that Love which will open the high gates to a prodigal who is brought in kicking, struggling, resentful, and darting his eyes in every direction for a chance of escape?[7]

Hidden

'You sometimes think you want to disappear,' says the musician Kid Cudi, 'but all you really want is to be found.' Yes, 'it is a disaster not to be found'. And there is anguish when, like the Psalmist's complaint, we feel it is God who is hiding from us. The consolation must be that 'You could not seek me if you had not already found me'. Moses, too, was puzzled by God's rejection of his request to see God's glory. But our seeking God is part of what it means to find him.

Now the role is reversed, and it's our turn to stalk God. Annie Dillard, in her novel *Pilgrim at Tinker Creek* imagines Moses turn to do the stalking:

> you can bang at the door all night till the innkeeper relents, if he ever relents; and you can wail till you're hoarse . . . I sit on a bridge as on Pisgah or Sinai, and I am both waiting, becalmed in a cliff of the rock and banging with all my will, calling like a child beating on a door: Come on out! . . . I know you're there!'[8]

The fact that God hides provokes us passionately and energetically to seek to find him, like children who can't stop themselves from seeking when they know someone is hiding from them.

Found

We are hidden in the waters of baptism to represent being found in God, heirs to the rich lexicon of phrases that describe what it means to be found. We 'abide in Christ', as John expresses it, or in Paul's pregnant phrase, we are found to be 'in Christ'. Being found by God, we find ourselves; being his captive we discover our true freedom. As R. S. Thomas puts it:

> I am the bush burning
> at the centre of
> your existence; you must put
> your knowledge off and come
> to me with your mind
> bare.[9]

Yes, we like to hide, from God, from ourselves, but we can never get over the joy and thrill of being found and to have, in Newman's words, 'a secret channel of communication with the Most High, a gift the world knows not of, to have their life hid with Christ in God'.

Roger Spiller

Hymn suggestions

Rock of Ages; Jesu, lover of my soul; Come, O thou Traveller unknown; Safe in the shadow of the Lord.

Lent

Ash Wednesday 6 March
Facing Mortality
Joel 2.1–2, 12–17, *or* Isa. 58.1–12; Ps. 51.1–18; 2 Cor. 5.20b—6.10; Matt. 6.1–6, 16–21, *or* John 8.1–11

No one speaks to us as we shall be spoken to tonight during the course of this service. We will be addressed with words that create a visceral impact, may strike fear and panic into our lives. But they are words that are, and must be, spoken to each one of us, personally. They face us with our mortality, which we can spend our whole lives trying to deny. 'You are dust and to dust you shall return.' And then two lines are drawn on our forehead with the weightless blackened ash, so that we can see and show and feel the mortal remains that we ourselves will become.

Not facing reality

In the light of this, giving up chocolate, alcohol, sugar, newspapers, or even some of the practices proposed in our Gospel are acceptable, even welcome, responses to Lent. But we know that such Lenten disciplines can serve as a soft option from facing the ultimate issues that confront us. 'Humankind cannot bear much reality,' says T. S. Eliot, speaking of 'one end, which is always present',[10] which is usually taken to mean our own deaths. And Eliot's assessment is all too evident in the way we privatize, sanitize and medicalize death in our western culture. We cannot bear too much reality. But Christians, whose sign is the crucified and risen Lord, and who live under the cross, should of all people be willing at least to reckon with death, believing that death is the necessary dark face of coming alive.

The season of Lent represents the 40 years the people of Israel wandered in the wilderness on the way to the land that God promised they would inhabit. That sojourn through dry, barren, inhospitable land became the training ground for the Israelites, and then for Jesus during his 40 days in his own wilderness experience. Free of external distraction, it's where the bare issues of existence can be confronted.

We might, of course, respond that 'we believe in the resurrection of the body and the life everlasting'. Yes, but believing as a form of assent to a proposition isn't the same as living our lives in and out of the hope of life eternal. Believing in beliefs can even assist us to deny the fears, doubts, questions that the fact of death awakens in us. The thought of death can be every bit as real and frightening for religious people, Christians included, as for non-believers. St Paul himself felt the fear of death's exposure even while he longed to be clothed in his 'heavenly dwelling'. We can be crippled, immobilized, by the terrifying inevitability of death, even if we entertain hope for an eternal life.

Annual stocktaking

The response is not to seek for grief support or counselling, or even to eat cake, drink tea and discuss death in a Death Cafe, though such resources may be helpful and necessary for some people. We're not primarily about reducing our fears and seeking our own well-being, nor about self-help to overcome the fear of death. Instead, Lent is the season when we return to God, conscious of our mortality, our nakedness, our regrets, our sin. Lent is the Church's annual stocktaking season, the time to overhaul our lives in God's presence, the season for undergoing more strenuous, intensive exercise in prayer, study and worship. It's our own voluntary wilderness experience.

This urgent mood is summoned by the prophet Joel in our Old Testament reading: 'Blow the trumpet in Zion; sound the alarm on my holy mountain! Let all the inhabitants of the land tremble, for the day of the LORD is coming, it is near.' Our inclination is to pass by this annual summons, this call to rend our hearts and not our clothing, and to return to the Lord our God. But if we heed the call, we may know the grace and love of God that can begin to release us from our deepest fears.

St Paul is no less urgent and insistent in today's Epistle: 'Now is the acceptable time . . . now is the day of salvation!' There's a sense of urgency he wants us to feel and respond to that is critical for our life and future. He's urging us 'not to accept the grace of God in vain', not to take it for granted, not to treat it lightly, not to use it as a guarantee against a serious engagement with the new life to which God is calling us. And that engagement is one, as Matthew's Gospel indicates, before the One 'to whom all hearts are open, all desires known'.

'You are dust and to dust you shall return.' Lent, then, invites us to recognize that we stand naked and exposed before our gracious God; who called us into being, made us in his image and loves us into a relationship with himself. Enjoying God, we begin to experience a renewal of ourselves that gives us hope of a fuller life to come. Making the most of the time we have will persuade us that 'Neither death nor life . . . nor anything else in all creation, will be able to separate us from the love of God in Christ Jesus our Lord'.

Roger Spiller

Hymn suggestions

Come, let us to the Lord our God; Rock of ages, cleft for me; Jesu, lover of my soul; From ashes to the living font, your Church must journey, Lord.

First Sunday of Lent   10 March
Principal Service   **Jesus' Vocation Tested**
Deut. 26.1–11; Ps. 91.1–2, 9–end [*or* 91.1–11]; Rom. 10.8b–13;
Luke 4.1–13

It's a condition today, it seems, that everything has to establish its relevance to us if it's to deserve our attention. So when we hear the account of the temptations of Jesus, it's usual, tempting even, to try to apply them directly, as a checklist for us. And it's not difficult nor is it wrong to try to do so. After all, what confronted Jesus boils down to three temptations, and they concern our most pervasive human appetites: possessions, power and popularity. I can't think of any temptations that don't fall within the scope of those propulsions.

Scaling down or scaling up? The risk is that we might 'scale down' the unique character of the wilderness experience so as to suggest that the unique and incomparable event that faced Jesus is directly applicable to ourselves. Jesus did indeed share our temptations, but we cannot fully share his. Coming immediately after the affirmation of his divine vocation, at his baptism, the Gospel writers set out the parameters Jesus established for his own unique ministry. So let's 'scale up' to the remarkable event Luke brings to our attention, and behold the character of Jesus spread out before us, and discern the hard and narrow path he lays out for us too.

Beware of the 'If?'

The three temptations, brief as they are, expand on the little word 'If'. 'If you are the Son of God?' This tactic is designed to sow doubt in Jesus' mind on the vocation that his Father had earlier confirmed at his baptism. It's often suggested that Jesus is following some predetermined plan, but that doesn't quite accord with the fierce self-questioning and tortuous prayers that marked key points in his life. The possibility seemed real enough that Jesus could have chosen, if not another path, then at least other routes to arrive at the outcome his Father had for him. The tempter's finely targeted temptations seem designed to offer the chance to 'do the right deed for the wrong reason'.

An economic Messiah?

The first temptation is for Jesus to be an economic Messiah; feeding his people by turning stones into bread. The Grand Inquisitor, in a novel of that title by the Russian writer Dostoyevsky, says that most people are too weak to live by the word of God when they are hungry. Christ should have taken the bread and offered humankind freedom from hunger rather than freedom from choice. 'Why doesn't God act to alleviate the plight of the hungry?', we ask. This temptation is the snare of the shortcut. It 'heals my people lightly', it suggests that there's a quick fix to the large systemic problems of hunger and homelessness. Jesus knew that people would come to him for food, but not for the living bread in whom 'all our hungers can be satisfied'. The temptation miraculously to produce bread here and there can distract from the miracle that comes when God's spirit creates a generosity for the needy that will bring about a redistribution of human resources.

A political Messiah?

The second temptation tries to paint Jesus as a political Messiah. Christ should have taken power, said Dostoyevsky's Inquisitor, but, since he refused, the Church has now taken it in his name in

85

order to convince people that security in an institution is preferable to freedom of choice. The devil offers him a pact so that Jesus can bring in his kingdom, without suffering, struggle and delay. Didn't Jesus break the Sabbath so that not a day's delay could hinder the coming of the kingdom to a sick person? It's attractive this, the 'art of the possible', to wheel and deal, cut and trim, not be too fussy about the means or the ethics of the folk we work with, as long as the big prize is secured. Work with the powerful, engage in real politick, without letting theological scruples hold us back. We want a viable church and we're not too fussy how we get it.

A celebrity Messiah?

The third temptation is for Jesus to be a celebrity or miracle-giving Messiah, someone who will 'play to the gallery'. The Inquisitor says that Christ should have given people a miracle, for most people need to see the miraculous in order to be convinced about the truthfulness of the Christian faith. 'What sign are you going to give us . . . so that we may . . . believe you?' 'If you are the King of the Jews, save yourself'; 'Come down from the cross.' If Jesus had put on a spectacle for Herod, he might have saved himself. Yes, spectacle, entertainment, photo opportunities sell, and if there are images of Jesus that are marketable, they can be used, and no one need worry if they are divorced from what we actually know of Jesus. Appearances, images, matter more than substance; what we do and get credit for doing comes to matter more than what is actually achieved.

The temptations tell us that Jesus refuses to be the Saviour we want him to be. He refuses the options that can bring short-term success to the life of the Church, but that derail his true ministry. Let us during Lent identify the choices and strategies that he repudiates and keep faith with him in our wilderness wanderings.

Roger Spiller

Hymn suggestions

Be thou my guardian and my guide; May the mind of Christ my Saviour; Forty days and forty nights; O love, how deep, how broad, how high; All my hope on God is founded.

First Sunday of Lent   10 March
Second Service   God's Goodness Is for All, Not Just for Some
Ps. 119.73–88; **Jonah 3**; Luke 18.9–14

The story of Jonah has so many twists and turns. It is easy to find humour and pathos in it. Yet, it is a story that offers insights into the nature of God that sit well in this season of the Christian year.

It is hard to categorize this story. It is possible that this is a story that was written as a counterpoint to the books of Ezra and Nehemiah, where the returning exiles are urged to purge themselves of all the foreign influences from their time in Babylon, including their foreign wives and children. Historically, there is no evidence of the repentance of the city of Nineveh as outlined in the story, nor is it as large as the narrator of the tale suggests.

All of this leads us to more questions. Whatever the purpose of the book, it is a story that challenges us to look again at our understanding of God.

The story outlined

Let's take a look at an outline of the story: Jonah is told by God that he is to take a message to the people of Nineveh, warning them that their ways have come to God's notice and God will send down punishment upon them. So, what does Jonah do? He gets on a ship that is going in the opposite direction to Nineveh so that he can avoid doing God's command. Of course, we know about the storm that engulfs him and the ship, and how he persuades the sailors to throw him into the waves to save the ship. We know that he is saved by the big fish – often we refer to it as a whale. Three days later, Jonah is spat out onto dry land and again God commands him to go to Nineveh. A very reluctant Jonah goes and warns the people of the town of God's judgement on their conduct.

Now we get to the crux of the story. The people of Nineveh repent and put on sackcloth and ashes. They have a change of heart, and so does God. The revenge that Jonah had prophesied did not happen, and Jonah sits outside the city and sulks.

Jonah's actions have brought the foreign sailors of the ship to recognize and to worship the God of Judah. Jonah's warning has led to a change of lifestyle in the people of Nineveh, who turn to

God in repentance. It is only Jonah who seems to be unaffected by the things going on around him. He complains that he didn't want to go to Nineveh because he knew God was compassionate, and if people repented then God would not seek retribution. He complains when the plant in the desert that brought relief from the sun dies. Clearly Jonah feels that God has let him down.

Jonah was a Hebrew prophet, and what he prophesied did not happen. This might mean people saw him as a false prophet. So Jonah continued to hope for God's destruction of Nineveh and its people, just as we in our time have been able to destroy Hiroshima and many other cities since.

The goodness of God

This wonderful little tale reminds us of the goodness of our God. It reminds us that God didn't just create us, or our little groups of people, people who live and worship like we do. God created all of humanity in its wonderful diversity; and God declared that this was good; not just a part of it, but all of it. We may have messed up God's creation and our relationships with those around us, but the message of Jonah seems to be that God's love for us has not changed. Rather like the father in the story of the Prodigal Son with the older brother, we see God trying to get Jonah to perceive the world through God's eyes rather than his own. God has not given up on Jonah, in spite of all Jonah's stubbornness.

How might God be trying to encourage us to look differently at the world and our neighbours? Are we content to withdraw and be isolationist, seeking only the company of those who are like us? Or do we want to reach out and build bridges, opening up ourselves and others to exciting new possibilities in our understanding of the nature of God and of faith?

In a world that is so divided and where we are being encouraged to fear those who are different from ourselves, the message of Jonah's short story – a message of the overwhelming love of the Creator God for creation and all its people – is surely a message of hope.

Let us pray for the courage to be communities that welcome those who are different, so that together we may share the blessings and the hope that God wishes to share with all of creation.

Ann Jack

Hymn suggestions

In Christ there is no east or west; Restore, O Lord; Judge eternal, throned in splendour; O Lord, all the world belongs to you.

Second Sunday of Lent   17 March
Principal Service   **A Fox or a Hen?**
Gen. 15.1–12, 17–18; Ps. 27; Phil. 3.17—4.1; **Luke 13.31–end**

Would you rather be a fox or a hen?! The Gospel animal allegories throw up that challenge today – a challenge which sheds light on what it means to be a disciple of Christ.

Jesus is making his way to Jerusalem through the region of Galilee. Approached by some Pharisees he's asked to leave the area and warned that Herod Agrippa, the Tetrarch – the leader of the region – is out to get him. Is this true or not? We don't know! Certainly the Pharisees had their own reasons for getting rid of Jesus, and they have their own animal allegory too – they're a 'brood of vipers'. Jesus is not fazed by the threats, despite Herod having executed his cousin, John the Baptist.

Fox-like?

Jesus tells the Pharisees to report to Herod that he is casting out demons, healing the sick – working in the moment, transforming lives. Jesus isn't frightened by Herod. He calls him 'that fox'. In the Greek the image of the fox is very similar to our use of it today. We imagine the fox to be sly and crafty, not to be trusted, a loner who skulks around rubbish bins, getting fat on others' leftovers, breaking into the hen house – causing havoc and destruction. We teach our children that foxes are villains: Jemima Puddleduck is seduced by Mr Todd – the foxy gentleman. The little gingerbread boy travels safely across the river on the fox's nose, only to be gobbled up on the other side. Foxgloves are beautiful but poisonous. The foxhole is a secret firing point in battle. A foxed book has spots of mildew on the pages – it's gone mouldy. Jesus wasn't being complimentary about Herod!

Herod won't get the satisfaction of killing Jesus because Jesus' destiny is to be killed in Jerusalem – the holy city that kills the prophets and stones those who are sent to it. The reminder of that causes Jesus to lament over the city, and brings forth from him another animal picture: 'How often have I desired to gather your children together as a hen gathers her brood under her wings.'

Hen-like?

It's a beautiful but extraordinary image. In the Old Testament we have the picture of God caring for Israel as a mother eagle cares for her young – a similar idea. But the eagle is a magnificent, majestic bird – powerful and awesome. Jesus would have known this image – but he chooses to use the picture of the mother hen with her chicks to describe his longing to care for Jerusalem.

What do we know about hens? Hens are female. Hens are homely and domestic. They peck the earth. They live fairly harmoniously together – they are peaceful unless you threaten their chicks. They are productive. They sit patiently on their eggs, waiting for them to hatch. They are ordinary, everyday birds, common throughout the world: useful for eggs and meat and feathers. They are vulnerable to predators, and perhaps in our minds a bit silly and stupid.

What an interesting image for Jesus: the Lord of heaven and earth, of time and eternity, the Messiah – he sees himself as a mother hen. In Jesus, God was honouring the covenant of love and commitment made with Abraham and Sarah by being ordinary and everyday, laying aside majesty – being one of us, in touch with things earthly, vulnerable to the foxes of the world. Bringing to birth new life and teaching us that fallen and broken lives can be transformed.

St Paul warns the Philippians that many live as enemies of the cross of Christ. In the Roman Empire of which they are citizens there are many foxes – living for the now, thinking of their stomachs, minds set on worldly pleasures. But the Christian is first and foremost a citizen of heaven. While the Romans proclaimed Caesar as Saviour and Lord, these titles are now to be reserved for Jesus Christ. And though this Christian proclamation may lead to humiliation – perhaps being a silly hen in the arena of foxes – ultimately this will lead to being Christ-like, and hence to a new and transformed life in the light of the resurrection. The same holds true for Christians today. Being citizens of heaven means we will be uneasy in the world – at odds sometimes with our culture, not quite fitting in with the norm.

A sly fox or a silly hen?

So – would you rather be a fox or a hen? It's very easy to get into fox-like behaviour – wanting to be top dog at the expense of others, and using subtle and sly ways to manipulate the system and those around us. We can do it without even realizing it. The call to follow Christ requires a change of character – an honest, open assessment of ourselves and the ability to let go of self and allow God to lead and guide our being. It often means being small or silly in the eyes of the world – being the one who serves, being the littlest or the least.

This Lent, try naming and curbing the 'foxiness' within yourself. Would you rather be a fox or a hen?

Catherine Williams

Hymn suggestions

Safe in the shadow of the Lord; Father, who in Jesus found us; Meekness and majesty; God is love, his the care.

Second Sunday of Lent   17 March
Second Service   **The Cost of Discipleship**
Ps. 135 [*or* 135.1–14]; Jer. 22.1–9, 13–17; **Luke 14.27–33**

'For which of you, intending to build a tower, does not first sit down and estimate the cost, to see whether he has enough to complete it?'

There are times when the words of Jesus sound like a trumpet blast: the harsh, uncompromising notes sound out across our lives and we have to stop all that we are doing and just listen. Today's Gospel reading is one of those moments. The message is terrifyingly clear. Discipleship is not a cheap or easy option.

At which point I pause . . . because, if I am brutally honest with myself, I have to ask whether I have taken Jesus' words about discipleship into my life.

Let's begin with the easy bit. Jesus' injunction is based upon common, everyday human experience: can we afford to build a tower, or perhaps, to bring the story up to date, can we afford to buy a house? Before we go ahead of course, we sit down with a piece of paper and try to calculate our options. We calculate how much we have saved for a deposit, and then consider how much we will need to borrow. We try to estimate how we will meet the repayments, including the interest payments on the capital sum. We take account of risk and, in so far as it's possible, we allow for unforeseen circumstances. It's known in the building trade as a contingency fund. And then, in addition, we probably want to take into account any insurance we might need to cover all eventualities. All of this is hard-nosed stuff . . . and takes place as we also try to factor in the emotional stresses and strains of going ahead.

Location, location, location

Many of us know that sort of process all too well. It's the kind of calculation that keeps us awake at night, and, by the way, you may have noticed that it is part of the house-buying process that is never shown on programmes like *Location, Location, Location*. We are agog when Kirsty or Phil phone the agent with an offer, and that is part of the TV storyteller's skill: omit the difficult bits; concentrate instead on the dream and the drama. And, let's be fair, it makes good and gripping television.

But the reality is that trying to calculate all the upsides and downsides of buying a house is a very demanding business. It requires a cool head and steady nerves.

Translate that process across, as Jesus did, from the experience of buying a new house to the decision we once made to become a disciple of Christ. I suspect we spent more time in the calculations over house-buying than we did over discipleship.

Yet this is where the analogy breaks down, for being a disciple of Jesus is a lifetime's occupation rather than just a one-off event. We may have made a commitment to follow Christ some years ago, a commitment that was indeed huge, but the implications of that decision continue to be worked out in our lives day by day.

Which is not to say that being a disciple is an easy or a quiet business. We may be jogging along steadily but suddenly a choice confronts us that requires an answer. If I see a profoundly unethical thing happening in my place of work, should I ignore it or should I intervene? If I undergo a severe, life-changing illness, how should I try to react? If my relationships appear to be going awry, what should I do? If I am tempted to indulge in a dodgy bit of behaviour, what will my discipleship require of me? If I am nursing greed or anger or jealousy in my soul and find myself rather enjoying the self-indulgence of it, what should I do?

God's call

And maybe there will not just be inner, behavioural changes required of us, demanding though they are; it is also possible that God will call us to new lines of work; work for which we feel entirely ill-equipped and unsuited. But the call of God will not go away. His gentle voice deep in our souls persists. What then?

Discipleship is costly. That is a fact. And though we may try, like the house buyer, to calculate everything carefully there will come a moment when serious decisions and choices have to be made. The cool calculations have to give way to a trusting, faith-filled, affirmative and risky change. We have to set out on a new path with no certainty about where the path will lead.

But note this, note this.

While discipleship is undoubtedly costly, the promise of Christ is that he will be with us every step of the way. We are not on our own: 'And remember,' said Jesus, 'I am with you always, to the end of the age.' It's a verse that should be constantly on our lips and in our hearts.

Those of us who have tried (and frequently failed) to be disciples know that promise to be absolutely true, and if it weren't for the continuously loving presence of Christ we might have given up long ago. As it is, we have found that our lives have been enriched in ways beyond all telling. To be a disciple is indeed very costly, but it is also a stupendous joy and for all the blessings discipleship brings we sing our alleluias to God.

Christopher Herbert

Hymn suggestions

Take up the cross, the Saviour said; Take my life and let it be; Will you come and follow me; O Jesus, I have promised.

Third Sunday of Lent   24 March
Principal Service   **A Second Chance**
Isa. 55.1–9; Ps. 63.1–9; 1 Cor. 10.1–13; **Luke 13.1–9**

Are you running out of steam?

In the Gospel today Jesus tells the parable of the fig tree that has stopped producing figs. Perhaps it was once a very fruitful tree, but somehow it seems to have given up – to have run out of steam. The owner thinks it's time to get rid of it – make room for a better or newer model. But the gardener who knows his stock well and cares for it negotiates a second chance for the fig tree. He will tend it and feed it and see if he can get it going again. Does that speak to where some of you are today? Do you need to get going again in your faith – to listen again to God, to stir up again the gifts that God has given you? This season of Lent is a very good time to re-engage with a committed, living and active faith, and work on becoming fruitful for God.

Tending

Everyone here is gifted – everyone has something to offer, whether you've been here for years, or whether you've just started attending church. We are all capable of bearing good fruit. Sometimes what happens in churches is that a few people do everything and they get very tired and overworked, while others don't get the chance to use and develop their gifts. Some of us may need to get more involved in the life of this church and our community – while some may need to step back a bit and allow others room to grow. How can we encourage each other to serve? How can we pass on wisdom and knowledge so that others can be fruitful? What more could we be doing together throughout this community to enable new things to happen, and established things to happen better? Where does the digging and tending need to happen? What needs pruning? What needs more fertilizer? What or who needs a second chance?

St Paul writing to the Corinthians warns against complacency: 'If you think you are standing,' he says, 'watch out that you do not fall.' It can be easy to get slack in our faith – to go through the motions, to get comfortable, or to think all the requests for volunteers, or the opportunities to explore our faith, are for someone else. It's very important that we all keep growing deeper into God.

Abundant life

God gives us gifts so that the body of Christ can be strengthened and built up in order to witness to the world – telling everyone we meet about God's love and goodness. The prophet Isaiah in our Old Testament reading does just that. He is calling everyone to the abundant life that can be found in a relationship with God. He likens it to receiving the best wine and the richest food. God's everlasting commitment of love to all people is like a great banquet, and everyone is invited. I expect the figs at that feast will be the best and juiciest ever grown.

We are the holy people of God in this place, at this time. God has given all who live and work here into our care. What can we do as individuals and as a church to demonstrate in practical ways God's love for our community? We're called to pray, to serve, to fight injustice, to carry others on our hearts, bring hope and new life into this community – being God's agents through our prayers and words and deeds, calling all to abundant life. It's our task to invite everyone to God's banquet. And that may feel quite difficult and uncomfortable, but God says: 'My thoughts are not your thoughts, nor are my ways your ways.' God longs for everyone to come to him, and we all need to have a bigger vision of what might be possible.

Challenge

It takes courage to be God's people. We have to be brave to branch out and share the love of God with our neighbours. We need to take risks, and we might suffer opposition – but God will be with us. We are God's people wherever we find ourselves throughout the week. God loves all the people of our community, without beginning or end, whether they believe in him or not, whether they ever come to church or not, and he calls us to love them too in his name – wanting the best for them, sharing ourselves and the gospel of God with them, through words, actions and prayers.

There's a sting in the tail of the Gospel this morning – if after its second chance the fig tree fails to bear fruit, the gardener is told to cut it down. In another story, in Matthew's Gospel, Jesus curses a fig tree because it fails to recognize him and produce fruit. Isaiah prophesied that when the Messiah came all creation would blossom and be fruitful in celebration of God coming among it. Today we've been reminded that there's a second chance for those who have run out of steam. Let's take the offer, allow ourselves to be tended by God, and move forward in our faith to bear fruit for the kingdom. God trusts us to blossom and be fruitful. In the power of the Holy Spirit, let's rise to the challenge.

Catherine Williams

You are the vine, we are the branches; The fruit of the Spirit; For the fruits of his creation; May we, O Holy Spirit, bear your fruit.

Third Sunday of Lent 24 March
Second Service **How Lovely Is This Place**
Ps. 12, 13; **Gen. 28.10–19a**; John 1.35–end

How we love our church buildings. In every corner of this land they stand as a witness to Christ. Some are homely, some are well worn, some are vast and glorious. Some are dilapidated and dusty, some are new and shiny. When we walk into a church, any church, we are called to look further than the stunning architecture and further than its physical manifestation to what lies beyond. Churches can be thin places where heaven touches earth. But sometimes, in order to recognize them as such, we have to have eyes to see.

When Jacob journeys from Beer-Sheba to Haran, he does not find anywhere obvious to lay his head. He takes a stone and sets it down and goes to sleep. In his dream, God speaks to him and sets up a ladder on the earth, which becomes a door, a portal between heaven and earth, and a point of connection between God and humanity. Jacob wakes up and asks, 'Surely the LORD is in this place – and I did not know it!' But Jacob was not in a 'place', was he? He was in the middle of nowhere with a stone for a pillow. And yet he says, 'This is none other than the house of God, and this is the gate of heaven.'

Jacob was able to see beyond a mere stone set down on the earth. The house of God of which he spoke did not have walls, or pillars, or even a roof. In his dream he was promised that God would not leave him, wherever he went. God was always going to be by his side. God did not need a home as such. As much as place is important, God cannot be confined within four walls. God is living and active. God moves here, there and everywhere.

A temple made of living stones

When John and his two disciples see Jesus they begin to follow him. They want to know where he is staying. Wherever that may be, they want to go too. They want to be *in the place* where he is. Jesus

96

simply invites them to 'Come and see', and then in their turn they invite others to come and see as well. When Jesus goes to Galilee he says to Philip, 'Follow me', and Philip in turn finds Nathanael and tells him about Jesus of Nazareth, the one about whom the prophets wrote. Day by day a new kind of church is being built.

Nathanael speaks without thinking and without deceit, and utters those memorable words, 'Can anything good come out of Nazareth?' Nathanael doesn't yet have eyes to see the one who is so plainly standing there before him. He is as yet unable to recognize Christ in his midst. But this man Jesus sees and knows Nathanael before he was even born, and suddenly everything becomes clear. This man is the one upon whom the angels of God ascend and descend. Christ is to be the new house of God; he is now the gate of heaven. God will make his home not in a temple made of stone, but in a temple made of flesh and blood, a church made of living stones, which is to be built on the foundation of Jesus Christ.

A sure foundation

The physical churches we love are, then, only witnesses to the Church of Christ as it is called to be: a church that lives and breathes and moves; a church that laughs and cries and rejoices and mourns. A building is brought to life by the life of Christ quickening the lives of those who worship within it. The gate of heaven is the Son of God in whom we live and move and have our being. The house of God is the community in which Christ dwells.

When Christ began building his Church, the first stone that he chose to build upon was Peter. Peter who was sometimes impetuous, impatient and imperfect. The same Peter who denied the Lord three times. But Christ was able to see beyond all of this. He had known Peter, like he had known Nathanael, before he was born and he had eyes to see what was possible, and he named Peter 'the Rock' – upon whom he would build his Church. Christ understands that each one of us is capable of doing greater things that witness to his glory. And so the Church, the body of Christ, is always called to be more than bricks and mortar. Whether there is a concrete place in which we worship, or whether we are called to express our faith beyond the walls of our buildings, let us have eyes to see that God is at work everywhere and in each one of us, for we are a church made of people, built on the foundation of Jesus Christ.

Victoria Johnson

Hymn suggestions

Let us build a house where love can dwell (All are welcome); Christ is made the sure foundation; All my hope on God is founded; Christ is our cornerstone.

Fourth Sunday of Lent   31 March
(For Mothering Sunday, see the Second Service.)
Principal Service   **The Resentful Brother**
Josh. 5.9–12; Ps. 32; 2 Cor. 5.16–end; **Luke 15.1–3, 11b–end**

The elder brother was in the field. Of course, he was; that's where he could always be found, day after day, year after year, toiling away in the heat, keeping the family farm afloat. Now that he was alone, with just his elderly father, everything rested on his broad shoulders. As he trudged home to snatch some food and rest, he heard a sound that had never rocked his house before. He could just have gone ahead and entered his home and satisfied his curiosity, but this orderly man had no wish to be caught off guard by sudden change and surprises. So he asked one of the servants what was going on so he could prepare himself for what he might encounter. Yes, we know what followed! He heard that his long-lost brother had returned, safe and sound. Their father has thrown a party, pulled out all the stops, even killed the calf that had grown fat while his father kept waiting for a reason for a celebration. And now, after a long interval, his brother has returned, and his father's daily torment is at an end.

The response of the elder son

If we didn't know what came next, we might have expected relief and grudging satisfaction from the elder brother. Relief that his younger wayward brother had finally seen sense and returned to the family. Still more, that his father's anguish had ended and that he was over the moon at the reunion with his long-lost son.

But the elder son is angry, incandescent. He won't even enter the house, and when his father comes out to remonstrate with him, he rudely interrupts: 'Listen,' he shouts before offloading a well-rehearsed litany of resentments that have been accumulating over the years. Rewarding this renegade brother was the last straw, while all along he's been working like a slave, he's been a dutiful, obedient son, and he's never brought grief to his father. Yet nobody ever got excited over him. He never needed to come back home, because he was always at home; he didn't experience the thrill of being found, because he was never lost.

Has his father treated him as a slave, or has the older son chosen a slave-like existence out of a misplaced need to impress his father? Did his father take his dutiful son for granted and fail to show tangible appreciation of his service, or was it the son who preferred the regulated, rule-based life to the spontaneous loving relationship that was always there for him? Did he resent the restrictions and expectations to which, as the elder son, his parents subjected him, or was it his own lack of his brother's sense of adventure and confidence that held him back from the wild and riotous time in the 'far country' that he secretly wished he had experienced?

Forgiveness for the dutiful?

Jesus aimed the parable at the Pharisees and scribes, guardians of the rules and regulations that were meant to order all relationships. In conversation with one of their number, Simon, recorded in Luke's Gospel, Jesus made a remark that serves as a commentary on the elder brother: 'the one to whom little is forgiven, loves little'. It's love, not rules, that sets the elder brother apart from his father and younger sibling. And it's love and forgiveness that should distinguish God's people from those who have yet to take their place in his family. But how is the one whose world has not been turned upside down by sin to experience the tangible love that comes from unconditional, unmerited forgiveness? 'Should we abound in sin that grace may abound?' asked St Paul's detractors in the church in Rome. 'Of course not,' says Paul, we have no licence to sin. But you can see their point. One Christian writer, Monica Furlong, suggested that some people need a big sin in order to soften them. The father assured his angry son: 'Son, you are always with me, and all that is mine is yours.' But how could he, with all his dutiful, rules-based living, recover the one thing he most needed and desired, his father's love? And how can those of us who claim faith but whose faith no longer makes them warm, generous, joyful, outgoing, recover the love, forgiveness and generosity of God that we yearn for? We can begin by inhabiting this story, letting it interrogate us and persuade our hearts of the Father's love for us.

As Henri Nouwen puts it: 'Do we want to be not just the one who is being forgiven but also the one who forgives? Not just the one who is welcomed home, but the one who welcomes others home; not just the one who receives compassion, but the one who offers to others the same compassion that he has offered to us.'[11]

Roger Spiller

Hymn suggestions

How deep the Father's love for us; There's a wideness in God's mercy; I will sing the wondrous story; To God be the glory.

Mothering Sunday 31 March
Mother Church
1 Sam. 1.20–end; Ps. 34.11–20; Col. 3.12–17; **John 19.25b–27**

Mothering Sunday invites us to think not only of mothers but about the Church. After all, the idea of Mother Church has a longer history than that of Mothering Sunday. One of the early Fathers, St Cyprian in the third century, said: 'No one can have God for his father who does not have the Church for his mother.' We often visualize the Church today as a family, but that can make unmarried people, single parents, and those who want to get away from too many emotional ties, feel excluded. Church as mother is inclusive. It is there for everybody, accompanying us on our journey through life, as personified by Mary the mother of Jesus. And since our stages of life and faith need to be handled with tact and patience, the Church as mother compliments the masculine way of being church – as combative, resolute and vigorous. So let's follow the phases of Mother Church through life's journey.

Storyteller

What is it that gives us a map of who we are and where we belong, that forms and acclimatizes us from infancy to the mysterious world we all enter? What is it that consoles and entertains and extends the growing child? Surely it's stories told by our mothers that give us our sense of place and belonging? We live our lives out of the stories; indeed we are made by stories. Above all, it's the story of God's life with us, with Jesus at its climax, passed on by mothers in the home, that has nurtured the faith and hope of generations.

Mother Church is the storytelling community. It's the guardian of the greatest story ever told. While doctrines are statements on a page, stories are events in life. It's as we are given space to share our own stories that we begin to locate ourselves within the continuing story of the life of Jesus. As we do so, Jesus becomes part of our story, redeeming and enlarging it so that we can find ourselves as part of the bigger story of the life of God.

Midwife

The Church as storyteller makes possible the rebirth of our imagination. But that becomes a reality only when we experience church as midwife. The Church is a midwife because birth is ultimately God's work. It's there to induce and release the life that's there. The Church as midwife knows that Christian life follows a long gestation period within a loving and safe environment. It won't artificially force the pace, but it knows when an intervention is necessary to restore a person who is immobilized by indecision and fear. It has no desire to produce clones who think and act like one another. Instead, the Church as midwife respects the otherness of each person, with all their individuality and difference, even when that makes common life more turbulent and uncomfortable. New life is God's gift, as unpredictable and mysterious as our own journey to life and consciousness. We can't contrive it or comprehend it, but the Church that reflects his love is acting as God's agent to cradle new life.

Nurturer

Mother Church is involved not only in birthing but in nurturing. We've no right to encourage birth unless we can provide nurture. New life is like a tender, fragile seed; it has to be nurtured through the ages and stages of life. It's tempting to short-circuit the repotting process by planting fragile plants in pots designed for full-grown plants. But if we do, they wither away. People, as well as plants, cannot handle too much space and freedom. The Church as nurturer has to provide rich, diverse, graduated opportunities for people to be formed in Christ's likeness throughout the stages of their lives. They need to know that they will be supported when their lives unravel, when they 'lose the plot' and their faith is plagued by doubt and crisis. The Church as nurturer prepares and resources its people for the dispersed Christian witness in the wider world. Those who exercise heavy responsibility in the wider community need to know that they can depend upon the Church to be held and supported, without a job being foisted upon them. Those, by contrast, who are settled, healthy and with time on their hands can be expected to be coaxed to discover their gifts.

Host

The Church as host creates entry points for explorers and pilgrims. Such people don't want some predatory minister asking them to join the membership role the minute they set foot in church or to be made to feel uncomfortable because they have not attended more regularly. They may need mothering with restrained care; not nannying by over-attention. Mother Church hosts a diversity of people, many of whom wouldn't naturally relate to one another, but find themselves relating through their instinctive relationship with her Lord. She is the one who is there not for her own sake, but for the sake of others. She is there with a low threshold and an open door, avoiding resentment to those who drift in and out, or who 'use' the Church, She is attentive to those who are new and doesn't take for granted the dutiful elder brothers and sisters who have always been there.

Images for being church in a new age and culture. Church, like Mother, will not be redundant until we all come home to the God who is both father and mother of us all.

Roger Spiller

Hymn suggestions

God of Eve and God of Mary; What shall our greeting be? Jesus is Lord; Sing we of the blessed Mother; I will sing the wondrous story.

Fifth Sunday of Lent (Passiontide) 7 April
Principal Service **A Two-Bar Electric Fire, or the Sun?**
Isa. 43.16–21; Ps. 126; Phil. 3.4b–14; **John 12.1–8**

Imagine a warm summer's day. The sun radiates balmy heat to bask in. Now picture a person in a darkened room; the curtains are all closed, and they are huddled around a two-bar electric fire. A perfectly healthy person huddled around a two-bar electric fire when they could be warmed by the sun? Why? Two-bar electric fire, or the sun? Hold that question.

Ignatius of Loyola states that our purpose is to praise, reverence and serve God. All created things are there to help us do this. Rather than focus ourselves on the two-bar electric fire of our own power and possessions, we are to orientate ourselves around the Son. Not the big orange thing in the sky, but Christ himself.

Paul regards 'everything as loss because of the surpassing value of knowing Christ Jesus' as Lord. In comparison to Christ, all other things are 'rubbish'. He has turned away from the paltry heat source of his own resources, thrown open the curtains and stepped into Christ's light. Christ is his goal, his aim, his centre.

Are we worshipping competence, job, bank balance, comfort, control or self? Hunkered down in the gloom, kings and queens of our two-bar fire? Or are we worshipping God, the heartbeat of creation; the One who blasted off the doors of death and hell in a fanfare of resurrection power; he who knows us, and loves us, and calls us into his light?

The truth is we waver along between both positions. One day God is the centre. The next we are hunkered down in front of the two-bar fire. It's a battle of failure and forgiveness. Perhaps today we need a Lenten hoof up the proverbial? That hoof comes in the shape of our passage from John.

Mary turns to the Son while Judas turns away to his two-bar fire

We are at a dinner party, in Bethany. Jesus is at the heart of this gathering, with his friends, among them Lazarus – now very much alive – and his sisters Martha and Mary. The scene is set for a very beautiful action. Mary takes a pound of spikenard, an expensive perfume, and anoints Jesus' feet, wiping them with her hair. The perfume is top-notch, worth a year's wages. But Mary is not focused on the value of the perfume for itself but on the worth of her Lord. She praises, reverences and serves Jesus with her perfume. She anoints his feet in an intimate act of servanthood. The fragrance of the oil fills the house. The fragrance of her actions wafts across the centuries.

Judas didn't appreciate the aroma; to him it stank. 'Why was this perfume not sold for three hundred denarii and the money given to the poor?' Her generosity meets his calculation. With forked-tongued piety, Judas draws the curtains and turns to his fire. Not for him extravagant acts of love.

Judas pounces on Mary's act of love as an extravagant waste of resources. He is a two-bar electric fire person, while Mary turns her face to the Son and does what she can for him. She gives of her best, freely and joyfully. Judas just wants to rain on her parade. He's drawn the curtains and turned in on himself into that place of hiddenness, deception and self-justification.

Mary praises, reverences and serves God in an act of unqualified devotion that looks back to the raising of Lazarus and ahead to the death and burial of Jesus. Jesus understands the symbolism of her actions and defends her: 'Leave her alone. She bought the perfume so that she might keep it for the day of my burial. You always have the poor with you, but you do not always have me.' The implication is that Mary purchased the perfume to anoint Jesus' body, and she recognizes that now is the time to express her love. Now is the moment.

Now is the time to throw open the curtains

There is only now. Now is the time to love God, to turn to the Son. Now is the time to wake up and see the extravagant love of God for each of us. Now is the time to name the shabby two-bar fire for what it is, to draw back the curtains and turn to the light of God.

How do we do this? I am not Mary, and I don't have any spike-nard handy. I've never seen anyone raised from the dead, and Jesus isn't likely to be sitting at my dining table anytime soon. What might it mean for me to love God lavishly, to centre my life and attention on God? The answer to that question will differ for each of us. We all have our own versions of spikenard.

Maybe now is the moment to release the fragrance of love for Christ by forgiving someone?

Is now the moment to pour out the oil of love for Christ in the form of cash for someone in need?

Could now be the moment to seek confession, and love Christ with the truth?

Now is the moment to love Christ by attending to him in prayer.

Perhaps now is the moment to love Christ by offering him a place at your table in the form of friend or stranger.

Now is the moment to throw open the curtains and reorientate ourselves around the light of Christ.

Kate Bruce

Hymn suggestions

Jesus be the centre; The Spirit lives to set us free (Walk in the light); Here I am to worship; Take my life and let it be.

Fifth Sunday of Lent (Passiontide) 7 April
Second Service **Preparing for Sacrifice**
Ps. 35 [*or* 35.1–9]; **2 Chron. 35.1–6, 10–16**; Luke 22.1–13

Earlier today I was with a friend who is mother to three children under ten, and who recently learnt that she was pregnant again. 'It's wonderful, of course,' she said, 'but we had given away all our baby things . . . I thought I was too old! I was about to go back to work . . . We just don't have enough room at the moment . . . We'll have to get a new car, think about moving house, and our lad will have a third sister! So it's a great gift, but we'll have to put our thinking caps on . . .'

My friend knows full well the cost of bearing a child, and she's thoughtful about this unexpected blessing. She will do all she can to make her third daughter's life perfect – she'll prepare for her arrival, get things together carefully in good time before the due date, and steel herself for the labour. And then she'll be in it – again – for the long run. For her and her family's lives to change again, for ever.

Getting ready

We think hard about getting ready for Christmas. Advent is a season of preparation, even if it is often spent just thinking about Christmas – presents, guests, food, family. But what about getting ready for Holy Week, or Easter? It may not go much further than buying (and eating) Easter eggs.

It helps us as we move from Mothering Sunday last week, to Holy Week next week, to think about getting ready. A mother has to prepare herself for sacrifices ahead. And so did Jesus. Our readings today are full of it. From a Jewish perspective, there was a lot to be done in getting ready for the great feast of the Passover. In Luke, Jesus tasks Peter and John with getting ready for it. So they ask where they should prepare it. But Jesus doesn't give a simple answer – an address or the name of a friend. Instead, he tells them that when they enter the city, a man carrying some water will meet them, and they are to follow him. When they find his landlord, they are to declare that the 'Teacher' wants the guest room, where he and his disciples may eat the Passover.

Knowing what's around the corner

While the disciples are talking about making preparations, it seems that Jesus has got everything planned in advance. He knows the size and location of the guest room, and that it's already furnished. He knows how they will bump into this man (normally it was women who carried water, so while this was unusual it also helped them to identify the one they were to follow). Luke shows Jesus knowing the details of what's going to happen next. Luke's Jesus is in charge, even though it is all being done around him.

And he doesn't give them details about the preparations to be done, once they'd found where to do them. All good Jews knew what a Passover meal needed. It was all there in their Scriptures.

The model

King Josiah in the Old Testament was a model Jewish ruler. He reinstated many of the ancient religious practices and brought the people of Israel back to their God. One of the ways he did this was through carefully keeping the chief festivals. The Passover was one of them. So in 2 Chronicles we see the thought that he put into this important annual moment in the life of his Jewish community.

The date's set, the priests are appointed, the place is chosen, God is there. And now comes the great Passover sacrifice: Josiah himself gives the people 30,000 sheep and goats, and 3,000 cattle. His officials follow his lead and do likewise. And everything is done according to the great teachings of David, Solomon and Moses. The lambs are slaughtered, the blood of the sheep is sprinkled by the priests, and the Levites skin the animals. Nothing is wasted.

The perfect sacrifice

So Josiah knew what to do: he had studied the word of the LORD and was following it to a tee. Imagine how special it would be today to be in a community where they breed their own male lamb, bring him up for some months, slaughter him in Lent, and cherish every last bit of him: the great roast meal he will be for the community's Easter celebration, the ordinary meals he will add something to, the sheepskin rug that will be placed before the hearth. The preparations are so thoughtful that both the getting ready and the feast itself are precious parts of the whole.

But while Peter and John were doing the preparations as in 2 Chronicles, Jesus is steeling himself not only to preside over this sacrificial meal but even to sacrifice himself. He knows that as the Passover lamb set straight the Israelites' relationship with God each year, he is the most powerful Passover lamb that can be offered, once and for all. Josiah provided the animals for one occasion of cleansing; Jesus provides himself for a world to be restored to relationship with God for ever.

At the meal, Jesus will encourage his disciples to share the bread, saying, 'Take, eat, this is my body which is given for you,' and to share the cup, saying, 'Drink this, all of you, for this is the blood of the new covenant which is shed for you and for many for the forgiveness of sins.' Our Holy Communion service both re-enacts the Passover, which was to be Jesus' last supper, and retells the story of Jesus' own self-sacrifice.

Jesus prepares the sacrifice, and *is* the sacrifice. He sets us free to celebrate him as the great, the perfect, sacrifice. What care will you take in preparing for Easter?

Megan Daffern

Hymn suggestions

My song is love unknown; O sacred head surrounded; This is my body; Once, only once and once for all.

Holy Week

Palm Sunday   14 April
Principal Service   Gazing over Jerusalem
Liturgy of the Palms: **Luke 19.28–40**; Ps. 118.1–2, 19–end
[*or* 118.19–end]; *Liturgy of the Passion*: Isa. 50.4–9a; Ps. 31.9–16
[*or* 31.9–18]; Phil. 2.5–11; Luke 22.14—23.56, *or* Luke 23.1–49

St Luke was not much interested in geography. It's a shame, but there it is. He mentions a number of specific towns in his Gospel, including Bethlehem, Nazareth, Capernaum, Nain and Bethsaida, but for the most part he is irritatingly vague. He describes Jesus, for example, entering a 'certain town'. 'Yes,' we reply, 'but which one?' He states that Jesus had a meal in the house of one of the leading Pharisees (Luke 14.1), but doesn't say where the house was. He tells the story of Jesus taking Peter, James and John up a high mountain (Luke 9.28), but gives us no indication where the mountain might have been.

Now this vagueness might well have been because Luke simply did not know. The names of places were not mentioned in his sources, so he had nothing to go on. It's also possible that he had an overall schema for his Gospel in mind, in which Jerusalem had the central place and therefore the specific locations of other episodes in the story as he was unfolding it did not matter.

But then, occasionally and by contrast, Luke could be remarkably specific. And so it is in today's Gospel reading: 'After he had said this, he went on ahead, going up to Jerusalem.'

The significance of place

Earlier in the chapter, Luke locates Jesus in Jericho, the ancient city down in the Jordan Valley. It lies 258 metres (846 feet) below sea level; a place of intense heat, and, from Israel's perspective, a city of great historical and cultural importance. From there, Jesus and his disciples set out to walk the zig-zag road up to Jerusalem, a distance of about 15 miles, climbing from 846 feet below sea level up through a rocky, barren pass to Jerusalem, which is 754 metres above sea level. It was a stiff climb and would have taken them the best part of a day to complete.

But that same day, according to Luke, Jesus began his symbolic ride into Jerusalem. It began on the Mount of Olives, in the village of Bethany. From there (and there is dispute about the exact location of Bethany: some place it towards the top of the Mount of Olives; others say it was a little further down the hill), the road slopes very steeply downwards to the Kidron Valley, and then, having traversed the valley, winds its way up towards the walls of Jerusalem and the Temple Mount. It would have been not so much a stately, noble procession through a park as a skittering, sliding journey accompanied by the cheering disciples. They shouted words taken from Psalm 118, which the Temple priests traditionally used to greet pilgrims making their way to Jerusalem:

'Blessed is the one who comes in the name of the LORD.
We bless you from the house of the LORD.'

To make clear that this was the arrival of the Messiah, either the disciples themselves or Luke slightly altered the words of the acclamation and inserted the word 'king' into the chanting slogan ('Blessed is the King . . .'). The tension must have been immense for everyone involved.

The tears of Jesus

But when the procession had got to a point where the whole city lay visible ahead of them, Jesus stopped for a moment and, filled with emotion after a long, hot day, wept. A great and terrible lament tore itself from his lips:

'If you, even you, had only recognized on this day the things that make for peace! But now they are hidden from your eyes. Indeed, the days will come upon you, when your enemies will set up ramparts around you and surround you, and hem you in on every side. They will crush you to the ground, you and your children within you, and they will not leave within you one stone upon another; because you did not recognize the time of your visitation from God.'

It was an agonizing cry. Had not Jesus' birth been all about the arrival of the Messiah? Had not the angels hovering over the shepherds in the Bethlehem fields sung the same words that the disciples were now proclaiming? 'Peace in heaven, and glory in the highest heaven!'

Is it any wonder that Jesus wept? His heart was breaking because his own beloved people did not recognize the arrival of God in their midst.

At which point we need on this Palm Sunday to pause. Why? Because there will have been times in our own lives when we have failed to see Jesus the Messiah in our midst. Times when we have failed to recognize his profound humility; times when we have ignored his courtesy; times when we have closed our ears to his honesty and truth.

So now, hearing his stifled sobbing as he looks out over Jerusalem, pray that God will have mercy on us and that he will bring us by his infinite grace to rediscover the life of his kingdom.

Of course, the journey was not yet finished. The Jericho–Jerusalem part had been done, but a week of uncertainty stretched ahead.

Our task as his disciples in our generation is to walk that uncertain road with Christ . . . making our way with him to Gethsemane, to Calvary, and on to the empty tomb.

Christopher Herbert

Hymn suggestions

Ride on, ride on in majesty; Make way, make way, for Christ the King; O love, how deep, how broad, how high; From heaven you came, helpless babe.

Palm Sunday   14 April
Second Service   **Suffering God**
Ps. 69.1–20; **Isa. 5.1–7**; Luke 20.9–19

Jesus' entry into Jerusalem and the cleansing of the Temple led to the final showdown between Jesus and the Jewish leaders. It precipitated a week of intense teaching by Jesus, and questioning about his authority by the Jewish authorities. But what are we to make of it? What was going on? How are we to understand it? One of the parables that Jesus told after Palm Sunday helps us to understand how Jesus interpreted his fateful final visit to Jerusalem and death.

But we begin with Isaiah and his parable about a vineyard, which is a background for Jesus' parable.

Celebrating a friend's grape harvest

It's the end of a harvest, and there's a boisterous party atmosphere as people relax and rejoice after a strenuous year in the vineyard. The prophet is there, in his capacity as a friend to the vineyard owner, but he's off duty. The vineyard is the owner's pride and joy. He's married to it, as to a bride. There's a mood of celebration, and the prophet has no wish to introduce his usual dose of doom and gloom to the proceedings. Instead, he praises his friend for the diligent, painstaking way he's worked on his vineyard and details all the measures he's taken to build up his winery. So far, so good, as they say. But then his friend speaks up for himself. He's in a more sombre mood. His grape harvest has been a disaster, he says. Instead of a harvest of fine purple grapes, he has only inedible, literally 'stinking' grapes. And he calls all the citizens of Jerusalem to make accusations as between him and his vineyard. But then what shall he do? Will he wait in hope of a better harvest next year, after more pruning and hoeing? No, his patience has run out. Its hedge will be removed, its wall broken down, and it will be abandoned. A bit drastic, you may feel.

What does God's harvest yield?

But then the prophet and vineyard owner's friend delivers the punch line. The vineyard is none other than Israel and Judah. The entire nation has produced a bitter harvest The people who were chosen by God, loved by God, nurtured by God, have produced a harvest of bloodshed and corruption. They have become the faithless bride of God! So what will God do with his faithless people? The question is left hanging, but Jesus will pick it up.

Jesus' parable is often known as the parable of the wicked vinedressers, but, as we'll see, it's more about the vineyard owner and his son than it is about the tenants. Jesus tells the parable as an indirect answer to a question from a delegation of chief priests, Scribes and elders on the source of Jesus' authority. A direct answer to a hostile question is seldom heard. It's a story, a parable, that offers the roominess and enchantment to tease and to lodge in the mind.

God's initiatives to retrieve his harvest

Once again, there is the vineyard owner, but this time he let the vineyard out to tenants to manage it for him during a lengthy period out of the country. You need no reminding of what took place. The owner sent first one of his servants to collect some of the harvest, only to be beaten and sent away empty-handed. Then a second, who was treated more roughly than the first, and then a third, who this time was wounded and returned empty-handed. So we're now at the same point as the previous parable, asking, 'What will the owner of the vineyard now do?' We knew that the first owner trashed the unproductive vineyard, but we didn't know what God would do with faithless Israel. But now the owner has been insulted and shamed by the abusive treatment meted out to his servants. He is in anguish, indignant, shocked, and yet he holds all the cards. We know what would be the natural, obvious action to take. That would surely be to storm the vineyard, arrest and banish the wicked tenants and install new ones, or dismantle the vineyard itself.

But to the amazement of the hearers, the owner decides to send his beloved son. To send him alone, unarmed, without a protection force around him.

Another story

One night in the early 1980s the late King Hussein of Jordan was informed by his security police that a group of about 75 Jordanian army officers were at the very moment meeting in a nearby barracks plotting a military overthrow of the kingdom. The security officers requested permission to surround the barracks and arrest the plotter. After a sombre pause the king refused and said, 'Bring me a small helicopter.' A helicopter was brought. The king climbed in with the pilot and himself flew to the barracks and landed on its flat roof. The king told the pilot, 'If you hear gun shots, fly away at once without me.' Unarmed, the king then walked down two flights of stairs and suddenly appeared in the room where the plotters were meeting and quietly said to them, 'Gentlemen, it has come to my attention that you are meeting here tonight to finalize your plans to overthrow the government, take over the country and install a military dictator. If you do this, the army will break apart and the country will be plunged into civil war. Tens of thousands of innocent people will die. There is no need for this. Here I am! Kill me and proceed. That way, only one man will die.' After a moment of stunned silence, the rebels as one rushed forward to kiss the king's hand and feet and pledge loyalty to him for life.[12]

We know, of course, that when God sent his Son he was not spared death. God did not give up on his vineyard.

Who are the wicked tenants? The Jewish authorities? God's rebellious, faithless people? We ourselves?

The rightful owner of the vineyard takes great risk, foreswears violence, and acts in vulnerability and costly self-giving love. And his son is expelled and killed, and the wicked and faithless who deserve to die are set free. 'Let anyone with ears listen!'

Roger Spiller

Hymn suggestions

From heaven you came, helpless babe; Thou didst leave thy throne and thy kingly crown; When you prayed beneath the trees; When I survey the wondrous cross.

First three days of Holy Week   15–17 April
Journeying with Jesus
(*These are the readings for Monday of Holy Week but the sermon may be used on any day.*)
Isa. 42.1–9; Ps. 36.5–11; Heb. 9.11–15; **John 12.1–11**

Tragedy

As we enter into Holy Week, this most momentous week in the history of the world, we are invited to set out on our own pilgrimage. We try to keep company with Jesus by reading, or rather 'inhabiting', the recorded events that chart the fateful days that led to his brutal death. We have simply to make ourselves available to occupy and live imaginatively into the gospel stories. It's natural that we will want to fast forward to Easter morning. But that can remove us from the sheer sense of human tragedy in the story, something that Mark's account, in particular, preserves.

Fateful choices

The death of Jesus may at one level be rightly viewed as the outworking of a divine salvific plan, but that does nothing to reduce the tragic choices with which Jesus was tormented in the Garden of Gethsemane, and in his awesome words to his Father on the cross. There was no obvious sense of inevitability that could spare Jesus the anguish of hoping for a route that would avert the suffering and death that was closing in on him. To feel the force of the passion and crucifixion, it is helpful to follow the story as if the ending was unknown. Reading the story forward in the gathering darkness helps us to see Good Friday aright. Easter Day doesn't reverse Good Friday. It actually vindicates it. It tells us that the darkness of Good Friday is God's way of coming alive.

We will be confounded by the sovereign and single-minded way in which Jesus reckoned with the cruel plot that was unfolding. He had no wish to seek a martyr's death, and recoiled from it. But his love for his Father was implacable, and he would do nothing that would divert him from that path of self-giving love and obedience to his Father's will. We will be repelled and savaged by the impenetrable tragedy that will be played out. And we will be provoked to ask what meaning can be made of this stupendous act – when we ask not merely what happened, but what does it mean. We try to make the connection between Jesus' death and our own living and dying, and we begin to edge forward in discovering how we might interpret our own lives in the light of his cross.

Seeking sense

Making sense and finding meaning in the death of Jesus was the challenge that the early Church faced in the days and years that followed his resurrection. Why did Jesus die? That was more than an interesting theological question. It was a pressing, urgent question on which the future of the Christian mission depended. The death of Jesus would have seemed to be the final repudiation of the claim that Jesus was Messiah and Lord. There was never an expectation that suffering would be the lot of God's Messiah. God was surely able to avert suffering, not be its victim. He would exert his sovereign will to banish the world's violence and evil, not absorb it in himself. We, too, find ourselves asking, 'Why suffering?' Why did Jesus have to die? And did he die for us?

Love confronts power

Jesus' death took place at the Jewish festival of Passover. This was no accident. It was the elaborate ritual season for dealing with sin and all that separates people from their Creator. It commemorated the rescue of the Israelites from slavery in Egypt by

God's own action, and the expectation was that God would again intervene decisively and reverse his people's grim political occupation. But the crucifixion of God's Messiah undermines the violent and aggressive ways of power politics. It opens us to the path of self-giving, self-expending love. The cross of Christ shows the cost he bore in order to reconcile us to God. Nowhere is God more characteristically God, more truly himself, than in the events of Good Friday.

Put on trial by the cross

So we keep Holy Week by immersing ourselves in the events of that fateful week leading up to Good Friday. We trust the stories to work their way into our lives and, as they do, they challenge us and they put us on trial. The cross of Christ tests everything. It requires a little imagination for us to see ourselves in the characters who played their parts during Holy Week. 'Were you there when they crucified my Lord?' Yes, in one sense we were there. We were there in Peter, Caiaphas, Pilate, the other disciples, the curious bystanders, the priests and, of course, the crowd.

Holy Week draws us into a world of darkness, treachery, naked power and self-serving. Those who seek only for comfortable emollient words will be discomforted by the days that lie ahead. But our faith isn't an escape from reality. Rather, it draws us deeper into the reality that is at the heart of the world, as Jesus confronts the worst that humankind can do, and it does so not for the worst but often for the best of intentions, inspired by religious devotion. Jesus dies to all the acts of betrayal, misplaced ambition, abusive power that are the potential within each one of us.

If we are prepared to keep company with Jesus, reliving his fateful journey, we will begin to grasp the power of his death and the vindication and triumph of the resurrection. If we do, we will emerge out of Holy Week as those who have become more alive, more receptive and responsive to the joy of Easter Day.

Roger Spiller

Hymn suggestions

How deep the Father's love for us; O love, how deep, how broad, how high!; Morning glory, starlit sky; When you prayed beneath the trees.

Maundy Thursday 18 April
The Intimacy of Being Served

Ex. 12.1–4 [5–10] 11–14; Ps. 116.1, 10–end [*or* 116.9–end]; 1 Cor. 11.23–26; **John 13.1–17, 31b–35**

It's a bracing, unsettling drama in which we are caught up tonight. It has to be, because it mirrors the surprising, disorienting events of the Last Supper. There's the tender intimacy of foot-washing. And, in contrast, the dramatic stripping away of the furnishings, symbolic of that fiercer pruning that needs to occur in our lives if we are to flourish under the cross.

Foot-washing and the cross

It's the foot-washing of Jesus, however, that interprets the cross for us. It's the acted parable of servitude and self-offering that anticipates and explains the once-for-all cleansing from sin and self that Christ wrought by his cross. Well might it shock and surprise Peter. Not even Jewish slaves would be expected to wash feet, though disciples might wash the feet of their teachers. But Jesus once more subverts the settled order of relationships that we count on to give us the security of knowing our place. He pulls away the ladder that rewards age, experience, seniority. And he changes our sense of geography: the way up is the way down. To see the cross we have to bend lower on our knees. And he shames us by his condescension as he repudiates the bankrupt power structures that define so much of who we are and the manner of our relating to other people – the same vested power relations that will soon have their way with him.

Recoiling from being served

Is it any wonder that Peter drew back? 'You will never wash my feet,' he protests. It's the pride that will not own our incompleteness and masquerades as humility that asserts itself. It struggles to conceal the inadequacy of our lives and our deep need of healing. So it's hard to accept service, harder to receive service than to give it. Our whole socio-economic enterprise is directed to minimize our dependency upon each other and to develop autonomous, self-sufficient persons.

Dependency – religious, social, economic – is despised. Even those aged and infirm who depend upon others to wash and dress them are shamed in a world that values independence. And even the ritual

116

expression of foot-washing exemplifies a dependence we'd rather not have to own. 'I don't want anyone dying for me,' said Bertrand Russell. And none of us wants anyone doing anything for us if it exposes our dependency. 'Love bade me welcome, but my soul drew back.' The guest in George Herbert's poem refuses to accept love's gift, being ready to serve, but refusing to be served.

One vicar said to me: 'I can cope with Good Friday, the realism and stringency, but I find Maundy Thursday difficult; its too touchy feely for me.' So perhaps what we, like Peter, recoil from is the level of exposure and intimacy and tenderness that Christ asks of us. The Christian tradition hasn't always helped us to be comfortable with our bodies – though, goodness knows, we've had them for long enough. It's hard enough for some people to get used to a handshake at the Peace. I know of one church that has a hands-free zone – an area cordoned off, for people who don't want to share the Peace. And at a cathedral where I was due to preach, it was planned that we should settle for washing hands instead of foot-washing. That is, until someone asked if we were wanting to remember Pontius Pilate rather than Jesus!

Allowing Jesus to serve us

There can be no growth in the Christian life, no appropriation of Christ's own life, without a willingness for intimacy. At the heart of our fear of intimacy is the fear of encountering our own helplessness and vulnerability in the face of chaos. There's a fear of destroying our self-image, our capacity to control situations and master emotions. We live with the tension between the longing for intimacy and the fear that it arouses. Yet moments of intimacy, like moments of grace, bring us closer together and transform us. Christ offers what Rowan Williams calls the 'hospitality of truth', the searching, searing exposure of ourselves as we see ourselves both at our best and at our worst, in the image of the crucified Lord. Daring to let Christ serve us, we begin to change into his likeness. And only by receiving service from Jesus have we the resources to render service ourselves. 'Unless I wash you, you have no share with me.' Letting Christ serve us is the precondition for our own life of service. Our service will be an expression of self-seeking unless it comes from the overflow of God's grace.

There's a story of a museum, set in heaven, dedicated to Christ's life on earth, displaying the symbols of his ministry. There's the widow's mite, in a corner the carpenter's tools, a crown of thorns, a sponge dipped in vinegar, 30 pieces of silver. After touring the display, a visitor asked the attendant, 'Where is the bowl and the towel?' 'Oh,' he said, 'they're always in use.'

The foot-washing interprets the Eucharist as well as the cross. It's through the Eucharist that Christ serves us today, because it is here, where he is pledged to be, here where he gives himself to us. For this meal is never a mere commemoration, nor even a re-presentation of Calvary. It is Christ himself present as host and victim, ready to serve us. It's been said that the Holy Communion is like a bread queue, a line of people who are so poor and destitute that they are publicly prepared to acknowledge their need. So we come, holding up our empty hands, symbolic of our empty lives, knowing that if into our lives the love of Christ does not come, we go away as empty as we came.

Roger Spiller

Hymn suggestions

Brother, sister, let me serve you; Put peace into each other's hands; Now my tongue the mystery telling; Great God, your love has called us here.

Good Friday   19 April
The Words from the Cross in St John's Gospel
Isa. 52.13—end of 53; Ps. 22 [*or* 22.1–11, *or* 22.1–21]; Heb. 10.16–25, *or* Heb. 4.14–16, 5.7–9; **John 18.1—end of 19**

Here is your mother

'Meanwhile, standing near the cross of Jesus, were his mother . . .'. These words introduce a tender, intimate interlude in an otherwise brutal, public execution. Mary has been bemused by her son, as hints in the Gospels show; his life has been a mystery to her, but she has recognized that there is more to Jesus than meets the eye, and she has learnt to trust in him and to wait. Now his hour has come and mother and son are united.

And Jesus, who has himself been handed over, hands his mother over to his beloved disciple. We see the care of the dying Jesus for his mother and the provision he makes for her after his death. Always careful for others, he was indifferent to his own life and welfare.

But there's a deeper meaning, too, in the action of Jesus in relation to his mother: Jesus addresses Mary, not as his mother but as 'woman'. The effect is to give her a representative status. Mary is not just the son of Jesus. Mary represents the Jewish Christians, who with the Beloved Disciple will find a home in Gentile Christianity. 'Who are my mother and my brothers?' 'Whoever does the will of God is my brother and sister and mother.' So Mary is the New Eve, she shares the struggle for the hour, when the Prince of this world is defeated, and through her Jesus makes provision for the future of those who believe in him. And what of Mary herself? One of the great tragedies is that she has been the subject of disagreement in the Church: regarded as semi-divine by Catholics, whereas Protestants don't think of her at all.

But Mary matters, first because she was there. She says nothing, she does nothing. Disciples are all action, rather than being. But they are a dead loss when asked to keep still and keep company with Jesus in his silent vigil.

Peter's denial or Judas' betrayal are failures to be still and to be there. It's tempting not to be present unless you can do something or say something. 'I'll only turn up if you've got something for me to do.' When we feel helpless, powerless, we stay away. Quite often, relatives, friends of a dying person, absent themselves, because they feel powerless.

We can abandon the relationship and withdraw, or we can, like Mary, share another person's helplessness. In sharing their helplessness, the other person is more able to retain control by discovering inner resources, through the mutuality in the relationship. Whereas if they were trying to be strong they might take control from the one who is in need, so that they become a victim. There are different ways of being present. The biggest mistakes are all to do with not being there, alert, active, silent. The highest and holiest thing you can offer is to be present in all your helplessness and silence.

> Only pierced hands
> Are gentle enough
> To touch some wounds
> You need
> To have been crucified yourself
> If you would find the tenderness
> To stay and share the pain
> Again and yet again.[13]

Mary gives that to Jesus, and God gives it to us. It's not oppressive, nor is it idling. It is an active presence, a refusal to give up on us. And at the most vital, pivotal moment in her sons' life, Mary was there.

Mary was not just there, but there as a mother – weeping, grieving. She is the universal representative of mothers who grieve their sons' deaths; those who never come to terms with their loss but who refuse to give up hope. Mothers of sons killed in Iraq, Afghanistan and elsewhere. She represents many more; others whom you would expect to be there – Bartimaus, Zacchaeus, all the little people. Where were they? In a profound sense, they were there in the person of Mary. The greatness of Mary is her littleness. She gave birth to a son she never asked for, on whom so much depended. She speaks to so many, she represents all little people, those whose lives and love is trampled upon, those hurt, let down, baffled, but who do not give up.

I thirst

Jesus is thirsty. It is the only concession to his human need, or so the soldiers interpreted it, but still it is Jesus who takes the initiative.

He who is the source of living water, cries out in thirst, not primarily for his own needs but a thirst for the men and woman who will believe in him, those who are dry and weary and discounted, like the woman of Samaria, to whom he promised living water: 'a spring of water gushing up to eternal life'. But Jesus must die before he can dispense this living water: 'If I do not go away, the Advocate will not come to you . . . Am I not to drink the cup the Father has given me?' Yes, he must drink the bitter cup of suffering and death.

We too may have times when we have a deep thirst for God, a yearning for renewal and refreshment. We too may echo the Psalmist: 'O God, you are my God, I seek you, as in a dry and weary land where there is no water.'

The soldiers, like all the characters in John's Gospel, miss the deeper meaning, and take the words of Jesus on the surface level. So they hand Jesus a sponge of bitter wine, on a branch of hyssop. A hyssop was a small wall-growing plant well adapted for sprinkling, such as happens in some churches where a priest will sprinkle the congregation with water. But you can see that a hyssop is ill suited to raise a sponge to the lips of a crucified victim. Yet John insists it is a hyssop, so as to recall us to the Exodus when the blood of the pascal lamb was sprinkled on the doorposts of Israelite homes. Jesus is the pascal lamb of the new covenant.

But there's another fascinating note here too. Jewish tradition taught that giving strong drink to a dying man was a way of obtaining merit. 'If your enemies are thirsty, give them water to drink . . . and the LORD will reward you.' John does not record Jesus praying to his Father for forgiveness for his executioners. Instead, perhaps Jesus is giving his executioners an opportunity to gain merit, or at least showing he forgives them by accepting the wine they offer.

It is finished

The death of Jesus in John is not a protracted struggle, with anguished cries of desolation, as in the other Gospels, but a short and glorious finale, with Jesus in perfect control, reigning from the tree. The cry 'It is finished' is not of desolation but the beginning of triumph. Not 'I am finished' but 'It is finished'; the work entrusted to him by his Father is finished. The Latin conveys the note of triumph: *Consumatum est.*

But the Greek word, *Tetelestai*, is the word used to cancel a bill when it has been settled. It marks the end of debt and enslavement, and the promise of a new relationship opening up.

> O Tree of beauty, tree most fair,
> Ordained those holy limbs to bear
> Gone is thy shame, each crimsoned bough
> Proclaims the King of Glory now.[14]

We need to hear in our world, beset by fears and demons and threat of chaos, that Christ has redeemed the world. It is finished, complete. No more needs to be done to bring us to God. Then, when all was accomplished, Jesus bowed his head and gave up his spirit, literally 'handed his spirit over' – to God, yes, but also to those at the foot of the cross. To his mother, in particular, who symbolizes the Church, and to the Beloved Disciple, who symbolizes the Christian. As Jesus said, once he was glorified believers would receive the Spirit.

Holy living is the best preparation for holy dying, said Jeremy Taylor. The very attachments and encumbrances that make death so difficult a letting go are also impediments to the full enjoyment of living. But, as Canon Sydney Evans said:

> If we have been brought up in the worshipping community, we should all our lives be familiar with death. All these deaths we voluntarily die to self are rehearsals for that greater death when

we must hand ourselves over finally to the God whom we have been learning to hand ourselves over all our lives. To live the Christian life in this world is already to live in some degree beyond death, in a faith relationship to him who is alive for us beyond his own death.[15]

It's being ready to let go, in the knowledge that God will not let go of us.

Roger Spiller

Hymn suggestions

We sing the praise of him who died; At the cross her station keeping; My song is love unknown; When I survey.

Easter

Easter Vigil (20 April evening or 21 April morning)
Following Through

(*A minimum of three Old Testament readings should be chosen. The reading from* Exodus 14 *should always be used.*)

Gen. 1.1—2.4a *and* Ps. 136.1–9, 23–end; Gen. 7.1–5, 11–18; 8.6–18; 9.8–13 *and* Ps. 46; Gen. 22.1–18 *and* Ps. 16; **Ex. 14.10–end**; 15.20–21 *and Canticle*: Ex. 15.1b–13, 17–18; Isa. 55.1–11 *and Canticle*: Isa. 12.2–end; Baruch 3.9–15, 32—4.4 *and* Ps. 19, *or* Prov. 8.1–8, 19–21; 9.4b–6 *and* Ps. 19; Ezek. 36.24–28 *and* Ps. 42, 43; Ezek. 37.1–14 *and* Ps. 143; Zeph. 3.14–end *and* Ps. 98; Rom. 6.3–11 *and* Ps. 114; Luke 24.1–12

Some years ago, I was being given a lift by an elderly friend and colleague so we could both go to a funeral of someone from our community. It was winter, and there had been a lot of rain. It shouldn't have been far to go, but we began to doubt this when we tried for a second time to cross the Evenlode river, which was in spate. We reversed again up the lanes, and the service was about to start just the other side of this great flood. As we approached a third possible crossing, and again found the bridge covered by the river, this time my friend told me to pray, and he charged on through in his little car. I have never been surrounded by so much water – apart from in a boat. The car started moving sideways beneath us. But he kept driving forward, and by some miraculous chance we regained the grip of the tyres and made it safely to the other side. We got to the service before it started, and we took our time to go back a different way.

Courage in risk

Sometimes life feels like we have little choice – we've committed to a path and we should see it through. It can be a risky business.

Exams at the culmination of a course. That final push in child-birth. The last few hundred metres of a marathon. The moment of handing over a job application. We give it a go, we take a deep breath, and press on through. We might be on the verge of turning back, but something drives us forward. It might not look at all easy ahead, but we know it's got to be done.

Can you imagine how the Israelites would have felt? That momentous first Passover had just happened: the final plague on Egypt where the Israelites were slaves. Every firstborn male has died, except for the Israelites who had marked their houses with the blood of lambs, and eaten bread that hadn't had time to rise in their haste. The Egyptians were stunned, and Pharaoh had finally let the Israelites go. So here they were, escaped into the desert. A shocking enough set of experiences for anyone.

But now Pharaoh's army has decided to pursue them after all, to enslave them again. The Israelites are camped by the sea. And now the Egyptians are bearing down on them in haste and strength. The Israelites think Moses has been daft bringing them out here to die in the wilderness. This will be the last push in their escape.

The only way is *through*

We hear the saying 'The only way is up'. But the Israelites had only one choice. Let the Egyptians get them, or entrust themselves to the sea. God's angels are described as keeping his people in the light and the hotly pursuing Egyptians in the dark. Meanwhile, as Moses stretches his hand out over the sea, God drives the waters back so that the Israelites can move on through on dry ground. Once they are all safely through, God lets the water fall back upon the Egyptians; the threat is gone for ever.

It's one of those Old Testament stories that seems at once both gloriously triumphant and yet also rather unpleasant. We picture the struggling horses and chariots and horsemen of the Egyptians flailing and drowning as the Israelites look on from dry ground. Sometimes life is cruel. But we don't like to think of God as cruel. Here he has distinguished between those who are pushing on through the sea in trust in him, and those who are pushing on through the sea in their own strength. He won't let the latter harm or even threaten his people any more: they've done enough of that. Now he can give a clear sign to his people that he is in control. That they need to trust in him, and that's the only way anyone can get safely through.

124

Following through in trust

Jesus on Good Friday handed himself over to be tortured, crucified and buried. He handed himself over to those who had bodily power over him, and he entrusted himself wholly to God and his promises. It takes courage and strength to put ourselves in other people's power; it is a fearful place to be, and we wouldn't normally walk into such a trap. But Jesus had to follow through. He had had three intense and rich years of ministry in Galilee and Jerusalem, he had preached about the kingdom of God, and the outcome would be his own persecution at the hands of those more powerful than him, just as the Israelites at that first Passover were pursued.

But he was also entrusting himself to God; and the outcome of that would be his rising again to new life from the dead.

The Israelites had made their way through a chasm of despair and doubt, a place of death, drowning and destruction, as they crossed the Red Sea. Miraculously they found themselves safe the other side. Now Jesus, at this latest Passover, has crossed from life to death, and comes through death into new life that would be new life for all people.

Jesus has followed through, as we see in the empty tomb of Luke 24. Now all Jesus' followers have to follow through. The women first. Mary Magdalene, Joanna and Mary the mother of James, with some others, are the ones to find Jesus' tomb empty. Women wouldn't normally be seen as reliable witnesses in first-century Palestine. But they follow through on the words of the angelic men: they go and tell Jesus' disciples.

Then Peter follows through: he goes up to the tomb, and we see him trying to let it sink in . . .

Megan Daffern

Hymn suggestions

Within our darkness night (Taizé); This is the night of new beginnings; I will sing the Lord's high triumph; Guide me, O thou great Redeemer.

Easter Day   21 April
Principal Service   **When Hearing Is Believing**
Acts 10.34–43, *or* Isa. 65.17–end; Ps. 118.1–2, 14–24 [*or* 118.14–24]; 1 Cor. 15.19–26, *or* Acts 10.34–43; **John 20.1–18**, *or* Luke 24.1–12

'Early on the first day of the week, while it was still dark . . .' For John, that's more than a comment on the time of day. It's dark, too, in the heart of Mary, enclosed in grief and desolation. She stands for all whose lives have been benighted by loss and who cry out for justice, deliverance, liberation. No one is ready to encounter Easter until they have spent time in dark places. Easter comes while it is still dark.

Expectations

Mary's expectations were modest, to keep a vigil at the grave of her late, lamented Lord. But even that small comfort was denied her: the tomb was empty. Meanwhile, Peter and John ran to the tomb as if they were heading for a Primark sale, but then simply returned home.

Mary remained, and through her tears she notices a figure she takes to be the gardener. Why does she not see Jesus standing close to her? We are with her in her grief and share the suspense that Jesus is there, the risen, living Lord, and we long for her to see Jesus and to assuage her fears.

We can miss noticing the things we ought to be seeing when we're imprisoned in the world of our own making. We miss seeing aright when we dismiss the kind of evidence that would allow us to entertain the hope and promise of newness and deliverance in our world.

Misperception

In his masterly account, John is asking us, who have been surprised and perhaps a little impatient that Mary was unable to recognize her Lord, whether we too may be failing to recognize the one who is close to each one of us. Our sight, our vision, our capacity to be surprised, our scope for having our horizons enlarged, can be occluded by the limits of our expectations and the modesty of our hopes.

Spiritual pursuit

If you'd been in the street and Jesus walked by, you wouldn't have seen him. The raised Jesus was a transcendent reality, always greater than we can know or grasp or imagine. 'Persons appear to us according to the light we throw upon them from our own minds,' as Lara Wilder put it. There usually has to be a 'turning', a prior spiritual disposition, an openness, before the risen Jesus makes himself known. And we're to learn that his preferred means of making himself known is through hearing. For hearing has a gratuitous quality; it cannot be possessed, but neither can it be ignored. It's always receptive.

Disciples Peter and John had long left the scene, but Mary stayed. She stands for the determination we need in pursuit of faith. She's a witness to those who long to believe but fear they'll never be able to, or they're not good enough, or not loveable enough for God to take them seriously. She speaks for those who live with loss and grief and self-doubt, and she shows that the personal search for truth is worth going on with; that in the end we will meet our loving, lost Lord. St John says that we are able to know Jesus because we're known to him already. And we know the voice of the one who knows us and calls us by name.

A woman was struggling with her husband's Alzheimer's condition. 'How hard it must be for you to find you've really lost him,' she was asked. 'Yes,' she said, 'it's painful, but just as long as he recognizes my name, I know he's there.'

Hearing our name

Mary supposes Jesus to have been the gardener, and still fails to recognize him. Only when she hears him call her name, 'Mary', does she recognize him. She turns to greet her risen Lord. 'Mary' – 'Rabbouni'. Instantly she is reconnected with her lost Lord by the single word, 'Mary'. And that is the moment of her own resurrection. Her sorrow is turned to joy, she comes to life again. Mary lives because Jesus lives. And when we too hear the voice of Jesus, like Mary, we come alive, quickened and exhilarated by the surprise of recognition and acceptance.

But if we already hear God's call, and know his life within – what next? Is this a tender, reassuring presence that we want to keep hold of, all to ourselves, like Mary? But Jesus tells us not to cling to him. He says to us, 'Don't cling to the past.' Resurrection happened on the first day of the week. John links it to the first day of creation.

It's a new beginning. Easter doesn't return us to the past – it opens up a new future.

Following Jesus is losing him the moment we think we have captured him, only to discover him anew in even more unmanageable form – always ahead, going before us. And his followers are to be caught up in the reckless love and hope that works and witnesses for liberation and reconciliation in the dark and fearful places in our world.

Roger Spiller

Hymn suggestions

Jesus Christ is risen today; Now the green blade rises; Alleluia! Alleluia! Hearts to heaven and voices raise; Thine be the glory.

Easter Day   21 April
Second Service   **Secure Ground for Hope**
Ps. 105, *or* 66.1–11; Isa. 43.1–21; **1 Cor. 15.1–11**, *or* John 20.19–23

A misguided instinct

'We fool ourselves that we've all got a future,' writes the celebrated journalist Matthew Parris in a recent attack on belief in life after death. 'The whole of what we call religion is a consequence, not a cause, of our gut feeling that there's more to it than our own short lives,' he says. 'Religion rationalizes one of our deepest instincts that this cannot be all there is.'

Well, an instinct for life beyond death isn't wrong simply because it's an instinct, any more than Parris's instinct that death is the end is necessarily right. And that 'instinct' is held as much by people who profess no religious belief as by those who do. What Parris calls an 'instinct' is better described by Wordsworth as an 'intimation of immortality', and that has been remarkably consistent for many centuries. By contrast, belief in an afterlife falters among some people who think of themselves as Christians, as it did by some in the church at Corinth that Paul was addressing in our Epistle reading.

That's where Parris's challenge is timely. It serves to give us a jolt, on Easter Sunday, not to take the hope of resurrection for granted, not to rely on instinct or wishful thinking. It stirs us to reckon with evidence and arguments that affirm the grounds for Christ's resurrection and the hope that we too will be raised with him.

The impact on history

St Paul takes us back to the heart of the gospel. This consists of historical facts: the *fact* that this Jesus died; the *fact* that he was buried; the *fact* that he was believed to have been raised from death by God; the *fact* that this Jesus was proclaimed as Christ and Lord; the *fact* that the early Christians had a life-changing experience that convinced them that Jesus, not just the Spirit of Jesus, was alive in a new way. We can't strictly call the resurrection itself a fact, as if it were just like any other mundane 'fact'. The resurrection could only happen as an act of God, and that can't be demonstrated; nor, for that matter, can it be disproved. Not all processes in the natural order or in science can be observed, but we infer their cause from their effect. The resurrection of Jesus has left the biggest impact upon human history, and requires an explanation. Those who rule out the action of God need to account for the impact of this seismic event upon world history.

Witnesses to the resurrection

Paul's writing is the earliest in the New Testament. He is writing within 20 years of the resurrection, and he is citing witnesses to the resurrection. Some are named and known to those to whom he writes. Then there are more than 500 other witnesses, most of whom, Paul says, were alive and available to be questioned and to have their lives exposed to scrutiny. Is it credible that they would give false testimony; that they would risk facing a death sentence in defence of a deception of their own making? Last of all, says Paul, Jesus appeared to him. What more obvious explanation for his dramatic change can there be than his own testimony that he had encountered the living Lord Jesus, and for it he was prepared to sacrifice everything, including his own life?

Jewish expectations

Belief in a resurrection was shared by most Jews at the time of Jesus, but the resurrection they expected and hoped for was a general resurrection and one that ushered in the end time, the end of the world and the renewal of creation and humankind. So the resurrection of one man, Jesus, in the middle of time, with history still to run, was contrary to all expectations. In the circumstances, those who claimed to have encountered the risen Jesus also knew themselves to have been forgiven and renewed by the gift of new, supernatural life. St Paul reminds his fellow Christians that they had themselves died and been raised with Christ, that the dying and rising of Jesus had been reproduced in them by the Spirit of Jesus as the pledge and assurance that they will also be raised to live with Christ.

The life of the Church

The stories of the resurrection appearances of Jesus in the first century can, at best, only help to persuade unbelievers that it's worth investigating the evidence for the resurrection. But it's the existing company of believers, the Church, that, is the most compelling evidence that Jesus lives, risen and glorified, for ever in the Father's presence. The Church is narrowly based on the single claim that Jesus, who died, was raised by God. It's a community of the resurrection or it is nothing. And its vocation, which extends to every single one of us, is to be the evidence that the risen Jesus lives by his Spirit in the broken body of believers who gather in his name.

The hope of life beyond death looks less like the instinct that Matthew Parris described. True, we have reflected on Jesus' resurrection rather than our own hope of life after death. But the logic of Jesus' resurrection is that we too will be raised with him. If we have entered upon a loving, personal relationship with God, how can we not believe that he will guard it for all eternity? And if we have already been raised with Christ and experience the power of his Spirit, how can we not be driven to believe that we too will enter the fullness of his promise of eternal life. 'Christ in you,' says St Paul, 'the hope of glory.' Praise be to God!

Roger Spiller

Hymn suggestions

If Christ had not been raised from death; Christ is alive, let Christians sing; Now the green blade rises; Thine be the glory.

Second Sunday of Easter   28 April
Principal Service   **The Vision of St Thomas**

Ex. 14.10–end; 15.20–21 (*if used, the reading from Acts must be used as the second reading*), or Acts 5.27–32; Ps. 118.14–end, *or* Ps. 150; Rev. 1.4–8; **John 20.19–end**

It's hard not to feel a certain sympathy with St Thomas, in today's Gospel reading, when all the other disciples come and tell him smugly, 'We have seen the Lord' (as if to say, 'Pity about you!'), like children in a playground talking about an experience they have had to the one person who has missed out on it. Like most of us, he's too proud to say 'Really? Where?' Instead he replies, arms firmly folded, 'I don't believe it. Unless I see the mark of the nails in his hands . . . I will not believe.' Thomas the apostle, who earlier in the same Gospel is recorded as saying to the others, 'Let us also go [with Jesus], that we may die with him', here becomes Thomas the doubter, driven to proud cynicism because he's made to feel he's missed out.

Doubter to apostle

But Jesus is not deterred by either pride or doubt. He appears again; and this time Thomas is there with the others. Jesus shows the mark of the nails to Thomas, who responds with the fullest confession of faith to be found anywhere in the Gospels: he calls Jesus 'My Lord and my God'. Thomas the doubter has been reminted as Thomas the apostle again, not simply because Jesus has provided the evidence he asked for, but because Jesus did not give up on him despite his doubts. Indeed, Jesus makes what appears to be a special visit purely for Thomas' benefit. Yet there's a gentle sting in the tail, when Jesus reproves him: 'Have you believed because you have seen me? Blessed are those who have not seen and yet have come to believe.'

Blessed are those who have not seen

Now, those famous words were not only aimed at St Thomas. They were aimed at all those Christians for whom St John was writing his Gospel, all those who never saw Jesus in the way the first apostles did, and had to rely on faith instead – 'Blessed are those who have not seen and yet have come to believe.' John Hull, a retired professor, went blind when young, and in his book *In the Beginning there was Darkness*, he looks at the Bible and at Jesus from the perspective of a blind person. For him, the hardest part of the Bible has been the Gospel of John, because throughout that Gospel the story of Jesus is presented in terms of a struggle between light and darkness, with light being identified with goodness and darkness (or blindness) with sin. Throughout the Gospel, that is, until we reach today's reading. And there, as Hull points out, almost at the end of the Gospel, the tables are turned. Thomas is portrayed as the quintessential sighted person, who insists on seeing for himself before he will believe anything. Ironically, St Thomas came to be seen in later Christian tradition as the patron saint of those who were blind. He's someone who relies absolutely on his ability to see, unable to take anything on trust. John Hull points out that this is one of the greatest weaknesses of sighted people: that they rely only on appearances, only on what they can see for themselves, and as a result lose the capacity to trust. Being blind, by contrast, requires an ability to take a very great deal on trust. And in that context, as Hull says, Jesus' words to Thomas suggest that a 'special blessing is reserved' for those who are blind. 'Have you believed because you have seen me? Blessed are those who have not seen and yet have come to believe.'

The sure sign of truth of the resurrection

So the witness, the example of those who have managed to cling on to Christian faith when like John Hull they have had very good reason to give up on it, is in the end not only an example to the rest of us: it is the surest sign of the truth of the resurrection. On the one hand, we see in today's reading the fear and cynicism of Jesus' sighted followers, who had seen him many times, had heard first-hand reports of what had happened on Easter morning, and yet were huddled together in what sounds like the first ecclesiastical committee meeting with the doors firmly shut against the outside world. The Church, confident that it alone has a monopoly of the truth about God, ends up by becoming a holy huddle, entirely uninterested in the world outside it. But, on the other hand, as Jesus implicitly says to St Thomas, there will come many who will never see what you have seen, who will have to endure terrible suffering either in spite of or even because of their faith, and yet who will continue to believe in me against all the odds. It is their faith, not yours, that will change the world. And that is the evidence for the resurrection. Not the easy confidence of those first disciples who emerged from the safety of their little house for just long enough to say to Thomas, 'We have seen the Lord.' Not the existence of vast basilicas or the grandeur of cathedral liturgies, or the certainties of the professionally religious. The evidence for the resurrection is the discovery that, when we ourselves become most aware of our blindness and powerlessness in the face of what life will throw at us, we come closer to the presence of God than we had ever been before – or, rather, the presence of God comes closer to us. In the fragile, uncertain, doubtful yet enduring faith of those people who 'have not seen, and yet have come to believe', God can renew the world.

Gordon Mursell

Hymn suggestions

Jesus, these eyes have never seen; Light's glittering morn bedecks the sky; Christ is alive! Let Christians sing; At the Lamb's high feast we sing.

Second Sunday of Easter   28 April
Second Service   **The Emmaus Road**
Ps. 16; Isa. 52.13—53.12, *or* 53.1–6, 9–12; **Luke 24.13–35**

'Now on that same day two of them were going to a village called Emmaus, about seven miles from Jerusalem, and talking with each other about all these things that had happened.'

When Luke wrote his Gospel, he did so with care and with literary skill. Let me give an example. If you read the opening chapter of his Gospel you will find a number of named characters: Theophilus, Herod, Zechariah, Elizabeth, Gabriel, Joseph, Mary and John. That's eight in all. Then there are, like a Greek chorus, an unnamed group, the friends and relatives who gathered around Zechariah and Elizabeth, and who help the story along by raising their concerns. When Elizabeth stated that the child should be named John, they replied, 'But there is no one in your family who has that name . . .'

133

Keep that in mind as we now shift our attention to the closing chapter. Here there are also named characters: Mary Magdalene, Joanna, Mary, Simon, Cleopas, plus, like the Greek chorus, the apostles. They have the same dramatic function as the 'relatives and neighbours' in the first chapter. They help the story along. The opening chapter and the closing chapter are almost mirror images of each other – named characters, plus a kind of chorus. But there is one difference, and it's that one difference that is intriguing.

In the story of the road to Emmaus, one of the characters is named Cleopas. The other remains anonymous, he is unnamed. He was a part of the encounter; he listened as the risen Christ expounded the Scriptures; he was there at the breaking of the bread; he and Cleopas rushed back to Jerusalem; he was there when the Eleven reported that Simon had seen the risen Christ, but at no point is he named.

The naming of characters

Which raises a question. Why, when Luke is so specific in his opening chapter and his closing chapter to name names, why does he not name Cleopas' companion?

It's possible, of course, that by the time he had come to write his Gospel, the name had been forgotten: possible, but unlikely. If Luke himself had forgotten, he could surely have asked one of his sources.

It's also possible, and I think much more likely, that, as a careful author, this was a deliberate choice.

Let me put this another way: if we were to act out the Emmaus road episode as a radio drama, and you were asked which of the characters you would like to be, some would undoubtedly opt to be Mary Magdalene, or Cleopas or Simon, but a number, those who are shyer or more reticent perhaps, would opt to be the unnamed disciple.

And that, I suspect, is why Luke wrote the episode as he did. It gives each of us the chance to be part of the story. It gives us the chance to be the 'unnamed' one. In this story there is, as it were, room for all of us. And for me, it is the unnamed disciple I should like to know more about. My natural human curiosity wants to know where that person was born, what they thought, what became of them after the story . . . but Luke gives us nothing. He has provided only the briefest of outlines.

Too sacred for words

Now bring that story right into the heart of our community today. We can all sympathize with and understand how the risen Christ made himself known to those two disciples in the 'breaking of bread'. That experience is common to us all . . . but, but . . . suppose I decided to be unbelievably insensitive and asked each one of you when you returned from the altar what your experience of the risen Christ had been, you would rightly be horrified by the crassness of my question. There are some things that are too sacred, too precious, too profound, too mysterious, too holy, to be put into words.

The encounter between the risen Christ and our souls is too impossibly intimate, too filled with longing and hope and the darkness of the mystery of God for us ever to be able to find the right words. Let me remind you of a phrase in the story: 'he vanished from their sight'. That is how our Lord is with each one of us, impossibly close and yet also impossibly distant.

Well. We can take one other delightful and encouraging thing from this story of the unnamed disciple, which is all about being unknown, except to the loving heart of God. At a time when our world is saturated with celebrity, inside our Christian faith is something far more profound and true. It is in our very anonymity and our shyness that we can draw close to God and God to us. We can be entirely unknown to the jostling millions, but we are known to God. And inside that truth we can find much comfort and strength.

So, thank goodness for Luke's skill as a literary craftsman, and thank goodness that he provides for each of us in the Emmaus road story a silhouette of an unnamed person into which we can project ourselves. And let us thank God, with all our hearts, that it is in our anonymity and shyness that we are held within the grace and strength of God's infinite love and mercy. There, in the innermost recesses of our souls, we can be encountered by the immense and life-giving joy that is Christ himself. 'He had been made known to them in the breaking of the bread.'

Christopher Herbert

Hymn suggestions

Alleluia! Jesus is risen! Be known to us in breaking bread; Christians, lift up your hearts; Thine be the glory.

Third Sunday of Easter   5 May
Principal Service   Stranger on the Shore

Zeph. 3.14–end (*if used, the reading from Acts must be used as the second reading*), *or* Acts 9.1–6 [7–20]; Ps. 30; Rev. 5.11–end; **John 21.1–19**

> If I were trying to convince an unbeliever of the majesty and spiritual stature of the Risen Christ, I would take that person straight to the last chapter of St John's Gospel and ask them to look through John's eyes at the Son of Man standing alone on the beach in the light of dawn, with a fire at his feet, on which fish is cooking for breakfast.

So wrote a distinguished scholar and Gospel translator.[16]

Let's look, then, at a few verses in the hope that its truth will chime in our lives and help us to recognize the God and Father of the risen Jesus and secure our divine paternity.

Finding solace in the familiar

Peter was last heard of when he was vehemently denying all knowledge of Jesus in the garden of the high priest. And with the suffering and death of Jesus, Peter had found the last few days unreal, bewildering and fearsome. With other disciples, he's in a state of denial, and he goes back to what he knows to be real, familiar and secure. That's what we do after a calamitous shock and disappointment. Usually someone will say, 'Let's have a cup of tea.' Peter returns to what he knows, back to Galilee, back to his old occupation, back to nets and oars and ropes. And tries to eradicate the painful memory of his time with Jesus. But it doesn't work. He and the other erstwhile disciples that Peter enlisted to go fishing laboured all night and caught nothing.

Failing to recognize Jesus

But the Lord with whom we have to do is there for him and for us, the stranger on the shore, to greet and meet us in all our shame and failure and fickleness and unbelief. But they don't recognize Jesus. What is it about the risen Lord that makes it hard for people immediately to recognize him? As somebody said, 'We don't see things as they are; we see things as we are.'

Having a few minutes to spare before a meeting in London, I popped into an impressive church. After my brief tour, I sat down for a short reflection facing the Lady Chapel. I was distracted by another visitor, a young woman, who then came towards me, and, when she saw me face to face, she called my name. I still didn't recognize her, as was all too obvious to her. 'I'm Penny,' she said, 'your godchild.' Sometimes we can be so immersed in our own world that we cannot see the unexpected. But the mystery of the resurrection is beyond comprehension, beyond experience. Eventually the disciples recognize Jesus, but not Peter, not until he sees the net full of fish. And then, as they come to shore, pulling the net, Jesus takes bread and gives it to them and also the fish. That became the way Jesus' identity was and is revealed to us. God in Christ can be known, and is known, among his people because he makes himself known. Through the proclamation of the resurrection this encounter with the risen Lord is rekindled in every age. And now Jesus speaks and emboldens them to do what doesn't make sense; the result is a net filled with big fish. What had been fruitless becomes overwhelming.

Rehabilitating the past

Jesus is not done with Peter yet. There is unfinished business. The stage is set for a tense encounter. The past has to be faced, revisited and redeemed, it can't be ignored. There is the charcoal fire that was there when Peter was warming himself in the garden and vehemently denied even knowing Jesus. The fish are grilled, but so is Peter. 'Do you love me?' The threefold question undoes Peter's threefold denial. Peter is rehabilitated, but he's also recommissioned – 'Feed my sheep' – to be the carer and overseer of Christ's flock.

We are given back our identity, as children of God, and commissioned to serve in his name, when the risen Lord meets us.

In the evocative words of Albert Schweitzer:

He comes to us as One unknown, without a name, as of old, by the lakeside, He came to those men who knew Him not. He speaks to us the same words: 'Follow thou me!' and sets us to the tasks which He has to fulfil for our time. He commands. And to those who obey Him, whether they be wise or simple, He will reveal himself in the toils, the conflicts, the sufferings which they shall pass through in His fellowship, and, as an ineffable mystery, they shall learn in their own experience Who He is.[17]

Roger Spiller

Hymn suggestions

Take this moment, sign and space; Jesus calls us o'er the tumult; Will you come and follow me; To God be the glory.

Third Sunday of Easter   5 May
Second Service   **The Great Acclamation**
Ps. 86; Isa. 38.9–20; **John 11.[17–26] 27–44**

> Jesus said to her, 'I am the resurrection and the life. Those who believe in me, even though they die, will live.'

Let us try a thought experiment . . .

Imagine that when you came to church this morning you saw a man unloading what looked like some electrical kit from a white van. He carried the kit into the church and placed much of it near the pulpit. Intrigued by what he is doing, you watch closely and notice that he is attaching electrodes to the walls. He then stands next to a laptop, types a few instructions into it and waits for the computer to fire up. It does so and you notice that in his hand he holds what looks like a remote control held together with gaffer tape.

He is a man in his late forties dressed casually in a check shirt, a pair of jeans and scruffy trainers. There is a look of intense concentration on his face. He continues to adjust some of the electrical leads and then, after one final tweak of his remote control, he seems ready.

He speaks: 'Ladies and gentlemen. I am sorry to interrupt your worship but I have been given permission to show you something that I find very exciting. My work is at a very early stage, but it's all about what I am going to call the DNA of buildings. You must have heard people say, "If only these walls could speak." Well, I have found a way of tracing and analysing the tiny fragments of sound that have embedded themselves in these walls over the years and through the power of digitalization I can now play some of those sounds back to you.'

He presses a button on the remote control and a hissing sound emerges from two loudspeakers situated near the lectern. He tries another button and the hissing noise begins to reveal the occasional word . . . faint but definitely a word.

If only these walls could speak

He pauses, turns to his computer, types in some more instructions, and turns up the volume. Now things are much clearer. There is still some hissing, but words are beginning to emerge through the background noise. As you attune your ears you can make out the beginnings of sentences, and soon you notice that a pattern is emerging . . . some sentences are being repeated, but at odd intervals . . . it's all very strange, even a bit spooky, but one sentence becomes very distinct. It's a biblical phrase that is repeated, by different voices. You recognize the voice of your current vicar, and then you hear the same sentence pronounced by a former vicar of whom you were very fond but who had died over ten years previously, and then the same sentence pronounced by yet another, older voice . . .

Let's stop this thought experiment at this point.

The sentence being repeated by a range of different voices is one that you know. It's one of Jesus' sayings: 'I am the resurrection and the life . . . '

If such an experiment were really possible, and if the walls of the church really could speak, that sentence of Jesus is one that would be deeply embedded in the very fabric of this building. The phrase 'I am the resurrection and the life' has been read by clergy for century after century, because the words are those used at a funeral service as the coffin is brought into church. The words are sonorously majestic, immeasurably noble and resonate with eternal significance.

'I am the resurrection and the life'

Now listen to them again: 'I am the resurrection and the life . . . '

The two opening words, 'I am', are the very words used by God in his encounter with Moses at the burning bush. When Moses dared to ask God what his name was, God replied, 'I am that I am.' It's one of the greatest moments in the Old Testament, for the name 'I am' implies eternal Being; the name implies the constant and continuous presence of God, always, everywhere; the name implies that God creates, sustains, enfolds and challenges all that is; and it implies that our human 'I am' derives from the 'I am-ness' of God.

But in John's story of the raising of Lazarus even more is implied. You will recall that there was a dialogue between Martha and Jesus:

Martha said to Jesus, 'Lord, if you had been here, my brother would not have died. But even now I know that God will give you whatever you ask of him.' Jesus said to her, 'Your brother will rise again.' Martha said to him, 'I know that he will rise again in the resurrection on the last day.'

That dialogue centred on the traditional teaching of Judaism about the resurrection of the dead on the last day. But when Jesus said 'I am the resurrection and the life', he was claiming that the traditional teaching of Judaism was now to be found in himself. More than that . . . the last days were, as it were, present.

It is as though all time and all the panoply of eternity has been compressed into himself. His being and the Being of God are one and the same.

Is it any wonder that the profound beauty of those words should have been chosen as the verbal fanfare of the funeral service, or, as the imaginative thought experiment suggested, have embedded themselves in the very fabric of our churches? After all, if Christ is 'I am' and if God is 'I am', then, through our very existence, our own 'I am', we too are embedded in the very life of God.

Christopher Herbert

Hymn suggestions

Now is eternal life; The Spirit lives to set us free; I am the light whose brightness shines; Christ is the King.

Fourth Sunday of Easter   12 May
Principal Service   **The Master's Voice**
Gen. 7.1–5, 11–18; 8.6–18; 9.8–13 (*if used, the reading from Acts must be used as the second reading*), *or* Acts 9.36–end; Ps. 23; Rev. 7.9–end; **John 10.22–30**

There once was a small dog called Nipper. The dog was a loyal servant of his master, who was called Mark. When Mark called, Nipper came running. But tragedy struck and Mark died, leaving Nipper all alone. Mark's brother Francis adopted the little dog and also a box of his brother's belongings. In the box was a cylinder phonograph and recordings of Mark's voice. When he played the recordings it was as if Mark was there in the room, and he wasn't the only one who was moved. Nipper sat close to the phonograph, listening to his master's voice. Francis, an artist, decided to commit the scene to canvas, and in 1899 the picture was acquired by a newly formed gramophone company. You can probably guess its name. The picture that Francis Barraud painted was about listening – and about voice recognition.

Voice recognition

We might sometimes wonder what Jesus' *voice* was like? Would we recognize him speaking if we could somehow miraculously obtain a recording of him? We know so many of his words – his stories, his parables, his conversations. We know of his life, his death and his glorious resurrection – but what did he sound like? It is generally agreed by historians that Jesus and his disciples primarily spoke Aramaic (Jewish Palestinian Aramaic), the common language of Judaea in the first century AD, most likely a Galilean dialect distinguishable from that of Jerusalem.

But we learn nothing of the sound of his *voice*. Was it an authoritative voice? Did it lilt? Was it whiny? Was it gruff? Was it loud or quiet? High or low? Husky or smooth? We just don't know. We can probably assume that there must have been some quality in Jesus' *speaking* voice that made people listen. We know that people have been listening to his voice ever since, and people have been responding to his call.

Call and recognition

It is recorded in Luke's Gospel that Jesus stood up in the Temple and unrolled the scroll of the prophet Isaiah and read from it – and people listened. He was, after all, a preacher and teacher. His sermon on the mount and many of his dialogues also suggest he was a natural raconteur, a storyteller, a rhetorician, a public speaker – he could hold people's attention.

It's clear that he made people laugh and cry, but his voice also had the power to heal the sick and raise the dead to life. '*Talitha Cum*', he says to the girl who has fallen asleep – little girl, get up (Mark 5.41). 'Lazarus come out', he says to his friend already laid in a tomb (John 11.43). He orders demons to make haste; his voice turned water into wine, and created enough food to feed five thousand from five loaves and two fish.

141

Then in the garden on Easter Day we see Mary Magdalene, whose eyes are blinded by her tears. She cannot see Jesus standing before her, she thinks him to be the gardener, but when he says 'Mary' she suddenly recognizes him. The same is true in another resurrection appearance. As Jesus broke bread and spoke a blessing, the eyes of two of his disciples were opened. Then they remembered that, as he opened the Scriptures to them, their hearts were warmed within them.

My sheep hear my voice

Jesus says, 'My sheep hear my voice. I know them, and they follow me.' Jesus calls and people follow. This is true yesterday, today and for all eternity. Jesus still speaks to us, and if we choose to listen, the Good Shepherd promises to lead us through our life's journey from beginning to end, through green pastures, beside still waters and in the right paths. Even when we walk through the darkest valleys, we are still called onwards until we reach the house of the Lord where we will dwell for ever.

The book of Revelation goes further, Christ is both the Good Shepherd and the lamb who sits at the centre of the throne of God. The Lamb that was slain becomes the Lamb who leads us all to that place where we will hunger no more, and thirst no more, and every tear will be wiped away from our eyes. Christ the Good Shepherd leads us through life, through death and into the life to come. His voice calls us and leads us onwards on every step of our journey.

The Fourth Sunday of Easter is sometimes known as Good Shepherd Sunday, and more recently remembered as Vocations Sunday. The word 'vocation' derives from the Latin word *vocatio*, meaning a 'call' or summons. It is appropriate then to consider Christ's call to each one of us. We are presumably here because Christ has called us already, but what is he now calling us to be and do? Where might he be calling us to go? Will we follow him when he calls our name? Do we recognize our master's voice? Christ does not stop calling those who have ears to listen.

Victoria Johnson

Hymn suggestions

Will you come and follow me; The Lord's my shepherd (Townend); Jesus calls us o'er the tumult; Loving Shepherd of thy sheep.

Fourth Sunday of Easter   12 May
Second Service   **Remembering**
Ps. 113, 114; Isa. 63.7–14; **Luke 24.36–49**

I'm not always so good at remembering things. If I'm rushing around, trying to do lots of things all at the same time, there'll often be something that slips from my mind.

Remembering was very important to the Hebrew people. It was their remembering of their salvation history, their story with God, that helped them keep their identity as a people, as a community. Their rituals involved remembering. The Passover, for instance. It was crucial that they remembered the night when their ancestors escaped from slavery in Egypt, so they re-enacted it every year with a special meal. They ate food that had practical purposes. The lamb provided them with blood to mark their doorposts to keep the plague of the death of the firstborn males from their homes. The unleavened bread reminded them that they left in so much of a hurry that they didn't have time to let the dough rise. The bitter herbs stood for their bitter time in the wilderness. And during the meal a child from the household asked lots of traditional questions – like the 'Why?' questions that children ask. Why do we do this? What's this for? What does this mean? Every answer helped everyone else remember what it was they were celebrating in this meal that marked a turning point in their shared story.

It's not surprising then that Psalms 113–118 were sung during the meal. We hear two of them today. They are part of a 'Hallel' sequence, a series of holy songs that are about praising the Lord. 'Halleluia' in Hebrew literally means 'Praise' (Hallelu) 'the Lord', (Jah, short for Jahweh). And remembering is important in the daily, hourly praise of God that Psalm 113 calls for.

At the Last Supper, then, since it was a Passover meal, Jesus and his disciples would have sung Psalms 113–118. Jesus was remembering the story of God's people, and singing his praises, even just before his passion and death. He was also about to set something else up that was to be remembered: this Passover meal became the setting for the first Eucharist. The Thanksgiving is repeated frequently, like the ongoing praise of Psalm 113.

Remembering in praise

Psalm 114 explicitly refers to Israel's escape from Egypt, and it brings back images of the parting of the Red Sea, the crossing of the River Jordan, and the moment when, at God's command, Moses struck the rock at Horeb and water flowed out to give drink to his thirsty people. Remembering things like this is a good reason to praise God. There will be things in each of our lives that we can remember with gratitude, times when we have seen God at work in our lives or the lives of those near to us.

The prophet Isaiah in today's reading also wanted the people to remember. The speaker wants to remind people of the good, kind things that God has done for them, but they forget. They fall out with God. Then God gives them a prod, as it were, and they suddenly remember it all again – the days of old, the days when Moses brought his flock through the Red Sea. It's the Passover again. Praise will follow naturally.

Jesus encourages our remembering

Some Christians see Jesus himself in this passage from Isaiah (even though Isaiah was written centuries before Christ). It is Jesus who has his garments stained crimson, like blood, from the winepress, earlier in the chapter. It is Jesus who is bringing salvation and redemption to the people of God. So it is Jesus who is quoted speaking to remind his listeners of their story with God. It was the thing a good prophet, a good rabbi, would do.

And it's also what the risen Jesus does in fact do in today's reading from Luke.

There they are, the disciples, gathered together as dusk falls for the first time since Jesus' resurrection. The women and Peter have seen the empty tomb. Simon Peter, we're told in passing, has seen the risen Jesus. The disciples who encountered him on the road, listened to his retelling of the Scriptures, and only recognized him when he broke the bread for them, have hurried back from Emmaus to Jerusalem. They get together and share their stories. And then Jesus appears again!

First, he has to persuade them that he has a body, that he's not a ghost. So he shows them his hands, his feet, and eats a piece of fish in front of them. He's not a ghost; they don't need to be afraid of him. It's real.

Remembering helps things make sense

It's also true, and that's what Jesus goes on to next. It's like a gentle 'I told you so'. As he did earlier the same day on the road to Emmaus, now he talks to them all about their shared Hebrew Scriptures: the Torah, or Law of Moses (basically, the first five books of the Bible); the Prophets (like Isaiah); and the Psalms – they all talk about him, and his life, death and resurrection all fits in.

Sometimes we can only make sense of something with hindsight. A few hours, days or years after a puzzling event, something happens and that first moment suddenly means so much more. This is what goes on now with the disciples in that upper room. Jesus leads them from fear to amazement to understanding, and he will go on to lead them, through the Holy Spirit, to renewed commitment. But that's for another day.

We don't all have the blessing of remembering. People with dementia, with Alzheimer's, or with traumas that can block out memories, won't always be able to use their memories for good. But remembering, like at the Passover, like at the gathering where Jesus appeared, is a shared activity. It's something we can best do together. In conversation, over food, around the eucharistic table, we can remind one another, and let our remembering lead us to praise, understanding and new commitment. Praise the Lord!

Megan Daffern

Hymn suggestions

Alleluia! Alleluia! Hearts to heaven and voices raise; Jesus, remember me when you come into your kingdom (Taizé); Now is eternal life; You shall go out with joy.

Fifth Sunday of Easter   19 May
Principal Service   Transforming the Landscape
Bar. 3.9–15, 32—4.4, *or* Gen. 22.1–18 (*if used, the reading from Acts must be used as the second reading*), *or* Acts 11.1–18; Ps. 148 [*or* 148.1–6]; Rev. 21.1–6; **John 13.31–35**

Snow

Agent of Temporary Transformation I love snow. I know it's April and the hope of snow has melted, but run with me . . . I love it when fat flakes come swirling out of the sky like giant Quavers, transforming the landscape into a scene from Narnia. Those bags of rubbish fly tipped in a layby are transformed into giant marshmallows; the fag butts in the gutter are hidden, and all is transformed. Call me a hopeless romantic, but I just love snow; it transforms the landscape. I know, I know, the snowy transformation doesn't last. As it melts, all the filth underneath is revealed. The transformation, however beautiful, is only temporary. Not so with the transforming power of God's Spirit.

Spirit

Agent of Permanent Transformation Today we read of Peter's account of the transforming reach of the gospel. The power of the Spirit has fallen upon the family and friends of Cornelius, a Roman centurion. The landscape of their lives is transformed. Can we begin to feel the consternation of the Jewish Christians living in Jerusalem when they hear news of all this? The landscape of their lives is about to be transformed too. Peter has stepped beyond the bounds of what they felt was acceptable, eating with the uncircumcised! They want to hear his reasons. Step by step he explains, recounting his vision, the direction of the Spirit to go to Caesarea and the outpouring of the Spirit on the Gentile hearers. Peter's critics are convinced. They cannot put a boundary on the transforming grace of God, any more than you and I can command the snow to fall upon one part of the landscape but not another. It falls where it falls.

Having eyes to see

Sometimes, our prejudice affects our eyesight; it is hard to see the transforming power of God at work. All of us have roped-off areas, places where we don't expect the grace of God to be at work and therefore never see it: perhaps in the life of that family member who scorns the gospel. No possibility of transformation there. Maybe in the lives of certain groups in society – drug dealers, sex workers, pimps – nah, the transforming power of God won't be found there. In the lives of the cynical and indifferent – transformation? I don't think so. So easily we can ring fence the gospel: 'It's ours, found in the Church, for the right people who come to church, for the insiders, who speak the right language and know the territory.' Oh, we don't put it quite like that, not in so many words, but our attitudes easily betray us. Today's readings come with a gentle hoof up the backside for our parochial narrowness. Together they seem to say, 'Look up, look out with eyes to see the transforming power of God at work, all across the landscapes of our world.' But, as we look around us and see the oozing sludge of sin in the world – war, terror, starvation, abuse, violence, poverty – we can easily lose heart, and hope melts like snow in spring. St John urges us to lift our eyes. He paints a beautiful picture, a stunning image of the ultimate transformation of creation. Imagine – no more death, no more crying, no more mourning, no more pain. We are given the breathtaking image of God wiping away the tears of those who weep. The one seated on the throne says, 'See, I am making all things new . . . these words are trustworthy and true.' Expect transformation!

Hearts and hands to love

But is it enough simply to hope for a future transformed when so may suffer now? No. We need to read the wonderful vision of Revelation 21 hand in hand with God's call to love. That brings us to today's Gospel reading. Jesus is with his disciples. It's their final meal together. Judas has just left the table, on his way to enact his betrayal; with dramatic force John tells us 'it was night'. The powers of darkness are massing, and Jesus knows this. He gives his disciples a new commandment: 'love one another'. Here is the hallmark of people transformed who will be agents of transformation. 'See how they love one another!' How do we express love for each other? How do we love those with whom we disagree? Those who, frankly, get right up our nose? We don't have to agree, we don't have to like each other . . . but love is not optional. It cannot have boundaries. We are called to love those within the community of the Church and those not part of it. Love transforms the landscapes of lives. When we expect someone to launch in at us and have a go, how disarming is the peaceable word. The practical action unasked; the timely text; the gift of friendship, time, money, the quiet persistent prayer – these things bring transformation. The willingness to challenge on the basis of real love, the courage to risk conflict in the name of love – here are the seeds of transformation in the landscape of the world. Transforming the landscape, we need eyes to see and hearts and hands to love.

Drawing it all into prayer

God, you send the snow; it covers the landscape with transforming beauty; we see old things in new ways. Send us out, to love; to see old situations with new vision; that the landscapes of the people we meet, whoever they are, might be permanently transformed by the power of your Spirit at work in our hearts and hands. Amen.

Kate Bruce

Hymn suggestions

Christ is the world; A new commandment; O Lord, all the world belongs to you; There's a wideness in God's mercy.

Fifth Sunday of Easter 19 May
Second Service **An Intriguing Problem**
Ps. 98; Dan. 6.[1–5] 6–23; **Mark 15.46—16.8**

> So they went out and fled from the tomb, for terror and amazement had seized them; and they said nothing to anyone, for they were afraid.

One of the most famous opening sentences in English literature was created by Jane Austen. It's the beginning of *Pride and Prejudice*: 'It is a truth, universally acknowledged, that a single man in possession of a good fortune must be in want of a wife.' It's a beautiful sentence: elegant, witty and exquisitely balanced. One can imagine Jane Austen in her Hampshire drawing-room smiling to herself as she wrote those words on a sheet of paper. It must have been a moment of pleasing satisfaction.

While the opening of *Pride and Prejudice* is a joy, the final sentence of the book is something of a let-down.

> With the Gardiners, they were always on the most intimate terms. Darcy, as well as Elizabeth, really loved them; and they were both ever sensible of the warmest gratitude towards the persons who, by bringing her into Derbyshire, had been the means of uniting them.

To which the only response from the reader is an 'Ahh', an exhalation of gentle emotion. Story done. Completion achieved.

From novel to the gospel

Now, take that way of analysing an English novel back across the centuries until we reach another author: Mark. There he was, seated at his table with a blank papyrus scroll in front of him. He dips his reed pen into the ink-pot and writes the opening words of his Gospel: 'The beginning of the good news of Jesus Christ, the Son of God.'

There's a stark boldness about those words; a sense that something momentous is about to be revealed . . .

And from that moment on, speed and urgency inhabit Mark's writing. But then we read the end of his Gospel. Scholars are generally agreed that the Gospel ends with these words: 'So they went out and fled from the tomb, for terror and amazement had seized them; and they said nothing to anyone, for they were afraid.' It's not how one might have expected the Gospel to end, especially when the opening of the Gospel is so momentous.

Why does the Gospel of Mark end as it does? It's a problem that has teased biblical scholars over the years.

The sense of an ending

Some have suggested that the end of the papyrus scroll on which Mark wrote his Gospel was damaged and lost, and that might explain the abrupt and mysterious ending. But if that was the case, why didn't Mark himself, or one of his friends, re-supply the proper ending?

Others, more melodramatically, have suggested that perhaps Mark was arrested by Roman soldiers in mid-sentence and therefore could not complete his work. There are two responses to this. The first is to say that while ancient tradition claims that Mark wrote his Gospel in Rome, that tradition is not so firmly established that a Roman arrest would be certain; possibly Mark wrote his Gospel somewhere else, in Antioch or Egypt, for example; and, second, if Mark had been arrested or, even more dramatically, had suddenly died in mid-sentence, why did not one of his friends scoop up the scroll and add a few extra sentences to complete the work?

Yet other scholars have argued that Mark ended his Gospel at verse 8 deliberately. It was what he intended. He wanted to leave his readers in suspense: the women were afraid, says this argument, because they had heard the awesome proclamation of the heavenly messengers announcing that Jesus had been raised and would meet the disciples in Galilee . . . and so they ran away from the tomb trembling with the immensity of their experience. The inference is that the early readers of the Gospel would have understood Mark's theological intention. It's as though he had written: 'And now this same risen Christ is with you . . . Jesus has, as it were, met you in your own Galilee . . . '

Well, unless by some miracle Mark's original scroll turns up in an ancient library or is found intact in an archaeological excavation, we cannot solve the problem. We can only speculate, and as long as people continue to study Mark's Gospel, the arguments about the final verses will rage.

All of this is a useful reminder to us in the twenty-first century that the Gospels were, at one level, human constructs . . . just as *Pride and Prejudice* was a human construct and a reminder that lying behind the words was a human being poised over his writing table with a reed pen in his hand, facing, like all authors, the challenge of how he was going to tell his story. But there is one profound difference between the Gospel writers and all other writers. They were writing in the sure and certain belief that Jesus was the Son of God, that God had come to earth, that Jesus had died a terrible death and had then been raised from the dead. A story such as this, beyond all human comprehension, was unique in the history of humanity. The Gospel writers' task was to tell the story so that its power would change lives and communities, and would somehow enable God's revelation of himself to continue – it was a gigantic and humbling task. Imagine how much poorer our world would be if they had not had the courage and the inspiration to pick up their pens, look at the blank sheet of papyrus and write their stories.

We owe them so much.

Christopher Herbert

Hymn suggestions

Jesus meets us at the dawning; Sing my song backwards; Jesus lives; You, living Christ, our eyes behold.

Sixth Sunday of Easter   (Rogation Sunday)   26 May
Principal Service   **The Counsellor**
Ezek. 37.1–14 (*if used, the reading from Acts must be used as the second reading*), or Acts 16.9–15; Ps. 67; Rev. 21.10, 22—22.5; **John 14.23–29**, or John 5.1–9

With so many people struggling with stress, anxiety, loss, issues of identity and self-esteem, the skills of a counsellor are much in demand. Loss and bereavement is the concern of the disciples in today's Gospel from John 14, when Jesus breaks the news of his imminent physical departure from their circle as he takes his leave of them after being reunited with them after the resurrection. It's the situation in which counselling would be an obvious resource. It's hardly accidental, therefore, that 'counsellor' is one of the words for the resource Jesus promises that they will receive.

John introduces a word that is used only in the Farewell Discourse in his Gospel. The word is 'Paraclete,' and is usually translated as 'Advocate', 'Comforter' or 'Counsellor'. No one word does full justice to it. It's identified closely with the Holy Spirit, but focuses on only some of the functions of the Spirit. Counsellor at least suggests some of the characteristics that help us to edge closer to what his presence can mean for us, and what comparisons can legitimately be made between the human counsellor and the divine counsellor.

Alongside

The literal meaning of Paraclete is 'to call alongside'. The counsellor is there for the other person. The counsellor won't sit on a raised chair in a detached mode from the person with whom they work. But neither will they allow themselves to be manipulated by emotional gestures so as to evade the truth. The counsellor has to remain strong for the person they help and be prepared to shoulder any of the mental and emotional burdens that the person is facing, giving them some space until the person feels sufficiently strong to take them back and work with them again. The counsellor is there to release, guide and empower us.

Abiding

Jesus is reported in John's Gospel as saying, 'It is to your advantage that I go away, for if I do not go away, the Advocate (Paraclete) will not come to you.' What is it that the counsellor can do that is more advantageous than the sheer personal and physical human presence of Jesus? It must have to do with the inward and 'abiding' presence of the one who is sent by the Father. He is the personal presence of Jesus in our lives. The Spirit who was with us, will be in us, says Jesus. The divine Counsellor is the 'gentle voice we hear', interceding 'with sighs too deep for words', as Paul puts it. As such, he is our permanent accompanist, a presence who is both transparent and self-effacing, who brings the wisdom and memory of Jesus into the dialogue going on inside us.

Witnessing

The Counsellor takes Jesus' place in our lives. He is known also as the Comforter. But his role is less to console than to represent the mind of Christ in the judgements we have to make. The Counsellor does not call attention to himself: he witnesses to the presence of Jesus and strengthens his followers in their own witness to Jesus.

Defending

The Counsellor renews confidence. Not the false confidence based on human attainment, but 'confidence in self-despair', the confidence that is ultimately anchored in Jesus Christ; the confidence that enables us to love ourselves *as* we love our neighbours. The Paraclete or Counsellor is also called the Advocate. He is the one who speaks up for us so that we do not have to do so ourselves.

Finding

The Counsellor is also the Spirit of truth. The Counsellor works with us and for us, not to judge us or accuse us but to help us to find ourselves. The Counsellor is there to enable us to know ourselves 'as we are known'. He is the Spirit who 'searches everything'. The Counsellor will not permit us to avoid or evade facing the issues we would rather suppress or deny, and neither will he collude with us. But through the warmth of his Spirit in our hearts we are gently prised away from our fear and defensiveness to face and to discover the true self we otherwise try to hide. Together we can befriend our inner child, the parts of our childhood selves that still call for attention, and be led into the enchanting playful world that we felt we left prematurely behind. It's our fear and timidity that submerges the diversity of our personalities in a blanket of sameness. But the Counsellor's work is to intensify our individuality and to help us to know and accept ourselves within the love of God.

Addressing

The Counsellor is there to enable us to handle relationships responsibly and maturely. How do we address God? Fearfully, obsequiously, untruthfully or daringly, frankly and honestly? The Counsellor who brings us in touch with the Spirit of Jesus enables our human spirit to pray like Jesus and to address God with the filial love and intimacy expressed in the selfsame word by which the Son of God chose to address his Father: Abba, dearest Father.

Jesus tells us that the Counsellor can be more to us than even Jesus' earthly presence, not just to make Jesus real but to befriend and renew and guide and strengthen us. May he be our counsellor too!

Roger Spiller

Hymn suggestions

O God, you search me and you know me; Spirit divine, attend our prayers; She sits like a bird; Holy Spirit, truth divine.

Sixth Sunday of Easter   (Rogation Sunday)   26 May
Second Service   **The Art of Learning**
Ps. 126, 127; **Zeph. 3.14–end**; Matt. 28.1–10, 16–end

> At that time I will bring you home,
>   at the time when I gather you;
> for I will make you renowned and praised
>   among all the peoples of the earth,
> when I restore your fortunes
>   before your eyes, says the LORD.

In 1876, a 9-year-old girl called Janet Marion Kimbell, who lived with her grandparents in a small village in Buckinghamshire, was working on a sampler. She had embroidered on it all the letters of the alphabet in both upper case and lower case, plus all the numbers from 1 to 25. In addition, she had embroidered the phrase 'Fear God and Honour the Queen', and, as her penultimate flourish, had also added, in unfalteringly neat needlework, the biblical text 'Remember now thy Creator in the days of thy youth'. (It comes from the King James' translation of Ecclesiastes chapter 12, verse 1.) As her final gesture she added her name and age.

That sampler is slightly faded now but is, as you might imagine, a family treasure. However, it is more than that; it is a reminder not only of the remarkable needlework skills of young children in the Victorian age but is evidence too of the processes of the education of young girls in that century.

Janet Marion Kimbell probably did not realize that she was following a long tradition. In the seventeenth century, 200 years before, it was customary for girls in England to embroider samplers with moral texts. The Victoria and Albert Museum in London, in their large collection of samplers, has one created by an anonymous child with the exhortation 'Bow and bend to another's will that I might learn both art and skill to get my living with my hands'. If you want to learn more, go online.

Social media and mottos

Needlework exercises for girls have nowadays largely been supplanted by various forms of social media. But even in this new form, moral exhortation also continues to appear. Certainly for adults, that moral tradition, once expressed in samplers hung in pride of place in the marital bedroom or on the parlour wall, continues in electronic form. Look at any young technological company's Twitter account and you will find moral exhortation frequently used. The mighty Google used to have as its motto 'Don't be evil'. Facebook's motto used to be 'Move fast. Break things'; certainly it's a thought that could be defined as an exhortation (whether or not it's moral is another matter), but could have been dreamt up by a 2-year-old. Apple, not to be outdone, has as its motto 'Think different'.

It seems to be a human characteristic that we want to take the complexities of the world and try to reduce them to a single, memorable phrase.

There is plenty of evidence for this characteristic to be found in the Old Testament, particularly in the book of Proverbs. Bring to mind, for example, 'Go to the ant, you sluggard; consider its ways and be wise!' Or, in the Old Testament reading for today:

At that time, I will bring you home,
    at the time when I gather you;
for I will make you renowned and praised

among all the peoples of the earth,
  when I restore your fortunes
    before your eyes, says the LORD.

A call for change

This saying is couched as a prophecy in the book of Zephaniah, but it echoes and re-echoes the calls of various prophets to the people of Israel that they should seek the way of the Lord and not be seduced by the behaviour of their neighbouring peoples. It is not, however, simply a matter of moral exhortation, it is more than that. It is a call that the people of Israel should be in a right relationship with God. Again and again, century after century, that yearning cry breaks across the history of Israel like a wave crashing on a beach. It is not only a prophetic cry of judgement, it's also a shout of promise – the prophecy of a time in the future when God himself will reign and the fortunes of his people will be restored.

Inside the prophecy is a kernel of great importance. The prophecy is an expression of hope, a belief that if the people will only amend their lives, and if they will live as God wants them to live, the future will be good, for God himself will be in their midst. Their ethical behaviour will be shaped by God; exploitation will cease, peace will be established, and the lion will lie down with the lamb.

It's a cry that continues to have its resonances today. We cannot look at the broken and desperate state of our world and not yearn, as the prophets yearned, that society, if it turned to God, could learn to become just and good. Maybe this is a shouting into the wind; maybe the cynics and the sceptics will win. But if we do not keep the possibility of hope and transformation alive, our future will become very bleak.

So perhaps Janet Marion Kimbell patiently stitching her sampler in her small Buckinghamshire village was closer to the truth than we might wish to think. Perhaps remembering our Creator in the days of our youth is an exhortation that we should all try to follow.

Christopher Herbert

Hymn suggestions

Breathe on me, breath of God; Here is love, vast as the ocean; Holy Weaver, deftly intertwining; Restore, O Lord, the honour of your name.

Ascension and Pentecost

Ascension Day 30 May
Christ's Work in Heaven
Acts 1.1–11 (*must be used as either the first or second reading*), *or* Dan. 7.9–14; Ps. 47, *or* Ps. 93; Eph. 1.15–end; Luke 24.44–end

Where is Jesus now? He's at God's right hand, answer the Gospel writers. How then, we might ask, is Jesus' absence from the world to be understood as good news?

Jesus Christ has returned to the Father from whence he came. This announces that Christ's work of salvation has been completed and that his human incarnate life on earth has come to an end. He is now sharing the glory of the Father. But this shouldn't be taken to mean that Jesus had departed into a remote and distant region of the cosmos. The cloud that withdraws Jesus from sight is like the cloud that 'overshadowed' the children of Israel, Elijah, Mary, and Jesus at his baptism and transfiguration. This cloud presents Jesus' departure not as a journey to a distant planet but as his entry into the mystery of God, a different dimension of reality.

Lord of space

God isn't in one space rather than another. He is not in space. He is the ground of all space. He is Lord of all space. And as he is parted from his followers his hands are held high in blessing. His hands remain stretched over our troubled world. His is the sacred canopy protecting his world. And, said John Calvin: 'As his body was raised up above all the heavens, so his power and energy were diffused and spread beyond all the bounds of heaven and earth.'[18] The Ascension is good news, because Christ's work is completed and his power is no longer tied to a body on earth but loose in the world. That's why the disciples returned home from Bethany rejoicing.

Humanity in heaven

Jesus Christ is at God's right hand. The one perfect representative of our humanity, the humanity we were meant to be, is with God. 'There is a Man in heaven,' said the Swiss theologian Karl Barth. I thought I knew and believed the incarnation. But only when I heard those direct words of Barth did the awesome, staggering wonder of it reach me with revelatory force. 'There is a Man in heaven!'

After so much in churches, liturgies and preaching that has talked down men and women as if sin has rendered them virtually worthless, we've thought of the human and the divine as opposites, as antithetical to one another. This is not simply due to sin, but has extended in the popular mind to the view that humanity is intrinsically separate from God by an unbridgeable chasm. How could humanity, even redeemed humanity, appear in the presence of God? In Christ's ascent to the Father, humanity occupies and shares the rule and dominion of God. Humanity is not in opposition to the divine, but in a continuum with it. There's a great difference, of course, between God and humanity, and because of the difference there is a nearness.

We possess heaven

What then has become of human sinfulness? 'Since Christ has entered the sanctuary not made with hands, he appears before the Father's face as our constant advocate and intercessor,' as Calvin put it. And thus, 'He turns the Father's eyes to his own righteousness to avert his gaze from our sins. He so reconciles the Father's heart to us that by his intercession he prepares a way and access for us to the Father's throne. He fills with grace and kindness the throne that for miserable sinners would otherwise have been filled with dread.' So said Calvin. This then is good news.

By his ascent into heaven, Christ opened the way into God's kingdom, which had been blocked by sin. Christ entered into heaven not just in his own name but in ours too. And, says Calvin, it follows that we already 'sit with God' in the heavenly places. So we don't merely await heaven, but through Christ we already possess it. We who have died to sin, says St Paul, have been raised with Christ and so must set our minds on the things that are above. But this is not a feat of imagination, but the realization of the place already opened to us by Christ. Through the Spirit indwelling our hearts, Christ shares with us the gifts with which he is endowed. So we don't contemplate him from outside ourselves, from afar, because we put on Christ and are engrafted into his body and are made one with Christ.

Lift up your hearts!

The body of Christ remains in heaven. It's the Spirit who descends and who constitutes the connection between the glorified Christ and believers. 'No extent of space interferes with the boundless energy of the Spirit, which transfuses life into us from the flesh of Christ,' says Calvin.[19] But, in descending, the Spirit 'lifts us up to himself'. This being lifted up is evident in Anglican eucharistic worship. Worshippers are invited to 'Lift up your hearts', and respond, 'We lift them up to the Lord.'

The Blessed John Henry Newman summarized it in this way:

It is then the duty and privilege of all disciples of our glorified Saviour, to be exalted and transfigured with Him; to live in heaven in their thoughts, motives, aims, desires . . . even while they are in the flesh; . . . but the while to have a secret channel of communication with the Most High . . . to have their life *hid* with Christ in God.[20]

So, in the words of today's prayer: 'as we believe your only-begotten Son to have ascended into the heavens, so we in heart and mind may also ascend and with him continually dwell'.

Roger Spiller

Hymn suggestions

Before the throne of God above; Rock of Ages, cleft for me; Ascended Christ, who gained; Hail the day that sees him rise.

Seventh Sunday of Easter
(Sunday after Ascension Day) 2 June
Principal Service **Gifts from God**
Ezek. 36.24–28 (*if used, the reading from Acts must be used as the second reading*), *or* Acts 16.16–34; Ps. 97; Rev. 22.12–14, 16–17, 20–end; **John 17.20–end**

John is subversive. Not subversive in a bad sense, but subversive in the way he takes our normal understandings of things and reveals them in an entirely new light. In today's Gospel our awareness of the words and actions of Jesus are turned upside down. It is what makes reading John's Gospel such a perplexing struggle and delight.

Let me give an example. If I asked you to tell me how Jesus went about choosing his disciples, I guess you would remember the story of the call of Simon and Andrew, James and John.

This is how Mark tells it in his Gospel:

> As Jesus passed along the Sea of Galilee, he saw Simon and his brother Andrew casting a net into the lake – for they were fishermen. And Jesus said to them, 'Follow me and I will make you fish for people.' And immediately they left their nets and followed him. As he went a little farther, he saw James son of Zebedee and his brother John, who were in their boat mending the nets. Immediately he called them; and they left their father Zebedee in the boat with the hired men, and followed him.

All very straightforward: Jesus calls; the disciples respond. Now look carefully at what John writes: 'Father, I desire that those also, whom you have given me, may be with me where I am.' The Revised English Bible translation of this verse makes things even clearer. It says: 'Father, they are your gift to me . . .'

Disciples as a gift

The disciples were called – of course they were. But this is the point: they were also, according to John, God's gift to Jesus. Their calling does not fall into the category of demand and response, as the other Gospel writers suggest. It was far deeper than that; the disciples, that motley bunch of men, were God's gift to his Son; a strange and unstable gift, it is true, but a gift nonetheless. They weren't chosen after shortlisting, interviews and psychometric tests; they were simply received. They were a given; God's gift from himself to Jesus.

We know what they were like: some were hot-heads – think of James and John; some were used to creaming off their own income from the tax system – think of Matthew; some – think of Simon the Zealot – were radical freedom fighters; some – think of Peter – were all for fire and action but when it came to the crunch turned tail and ran; and one, Judas, turned out to be a traitor. Some gift . . .

But here they are in John's Gospel featuring as the major players in Jesus' prayer to God, in which he refers to them as a gift. From a worldly perspective it doesn't make much sense. But look at how the prayer continues: 'Father, I desire that those also, whom you have given me, may be with me where I am, to see my glory, which you have given me because you loved me before the foundation of the world.'

The circle of God

John seems to see the relationship between Jesus and the disciples as part of a great cosmic movement. It's like a circle standing up vertically. At the very top of the circle is God. He sends his Son Jesus into the world – that's the downward sweep of the circle. As Jesus begins his ministry, God gives Jesus the disciples – that's at the bottom of the circle. Then Jesus prays and the disciples are caught up into the upward sweep of the circle, for Jesus prays that they will see him in glory with God, at the top of the circle. The movement is from God downwards, through Jesus in the world, and then upwards returning to God.

It is a strange and wonderful way of looking at life that John offers us. He suggests that we should see our lives not as humdrum and ordinary, but instead we should see our meaning and human purpose in mystical terms. We, like those first disciples, are part not just of a local and particular time and place, but we are part of an eternal and universal dynamic. We are given as a gift from God to Jesus, and he in turn bears us back to God. We are, as it were, part of the procession of all the saints; we are, whether we realize it or not, dancers in the divine and universal drama; clumsy and awkward as we are, we are nevertheless part of the enfolding beauty and joy and pleasure of God.

But the recognition of that extraordinary truth might take us a lifetime to learn.

Christopher Herbert

Hymn suggestions

Put peace into each other's hands; Living God, your word has called us; Jesus, Lord, we look to thee; Eternal Ruler of the ceaseless round.

Seventh Sunday of Easter

(Sunday after Ascension Day)   2 June

Second Service   **Growing Up in Christ**

Ps. 68 [*or* 68.1–13, 18–19]; Isa. 44.1–8; **Eph. 4.7–16**; *Gospel at Holy Communion*: Luke 24.44–end

St Paul often talks about spiritual maturity when in correspondence with the young churches over whom he has pastoral oversight. When writing to the church in Ephesus, it seems he is encouraging them to 'grow up' in Christ. He prays that they may come to maturity in the full stature of Christ. They are now ready to advance from milk to solid food. Paul is calling members of the church to consider the gifts they have been given, and how they each might be being called to use them for the building up of the church. This, he says, requires them not only to receive but also to give generously of themselves for the sake of the gospel.

His advice is as useful today as it was 2,000 years ago. The Church of Christ is made up of extraordinary people with many and varying gifts, some very obvious, some less so, some yet to be discovered. Some are still called to be apostles, some prophets, some evangelists, some pastors and teachers – some are naturally hospitable, some sing, some arrange flowers, some sweep, some garden, some bake. In order for any church to thrive, its members are called to reach a level of maturity by which they are able to take on their share of ministry for the benefit of all. They move from being people who are primarily fed by others, to people who are themselves called to nurture others in the faith. Everyone has a part to play, and this is perhaps what Paul means when he talks about growing up in Christ.

What do we need to grow up in Christ? The writer of Psalm 68 assures us that God gives power and strength to his people. This is affirmed in the words of the prophet Isaiah, where God reveals our destiny as his children whom he has known from the beginning. God will take this seed of life and pour out his blessing upon it so that we each spring up like green tamarisk, like willows by flowing streams. There is an expectation of growth and development from a tiny seed or sapling into a tree in which the birds of the air may find a home.

Gifts to share

In Christ we are nurtured and fed and, as St Paul says, given grace according to the measure of Christ's gift. The measure of Christ's gift to us is without limit and it has the power to help each one of us find the gifts we have been given to then share with others. This is essentially how the Church continues to be built up from generation to generation. We still need apostles, evangelists, pastors and teachers, but perhaps more importantly we need to recognize the call to give without counting the cost.

Though Paul talks about 'growing up' and being mature, this isn't necessarily about seniority. Paul makes it very clear here, and famously elsewhere in his writings, that every member of the Church is part of the body of Christ, which is knit together so that every member 'promotes the body's growth in building itself up in love'. The young and the more mature have a contribution to make, and everyone in between. There is an expectation of reciprocity among the people of God. Experience is a gift but so too is enthusiasm, diversity and a fresh perspective. As the prophet Isaiah says, we all belong to the Lord, and we all therefore have a gift to share in his name.

Living in the community of Christ

Careful reflection on what it means to live as a Christian community is something that St Benedict also instituted in his rule. He talks about prayer, worship, study and how to say the psalms together, but he also talks about the very practical aspects of community life we often underestimate, cooking, cleaning, caring and how community life is to be managed. Living as a Christian community requires both humility and a level of maturity, but Benedict is always clear that everyone has something to contribute and all are called to be servants of Christ. The Christian life, then, is not something we passively observe. We are each called actively to participate and share in the life of the communities of which we are part. Every member of every church has a ministry, and the challenge for each one of us is to discern what that ministry might be and, vitally, how it can be shared to build up the life of the Church in this age.

Victoria Johnson

Hymn suggestions

Bind us together; Help us to help each other, Lord; I give my hands to do your work; For I'm building a people of power.

Day of Pentecost   9 June
Principal Service   **The Hubbub of Prayer**

Acts 2.1–21 (*must be used as either the first or second reading*), *or* Gen. 11.1–9; Ps. 104.26–36, 37b [*or* 104.26–end]; Rom. 8.14–17; John 14.8–17 [25–27]

Lost for words: or a new language?

'Everyone was amazed and perplexed . . .' I'm not surprised. They said, 'What does this mean?' Good question! I'm perplexed. Perhaps you're thinking, 'If you're perplexed, the confusion's all in your mind. Read Luke's account of Pentecost again, slowly and carefully, and all will become clear.' Yes? Well, I have read it slowly and carefully, and I'm still 'perplexed'. I may be confused in my mind, but – dare I say it? – I think there may be a confusion in Luke's mind too! The confusion seems to revolve around this business of speaking in 'tongues', or 'languages', or both. What exactly did Luke imagine coming out of the mouths of these hyper-excited people? What were the sounds filling the air? Were they unintelligible ecstatic noises? Suppose the coming of the Holy Spirit was such a novel, overwhelming experience that the followers of Jesus, packed into this room, were literally 'lost for words'; but they just had to respond somehow. So they all burst into wordless utterings. We know that sort of thing went on in the first churches. And we know that Paul, while not exactly dismissive, was a bit cool about it: 'If then I do not know the meaning of a sound, I will be a foreigner to the speaker and the speaker a foreigner to me.'

That said, Paul himself admitted to speaking in tongues sometimes. And in many churches today, worshippers still sometimes set the disciplines of orderly communication aside, gripped by an impulse to say a great big 'yes' to God, never mind what noises come out. And why not? Perhaps it all started that day in Jerusalem.

But maybe this story isn't all about unintelligible 'tongues' but about people communicating with each other, about language. It seems as though Luke thought it was. He understood the whole event as one big sign that the Holy Spirit had, on that very day, launched the gospel from Jerusalem on its journey to the farthest parts of the known world, transcending the barriers of language. It was a sort of reversal of what happened with the tower of Babel. There God put an end to the old common language of human arrogance; here he brings into being the new common language of the good news of his new kingdom.

So what are we dealing with – an experience genuinely over-whelming but beyond words; or the release of news so powerful and so transformative that it can bend any existing language to its purpose? Are we talking about dialogue with God among ourselves 'in one place', or dialogue about God with 'every nation under heaven', with people on the other side of the fences we all build around ourselves? Or both?

Intelligible international hubbub – in the cathedral

A few years ago I went to a service at Coventry Cathedral, in the shell of the old bombed building. The theme was peace through reconcili-ation. And there were people from different countries at the service. At one point in the worship the Dean invited us all to pray – out loud and in whatever words we chose. He called for a 'hubbub of prayer'. And hubbub it was. The broken walls echoed a great cacophony of noise. Altogether, it was entirely unintelligible. But anyone, from any one of a number of nations, moving in among the crowd, would hear someone speaking to God, or speaking about God, in his or her own language. 'Tongues' or 'languages' – it could be both. So it's possible for a church to be excited by God beyond words and to talk intelligibly about God, both at the same time. Indeed, I want to say that you can't talk intelligibly about God unless you're first excited by God. It's not just information about God's mighty deeds we have to share, it's God-given excitement as well.

Excitement – Christ's gift to his people; wait for it; expect it!

So what's excitement, Christian excitement, like? When and where does it come? It comes when a little church, locked into present habits for fear of the future, suddenly sees an unexpected future bursting through the locked door. It comes when something precious in church life, which people thought they'd lost for ever, suddenly returns. It's like when the ordinary routine transactions of everyday life – commonplace greetings like 'Good morning' or 'Peace be with you' – become suddenly filled with real warmth and deep meaning. It's like when the church that thought itself powerless suddenly feels empowered to do something new. In short, excitement comes into the life of a church when that church is suddenly filled with a vivid awareness of the presence of Jesus. John and Luke provide very different accounts of when and how the Holy Spirit first came upon the followers of Jesus. But both agree that the Holy Spirit was Jesus' gift to his people. Are we excited now? No? Well then, wait! Listen out for the sound of a mighty wind. Look out for flames of fire. The Spirit of Jesus is hovering over us. The Spirit of Jesus will not be kept out of this building.

Paul Johns

Hymn suggestions

O for a thousand tongues to sing; Come down, O love divine; Come, Holy Spirit, come!; Filled with the Spirit's power, with one accord.

Day of Pentecost   9 June
Second Service   **In Your Face?**
Morning Ps. 36.5–10, 150; Evening Ps. 33.1–12; **Ex. 33.7–20**;
2 Cor. 3.4–end; *Gospel at Holy Communion*: John 16.4b–15

We don't like having our space invaded. If someone gets too close, it feels uncomfortable. If someone puts their face too close to yours, it feels aggressive. If something's really obvious, a young person today might say, 'It's, like, *so* in your face!' It's a way of talking about something that's apparently evident, blatant, not to be questioned. And it's a way of talking that means no further questions are asked.

In the face of awe

We don't see the face of God in the Bible. Do we? After all, in our reading from Exodus today God says to Moses, 'But you cannot see my face; for no one shall see me and live.' In Hebrew, the 'face' of someone often stands for their very being (just like the 'hand' can stand for power and might, and so on). So to be face to face with someone is to be close to their presence. To see their face is to be near to them. The idea of being in the presence of God, for the great Old Testament mystic Moses, is awesome, and more. In fact, it is so awesome that it would be entirely overawing.

Awe is not a very 'First World' thing. We are capable – so we are unlikely to be in awe of those around us. We are in control – so who is there to be in awe of, really? But reclaiming awe is inspiring. Moses was in awe of God so much that his face shone with it.

A shining face

Paul, in his second letter to the Corinthian Christians, describes the awe that we can feel when we realize we're not capable by ourselves, but only through God. Our confidence, he says, should come not from our own self-sufficiency but from God. Confidence is literally 'trusting in', 'having faith in'. Where does our confidence come from?

Moses' confidence came from God. We saw him wavering at the beginning of Exodus as to how he could possibly represent the Israelites before Pharaoh. He had no faith in his own speech, or what he could do. God gives him his brother Aaron to help in his mission. And Moses has to rely fully on God. His people are unreliable, even Aaron is shown to be undependable, in the episode of the Golden Calf, which wasn't so long before our present passage. The only one Moses has to rely on in the wilderness, in his lonely position of leadership, is God, who gives him the stones engraved with the new covenant. His meeting with God fills him with radiance, and his receiving from God makes him overflow with God's glory, so much so that his face shines. In turn, the Israelites can't look him in the face, and Moses has to wear a veil.

Restored: face to face

Paul's words remind us how the veil separates us from the real presence of someone. The veil seems to be a little like the curtain in the Temple, which separated the place of the most profound presence of God that the Jews could imagine from everyone else. Only the High Priest could 'enter the curtain'. And it was this curtain that was torn down the moment Jesus gave up his spirit on the cross, according to the Gospels of Matthew, Mark and Luke. It is only in Christ, says Paul, that such separation can be removed, that God can be wholly with his people, see them face to face. So, for Paul there's the ministry of the engraved tablets of the covenant, kept in the Holy of Holies, that needs some kind of separation; and the ministry in Christ of the Spirit, where the veil is removed, and all can see God face to face. This is the true radiant-faced glory that comes from the Spirit.

Coming face to face with Jesus today

In today's passage from John, Jesus is preparing to leave his disciples, he's getting them ready to live without seeing his face every day. And because he is going away, he tells them he can leave his Spirit. This is the Spirit that fills those who receive him with truth. And this is the Spirit that truly shows God's glory in Jesus.

We can sometimes read one another's faces. We can tell when they're very sad, or filled with delight. The Spirit that 'glorifies' Jesus makes Jesus for ever present in the life of the believer. We can be with Jesus face to face if we choose. Prayer is a good time for that. So is study, reading the Bible, or being inspired by the writings of saints past and present. And Pentecost, when we celebrate the coming of that Spirit that means we can be face to face with Jesus eternally, is a time truly to celebrate God's glory. God's glory may not always be evident to us in every part of the world, but it is for us to let our faces shine with God's radiance, Jesus' Spirit.

Megan Daffern

Hymn suggestions

O Lord, we long to see your face; Lord, the light of your love is shining; Can we by searching find out God; Love divine, all loves excelling.

Ordinary Time

Trinity Sunday   16 June
Principal Service   **A Trinity-Centred Life**
Prov. 8.1–4, 22–31; Ps. 8; Rom. 5.1–5; **John 16.12–15**

Father-centred

There are Father-centred Christians, who have a sense of a supreme being, analogous to a perhaps distant father figure, the
source of power and wisdom; the Creator whose handiwork can
be recognized in the natural order, in the expansive and mysterious universe. Father God is often the default belief for those who
believe there must be 'someone', even though this being appears
remote, distant and perhaps also absent and judgemental, and
one who doesn't make too many demands but, for all that, can
elicit a sense of insecurity and fear. We are left wondering where
we stand before him; what he thinks of us.

Father-centred Christians need a relationship with Jesus the
Son if they're to know God as Father. Without the relationship
offered through Jesus Christ we could never know for ourselves
that God loves us unconditionally. There's nothing that the
Father withholds from us to bring us home. But without the Son,
how could we know this? And without his ignominious death,
how could we ever persuade ourselves that God sent his Son to
bring us back to himself and throw open his storehouse, shower-
ing upon us his grace and love? It's through Jesus the Son that
God came down to earth. He is the window, the icon into the
heart of God. What Jesus was, God is. God is Christlike, and the
God that he reveals is one who is hidden in the sufferings of Jesus
on the cross.

And Father-centred Christians need also the Spirit, God's hidden
agent, who seals our adoption as sons and daughters of our heavenly Father. His Spirit is poured into our hearts so as to fashion our
family resemblance to God through the Spirit's own life.

Jesus-centred

There are Jesus the Son-centred Christians. They attest a special, personal, intimate relationship and act as those who have already entered upon their Christian inheritance. But the focus on Jesus may eclipse the awe-filled relationship offered by the Father God. Jesus reveals God, but this makes no sense and is a tautology unless we have some knowledge of the Father apart from Jesus. Jesus-centred followers need to be rooted in the Father's human history, otherwise Jesus looks like a solo religious guru around whom a personality cult is built. A proprietary attachment to 'my Jesus' can disregard the universal dimension that God has with the whole of creation.

Jesus-centred Christians also need the Spirit to release them from a rigid, literalistic, infallibilist attachment to the Scriptures, and to enable them to discover the subtle, poetic and storied character of its language that alludes to, rather than captures, Christian truth. Teaching and sound doctrine can become shibboleths, and Jesus-centred Christians can seem captive to legalism and to finding simple solutions rather than relishing uncertainty and mystery. Jesus-centred Christians need the Spirit to release them into the freedom of the Spirit who leads us into all truth.

Spirit-centred

There are Spirit-centred Christians. They emphasize the experience of the Spirit and its supernatural manifestations and gifts. They are refreshed by the freedom and spontaneity of life in the Spirit. But Spirit-centred Christians need the Son to teach them that the heart of Christian discipleship is self-denial rather than the pursuit of exalted spiritual experience. And they need theology as their map and guide if they are to channel and mobilize the Spirit's power. Spirit-centred Christians can act like orphans, subject only to themselves and their self-validating spiritual experiences. This has sometimes resulted in factionalism and divisiveness. Spirit-centred Christians need the Father God as their reference if their individualism is to be tempered by the community of the Spirit within the disciplines of the Church. A relationship with the Father ensures their life is grounded in God's faithfulness and not the fleeting sequence of religious experiences. They, too, need the Father if their exuberance is to be chastened by a recognition of the intractable experiences of the human condition. For the Christian there are desert times, times of godforsakenness, when the Spirit does not lead to ecstasy and inspiration.

We are who we are by virtue of our relationships, and to be developing as disciples of Christ we need to relate to Father, Son and Spirit. The whole of Christian thought and living is quite simply the explication and working out of the Trinity. That is what defines our faith; that is what shapes our lives. Where God is known only as Father, there is a remoteness that can lead to atheism; where the emphasis of God is exclusively on Jesus, there is the risk of idolatry; and where the Spirit is sought for heart-warming experience, there is scope for division. God is the relationships God has, and we need a relationship with all three persons in order for us to come fully alive.

The Trinity is not a puzzle to solve, but a community to be drawn into. Not so much an article of belief as a way of life. It is the sublime demonstration of the full panoply of God's dynamic, communal life, reaching down and through and into every life that we too might share the wonders of his divine life.

Roger Spiller

Hymn suggestions

Affirm anew the threefold name; We give immortal praise; Father of heaven, whose love profound; Father, Lord of all creation.

Trinity Sunday   16 June
Second Service   **The Importance of Names**
Morning Ps. 29; Evening Ps. 73.1–3, 16–end; **Ex. 3.1–15**; John 3.1–17

In one of my earliest courses in listening skills, we had a session about asking people's names, remembering them, and the conversations that can flow from a name. Names matter. So when a whole intake of new students comes to our college each October, I throw myself into learning their names. That can be in the form of studying the sheets of photos that we get a few days before they arrive. It can be through high-energy conversations with groups or individuals, in the lunch queue or at the chapel door. And it's through frequently testing myself, in their presence (if I'm prepared to be embarrassed sometimes), or back with their photos at my desk. When I meet students with a name I haven't come across before, I'll ask them about what it means, where it comes from, how it's spelt. And then their surnames. It's all a good way of engraving it in my memory, while finding something out about them, and beginning to build a relationship.

Names and relationship

Getting to know someone's name is an important, early part of getting to know them. When we know someone's name, and they know ours, we can call to them at a distance, we can address them when they are close by. We can offer them coffee, or ask them what's wrong, or request help, or guide them in some way. Then we can get to know the person who holds that name.

Knowing how to call upon God is a big part of prayer. Sometimes, it might just be enough for our prayer to be 'Jesus!' or 'O, God!' We can leave God to work out what we need to say to him even if we can't put it into words ourselves. It's like any kind of relationship. Sometimes a wife just needs to say 'Darling!' to her husband, and a whole conversation is contained in just that one word of relationship, of address, of name.

Being a name, naming a being

Moses' early encounter with God, at the burning bush, was his chance to ask God his name. Moses could see how totally crazy it all might look to someone else. A weird burning bush that is not consumed in the flames? *Talking* to him? No one would believe him. Especially not if he couldn't even give it a name! OK, so this is the God of the Israelites' ancestors; but doesn't he even have a *name*? Doesn't Moses know him even *that* well?

So God gives his name to Moses. Back at the beginning of Genesis, names were important: God asked Adam to give names to all his creatures. God now reveals his name. It's a pivotal moment in the relationship between Creator and created.

'I am who I am.' Or, 'I will be who I will be.' Or, 'I am becoming who I am becoming'. It's a Hebrew phrase that's both profoundly simple and deeply complicated at the same time. (Hebrew verbs have a whole range of how they can be translated in terms of tense, which is why it can be understood both as present and future, and really anything in between too.)

Above all, this is a name of Being.

Knowing God's name

The idea of God simply as 'Being' or 'Existence' or 'Life itself' is something of a conundrum, puzzling one to get one's head round. But it does relate to God as Creator, the one who gave life. It also reveals God as Sustainer, the one who continues to give life, continues to re-create. At the same time, God expresses his care for generations past, and vows care to future generations. This is a God who simply *is*, and always *will be*.

This means making this name known to the wobbly human race, always so ready to go off-track, that this is also a God who is always and will always want to be in relationship. He will always go back and rescue them. He will uphold that relationship through thick and thin. He will be their Redeemer as well as their Creator and Sustainer.

Simple and complex: the life of love

The Trinity is at one and the same time both unity and united. That seems like a complicated thing in itself. Yet how true! At the heart of God is relationship. Relationship between Creator, Sustainer and Redeemer. Relationship between God the Father, God the Son, and God the Holy Spirit. The Gospel of John today tells us, through Jesus' words to Nicodemus, about the Spirit as crucial to being in the kingdom of God. And that through the Father giving his Son, the kingdom of God is opened to all who receive that Spirit. That is the most wonderful love.

The Trinity then is a sign of love: the Spirit of love between the three persons of God, and love in their actions, and love in their being. And many of us know how love can be both simple and complicated; it can enrich us, inspire us and make us whole. All because we know we can call upon God by name, God, who is love, within and through his very being.

Megan Daffern

Affirm anew the threefold name; I bind unto myself today; How sweet the name of Jesus sounds; At the name of Jesus.

First Sunday after Trinity (Proper 7) 23 June
Principal Service **The Man with Many Names**
(*Continuous*): 1 Kings 19.1–4 [5–7] 8–15a; Ps. 42, 43 (*or 42 or 43*); *or* (*Related*): Isa. 65.1–9; Ps. 22.19–28; Gal. 3.23–end;
Luke 8.26–39

This is a humdinger of a Gospel reading to preach about because it presents so many difficulties for our twenty-first-century minds. We struggle to make sense of it.

Let's be honest: there are a number of problems. The most basic problem is that biblical scholars cannot even agree about where the events described actually took place. Some say that the story might have been set in a small village called Khersa on the eastern side of Lake Galilee. Others say the story was based in Gerasa or Gadara, small cities some distance from the lake. Khersa seems the most likely and fits the narrative the best. But you'll notice that Luke, with his enchanting geographical vagueness only states that the events took place in 'the country of the Gerasenes'; suitably vague, a kind of dismissive, fluttering sweep of the hand indicating 'Somewhere over there . . . on the eastern side of the lake'.

And then there's the problem of the demoniac's possession. There are some who take the story literally and see it as a dramatic and powerful exorcism, a battle between good and evil; others, not sharing the literalist view, say that perhaps the man was suffering from what in the twentieth century used to be called 'multiple personality disorder'. It's now known as 'dissociative personality disorder'. The journal *Psychology Today* describes it like this: 'It is a severe condition in which two or more distinct identities, or personality states, are present in – and alternately take control of – an individual. Some people describe this as an experience of possession.'

Yet others say that they struggle intellectually with the whole concept of 'possession' and are deeply troubled by contemporary instances of 'exorcism', which seem to be characterized by arbitrary and cruel abuses of power. Nevertheless, they acknowledge that they have also seen situations in which people behave in ways that are utterly appalling and brutally sadistic where only words like 'evil' to describe them will do. Think of the horrors of Belsen, for example, and you can see that the anodyne vocabulary of psychology is inadequate to convey the depths of depravity witnessed in that concentration camp. This is not the place to discuss this problem further; perhaps all we can say with any degree of certainty is that our ideas of what constitutes 'health' and 'illness' are strongly influenced by the cultures in which we live. And so, at the time of Jesus, when demon possession was part of day-to-day discourse, it is not surprising that this story of a dramatic healing should have been couched in those terms.

Legion

What all can agree on is that the man wandering around the graveyard dressed in rags, rattling his broken chains, was a profoundly disturbed soul; a man who terrified his neighbours, a man so deranged, and so disruptive of himself and others, that he could only exist on the farthest outskirts of civilization, in a graveyard.

Then notice what happens: Jesus asks him his name. He recognizes that the man has a precious identity; he is 'named' by Jesus as a fellow human being. The man replies to Jesus' question with a kind of dark wit: 'My name is Legion.' In other words, he sees himself as being thousands of people . . . his identity is the size of a Roman legion. It's a subtle, powerful, dramatic moment, for the man who is possessed calls himself by the name of the occupying power, the political power that 'possesses' the land. No other words are spoken, either by the man or Jesus, but in that encounter with Jesus the man's innermost, raging, tumultuous self is brought to stillness and peace.

At which point let us also recognize the subtlety of Luke the author. Unfortunately, the lectionary-makers have done us a disservice today. How? They have detached the previous story in the Gospel from its rightful place. It should have been read in conjunction with this one.

Let me remind you that in the verses prior to the story of Legion the story is about Jesus and the disciples crossing the lake and encountering a vicious storm, which Jesus calms. The disciples' response is one of awe: 'Who then is this, that he commands even the winds and the water, and they obey him?'

The calming of the storm on the lake and the calming of the man called Legion are profoundly interconnected. Luke's message could not be clearer: Jesus is the one who brings peace, who, like God at the creation, brings order out of chaos. And if Jesus has this power, then who is he? What are we to make of him?

Let's return for a moment to the story of Legion. Is it any wonder that the townspeople seeing Legion calm, clothed and in his right mind are terrified? They simply cannot cope with the radical power of Christ. Ironically, whereas his authority has been welcomed by the deranged but now healed man, the townspeople cannot live with it. It's too much. It casts into doubt their entire understanding of the world. Better to remain in a safe, binary system in which the deranged are banished to the edge than a world in which the previously mad are given back in their right mind to the community.

It is, as I said at the beginning, a humdinger of a story . . . and we have to take away from it what we will.

Christopher Herbert

Hymn suggestions

Great God, your love has called us here; O Lord, whose saving name; My God and is thy table spread; And can it be.

First Sunday after Trinity   (Proper 7)   23 June
Second Service   **A Wife for Isaac**
Ps. [50] 57; **Gen. 24.1–27**; Mark 5.21–end

Are you the kind of person who picks up a novel and immediately turns to the back, speed reading the ending in order to decide whether to buy or borrow it? It feels like choosing this Old Testament reading is a bit like that. If the story of Abraham was to be made into a drama serial this would be one of the closing episodes.

So, what's of interest in this part of the tale of some Mesopotamian nomads? Quite a bit as it happens.

Unpacking the passage

At first glance, there is a sense of sadness. The long-widowed Abraham realizes that his life is ebbing to a close and he sets about ordering his affairs. Since the land in which Abraham lives was given to him by God, for him and for his descendants, Isaac, the cherished only son of the promise, must carry on the family line. So, if Abraham is to enable him to fulfil his duty to the promise, he needs to find his son a suitable wife.

Abraham is determined that his daughter-in-law will be from among his relatives; she will not be a Canaanite. You might argue that Abraham is racist, so intent is he upon keeping the bloodline pure. Pause a while and think about how this episode fits into the wider (Jewish) story of the salvation history. Let's give Abraham the benefit of the doubt rather than applying twenty-first-century Western cultural norms. If you're a parent (or grandparent) and a young member of your family is to be married, what kind of partner do you want for him or her? Isn't it natural that Abraham should be pro-Aramean? He wants his son to have a wife who will share the same religion, be compatible culturally, and (yes) be of the same ethnicity. Most important to him as a devout man is that, through marriage to a Canaanite girl, his son will not be led astray from the worship of God.

This story implies that though the patriarchs dwelt in Canaan, regarding it as the land promised to them in perpetuity by their God, they lived there as incomers, as resident aliens, still thinking of Mesopotamia, the place from whence they came, as the 'home country'. Isaac's bride must come from their spiritual home.

You might ask why Isaac, now aged 40, can't go himself and select his bride. Perhaps there's an explanation to be found in who Isaac is: Isaac is the embodiment of the promise, God's promise of land and descendants. He is inextricably bound to the land. He must fulfil his destiny. If you read his entire story you'll realize that of all the patriarchs he is the one who never leaves Canaan.

As no longer physically able to carry out his final mission himself, Abraham calls upon his loyal servant (unnamed in the story) to go and act on his behalf. Commissioning his servant we have Abraham's last recorded spoken words: 'If the young woman is not willing to come with you, you will be free from this promise. But you must not under any circumstances take my son back there.'

You'll notice that the servant's concern was not that he might not find a bride for Isaac but that she would not be willing to leave her home and family. Maybe the servant's confidence that he would find a woman willing to marry his young master was justified by the impressive bride price with which he was to travel: 10 laden camels were a display of Abraham's great wealth.

The text tells us nothing of the servant's lengthy journey, but our next scene in the story features the servant and Rebecca. Arriving at a well, a watering hole for beasts and humans, essential for nomadic life (and natural 'fixed' meeting places), Abraham's servant prays to his master's God. So the forthcoming encounter between the servant and Rebecca is grounded in prayer.

Even before the servant has finished his first heartfelt prayer, in which he reveals his plan to test any potential bride, Rebecca appears. We're told that she is young, beautiful and still a virgin. She passes his test with flying colours. Success! Then she accepts the gifts and offers him hospitality in her father's home, confirming to him that he has, indeed, found his master's kinfolk. Mission accomplished.

Making sense of the story

So, what do we make of this part of the 'Abraham cycle'? Perhaps we should begin by reference to those parts of the text that I have thus far largely ignored – those that implicitly and explicitly make reference to Abraham's (mature) relationship with his God.

Looking back, he knows 'the LORD had blessed him in everything he did'. He realizes that everything happens in accordance with God's will. So, God will not now fail him. God will bless the wife-hunting mission upon which he is sending his servant, because Isaac is the instrument through whom the promise to Abraham of descendants will be fulfilled. Abraham assures the servant that an angel of God will go before him. This is Abraham's faith; he is determined and believing. Blessed assurance, God loves him and his.

The hidden and most significant actor in this story is God. He's also the hidden and significant actor, the prime cause, in our lives and stories too. Abraham's life story shows that God cares about land (which represents home, safety and sustenance) and family (love, loyalty and survival). All life, the humdrum and the exciting, is under his providential care. Nothing can separate us from God's love.

The challenge to us

If, like Abraham, we can grow to love and trust God, we will receive assurance. If, like the servant, we can act and pray in accordance with his plan, we will see his answer to prayer. If, like Rebecca, we can show an inner beauty, evidenced in generosity and hospitality to the weary traveller, God will be the author of our life stories. May he be with us now and for ever.

Wendy Kilworth-Mason

Hymn suggestions

Deep in the shadows of the past; God it was who said to Abraham; The God of Abraham, praise; Make us your prophets, Lord.

Second Sunday after Trinity (Proper 8) 30 June
Principal Service In the Shadow of the Cross
(*Continuous*): 2 Kings 2.1–2, 6–14; Ps. 77.1–2, 11–end [*or* 77.11–end]; *or* (*Related*): 1 Kings 19.15–16, 19–end; Ps. 16; Gal. 5.1, 13–25; **Luke 9.51–end**

People come up with some wonderful excuses. Here are some genuine ones people have given for not going out on a date: 'Can I reschedule? I have another date tonight.' 'My cat needs me. Sorry.' 'I'm under house arrest.' 'I got married today.' In our Scripture today something more important than going on a date is at stake. It is the challenge to follow Jesus with the whole of our lives. But the excuses are just as ingenious. But before we get to these, we need to pause to set the scene.

The very first verse in our Gospel reading does this for us: 'When the days drew near for him to be taken up, he set his face to go to Jerusalem.' We have reached a turning point in Luke's narrative. Twice in our chapter Jesus has revealed to his disciples that he is going to be betrayed and murdered. He has also spoken of his rising again. Now Jesus sets his face for Jerusalem, and heads for the defining acts of his ministry. He is heading for his crucifixion, the cross where he will 'give his life as a ransom for many'. It is under the shadow of the impending cross that the excuses of those we read about in this chapter have to be seen.

A plethora of ways to avoid the cross!

First, for the Samaritans, they couldn't let go of the past. We read that the people there did not welcome him, 'because his face was set towards Jerusalem'. They refused to acknowledge Jerusalem as the legitimate place for worship. Yet Jerusalem was the place of the cross and resurrection, the heart of Christ's ministry. So past hurts and arguments prevented them from receiving Christ. They couldn't let go of the past, so they could not receive the future God had for them.

Next comes the first would-be disciple. It appears that he had not counted the cost. Although he seems keen to follow Jesus, Jesus' reply should make us stop and think. Why 'foxes' and 'birds of the air'? Elsewhere in Luke, Herod is referred to as a fox, and the local Amonite nation were also known as 'foxes'. 'Birds of the air' was a common title for the Gentiles, referring to their unclean status. So it's as if Jesus were saying, 'Look, the foreigners and invaders who are here have places to live, but Israel's true Messiah has nowhere. Are you sure you want to pay that kind of price?' Indeed, not only has the Son of Man nowhere to lay his head, but the city that ought to embrace him will actually murder him on a cross. The call to follow Jesus is cross-shaped, it is costly. It will bring hardship and difficulty, today just as then.

The second man had a different problem. He was trapped by other duties. It is doubtful that his words, 'Lord, first let me go and bury my father' mean that his father had just died. For a start, such a burial would have happened very quickly, and second, in the event of such a death, it is most likely that he would have been at home with his family mourning. Instead, as most eastern commentators have shown, it carries the sense of 'My father is old and frail. Let me wait till he's gone, and then I will follow you.' It is the 'and then' that is the problem!

The cross will not wait. If the man wishes to follow, he must follow now, on the way to Jerusalem. The call to follow Jesus is urgent. Indeed, it is positively inconvenient! Today there are too many of us who wish to follow Jesus when it suits us. The last man's request seems innocent enough. However, within the culture of the day, it carries more the sense of a request to 'take my leave with my parents' permission'. Many Arabic translations of this passage read, 'Let me go and explain my case to those in my house.' In other words, he felt he was under a greater authority, namely, needing his parents' permission. But Jesus will have none of it. In the light of the cross, his is the highest authority. The call of Jesus is pre-eminent over all others.

Responding to the call

Such simple things, yet they stopped people responding to the call of Christ – not being able to let go of the past, not counting the cost, wanting to wait until a more convenient time, not putting Christ first. Have times changed that much? Are we any different? Today his call is still costly, urgent and pre-eminent. Above all, it is still a call that is made in the shadow of the cross. 'For whoever wants to be my disciple must deny themselves and take up their cross and follow me. For whoever wants to save their life will lose it, but whoever loses their life for me will find it.' And that is what most of us would like to avoid.

Darren Blaney

Hymn suggestions

Will you come and follow me if I but call your name; Above the voices of the world around me; Hope of our calling; Forth in thy name, O Lord, I go.

Second Sunday after Trinity (Proper 8) 30 June
Second Service **What a Story**
Ps. [59.1–6, 18–end] 60; **Gen. 27.1–40**; Mark 6.1–6

What a story

It's a story with a plot line worthy of a modern TV soap. We've got a father on his sickbed, an eavesdropping wife, conniving with one son against his brother, all set against the background of the Ancient Near East.

So let's recall the gist of the story we've heard read: Isaac, old and blind, sends Esau out to hunt and then cook a meal for him, promising him that he'll then bestow his blessing upon this his eldest (and favourite) son. However, Rebecca eavesdrops upon the conversation and plots to ensure that her favourite son, Jacob, will be the recipient of the blessing. At first, Jacob has reservations about his mother's plan: Esau is hairy, whereas he is smooth skinned. What if Isaac were to realize the substitution? He worries about the possible consequences of being caught out (not about the morality of the plot). In the dialogue between Jacob and his mother it is clear she is the mastermind and that hers is the upper hand.

Jacob soon caves in to the more forceful personality of Rebecca (he is revealed as a real 'Mummy's boy'). After Rebecca has cooked the meal, used the goatskin to disguise Jacob's smooth skin (so that he will feel like Esau) and persuaded him to dress in his brother's clothes (so that he will smell like his twin), she sends him in to his father.

Despite some hesitation, Isaac is convinced that the gift-bearer is his beloved son, Esau, and so he speaks his blessing.

When Esau returns from the hunt and takes his meal to his father, the treachery is revealed. Isaac trembles. Esau rages and rails. The blessing has been bestowed and cannot be withdrawn. Isaac has made Jacob, irrevocably, master over his brother. The secondary blessing that is bestowed upon Esau is no consolation. So, Esau vows that after Isaac's death he will wreak revenge upon his cheating brother.

Did you notice how carefully the passage is constructed. It's made up of four scenes, so if we were planning to dramatize it we'd begin with Isaac speaking with Esau and the preparations for the expected blessing. The second scene would show Rebecca scheming on Jacob's behalf. The most significant scene would be the third one, where Jacob deceives Isaac. This episode in the patriarchal history would then conclude with Isaac grieving with Esau over the loss of his blessing. So, the thwarted hopes and dreams of Isaac and Esau frame the triumph of the deceivers, Rebecca and Jacob.

The structure of text shows that it revolves around inter-relationships of the characters. So let's meet them.

Meet the ancestors: Isaac and Rebecca

I find the adult Isaac of our story a rather two-dimensional character. Maybe he suffers the fate of all too many sons of famous fathers: he is not the man his father was. Perhaps he is the forgettable Patriarch? Isaac is just a weak link in a genetic chain. As the son of the promise (the covenant between God and his people), he must pass on the blessing. However, he is now old and blind.

Rebecca is no longer the virtuous, hospitable woman we were shown earlier in the story; she is scheming and conniving. She sets out deliberately to deceive her husband on behalf of her favourite son.

Esau and Jacob: the terrible twins

The adult twins suffer from an advanced case of sibling rivalry. That rivalry began in the womb. Rebecca was told that the struggle in her womb would result in the birth of two rival peoples. The older brother would serve the younger. Esau was her firstborn, but his brother Jacob was born holding on to Esau's heel. Esau was red-skinned and hairy. Jacob was smooth. Esau was a huntsman who loved the outdoors; Jacob was a mild, quiet man. They're a study in contrasts.

In our passage, Esau is hapless. Jacob, manipulated by his mother but raising no moral objection to her direction, is grasping, cheating and slippery. He's a con man, a deceiver of his own father, a trickster. This story shows one should not ignore the quiet ones: still waters run deep.

The Bible has some unpleasant heroes.

Birthright and blessing: the underlying theme

Esau was far from being an ideal son. Earlier in the story, Esau sold his birthright, the privilege of the firstborn son; he gave it up lightly for a 'mess of potage'. The birthright would have afforded Esau a double portion of the inheritance upon the death of his father. Jacob tricked him out of future financial security.

Esau further revealed his unsuitability to assume the responsibilities of the firstborn by marrying foreign wives who made family life miserable.

The loss of the blessing was still more significant than the loss of his birthright. It's not just loss of property, but of status. The recipient of the blessing would be the head of the family. This, however, is no usual family. This is God's chosen people. Hence, the recipient of the blessing, the chosen one, will be the bearer of the promise. The blessing is not for the individual but for the people for whom he will be responsible.

The blessing has power. So it cannot be taken lightly. Once given it cannot be withdrawn.

The consequence of this episode in the story of the Patriarchs is that Esau is condemned to wander (like Cain or Ishmael).

Jacob, albeit by means of trickery and duplicity, has received the blessing. Thus, the priority of birth has been set aside. Isaac's words have made Jacob the successor to the promise.

What's it all about?

What makes the Patriarchal narratives so interesting is, in part, their intricate plots and diverse characters. Isaac, Rebecca, Esau and Jacob, the heroes, are flawed human beings. The background details of the stories may reveal a nomadic Ancient Near Eastern culture, but the character traits transcend time and place.

From the human perspective, this story could be regarded as a cautionary tale: be careful what you wish, or pray (or scheme) for: Jacob learns that the blessing can be a burden and that it brings heavy responsibilities. In the biblical story, both Jacob and Esau pay the price for the blessings they have received.

God's plan for his people forms the foundation for this story. God will bless his people, though they may be flawed instruments. God can use even us as bearers of the promise. We should rest assured that the future of the kingdom is not in our hands but in his.

Wendy Kilworth-Mason

Hymn suggestions

God moves in a mysterious way; God is working his purpose out; Thy way, not mine, O Lord; Great is thy faithfulness.

Third Sunday after Trinity (Proper 9)   7 July
Principal Service   **Travelling Light**
(*Continuous*): 2 Kings 5.1–14; Ps. 30; *or* (*Related*): Isa. 66.10–14; Ps. 66.1–8; Gal. 6.[1–6] 7–16; **Luke 10.1–11, 16–20**

Turn out your pockets, empty your handbags. No mobile phone. No credit card. No travel insurance. No suitcase. No protection, no resources. And no cheating! Travel light.

Done that? Now you're ready for off, says Jesus. Would you go? Honestly? Most of us would think at least twice. Why is he so particular? Why so definite? Mission partners today think nothing of taking toiletries to last the full three-year stint and books to read on time off. And why not? They deserve it. Some have even transported fridges to Papua New Guinea. Not that we'd go that far, of course, but no resources at all? It will seriously hamper our mission – *your* mission, Lord – if we travel that light.

But there's more: On your journey, Jesus continues, receive whatever hospitality you're offered.

Whoa! Not so fast, Lord! We're Jewish and kosher; we can't share a table with just anyone. Some of us have allergies; we can't eat just anything. Some of us have issues, we can't mix with just anyone. What if a gay couple offers us hospitality? Or an Asian couple provides curry? Or it's a house that is, quite frankly, dirty? Must we eat together, pray together, share your table together?

Yes, says Jesus. All share in the one bread, whether you're naturally comfortable with each other or not; whether you agree with each other over points of doctrine or not.

But, Lord, what if someone gets violent? The last person who tried to prepare the way for you got his head chopped off. Can't we leave it to the professionals, the confident evangelists, the Twelve?

No, says Jesus. Rejection? Handle it.

The mission of the Twelve (note the symbolic number) was to the people of Israel. The mission we're part of now, first- and twenty-first-century disciples alike, has grown, and is to all the nations of the world – 70 in the then known world if you're reading Genesis 10 in Hebrew, 72 if you're into the Greek version! But that's not the point.

The point is, it's down to us now. Ordinary disciples, mostly nameless, unimportant followers of Jesus; it depends on us. Most of us won't be knocking on doors or travelling from place to place, but for all of us, all the time, mission *is* about how we live our lives, how we radiate the kingdom wherever we go. And if people receive us, they receive Jesus. If they reject us, they reject Jesus. Lambs among wolves is dead right! Are we up for it?

Travelling light means leaving things that weigh us down. It's something I'm not good at. Ask my family. Suitcases hover dangerously near the limit, especially if I'm visiting my daughter in America, as she suffers from English chocolate deprivation! It's not only about holding our possessions lightly, things we think we can't do without, but our cultural baggage too. We may think we have none, but ask someone from a different culture to give you an outsider's view, and you'll be surprised at how others see us.

Take consumerism. How do we radiate kingdom freedom if we give in to our 'must have' society and allow possessions to have power over us?

Take individualism. How do we radiate kingdom community if we insist on going it alone, priding ourselves on our independence, doing it 'my way'?

Take our blame culture. How do we radiate kingdom forgiveness if we off-load blame on to others – or God – all the time?

Take the 'rights' ethos. How do we radiate kingdom peace if all our energy goes into making sure we get what is ours 'by right'?

Take the indifference to worldwide need, oppression and slavery. How do we radiate kingdom justice if we care nothing for situations beyond ourselves?

Travel light and people will see what we *are* carrying and want to give away – the kingdom: healing and wholeness, peace, freedom, forgiveness, grace, love.

The reward? They return, not empty but full: full of wonder, joy and excitement. Yes, they need to adjust their priorities, but they have a smile on their faces.

Barbara Steele-Perkins

Hymn suggestions

Go forth and tell! O Church of God awake!; God's Spirit is in my heart; Send forth by God's blessing; Forth in the peace of Christ we go.

Third Sunday after Trinity (Proper 9) 7 July
Second Service **God at the Dinner Table**
Ps. 65 [70]; Gen. 29.1–20; **Mark 6.7–29**

Family favouritism

Families can be delightful and difficult; full of fun and full of fury; sources of tenderness as well as tension. Imagine the dynamics around many a Christmas dinner table! Our Old Testament reading draws back the curtain on a problematic family. We zone in on Jacob, who has just arrived at his Uncle Laban's place. To understand why he is there, we must rewind and focus on Isaac and Rebecca and their two sons: Esau, the red-haired hunter, apple of his dad's eye; and Jacob, Mummy's precious boy. This favouritism feeds a family dysfunction that leads to birthright sold and blessing stolen. Rivalry, deception and resentment are often guests at this family's table. Having been betrayed by his wily brother, and lost his rightful inheritance, Esau is enraged and is, perhaps understandably, contemplating murdering his little bro. Mum and Dad, both complicit in this dire situation, pack Jacob off to Mum's side of the family – in the hope that time will heal the sibling rift. Jacob hefts his rucksack and heads off to Uncle Laban in Haran.

God at the dinner table

Perhaps you look at your own family and see some of the themes identified in the story of this Old Testament brood. Favouritism, tensions between siblings, acts of sabotage, resentment and bitterness. What I find so encouraging is that God does not write off this family. Rather, God is present in all the tension, right there at the dinner table. We might look around at families who seem somehow perfect, and think God is only interested in them, with their polished round-robin letters, telling of great achievements, presenting us with golden boys and girls, perfect teeth and apple pie moments. Make of such missives what you will, but never be fooled into believing that God isn't to be found right in the midst of ordinary family dysfunction, right there at the heart of the dinner table.

Just before the reading set for today, we see Jacob on his own trudging towards an unknown future with the other half of the family. He camps out for the night, and in the midst of all his trouble he has a remarkable dream in which God encounters him and promises him descendants, blessing and presence. Jacob is not written off or abandoned. In response, Jacob reaches towards God in a vow that expresses trust in God and commitment to God.

Dysfunction revisited

Now we can focus in on the main scene. Jacob arrives at a well, the time-honoured meeting place. Local shepherds gather the flocks and don't open the well until all livestock are there, along with a representative of the landowner's family. Rachel, Laban's daughter, arrives, and Jacob rolls the covering of the stone away for her. There is a touching scene as Jacob meets relatives and weeps openly. What will this new home bring?

We are given a snapshot into this side of the family. It's a picture in which it is easy to see comparison, jealousy and favouritism.

Leah, the older daughter, is described as 'weak eyed' compared to her sister Rachel who is 'graceful and beautiful'. How often did Leah have to deal with the comparison, the humiliation of being overlooked as Jacob fell for Rachel. For seven years Leah observed love's young dream living under the same roof as her. I wonder how she felt?

Glancing into the next part of the story we see that it gets worse. At the end of seven years, Laban deceives Jacob and places his daughter Leah in the lovers' tent, in Rachel's place. Notice how the women are treated as objects in the text; Rachel and Leah are controlled by the men around them and seem voiceless and powerless. We need to acknowledge that what is taken as the cultural norm within the horizons of the Old Testament text has also often been the norm for countless women across the centuries and to our own day.

Leah is handed over by her father in order to avoid upsetting the cultural norm of the eldest marrying first. She is abused, having no agency or choice. What of Rachel? Pushed aside and humiliated. Again, the actions of the parents create rivals of the siblings, and family dysfunction seems to have the day. As we read on we witness lovelessness, childlessness and rivalry. But we also see God present in the midst of this dysfunction and pain; always present at the dining table.

God present in the pain

This has always been the way. God sees the pain of his beloved; often a pain that is self-inflicted, sometimes coming as a result of maltreatment. Looking ahead in the narrative we will see more accounts of favouritism, leading to Joseph – Daddy's special boy – being thrown into a pit and abandoned by his disgruntled, jealous brothers. But God protects Joseph and watches over him through all the trials he faces.

Many people look at their situations and wonder where God is; where was God when X or Y occurred? Perhaps we feel angry with God, or angry with ourselves? Perhaps we can identify with Esau, conned out of his inheritance; maybe we understand Jacob – manipulated by a parent, then sent away. Maybe we know what Leah felt like – an object abused and left on the sidelines; or Rachel, who knew the pain of childlessness for such a long time; or Jacob, the deceiver who is deceived.

Take comfort today that God has compassion beyond all human compassion. Trust that God shows up when we least expect. Hope in the God who never abandons, not even his flakiest of children. Believe in the God who does not overlook women, the powerless or the abused. God sees, knows and is present, even when we can only see darkness. God is present. Present at the dinner table of dysfunction – especially present here.

Kate Bruce

Hymn suggestions

Great is thy faithfulness; Christ's is the world in which we move; Empty, broken, here I stand; The Lord's my shepherd.

Fourth Sunday after Trinity   (Proper 10)   14 July
Principal Service   **Unlikely Defendants?**
(*Continuous*): Amos 7.7–end; Ps. 82; *or* (*Related*): Deut. 30.9–14; Ps. 25.1–10; Col. 1.1–14; **Luke 10.25–37**

A man was going down from Jerusalem to Jericho, and fell into the hands of robbers, who stripped him, beat him, and went away, leaving him half dead. Now by chance a priest was going down that road, and when he saw him, he said to himself: 'I have no first-aid skills with which to help. I can do more for that man by praying in the Temple. I will not indulge my morbid curiosity by taking a closer look.' And he crossed over on the other side and sped on his way to the place of prayer.

So likewise also a Levite, when he came to the place. But a *Samaritan*, when *he* saw him, welcomed the opportunity to burnish his reputation and ingratiate himself with his hostile neighbours. So he went to him, bound up his wounds with unsterile cloth and poured over contaminated oil, then set him on his own beast, which, because of the man's spinal injuries, caused permanent paralysis.

Speaking up for the priest and Levite?

It's disorientating, disturbing really, to hear a familiar parable turned upside down. Some of you may feel I am taking liberties with the text. But I'd plead that this is just the sort of reading that those listening to Jesus for the very first time might have expected and hoped for: putting the Samaritan in his place and affirming the worth of the invisible religious practices of the priest and Levite.

Instead, just when we imagine his hearers began to relax their guard and settled down to hear a good story, Jesus delivers a shock and surprise that blows their settled world apart. It's the new story that Jesus told that has become so familiar to us that it no longer shocks us. Reversing the familiar story line and making a case for the defence of others whom we cast as villains in Jesus' parables – publicans, tax collectors, Pharisees – demonstrates the outrageousness with which Jesus' message was received, and fuels these familiar stories with new explosive force. But, then, the parables are meant to blow apart the settled, predictable worlds we have created for our own security. Try making a defence of the priest or Levite, or any other target of Jesus' scorn, and the choices become less clear.

Defending the lawyer?

The lawyer earned his living by defining responsibilities and rights in clear and uncontested definitions. How then could he cope with the unlimited, universal, unconditional character of the law of God? How, on that basis, could he ever be sure that he had secured the eternal life that he sought? So he asks a supplementary question: 'Who is my neighbour?' He's looking for a water-tight definition so that he can know precisely what's expected of him and whether he can fulfil it.

Does he have grounds for trying to nail down the limits of neighbourliness? There's a perennial debate over the appropriateness of universal and particular ways of discharging neighbourliness and serving the common good. An unlimited obligation to some universal notion of neighbourliness can sound good: 'A truly virtuous man would come to the aid of the most distant stranger as quickly as to his own friends,' said Montesque. Yes, but the demand can overwhelm and disable us. And it can be an avoidance strategy. It's easier to love humanity in general than it is to love the particular neighbour: 'My problem's not the world I hate, but the neighbour next door.' So, does charity begin at home? Do Christians, for example, have a particular obligation to the 'brethren', the local Christian community? In limiting and particularizing who counts as neighbour is the lawyer making a bid for realism, for commitment to particular groups and identities in which the costly obligation to neighbours is honed and practised? Or is he trying to define his obligations within the narrow parameters of his tight religious and racial identity?

The lawyer who spent his life defending others wanted also to defend and justify himself. He hoped he could define in advance the limited claims that he was expected to be set. If he could assure himself of that, then he could know that he had secured a binding agreement that gave him the right of eternal life.

The lawyer should have realized from the summary law that Jesus recited that he could never hope to justify himself before God, and no more can we. We don't even have to try. Justification is God's work, secured for us through the perfect life of Jesus.

The scope of the neighbour

It's not the grand gestures on behalf of the world's poor in the Sudan, or Christian Aid, or caring for sick friends and relatives, that catch us out. It's not so much the planned pattern of our lives, the established relationships, that find us wanting. It's the unexpected, unplanned, unlikely people and events that cross our path, that challenge and test us most and put our faith on trial. 'When I needed a neighbour, were you there?' Ubiquity isn't expected. We can't be everywhere. And often it's tempting to be somewhere other than where we are, but we are invited to be neighbour where we are. Christian faith is often a matter of geography. Being a neighbour is defined by space and time. Where we and those we have a capacity to assist meet. It's being near, it's staying where we are, rather than crossing over to be somewhere else, attending, loving, giving.

Roger Spiller

Hymn suggestions

When I needed a neighbour were you there?; Love is the only law; Brother, sister, let me serve you; To you, O Christ, the Prince of Peace.

Fourth Sunday after Trinity   (Proper 10)   14 July
Second Service   **Wrestling with God**
Ps. 77 [*or* 77.1–12]; Gen. 32.9–30; Mark 7.1–23

Wrestling is not something that might come to mind in the Christian life. I do know of some wrestlers in church, but it wouldn't be a sight we would expect during a service, in a church meeting, during a Bible study, or in a pastoral visit. Wrestling for many church-going people in England might be more likely to happen with an overgrown shrub or with a wriggly child with a mind of her own!

But spiritual wrestling can happen – and maybe should happen – in church services, church meetings, Bible study, and pastoral visits . . .

Wrestling in prayer

When we're down or having a hard time, we are likely to ask God, 'Why?' Or when we see the news, another violent crime or unjust regime causing fatalities and suffering, we are likely to think, 'I don't understand how a good God, a powerful God, a God who knows everything, can let that happen.'

Today's psalm is a picture of just that. At the very opening of this prayer, we've got the Psalmist lamenting, repetitively raising his voice to God, in his troubles both day and night. He remembers God and he groans; he meditates on him, and his spirit is worn out. We aren't told what the matter is, but we know what it is like to feel these things.

His redemption comes by voicing it. His voice is really important, it gives him freedom to speak out, to address God, to let his words even be heard by the generations who now read, sing or pray this psalm. He puts his feelings into words, he looks at them face on, and he invites God to look upon them too. Has God gone away? He used to be so great . . .

Asking the hard questions

So we see the Psalmist tackling God, charging at him again and again with his questions. 'Has God stopped caring?' These questions are important questions to ask in faith. Asking questions is a good way to get to know someone, and we can learn a lot about ourselves too when we have conversations like these with other people. So why not ask questions about God, and to God?

It's hard work, having unanswered questions. It can leave us feeling down. But it's also a good way to go *deep*. Not just to accept faith on the surface, taking the bits we like and ignoring the bits we don't like. Not just to accept faith without thinking about it. After all, faith is bigger than knowledge: it always allows for more. Faith is richer than absorbing any kind of textbook or lecture about God: it allows for questions and conversation. Faith allows for doubt, just as we hear in the man whose son is healed, who says to Jesus, 'I do believe; help my unbelief!'

Faith asks for questions.

Finding answers

Asking questions can be the best way to find answers. Although we don't hear God giving any answers to the Psalmist of Psalm 77, we see the Psalmist coming to his own answers. He remembers God. He remembers that God is loving. He remembers that God is good. He remembers that God has done great things in the past. He remembers that God has made promises to his people. So the end of the psalm oddly has quite a lot of hope about it. He remembers all this – so he knows that God *will* answer, God *will* act. He just doesn't know when, or how. But he knows that that's the end of the story.

Peace after wrestling

The Old Testament story today was all about Jacob wrestling with God. Jacob's about to have a life-changing encounter with his brother Esau, whom he cheated so badly that he took what should have been Esau's inheritance. It's a kind of family battle that we see today as people fight over wills and legacies. They've been apart ever since – until now. Now they are very close to one another, and about to meet up again after all these years. Who knows what will happen?

So Jacob sends a lot of softeners to his brother first. Plenty of gifts – and advance warning. He does all this in the context of prayer. And then when he has sent everyone else on ahead, across the river, he stays behind, by himself, and is caught up in an all-night-long struggle.

The mysterious man puts Jacob's hip out, but, even so, Jacob won't let go. He won't let go until he receives a blessing from the man. The man asks Jacob's name, and then gives him a new name, and with it a blessing.

Explanations

The whole story is about explaining things: why Jacob gets the name Israel, why the place Peniel is so-called, smaller details about a Jewish ritual vessel, and various rules connected with the hip bone. Untangling things, understanding why – all are important outcomes of this monumental wrestling.

As Christians, there are lots of questions we can be asking ourselves, each other and God, and lots of wrestling we can be doing. Whether it's wrestling with a difficult passage of the Bible, or wrestling with God in prayer, or wrestling with others as we try to find meaning and the directions of our callings, we're called to engage with God. Jacob who becomes Israel gives us a very good example – and a very good reason why we should join in the struggle.

Megan Daffern

Hymn suggestions

O God of Bethel, by whose hand; Come, O thou traveller unknown; O Love, that wilt not let me go; Be thou my guardian and my guide

Fifth Sunday after Trinity   (Proper 11)   21 July
Principal Service   **A Tale of Two Sisters**
(*Continuous*): Amos 8.1–12; Ps. 52; *or* (*Related*): Gen. 18.1–10a; Ps. 15; Col. 1.15–28; **Luke 10.38–end**

Whose side are you on?

Martha and Mary, the only characters in today's Gospel apart from Jesus, can be divisive figures. Mary, says Jesus, has chosen the better part, but many, if not most, people would take Martha's side: after all, she has been left with all the housework, while Mary sits around at Jesus' feet, hanging on every word he says! Schools of spirituality have lined up on the side of one sister or another depending on whether their proponents consider themselves to be 'active' or 'contemplative' in their pursuit of discipleship. These disputes, though, might well prompt us to ask whether or not the Evangelist Luke had any such notions when he, uniquely among the Evangelists, included this story of the two sisters in his Gospel.

Unpacking the story

The first question we should ask is not what to make of Martha and Mary and their relative merits, but what does the Evangelist suggest we make of them? If we are to understand the importance of Jesus' visit to the house of Martha and Mary, we must understand something of the journey that takes him there. In Luke 9.51, part of a sentence sets the scene for the remainder of this Gospel. We are told, 'When the days drew near for him to be taken up, he [Jesus] set his force to go to Jerusalem.' In those few words, Luke introduces the journey that Jesus will make as the prophet whom Moses foretold in Deuteronomy. 'The LORD your God will raise up for you a prophet like me . . . you shall heed such a prophet.' From this point on, Jesus journeys to Jerusalem where he will fulfil his destiny in his death. Later, Jesus will say, 'It is impossible for a prophet to be killed away from Jerusalem.'

So the visitor now in Martha and Mary's house is no ordinary guest, and he is on no ordinary journey. Mary grasps the opportunity to sit at the feet of the ultimate prophet and listen to what he has to say. In this Gospel, he will not pass that way again, although John's Gospel suggests that Jesus knew Martha and Mary and their brother Lazarus rather well. Martha's response to her guest is different from Mary's: Martha has better things to do – like attending to all the serving. Not content with failing to listen to the prophet, however, Martha also breaks a very important rule of hospitality. Semitic etiquette dictated that no honoured guest should be insulted by being drawn into a family dispute, but Martha wants Jesus to intervene and tell her sister Mary to help her.

One final important strand of background should be noted. Many writers have commented on the fact that it seems out of place. Before and after this episode Jesus is on the move, followed by disciples and surrounded by crowds. Now, he is alone in the house with the sisters. Did Luke decide to take this story from another point in Jesus' life and add it here to the journey narrative – and if so, why?

One possibility is that Luke wants to link the Martha and Mary story with what has gone immediately before, which in this case is

194

the parable of the good Samaritan; but before Jesus launches into that parable, a lawyer tries to disconcert him by asking what he must do to inherit eternal life. Jesus asks the man what he reads in the law. Without hesitation, the lawyer quotes the commandments from both Deuteronomy and Leviticus about loving God with all our heart, soul, strength and mind, and about loving our neighbour as ourself: words we are probably more used to hearing from Jesus' own lips as his expression of how to sum up the entire Law of Moses. Jesus approves of the lawyer's answer, but the lawyer, anxious to justify himself, asks, 'And who is my neighbour?'

Self-justification made easy

The lawyer wants to 'keep himself right', as the saying goes. He seeks a standard of minimal obligation. The question for him was not so much 'Who is my neighbour?' but 'Who can I regard as not my neighbour?' Jesus' good Samaritan parable makes it clear that nothing less than total commitment of self to God and to neighbour – that is, anyone in need – is what the law is all about. Martha appears to be doing something similar: justifying herself for not listening to the words of the prophet speaking in her own home. The suggestion of a similarity between Martha and this lawyer may come as a surprise, but Martha indulges in self-justification just as much as he does. The question then is – how readily do we fall into a similar pattern? Is it in the way we find perfectly good reasons for less than total commitment to God in prayer, or in time spent listening to God's word? Or might it be found in excuses for not helping someone in need, 'If I give him money, he will only spend it on drink'?

Do we justify ourselves for forcing on others what they neither need nor want? Martha is set on forcing a well-prepared meal on Jesus. He only wanted her attention while he was in the house: perhaps the equivalent of a cup of tea would have suited him better!

Robert Hill

Hymn suggestions

To be in your presence, to sit at your feet; Brother, sister, let me serve you; Put peace into each other's hands; Be still, for the presence of the Lord.

Fifth Sunday after Trinity (Proper 11) 21 July
Second Service **The Foolishness of the Cross**
Ps. 81; Gen. 41.1–16, 25–37; **1 Cor. 4.8–13**; *Gospel at Holy Communion*: John 4.31–35

When you are steeped in church it all begins to make sense. Even the audacious Christian beliefs sound reasonable. But perhaps that's the time to take a reality check. Join a Good Friday procession, following a large wooden cross, through the busy streets of one of our towns. People stare at you with expressions of incredulity, scorn, ridicule, contempt. You are made to feel you are a reluctant player in a public spectacle that is destined to make you feel foolish.

Why foolish?

That, at least, confronts us with the inescapable foolishness of the cross, which preoccupied St Paul in his letters and his visits to the church he founded in Corinth. The missionary statesman Lesslie Newbigin identifies the precise cause of the foolishness: 'How is it possible that the gospel should be credible, that people should come to believe that the power which has the last word in human affairs is represented by a man hanging on a cross?' How indeed. And yet we're often told that we have to make faith relevant and reasonable if we're to arrest or reverse the sharp decline in Christian belief and practice. But, as St Paul reminds us, it's the message of the cross that is the power of God. And those who dare to share the message of the cross with others are likely to be called foolish and make life uncomfortable for themselves.

Reducing foolishess

There are ways that we, like Paul, may be tempted to minimize our foolishness. We can, like any failing enterprise, diversify and broaden our appeal. We can invest in activities that win us credibility and speak less of cost, suffering and death and more of appealing abstract ideas that most people share, of peace, love and victory. We can play with the ideas of 'dying and living' as a semantic game, or engage in the dialectics of opposites, so as to make out that the cross can be a respectable and sophisticated subject for discussion. But St Paul resisted these human subtleties. Instead, he insisted that he must remain single-minded, 'knowing nothing among you except Christ and his cross'. Where we latch on to aspects of the good news that unite us by their credibility and conviviality, Paul alights on the message that threatens to divide and send us into an intellectual tailspin.

Again, Paul could improve his preaching, which his accusers called 'contemptible'. He could, surely, rise to the sublime rhetorical flourishes of Greek culture that he demonstrated in the best of his writing. He could stand up with confidence to preach, buttressed by his intellectual brilliance and by his superior natural, family and religious credentials that he occasionally mentions in his letters. Instead he shakes and trembles like a willow tree when he rises to preach under the weight of his commission.

The weakness of power

Paul refuses to conceal the folly of the cross. If he preached 'lofty words of human wisdom' it would be only the power of a person's preaching and not the power of God that would be evident and active. 'We have this treasure in clay jars,' says Paul. We are the 'crackpots'. And why? 'So that it may be made clear that this extraordinary power belongs to God and does not come from us.'

Sometimes a composer's music is sabotaged by inadequate performers. But just as often the music will suffer as a result of the self-conscious perfectionism of the performers. The lavish, beautiful sound of a great orchestra can conceal the disturbing elemental power intended by the composer. In the same way, the nervous, tongue-tied, reluctant preacher can be a more eloquent witness to the gospel than the self-confident, experienced preacher.

Making the gospel credible

In our day, we are still drawn to human wisdom, as defined by what can be established by argument and evidence. What doesn't meet the stringent demands of the scientific paradigm risks being dismissed as foolish or as just private opinion. It's an erroneous view, we may say, but not one that can easily be dislodged from the popular mind. So we try to demonstrate that intelligent people can and do believe the gospel. We wheel out and name-drop the odd Christian Nobel Prize winner in physics, or Fellow of the Royal Society, to lend credibility. Last week a newsletter from one of the theological colleges appeared: 'Outstanding First-Class degree results', it proclaimed with pride. No one would deny the need for more and better intentional teaching and learning in our churches. But can we be too impressed by academic achievements? Can they tempt us to engage more comfortably in human wisdom than in divine folly?

The gospel given not discovered

Christian faith is something that is revealed not learned, given not discovered. It appears foolish until we inhabit its truth. The gospel, says Paul, can only be grounded in the wisdom of God. It can only be received by his Spirit. How, then, can we defend the gospel by that which is other than the gospel? We need the best of scholarship to help us to translate and interpret the Bible, but the message of the gospel is self-validating. It's the lives of its adherents, their love, generosity, joy, hopefulness, which is the most persuasive proclamation of the good news.

Roger Spiller

Hymn suggestions

We have a gospel to proclaim; All praise for wisdom, great gift sublime; Can we by searching find out God; O for a thousand tongues.

Sixth Sunday after Trinty (Proper 12) 28 July
Principal Service: **Lord, Teach Us to Pray**
(*Continuous*): Hos. 1.2–10; Ps. 85 [*or* 85.1–7]; *or* (*Related*): Gen. 18.20–32; Ps. 138; Col. 2.6–15 [16–19]; **Luke 11.1–13**

If you have visited the catacombs in Rome, or if you have explored them on the internet, you will know that you can discover in those underground tunnels and rooms some of the earliest Christian paintings; for example, images of the Good Shepherd, of loaves and fishes, or of an anchor. Some of the images in the Christian catacombs are drawn from the Old Testament – Jonah was a particularly favourite motif, and you can also find frescoes of people praying; technically, such images are known as 'Orants'. The word comes from medieval Latin and means 'one who prays'.

It shows a person standing upright, elbows tucked into the body, with the lower arms and hands outstretched.

Prayer's posture

This was the actual physical pose adopted by many ancient people as they said their prayers. It wasn't original to Christianity; most religions in the Middle East at the time of Jesus, including Judaism, had adherents who prayed using that particular physical posture: all a very long way from 'hands together and eyes closed'.

So when Jesus, according to Luke's Gospel, had finished praying, it would have been entirely obvious to the disciples that that is what he had been doing. He had probably been standing nearby, elbows tucked in, lower arms and hands outstretched.

But when you think a bit more about it you can see that there is a slight puzzle in the story. The disciples said to Jesus: 'Lord, teach us to pray.' But they knew what prayer was, didn't they? They were Jews who had attended the synagogue where prayer was offered on a regular basis. What they presumably meant by their question, as you can see from the second part of their request ('as John taught his disciples'), was a special prayer. They wanted their own prayer; a distinctive prayer; a prayer that would encapsulate all that Jesus was teaching them. We all know what Jesus replied.

So far, so good. But let's just stay for a moment with the physical posture and place of prayer. It is a matter of record that Jesus did not confine prayer to the synagogue – his own prayers sometimes took place out of doors. But he was doing nothing particularly radical in that. You will remember that Jesus drew attention to his fellow Jews who also prayed outside: 'And whenever you pray, do not be like the hypocrites; for they love to stand and pray in the synagogues and at the street corners', but he added a sharp reminder that prayer should not be about outward display, it was a matter of the heart, a matter for quiet and unostentatious behaviour, well away from the public gaze: 'Truly I tell you, they have received their reward. But whenever you pray, go into your room and shut the door and pray to your Father who is in secret; and your Father who sees in secret will reward you.'

Abba: Father

But to this instruction about inwardness Jesus added another dimension. It was his opening phrase in the prayer that was so startling. Where we use the word 'Father' Jesus used the word 'Abba': it's an Aramaic word, the language that he used on a daily basis. It too means 'Father', but it carries with it a sense of intimacy, of closeness and of profound respect.

We are bidden by Jesus to learn what it might mean for us to think of God in such intimate, personal terms. It implies, doesn't it, that God is in a relationship with us that is akin to the relationship of a father with his beloved child? But that is so difficult for us to internalize. It does not imply an unhealthy dependency, nor does it imply childishness on our part; instead, it nudges us away from our own self-centred preoccupations and vanities into the very heart of who God truly is. In that sense, learning the truth summarized in that one word 'Abba' is a lifetime's occupation because in our pride and sin we always want to slip away from it. We want to be self-sufficient. We want to stand on our own two feet. We want to express our own uniqueness. Yet in 'Abba' we find that we are held in a relationship. We are not atomized individuals; we are persons who find our ultimate meaning and purpose in God. We find our destiny in being in a quiet but deep relationship with him.

And it is this truth that must be at the heart of how we pray. It's not about being on our knees (though no doubt that should sometimes happen; after all, Jesus prayed on his knees in the Garden of Gethsemane); it's not about adopting a particular set of postures for our prayers; it's about consciously and deliberately bringing ourselves on a daily basis into the presence of God our Father. As we do that, we can discover and rediscover that his relationship with us is one of love – with all that that also implies about our relationships with our fellow human beings. As disciples of Christ, waiting in stillness and silence on God is central to our vocation. May we have the courage, perseverance and patience to live in that truth, this day and always.

Christopher Herbert

Hymn suggestions

Lord, teach us how to pray aright; Jesus, where'er thy people meet; Prayer is the soul's sincere desire; Father, who in Jesus found us.

Sixth Sunday after Trinity (Proper 12) 28 July
Second Service Inhabiting the Story
Ps. 88 [*or* 88.1–10]; **Gen 42.1–25**; 1 Cor. 10.1–24; *Gospel at Holy Communion*: Matt. 13.24–30 [31–43]

There are seven forms of story, I'm told, but the commonest starts with a problem, introduces further complications, and ends in some form of resolution that may be partial or complete.

The issue or complication that got this long story of Jacob and his brothers underway is a family drama – parental favouritism that leads to sibling rivalry and escalates into violence, pitting 11 brothers against the favoured son. The brothers, too, are irritated by Joseph, whom they nicknamed 'the dreamer' for relating dreams that suggest he's getting 'above himself' and anticipating that they will one day prostrate themselves before him.

God's agent

We know of Joseph from the musical, *Joseph and His Technicolour Dreamcoat*, if not from the Bible. He faces an uncertain future when his brothers get rid of him from their home by selling him to some traders. He is taken to a far-away country where he can be forgotten, presumed dead. Of course, his father is left to weigh his own responsibility for encouraging Joseph to leave the house and set off to find his brothers on that fateful day. It's a stiff test to see how that situation can ever be redeemed. Many years pass and Joseph has ingratiated himself in the court at Egypt and now oversees the whole country, including the supply of grain on the international market.

Meanwhile, Jacob and his brothers are facing starvation. Hearing there is a plentiful supply of corn in Egypt, their father despatches his sons to that country, where they come face to face with Joseph. But they don't recognize him after so many years, and, besides, he uses an interpreter to feign ignorance of their native tongue. Meanwhile, Joseph recognizes them and must adopt a severe public face and keep his emotions under a tight rein. This is where the tension is heightened for the reader until the final identity of Joseph is revealed.

Testing and reassessing past conduct

How will Joseph react now that he finally has his brothers in his hands, just as they once did of him? How will he exercise power? How can he satisfy his curiosity about his father's well-being and about his brothers' reflections on their conduct and care for each other without giving himself away? He claims the visitors are spies. Their only defence is that they're a family unit and families have no use for espionage, which gives him an opening for learning more about his family. But they can't dislodge the spying charge, and are told that one of the brothers must go home and bring back the youngest brother who remains at their father's side while the other brothers are detained in Egypt.

After three days of imprisonment, Joseph declares that only one brother must remain behind; the others can return with the grain. Joseph has overheard the brothers, whose guilt comes home to them with force, leading them to acknowledge the reason why they are now facing punishment. Joseph's emotions have got the better of him and he is forced to withdraw from public view.

With the youngest brother remaining behind, the rest of the brothers set off for home. One of them finds the money he paid for grain at the top of his feed bag, and all the brothers fear what consequences might befall them as a result of this inexplicable discovery. They are now acting like responsible brothers, bearing each other's burdens and not pursuing their individual interests.

Spotlighting their father's dilemma

When they arrive home they are sparing in the account they give their father, to avoid adding to his distress. Once home, they discover that they all had money returned to them hidden in their sacks. And they and Jacob react with dismay and consternation. And reacting to Joseph's demand to bring to him the missing brother, Benjamin, the father laments his loss: 'Joseph is no more, and Simeon is no more, and now you would take Benjamin. All this has happened to me!' When Reuben pledges to act as surety for Benjamin, he refuses, saying that, with Joseph dead, Benjamin 'alone is left'.

The sequence ends with the outcome hanging in the air. A heartfelt dilemma has been uncovered. Jacob is presented with an invidious decision, with both choices leading to the potential for great loss. But the decision couldn't be postponed for long. Soon the grain that they had brought with them was used up and they had to return to Egypt. This time they receive a royal welcome. The brothers are invited to eat at Joseph's table, while Joseph struggles to keep up the pretence and hold his emotions in check.

Letting the story read us

Stories do not need to be explained and usually lose their power when an attempt is made to do so. But neither do we need to make those hints and references to God more explicit than they are already. The restraint of the storyteller confers a particular power on those theological explanations. But stories always beckon us to occupy other shoes, and challenge our attitudes and actions in the light of the other actors in the drama: the exercise of power, the way of forgiveness and healing. And we're left to wonder at the providence of God who deftly weaves the threads of lives and nations over vast distances and tracts of time. Thanks be to God.

Roger Spiller

Hymn suggestions

Lead us, heavenly Father, lead us; Guide me, O thou great Redeemer; Put thou thy trust in God; Thou art the way.

Seventh Sunday after Trinity (Proper 13) 4 August
Principal Service **Attend to the Frame!**
(*Continuous*): Hos. 11.1–11; Ps. 107.1–9, 43 [*or* 107.1–9];
or (*Related*): Eccles. 1.2, 12–14; 2.18–23; Ps. 49.1–12 [*or* 49.1–9];
Col. 3.1–11; **Luke 12.13–21**

Every picture has to be framed. A frame improves a picture no end, and my pictures need all the help they can get. Put a mediocre painting in a frame and it begins to look much better. Photographers know about this because the frame is part of the picture, whether it's a tree or an archway or an open door. The frame directs your eye to what needs be seen. Some say the frame is the most important part of the picture. Well, the pictures Jesus paints in stories and parables are nearly always framed, by a conversation, a discussion, a question put to Jesus. It's often not so noticeable or as gripping as the parable, and we often discard it once we've found our way into the story proper. So before we see into the picture of the rich man, we need to give attention to what framed it.

The frame of the story

The frame that guides us to the parable is a dispute between two brothers over their father's inheritance. It appears that their father has died without leaving a will. So according to the law the inheritance couldn't be divided until the elder brother agreed. This he was unwilling to do. The younger brother therefore petitions Jesus to press his older brother to divide the estate.

But Jesus will not play his game. 'Who set me to be a judge or arbitrator over you?' There is no reason to think that the younger brother would have anything less of an insatiable, single-minded appetite for wealth and security than his elder brother. If Jesus had adjudicated in favour of the younger brother, the materialist, self-enclosed lifestyle would have remained intact. And his narrow, self-serving, uncritical view of his rights would have been vindicated. Even if the brother gained his inheritance, he will not have the security and happiness that he craves.

The story

So now we can get into the story. The land of a rich man produced abundantly – well, that can't be bad. A bumper harvest compensates for those years of drought or pestilence. So he decides to pull down his barns and build bigger ones. Well, what else is he expected to do – let it go to waste, flood the market so that the price of grain falls and hardworking farmers receive less reward for their labours? Oh, you say, give it to the poor. But he will have already fulfilled the requirement to leave a corner of the field for the hungry, which is calculated to be more than sufficient for their needs. So, building larger barns seems a sensible idea. And, moreover, since he has got sufficient provision for his pension, he decides to retire, take life easy and enjoy the fruits of his labour. Well, when people take themselves off the labour market they create employment for others, so that can't be wrong. What else could he have done? Would it have been better that he should have blown it all in feckless, indulgent living?

The analysis

This man has no friends to talk things over with. He is alone, a pathetic figure, talking to himself. But now he hears the voice of God addressing him. Why is this man condemned? Not surely for his prudence, in safeguarding the fruit of his labour. Not for his foresight, in planning for his future. Not for his enterprise, in planting for a harvest. Not for his indulgence, in taking life easy after years of work and worry. Not even for failing to share his wealth with the poor. Nothing that he did, but what he failed to do. In a word, he committed idolatry! That's the cause and consequence of greed, set out in Paul's letter to the Colossians. In reckoning with his material life, he didn't reckon with his life before God. He mistook life as a possession, when it is a gift. So he made no effort to be rich in spirit, rich before God: 'Soul, you have ample goods.' His wealth has consigned him to solitary confinement – no friends to talk to and no recognition of the God to whom he is accountable. He lost his possessions and his life.

O yes, and what about the younger brother? Well, he would have received all of the inheritance. Let's hope that he learnt from Jesus to be rich before God!

Roger Spiller

Hymn suggestions

Take my life and let it be; Jesu, lover of my soul; Seek ye first the kingdom of God; All my hope on God is founded.

Seventh Sunday after Trinity (Proper 13) 4 August
Second Service **Weaver God**
Ps. 107.1–32 [*or* 107.1–16]; **Gen. 50.4–end**; 1 Cor. 14.1–19;
Gospel at Holy Communion: Mark 6.45–52

Just when we thought the family soap opera of Joseph, his brothers and their father had finally been happily resolved we are given a sharp reminder of the power of mistrust that can challenge any relationship.

The story recapped

Joseph is their father's favourite son, and that provokes the brothers to hate not their father but the brother on whom such lavish attention is poured. And to rub salt into the wound, Joseph relayed to his brothers the contents of a dream, that one day it would be they, his already jealous brothers, who would be prostrating themselves before him as their saviour. They would take steps to eliminate this hated brother, but their wicked actions served only to initiate a chain of events that would enable Joseph to attain a commanding position in Egypt, subordinate only to the Pharaoh. Meanwhile, facing a severe famine and starvation, his father packed all but his favourite son off to Egypt to purchase grain, where they unwittingly fulfil Joseph's dream as they place themselves at the mercy of their hated brother. Of course, many years have passed, and it's therefore no surprise that his brothers don't recognize Joseph. But Joseph recognizes them, and keeps us in suspense to see when he will reveal his true identity.

Meanwhile, Joseph sets his brothers a series of challenges and tests by which they re-examine their past and own their guilt. Joseph has struggled to control his emotions, but, at a third meeting with the brothers, he can no longer keep up this pretence and discloses his identity at a great feast at his table in honour of his brothers, 'kissing all his brothers' and 'weeping upon them'. On a fourth visit, this time joined by his father Jacob, a lavish arrangement is agreed by the Pharaoh and the story comes to a dramatic end, or so it seems.

Are the brothers secure and forgiven?

In today's reading, concluding the book of Genesis, we hear of Jacob's death, the last of the three Patriarchs. But does this new fact release Joseph from loyalty to his father, which constrained him from taking revenge upon his brothers for what they did to him? Some read the story in a darker light: the brothers are still self-serving and manipulative. They play on Joseph's deep love for his father and they beg for forgiveness, not in their own voice but by invoking the intent of their dead father. Perhaps they even invented their late father's instruction that guaranteed their safety. On this reading, Joseph's testing was not born out of an educational desire for their self-understanding and rehabilitation; more a wilful act of retribution.

Great epics often give space for readers to read and construct their own interpretations within the loose framework of the story, and this is possible here. But the evidence leans, by contrast, to a more hopeful reading in which Joseph has proved himself ready to make the arduous journey of reconciliation.

His response to the mistrust his brothers show to him, and their reluctance to accept the transparency and liberation that has occurred, brings him sadness and weeping. And when they acknowledge that they are no more than his slaves, Joseph will have none of it.

The agency of God

Does Joseph forgive his brothers? There are his costly tears of devotion and healing, but there's another player in this drama and Joseph will ensure that he is included in the narrative. God doesn't have a voice in this long story. The Egyptian officers alone recognize the activity of God in the gifts and success of Joseph. The brothers want only to know whether Joseph will forgive them. They're not troubled to know what God thinks. But Joseph tells them that God is the great actor in this whole story. 'Am I in the place of God?' he asks them, as if forgiveness is a personal, local issue that need only involve men and women. And then, in the space of a verse, he reveals the theology not only of this story but of the purpose of the whole book of Genesis.

'Even though you intended to do harm to me, God intended it for good, in order to preserve a numerous people, as he is doing today.' He's not, of course, saying that Joseph's sufferings were part of God's plan or that any harmful, evil deeds can ever be intended by God. They were the actions of human agents acting freely. But even the evil machinations of humankind can be turned to serve God's purposes.

Does God have a plan?

People take comfort from the idea that God has a plan, a single, master plan. A plan would suggest something predetermined, but there's no suggestion that God's decision to use the evil intentions of the brothers for good was made before creation or before the brothers developed their own particular character traits. No, there is no evidence in the Hebrew Bible that God had a specific and immoveable plan. It's more accurate to think of God as having an intention, with which God persists until it is realized.

The word in Hebrew that can be translated as 'plan' is rooted in the concrete meaning 'to weave'. It's a little bit like a Persian rug-maker who enlists his children in his work. The children work at one end of the rug, the father at the other. Of course, the children don't always carry out their father's instructions. But he adapts his design to take in the mistakes of the children and work them into a new pattern.

As our story suggests, God's intention doesn't always proceed in a smooth, monolithic way. It takes surprising twists and turns because the divine–human relationship involves a genuine give-and-take dynamic. But through God's hidden agency, Joseph secured his descendants a safe passage and a privileged lifestyle in an alien land in Egypt, which will become their home for some 400 years. And then, when the size of their population spreads alarm and they become ill-treated, God will raise up Moses, to secure their release and lead them to their promised homeland. So, the book Genesis, culminating in the heartfelt story of Joseph, proclaims that God's loving purpose cannot finally be thwarted.

Roger Spiller

Hymn suggestions

Thy hand, O God, has guided; God is working his purpose out; Inspired by love and anger; Put peace into each other's hands.

Eighth Sunday after Trinity (Proper 14) 11 August
Principal Service **Chasing Preachers?**
(*Continuous*): Isa. 1.1, 10–20; Ps. 50.1–8, 23–end [*or* 50.1–7]; *or* (*Related*): Gen. 15.1–6; Ps. 33.12–end [*or* 33.12–21]; Heb. 11.1–3, 8–16; **Luke 12.32–40**

Chasing preachers?

The headline said, 'Preacher chased over poor preaching'. Surely a thought that's bound to stir anxiety in any preacher's mind! If this catches on, should I always wear running shoes in the pulpit, just in case? Christ's words in today's Gospel, 'be dressed for action . . . you also must be ready', suddenly had a resonance that wasn't apparent to me before.

I thought, what if sermon feedback did indeed become more physical than the polite 'Thank you for your message'? How would I temper my words and my way of speaking if booing, rotten tomatoes, or being chased out, was a likely response if I got it wrong? Perhaps I would indeed be alert in a way altogether different from my previous sermon style.

Not quite what it seems

These were my musings on seeing the headline, but then I read the article that followed. It turns out that the hapless preacher wasn't in fact chased out for poor preaching in terms of the quality of what was being said. What caused the kerfuffle was the content of the sermon. According to the reporter, the preacher had required worshippers to pledge no less than a certain sum per year in order to remain members of the congregation. So outraged were a hundred of those present that they chased the preacher out of the pulpit and down the street.

In the light of that report, I now look at the Gospel reading in a different way. My attention turns towards Christ's words about possessions and about giving. Had the preacher asked too much in an overbearing way? Or, was it that those who responded so physically were less than wholehearted in their commitment? The incident happened in a country far away and in circumstances of which I know little, so I'm not able to judge. According to the paper, the bishop has been called in. No doubt he'll have more idea of what really lay behind the chase.

Many stories

The incident, the headline and the way it was reported have changed the way I think about today's Gospel reading. Did you notice that similar things are happening in those verses from Luke? At first sight this is a passage of direct teaching. It's as if Christ offers straightforward advice – don't be fearful, get your priorities right, be always ready for God. But, if you read on, in verse 41 Peter says, 'Lord, are you telling this parable for us or for everyone?' So the part about the house owner and the thief is a parable. And the earlier verses are tiny parables as well: one about a flock, one about purses for money, and two about the lives of slaves.

Many circumstances

And just like the story of the preacher being chased, there are different ways of understanding what those tiny parables are saying to us. Did Jesus first speak them to peasants and slaves? Landless labourers who knew a lot about trying to keep alive a tiny flock, or who had to keep what few coins that came their way constantly on their person? These were people who didn't actually have any possessions to sell. And did Luke then understand these parables anew in an urban setting where the disposal of wealth was a real possibility? In circumstances where some slaves were people of considerable responsibility and authority?

Walking with Christ's words

Are we to draw from these tiny parables the promise of God's care and concern in the most poverty-stricken of circumstances? Or, are we to take from them his call to those who have the privileged choices of wealth to exercise those privileges always for the purposes of the kingdom of God? Are these parables demanding of us an ever present godly alertness? Or, are they overturning all our commonplace understandings, and reordering the world into a place where the master must pull up his tunic under his belt and be ready to labour for the lowliest?

For certain, all these things and more are in these little tales. Every time we let these words loose alongside our own experience and imagination, Christ speaks anew.

The biblical scholar Hans-Ruedi Weber used to tell a story of an East African villager who constantly carried her Bible with her. She was repeatedly teased by her neighbours, who thought her foolish to make her chores all the more difficult by always carrying the big book. She was never angered or distressed by their taunts. Finally, however, one day she knelt in the middle of those who laughed at her and, holding the Bible about her head, said, 'I carry this book always because it is the only book which reads me!'

We must let ourselves be read by Christ's stories.

Christopher Burkett

Hymn suggestions

Wake, O wake! With tidings thrilling; Come, thou long expected Jesus; Thy kingdom come! On bended knee; Do not be afraid, for I have redeemed you.

Eighth Sunday after Trinity (Proper 14) 11 August
Second Service **Always 'Yes'!**
Ps. 108 [116]; Isa. 11.10—end of 12; **2 Cor. 1.1–22**; *Gospel at Holy Communion*: Mark 7.24–30

Jeremy Clarkson has recently had 'Brummies' in his line of fire. He stereotypes Brummies as people with an inability to say 'yes': 'That is amazing.' 'Their emotions', he writes, 'are not just hidden, they are locked in a safe and buried under 20 tons of concrete, in a well, at the bottom of the garden. Show a Brummie an amazing garden, and he will say, 'I bet that takes a lot of digging.' He has a point. I can speak as one fortunate to have been born in that cultural heartland but with a congenital capacity to say 'yes'.

No

A few years ago, a small group of us from Birmingham got together to meet the city's officers from the education department. We were to hear whether the long battle for a new school building had been given the green light. We were anxious as we waited for this momentous decision to be revealed. 'Yes' – the news was great, millions of pounds would be spent. A drawing of the proposed new school was unfolded before us, revealing an imaginative building that would combine two separate schools. Excitement was palpable, except for one poker-faced, elderly man. His response to the splendid news was that there were too few toilets in the plans!

Saying 'no' is the default response, the safe option, it cuts down risks and limits responsibilities. There's a negative bias, which spreads like a pernicious disease. Unless you've overdosed on Steven Pinker, who insists that things are getting better, we're likely to be feeling a sense of negativity and foreboding as we contemplate the big picture. Our belief in God, if we have one, may also be telling us that God's response is 'no'. After all, the Ten Commandments are an assemblage of 'nos'. And where new pleasures, lifestyles and sexuality are concerned, it's expected that the response will mirror large sections of the Church and register a predictable 'no'.

Yes and no

When I needed a few years ago to employ a garden designer, there were lots of questions – soil levels, the location of paths, the introduction of big rocks, a water feature, creating 'rooms', building pergolas and, of course, the planting.

I soon realized that the designer's answer to every question was prefaced by the same phrase: 'Yes and no'. I don't think the man had had training in Hegelian dialectic, but his own learning equipped him to see the complexity lurking in any question and to deride clear and unambiguous responses. All the same, it became a satisfying challenge to try to frame questions that couldn't be answered 'Yes and no'.

But saying 'Yes, yes' and 'No, no', at the same time was exactly what St Paul thought his opponents were accusing him of. They said he had failed to carry out the plans he announced for visiting them. He planned to visit Corinth twice on a journey he was making to Macedonia, once on the outward journey and then again on his return. He changed his plans, cancelling his visit, not out of self-interest but because his visit would have brought them grief, as happened on his last visit, and he didn't wish to repeat it. Paul knows that the gospel is always 'yes', and so his conduct must be rooted in his message, in which there is no ambiguity.

Yes!

For, says St Paul, in Christ, 'every one of God's promises is a "Yes"'. Isn't that wonderful news? God is unchangeably yes, unchangeably loving. He is always saying 'yes' to you, always affirming you, always holding you in existence. Of course, it doesn't always feel that way. And St Paul knew better than most the depths of human suffering. 'We were so utterly, unbearably crushed', he said, 'that we despaired of life itself.' And that compelled him to rely on God, who raises the dead. He can go on in the same chapter to tell us that, despite his sufferings, 'Every one of God's promises is a "yes".'

Amen

And so what is our response? St Paul's response was to say 'Amen' to the glory of God. And so we too speak back to God's 'yes', acknowledging his grace. If we're united in Christ we will always say 'yes' to him. But then, we're to be God's unchanging 'yes' to other people, carriers of God's love, hope, affirmation and generosity.

Roger Spiller

Hymn suggestions

In the Lord I'll be ever thankful; Go to the world! Go into all the earth; Hope of our calling: hope through courage won; What shall our greeting be? Jesus is Lord.

Ninth Sunday after Trinity   (Proper 15)   18 August
Principal Service   **Reordering Relationships**
(*Continuous*): Isa. 5.1–7; Ps. 80.1–2, 9–end [*or* 80.9–end];
or (*Related*): Jer. 23.23–29; Ps. 82; Heb. 11.29—12.2;
Luke 12.49–56

They didn't speak to her again, not her father, her mother, her sister or even the younger brother with whom she'd been so close. When their eyes met, the family walked on the opposite side of the road. Cut off, considered as good as dead, the cost and consequence of declaring that she was now following Christ. A scenario repeated in countless homes throughout the generations reaching back to the life, death and resurrection of Jesus himself.

Jesus is pre-eminent

It happens to converts from other religions, too, but for Christians it's not beliefs and creeds and values, but the sheer towering, luminous, person of Jesus that is the gravitational centre around which our most cherished, challenging and supportive relationships are realigned. Jesus is not undermining the family, but neither is he lending support to the view that church and family are twin pillars of society. The family can consume us. It has to be subordinate to him, otherwise it can be self-serving and even idolatrous. Jesus asks not merely to have a presence, or even a prominence in our lives, but to be pre-eminent.

Having divided the natural family, Jesus' challenge has implications for the rebranding of church as family. We inherit our family; we expect to choose our church as we choose our washing powder or toothpaste, aided perhaps by *The Good Church Guide*. The church of choice is the one where we find those who think and speak like us. But – followers of Jesus aren't meant to replace one exclusive set of relationships with another.

We're not meant to pick who we're standing with as we worship. It's a hand of cards that's randomly dealt to us; people who have nothing in common, whose paths would never, ever cross, except for one thing: each one has an individual allegiance to Jesus Christ. The result is that they pledge, as in a marriage covenant, to work out their relationship with Christ with one another. And they renounce their right to walk away whenever they meet someone they don't like. As one recent convert said: 'You'd never have caught me with this bunch of people a few months ago.'

Embracing those who are different

Mabel is a woman with a heart as big as the Grand Canyon,[21] with arms and mind to embrace all kinds of people. She throws a party, for no better reason than to celebrate being alive. A wide assortment of people turn up who would never normally be seen in one room together: sworn enemies and adversaries, casualties of personal feuds. Ian Paisley is there, as is Gerry Adams. Because of the mix, there's a high level of tension. But because Mabel is there, and because everyone respects and loves her, the guests are willing to engage with one another in a way that would be inconceivable without her.

The mix of people can only come together around one person. Everything depends upon her presence. That's a faint reflection of the way the figure of Jesus Christ works to draw all people to himself and to one another. Nothing holds us together except the shared significance of Jesus Christ. That is likely to include people who have still not decided what significance Jesus has for them, but who, nevertheless, are prepared to immerse themselves in the life of the church, voice its prayers and sing its praises, along with those more assured of their beliefs and commitments than themselves. And those for whom Jesus is significant, as explorers and disciples, however uncomfortable and challenging and unlike ourselves, they have a claim on our lives that we have no right to refuse.

Jesus challenges our comfort zone

The fact of Jesus divides all forms of social cohesion that serve our own comfort and self-satisfaction. His gifts come in awkward packages. And the awkward and unlike and different compel us to address the hiding places within our lives that we would most wish to ignore. They offer us alternative ways of thinking and acting. They release us from our enclosed and narrow worlds. They contest the religious clichés we use that serve as a moratorium on our future growth. And they become bracing fellow travellers on our journey of discipleship.

Dividing and realigning our family relations strengthens rather than undermines the relationships we most cherish.

Roger Spiller

Hymn suggestions

God of grace and God of glory; Here from all nations, all tongues, and all peoples; Come build your church, not heaps of stone; Painting many pictures, in the hall of faith.

Ninth Sunday after Trinity (Proper 15) 18 August
Second Service **Giving God's Gifts**
Ps. 119.17–32 [or 119.17–24]; Isa. 28.9–22; **2 Cor. 8.1–9**; *Gospel at Holy Communion*: Matt. 20.1–16

A Christian teacher who got his face on the cover of *Time* magazine for being the best theologian in the world was asked what the Church should do if it wanted to become a truly caring and disciplined community. He replied that the Church should start by requiring all those currently in the Church, as well as anyone who wished to join the Church, to declare in public what they earn. Predictably the suggestion was treated with derision. It's assumed that no one should be expected to declare their income in public. But the speaker's point was that if the Church is a divine community, and if it is concerned with salvation, then it has some claim over us. We can't, then, have sole ownership over our possessions and even our lives. We should be under the discipline of the Church.

Keeping income and giving under wraps

This is not, of course, how it is. There's a reluctance to talk about giving, which, considering the centrality of the language of giving and receiving in the Christian vocabulary, seems odd. And the notion of money seems to belong on the wrong side of the fault line we have invented between the secular and the sacred. There's no pressure for us to 'cash out' our Christian faith in terms that really cost. It's been said that the wallet is the last item to be converted.

215

But how far do we know ourselves to be blessed, enriched, loved, if we are reluctant to dispense the currency of the world?

Well, St Paul himself found it hard to 'beg' even in the church in Corinth that he founded. But circumstances dictated that he must, and his treatment of the subject stretches into three whole chapters.

The generosity of the poor

The obvious starting point is to offer an example. The church in Macedonia served the purpose. They suffered both poverty and affliction but, so far from turning inwards, they wasted no time in arranging to make payments and were keen to be generous. They, as a poor church, contrasted with the more prosperous church in Corinth, who needed Paul's letters to convince them to part with their money. The disparity between the generosity of the poor and the tightness of the rich, epitomized in such stories as the widow's mite, is still replicated today from the evidence collected. It's usually the poorer churches, struggling in tough areas, who are the most willing to give generously.

Paul can't resist drawing out the contrast with the Corinthians. He deploys shaming, encouragement and flattery to win his hesitant converts. What an impressive account he has to give of the Macedonians! He extends his vocabulary to make sure he does them justice. Theirs has been a ministry of 'grace, blessing, priestly service, relief work, participation and fellowship'. The issue is not merely about the transfer of assets, it's that the gift of money has served to extol and exemplify the generosity of God. The Macedonians, says Paul, have transposed the giving of relief into an opportunity for self-giving and for an outpouring of joy and blessing.

Encouraging giving

The oblique way in which the Corinthians overhear the Christian gospel of grace may trigger some soul-searching in Paul's converts. But he knows that flattery and encouragement is also needed if they are not to feel out of the game and dismissed to the sidelines. Yet there are plenty of positive grounds for encouragement that he can spell out to his Corinthian congregation. He praises them: 'You excel in everything – in faith, in speech, in knowledge, in utmost eagerness, and in our love for you – so we want you to excel also in this generous undertaking.' What a persuasive appeal – who could resist it?

216

Recipients of Christ's self-giving

But St Paul has one final clinching argument. This practical, mundane, local concern must be subjected to the life of Jesus Christ. Dealing with both the poor and the rich gives him the vocabulary with which to interpret the life of Jesus. He writes: 'For you know the generous act of our Lord Jesus Christ, that though he was rich, yet for your sakes he became poor, so that by his poverty you might become rich.' The life of the Son of God could be depicted in terms of the wealth that he forsook in becoming human. And that life was cruelly terminated in the poverty of crucifixion. Jesus Christ assumed poverty so that the Corinthians and we too 'might become rich'. If that is the costliness of God's self-giving, how can it not determine and inspire our giving and the generosity by which we live? Paul will take that forward, without repeating himself, in the next chapter.

Maybe more transparency about what we earn, and especially what we give, may not be as outrageous as it first seemed.

Roger Spiller

Hymn suggestions

Long ago you taught your people; Thou who wast rich beyond all splendour; For the healing of the nations; Praise and thanksgiving.

Tenth Sunday after Trinity   (Proper 16)   25 August
Principal Service   **Walking Tall**
(*Continuous*): Jer. 1.4–10; Ps. 71.1–6; *or* (*Related*): Isa. 58.9b–end; Ps. 103.1–8; Heb. 12.18–end; **Luke 13.10–17**

John Bishop, the comedian, told his audience that he'd bought a new fridge. So he took the old fridge to the recycling centre.

> The man at the site said. 'What have you got there?'
> 'A fridge,' said Bishop.
> 'You can't bring that in here. Fridges have got ferons on.'
> 'So what do I do with it?' enquired John Bishop.

'You have to ring up.'
'And then what happens?'
'We'll come out and get it.'
So Bishop got back in his car and rang the number.
'I've got a fridge,' he said.
Where are you?' said the attendant.
'I'm just outside the Recycling Centre.'

That ludicrous interaction with rule-making bureaucracy gets us close to the thrust of the conflict reported in our Gospel where Jesus is attacked for healing a woman on the Sabbath day. Jesus is teaching in the synagogue. You may expect him to be preoccupied. The unnamed woman makes no attempt to ask for healing. She has a curved spine, she's unable to lift herself up straight. She's been forced to look down at the ground as she went through life. But Jesus notices her and calls her to him, telling her she is delivered from her infirmity. As he lays hands on her, she is made straight.

Rules that oppressed our Sundays

But this occurs on the Sabbath. The Sabbath command wasn't intended as a killjoy, but a day for play and delight and space to develop; an interruption from the purpose-filled weekdays. Sabbath reminds us to see ourselves not in terms of what we do but who we are. Keeping the Sabbath is intended to help us to preserve the image of God in our lives.

For many of us growing up in the 1950s and 1960s, Sunday was a grim day. 'Church was somewhere you went before garden centres were invented,' said Victoria Wood.

In order that the Sabbath commandment was kept, it became hedged around by a dense thatch of minor regulations, which set out in precise detail what could and could not be done. By adhering to these rules it was intended that the Sabbath commandment wouldn't be inadvertently transgressed.

The leader of the synagogue is the law enforcer. Those involved in enforcing rules can easily come to see people as law-keepers or law-breakers. Exceptions are kept to a minimum so that the structure is not undermined. We've seen recently how the Home Office has been so rule-bound that large constituencies of people have been treated unjustly. But the issue here with the leader of the synagogue looks more straightforward.

'What's the big hurry? he asks. Why can't a woman with a curved back she's had for 18 years not wait one more day to be healed? After all, she's not in mortal danger. So if the Sabbath is part of the rhythm of life, a source of renewal, an expression of the grace of God, is Jesus flouting it?

When rules must be set aside

Jesus infringes Sabbath observance for the most pressing reason. It's that this woman's condition is a symptom of a deeper disorder. And for Jesus there is no time to be wasted. When rules, traditions, habits and even commandments designed to make us walk tall are used to weight us down, they thwart the purpose they were intended to serve.

Jesus cites one of the 40-odd rules that surrounded the Sabbath command itself. The one that permits a person to take his ox or ass from the manger and lead it away to water. Everyone in the room had, that morning, taken animals out of their houses and tied them up outside. His point is that today on the Sabbath you untied an *animal*. I untied a *woman*. How can you blame me? This story is followed by two short sayings about the kingdom of God. Where Jesus is, the kingdom is present, bringing healing and wholeness.

There's another irony. Keeping the Sabbath was intended to mark the liberation of God's people from Egypt. But rules and commands can easily become the very means to enslave people. The ministry of Jesus is for fullness of life, for liberation from all that stultifies and cramps our lives; for 'bringing us into the glorious liberty of the children of God', for enabling us to stretch to our full height as God's children. It won't happen by discarding all rules and commandments. But neither will it happen when we're more concerned to be safe, consistent, conformist than to be celebrating creation and working with God to renew his image in his human family.

I'll think twice before turning up with an old fridge at the recycling centre. But I'll keep rejoicing that at the heart of faith it is not rules and customs and habits but the towering person of Jesus who stops at nothing to liberate and heal all of us who are crippled by forces that grind away our hopes and deface the image of God imprinted on our hearts.

Roger Spiller

219

Christ is our King; I danced in the morning; Stand up and bless the Lord; King of Glory, King of Peace.

Tenth Sunday after Trinity (Proper 16) 25 August
Second Service **The Generosity of God**
Ps. 119.49–72 [*or* 119.49–56]; Isa. 30.8–21; **2 Cor. 9**; *Gospel at Holy Communion*: Matt. 21.28–32

The point is this: the one who sows sparingly will also reap sparingly, and the one who sows bountifully will also reap bountifully.

It was a wet afternoon in an East Anglian market town. Flags that should have been blowing happily in a spring breeze were held horizontally aloft by wire frames. It should have been a warning to us. The hoarding outside the Retirement Apartments announced an Open Day and that everyone was welcome to come in. So we took them at their word.

The welcome was warm. Champagne flutes were at the ready; brochures were laid out on coffee tables in the reception area. We were guided to the show flat by a delightfully loquacious woman who pointed out the 'bijou' kitchen and the lounge, complete with a tiny alcove, which was designed, she said, for 'the gentleman of the house, so he has somewhere to put his computer'. She did not mention that the wife's computer might also need a space. In the bedroom she opened a wardrobe door. On one shelf was a single handbag; on another shelf a pair of high-heeled shoes. Having been shown a room arranged as a dining room we asked where the second bedroom was. 'This room', she said, extending her hand in a careful gesture, 'could be your second bedroom.' 'So,' we replied, 'if this is not really a dining room, where would the occupants of the flat eat?' 'In the kitchen,' she replied, and took us back to the 'bijou' kitchen to show us a Lilliputian glass table with two matching Perspex chairs.

Claustrophobia was beginning to hover close by. It was all show, bright lights and polished mirrors. Everything had been arranged to give the impression that the crammed space was really much larger than it actually was. We left. They did not make a sale. And we were faintly depressed.

A lack of generosity

Trying to analyse my sense of depression I came to the interim conclusion that the emphasis of the developer was primarily and unsurprisingly on making a sale. Fair enough. The flats had been constructed to maximize the number that could be fitted on to an extremely small site. But the more I thought about my depression the more I realized that it was not the sales pitch that troubled me; it was the underlying philosophy of the developer. There was no sense of generosity: no generosity of space; no generosity of architecture; no generosity of design. The foundational concept was a combination of meanness and greed. The imagined needs of the prospective older residents centred on fears being ameliorated. So the proximity to the police station was proclaimed as a plus point, and the entry systems would have been envied by Fort Knox.

Well. All a very long way from my ideal housing for elderly people, which should be about community (of all ages), outdoor space (does an uninterrupted view of a car park count as beauty?), flat access to shops, areas for socializing, rooms of a reasonable size, plenty of storage, a caring warden who might just keep a loving eye on things . . . and, of course, access to a church.

That housing complex we visited was a million miles from St Paul's elegy on the theme of generosity that we heard in today's reading from 2 Corinthians.

St Paul's sales talk

Mind you, St Paul engaged in some fairly manipulative sales rhetoric as he tried to persuade the young church in Corinth to develop gifts of generosity. He was asking them to contribute to the needs of the church in Jerusalem and reminded them of the great example of sister churches in parts of Macedonia, which had already demonstrated a very generous attitude to their fellow Christians who had fallen on hard times.

'God', he proclaimed, 'loves a cheerful giver.'

It's the kind of slogan you sometimes see, slightly irritatingly, on stewardship envelopes . . .

But St Paul is surely right. Knowing our human propensity for meanness, selfishness and greed, his trumpet blast about generosity is sorely needed. Generosity, however, except among the saints, does not always come naturally to us.

And yet . . . think of the very nature of God. The creation is prodigally generous in all that it gives us. The life of Christ overflowed with generosity of love and care for those in need. The first disciples were generous in sharing their experience of the risen Christ with their fellow citizens. Our forebears in the faith were generous in creating churches in which we can now worship. Think of composers of music, artists, teachers, engineers, doctors, nurses, social workers . . . all of whom through their generosity have enriched and sustained our lives. Push the idea a little further.

Generosity: an unsung virtue

When you and I are in our last days, shall we not hope to be ministered to by people who are profoundly generous in the care they offer?

Generosity is one of the great and unsung virtues, and one that does not need any qualifications or diplomas to practise. It is simply an act of will.

Designing generous space into buildings is relatively easy, though, as we have seen, it requires generosity of mind and soul to bring *good* buildings into being; designing generosity into our lives is a much more challenging task . . . But, after our experiences of God's generous outpouring of love towards us, should we not resolve to respond in such a way that the practice of self-giving generosity on a daily basis will become part of our lives?

Christopher Herbert

Hymn suggestions

Praise and thanksgiving, Father, we offer; O Lord of heaven and earth and sea; In the Lord I'll be ever thankful; Give thanks with a grateful heart.

Eleventh Sunday after Trinity   (Proper 17)
1 September
Principal Service   Knowing Our Place
(*Continuous*): Jer. 2.4–13; Ps. 81.10–end [*or* 81.1–11]; *or* (*Related*): Ecclus. 10.12–18, *or* Prov. 25.6–7; Ps. 112; Heb. 13.1–8, 15–16; **Luke 14.1, 7–14**

Where we choose to sit in church can say a lot about us. People who sit right at the back or at the side may be expressing their detachment and may need watching. Those who perch themselves right at the front, may be showing commitment, but they might have a mischievous wish to intimidate the minister.

Who sits where?

Once you could buy your pew, a Victorian money spinner, this, and then you had your place and knew where you were in relation to everyone else. It's like that at most formal sit-down meals at weddings where place names are used. And the only challenge, apart from finding your place, is to know whether you're as close as you feel entitled to be to your host. When it's left to the guests to decide for themselves where they sit they might, as in our parable, occupy places intended for more prominent guests. Or they might hang back for others, and then resent being left with only seats at the margins by those they judged to have been presumptuous in taking the better seats.

A number of seats in our churches are already assigned to ministers and other participants in the worship. It's been suggested that the Church needs to move, mentally at least, from long tables, 'longtabling', as a poet called it, to roundtables, where there are simply no places of honour. But in the gospel story, Jesus is not dishing out rules of etiquette. He's challenging the self-regarding love of status.

A place for all

The good news is that we're all invited, all given a place, symbolized by our baptism. We are all included in God's banquet by grace. We can't earn it, we can't be sorry enough to win it, we don't deserve it. Grace, it's been said, means that 'there is nothing we can do to make God love us less'. But that doesn't seem enough for us. We seem to need gradations, set places, a pecking order where we can be on top. Cardinal Suenes said that clergy will find their place when they have succeeded in helping others to find theirs. The business of ministry is to enable all of us to find our place, and the work of evangelism is to convince us that we all have a place.

The first parable shows us as guests, the second shows us as hosts. We are as Christians hosts of the all-inclusive, accepting, unlimited grace of God. But what has become of the Church's inclusive banquet? Has it become a club for the temperamentally religious, for people like us, a fellowship of the like-minded, who play by our rules, and return favours? We're proud to call the Church a family – but Jesus says do not invite your friends, your brother, your relatives, or rich neighbours. Yes, we like the image of family without thinking that in our day of alternative lifestyles people can feel excluded by the emphasis of church as family, family worship – single parents, childless couples, gay or lesbian people.

Summoned by Jesus to his table

The Church of Jesus Christ is meant to be a menagerie of people who have nothing in common, would not naturally meet or talk with one another, still less share the communion meal together, except for the allegiance that every one has to Jesus Christ. But that allegiance is so decisive in shaping lives that we are drawn inexorably to one another, and it constitutes a set of relationships that go deeper than those between blood relations and friends. That's the point of Jesus' words, 'Whoever loves father or mother more than me is not worthy of me.' They say you inherit your relations and you choose you friends, but we say we are chosen to be friends and co-workers together, gathering around the person of Jesus and sharing his Spirit.

In parishes we don't get to pick who will be worshipping with us. It should include a heterogeneity of styles, temperaments and backgrounds, as far as practicable, a 'rainbow people'. To be the Church, it isn't necessary that we are emotionally or ideologically compatible with others. It is to stand shoulder to shoulder, hand to hand, with people who are very different from ourselves, and with them hear a common word and break the common bread. The Church is not an outfit for the temperamentally religious. Not a mutual support club for the like-minded, but a gathering for many different kinds of people who can show unselfconsciously that their differences strengthen rather than impede their 'oneness in Christ Jesus'.

Shaped by shared meals

The stories of meals Jesus told are parables that get to the heart of our relationships with others. They show, for example, that where some eat and others do not eat, the kingdom is not present. The real test in the early Church was not about who to baptize but who to eat with. Just as human families keep themselves from falling apart by eating meals together, so the Christian Church holds its members together by the repeated ritual of the Eucharist.

In our world menaced by mistrust and fear, what could do more to remove the stain of selectivity and tribalism from the Church and signal the gospel basis for shared living than to take seriously the implications of our gospel? We line up to come to communion as in a bread queue. We know our need and have been brought so low that we are publicly prepared to acknowledge it. We offer up our empty hands, symbolizing that if, into our empty hands, our empty lives, the bread of life does not come, we go away as empty as we came. We who know ourselves to be invited as guests are hosts too of God's banquet, Christ making his invitation through us.

Roger Spiller

Hymn suggestions

I come with joy, a child of God; Jesus calls us here to meet him here; We need each other's voice to sing; Church of God, elect and glorious.

Eleventh Sunday after Trinity (Proper 17)
1 September
Second Service   **He Must Increase, but I Must Decrease**
Ps. 119.81–96 [*or* 119.81–88]; Isa. 33.13–22; **John 3.22–36**

In the small town of Colmar in Alsace is a very beautiful museum; it is known as the Musée Unterlinden – the Museum under the Lime Trees. It was once a Dominican convent but, as a result of the French Revolution, when many religious orders were shut down, its buildings remained empty. Then, in 1849, it was decided that it should become a museum, and only three years later one of the greatest works of art in the world was moved there. It was the Isenheim altarpiece, created between 1512 and 1516 by an artist called Matthias Grünwald.

It was originally commissioned for the hospital at Isenheim, just upstream of Colmar, and was the central and haunting feature of the hospital ward run by the Antonine monks. The patients in their hospital suffered from what was then called St Anthony's Fire, a terrible infection that led to gangrene and was accompanied by terrifying hallucinations. We now know that the underlying cause of their illness was ergotamine poisoning, which derived from a fungus that contaminated rye bread.

The patients looked from their beds towards the altarpiece. The central scene of that altarpiece was a harrowing painting of Christ on the cross, his body twisted in pain, his hands and feet contorted by the nails that held his body fast. To one side of the crucifix is Mary, the mother of Jesus, swooning in grief and being supported by John the beloved disciple. Kneeling on the ground next to them is Mary Magdalene, her hands knotted in an agony of beseeching prayer. On the other side is John the Baptist, accompanied by a small lamb carrying a cross; from the lamb's chest, blood is expressed into a chalice. John points with strangely elongated fingers towards the crucified figure of Christ . . . and painted on the canvas are the words, 'He must increase and I must decrease'.

The power of the painting

It is an immensely powerful painting and is layered with meaning. But let's just concentrate on the words that John the Baptist has uttered (we heard them read in John's Gospel). First of all, we need to realize that when the Isenheim altarpiece was painted in the sixteenth century, it was the practice of those who could read to read words aloud, not, as it were, under their breath or silently in their minds. In our contemporary jargon we might describe, a bit lamely, that what they were doing was an immersive experience.

But then think of the patients in the ward who gazed on this painting daily. Those words addressed by John the Baptist to Jesus, 'He must increase and I must decrease', had a dreadful, existential resonance. The chances were very high that because of their illness they would indeed decrease; most of them were moving inexorably towards death.

'Increase' as the predominant message of our society

And now let's try those words on ourselves: 'He must increase and I must decrease.' They don't fit easily, do they, into our culture in which 'increase' seems to be of the essence? Think of all the weekend newspaper supplements filled to overflowing with foods we are encouraged to consume: the net result, of course, is obesity. It's the predominant and classic result of the cult of 'increase'. And that then leads to concern about what we should be doing to beat the growing (note the word) obesity epidemic. Try another example: have you noticed our local car parks? Cars have become, perhaps unconsciously, symbols of our gluttony. They are getting larger and larger, and overflow, front, back and sides, the parking bays. Or try all those glossy travel brochures: they too are devoted to 'increase' – increasing our desire to be somewhere other than where we are.

But what if some of this cult of 'increase' is a sign not simply of the inevitable out-workings of the capitalist system, but also of our deep unhappiness and of our inability to discover what it is to be content? Or, perhaps, at an even deeper level, a sign of our unwillingness to consider our own mortality. The raw fact of the matter is that you and I are destined to die. And because that is the case, should we not consider how we are going to approach the end-time of our lives? If we, quite rightly, prepare very carefully in our society for birth, should we not also consciously prepare ourselves for death? If, in the long term, we are destined by our very nature to decrease rather than increase, should we not take time to consider how we might approach the decrease-time of our lives?

When the Isenheim altarpiece was first created, many churches had rough-and-ready frescoes about facing the reality of death. Those images had none of the beauty of Grünwald's masterpiece, but they had a clear message. The frescoes showed three handsome young men in the prime of life hunting and enjoying themselves out in the greenwood. There they were suddenly confronted by three skeletons who spoke to them. The skeletons chanted: 'As you are now, so once were we; as we are now, so you shall be.'

All very stark and not to our taste, and perhaps a bit over-morbid. But surely it is worth considering whether our society, obsessed by 'increase', should not also give time to consider the realities of 'decrease'? And isn't it true that from the perspective of our faith, we have many riches that we are failing to disclose and proclaim? Through the death and resurrection of Jesus Christ we know that death is not actually the end; beyond the grave there is abundance of life and joy to come.

That should be worth, at the very least, a gentle alleluia, shouldn't it?

Christopher Herbert

Hymn suggestions

Jesus is Lord; O Christ the same, through all our story's pages; The kingdom of God is mercy and peace; On Jordan's bank the Baptist's cry.

Twelfth Sunday after Trinity (Proper 18)
8 September
Principal Service **God's Living Temple**
(*Continuous*): Jer. 18.1–11; Ps. 139.1–5, 12–18 [*or* 139.1–7];
or (*Related*): Deut. 30.15–end; Ps. 1; Philemon. 1–21; **Luke 14.25–33**

From the Tower of Babel down to our own times, building a tower is the ultimate sign of success and prestige. Countries as well as individuals vie with one another to erect the tallest, most impressive towers. Trump Tower is one man's flamboyant display of pride in the tradition of the original Tower of Babel. It was evidently so, in the time of Jesus, so that it illustrated a clear warning to his would-be followers. One condition has to be met when building a tower. The tower has to be completed, otherwise it becomes a monument to human folly. Unfinished towers are to be seen over our cities, announcing the folly of the building contractors who failed to count the cost.

Counting the cost

'Which of you,' says Jesus, 'intending to build a tower, does not first sit down, and estimate the cost . . . Otherwise, when he has laid a foundation and is not able to finish, all who see it will begin to ridicule him, saying "This fellow began to build and was not able to finish."'

Who would act like that? If we know ourselves at all, we know how easily we can overstretch ourselves. We can embark upon a project but then run out of time or money, and have to withdraw, leaving ourselves open to ridicule.

Large crowds accompanied Jesus, they hung on his every word, and they joined in what they hoped would be his victory march on Jerusalem. To this day, people have sought to follow Jesus in the hope that it will bring them prosperity, or healing, or protection against suffering and loss. Weighing the cost, with the sombre calculations of a building contractor, might seem to postpone or abandon a decision to follow Jesus Christ. We might have expected that Christ's cross would enable us to avoid facing the cross ourselves. Where, we might well ask, does this fit with the promise of grace, God's free, unconditional gift? Is there a price to pay for that too?

228

Free and costly grace

God's grace is, indeed, free, but it will cost us everything to receive it. A few years ago I bought my wife a flute for Christmas, and she bought me some paints and brushes. They were free gifts, but the gifts could only be received as gifts by entailing a cost. They had to be taken up, put to use, and that involved a cost that is continuous. Edging closer to an answer, we recall that human love is a gift, but to love truly costs us everything, as we find reflected in the marriage vows. Pope Benedict expressed this tension when he wrote: 'To be a Christian is primarily a gift, which then unfolds in the dynamic of living and acting in and around the gift.'

The call to follow Christ requires the kind of detachment entailed by any commitment, whether to a building or to a relationship. One young man, who was preparing for ordination, prided himself on his extensive CD collection, lovingly built up over a number of years. But he realized it had become a distraction and was enslaving him, and so he disposed of it all. Another person maintained sports cars as his pride and joy. He, too, felt they took too much of his time, and decided to hand them on to his children. Another, who was a news geek, decided to limit the time allocated to television viewing and cancel his daily newspaper, so as to escape the often-warped mindset and to make time for Christian activity and study.

Budgeting for the loss of life

There are no rules, no predetermined conditions as to what following Christ may mean for any one of us; the readiness to count the cost and be captive to Christ is all. But to follow Jesus means, as one New Testament scholar put it, 'to budget for the loss of one's very life'. But this must be expressed positively in terms of a daring love and generous embrace of all that brings healing and newness. A hymn by John Bell and Graham Maule offers a beautiful exposition and check list of what this involves:

Will you care for cruel and kind and never be the same?
Will you risk the hostile stare should your life attract or scare?
Will you kiss the leper clean and do such as this unseen?
Will you use the faith you've found to reshape the world around,
through my sight and touch and sound in you and you in me?[22]

If we've said 'yes' to such demands, then we are ready, as the letter to the Ephesians puts it, for us to be 'built together spiritually into a dwelling place for God'. Unlike the stunted buildings, God will build us into a living temple.

Roger Spiller

Hymn suggestions

Will you come and follow me; Take up thy cross, the Saviour said; Make me a captive, Lord; Let us build a house where love can dwell.

Twelfth Sunday after Trinity (Proper 16)
8 September
Second Service **The Future God**
Ps. [120] 121; **Isa. 43.14—44.5**; John 5.30–end

Are we living in the past, enslaved to traditions, dutifully following inherited practices? I suspect a lot of people outside of church life think that we are. And many on the inside would be only too happy to keep things 'as they always have been'. Protecting the past from change and innovation can lead to ludicrous conduct. I recall a former headmistress crossing out the word 'President' and other changes that had been introduced into the service book, working her way Sunday by Sunday through all the service books. Another, a prominent member of the choir, pointedly recited the traditional creed in competition with its modern version. And one church I visited had an area cordoned off for those who refused to exchange the Peace.

'Do not remember the former things'

There's a handy text for preachers from today's Old Testament reading, which some preachers take as authority for challenging us to leave the past behind: 'Do not remember the former things, or consider the things of old.' However, the text, doesn't support such a blanket interpretation. Isaiah, more than any other prophet, was instructing people to *remember*, not to forget, the past. Over and over again he reminds his hearers to remember God's mighty acts in the past, as the ground for believing that God would deliver his people from the suffering and devastation of the exile. By selectively remembering the past and overlooking the fact of God's continuous, unfinished work we can be unprepared to embrace God's future. It's in that spirit that we are to interpret and embrace God's promise, 'I am about to do a new thing.'

The 'new thing'

The 'new thing' that God promised now lies in the past, so we can only access it through the record of Scripture. The nation of Israel had been crushed, its people driven off into exile, its Temple and infrastructure destroyed, and faith in God and faith in any future had evaporated. It was to this crushed and abandoned people that Isaiah addressed some of the most exalted poetry in all literature. God will make a way through the desert, the exiles will return home with joy, Jerusalem will be restored, and all the nations will come flocking to it. This is the 'new thing' that Israel had stopped expecting, or believing could be possible. She thought that God's saving acts were now at an end. So what Isaiah was trying to say was, 'Stop looking back in despair and grief; don't cling to the past; open your minds to the fact that God is about to bring about a new act of deliverance.'

The reality of the new

It did seem that a 'new thing' was about to happen. The proud, cruel empire that had inflicted defeat on Israel was shortly to fall to the Persian Empire, and a bright future seemed to beckon. One of the most enlightened rules of ancient times now directed the rebuilding of the Temple and the return of all the Jews who wished to return to their homeland. God was doing a 'new thing'. The historian Simon Sebag Montefiore comments in his history of Jerusalem that 'Jewish history is filled with miraculous deliverances. This was one of the most dramatic.' True, the glowing picture of a new exodus voiced by Isaiah didn't match the reality. But the new thing God promised isn't restricted to our foreshortened time frames. God was 'about to do a new thing', again just when the promised restoration looked like collapsing. And then came the inauguration of the reign of God through the coming of Jesus, which exceeded all the promises. It's the fact that God is both agent and actor in human history that enables us to trust that God is working to bring newness into our world.

The need for 'new things'

Our time, too, appears like another watershed in human history, a period of turbulence, when all the trusted institutions of the past seem tired and discredited. Trust seems to have drained away, as the book of that name by Anthony Seldon has persuasively argued. The loss of Christian story, too, has lost its hold on the public imagination. Faith, in a society believed to be increasingly secular, is attacked and marginalized.

Faith, as Isaiah demonstrated, has to be in God if it is not to be suffocated by the present, outward, uncongenial social, political and religious conditions. Ours is a countercultural language that seeks to match the God who meets us from the future, from the source of newness.

Barak Obama describes in his autobiography the times when it looked as though he 'wasn't going to amount to anything'. At the age of 15 he was arrested for larceny and car theft. Still he was puzzled that his momma and daddy, as he affectionately called them, would break into a song: 'Thank you, Jesus. Thank you, Jesus. You brought me from a mighty long way, mighty long way.' It made no sense to him; they were thanking God in advance for all that he would bring to their son. It makes sense now.

Where are the new things, the green shoots, the small pools that offer refreshment, the streams in the desert places in our lives and churches? Where are the places of turbulence and disturbance that hint at surprise? Where are the new things that signify God's activity? And are we perceiving them, hoping, praying, investing in the new things that our God of the future is bringing forth?

Roger Spiller

Hymn suggestions

Guide me, O thou great Redeemer; The Lord's my Shepherd; Do not be afraid; All for Jesus!

Thirteenth Sunday after Trinity (Proper 19)
15 September
Principal Service   **A Party in Heaven**
(*Continuous*): Jer. 4.11–12, 22–28; Ps. 14; *or* (*Related*): Ex. 32.7–14; Ps. 51.1–11; 1 Tim. 1.12–17; **Luke 15.1–10**

The lost sheep

Miriam is a sinner. Once, she was on the streets, forced from home by her parents, who were shocked when she got herself pregnant at 14. The shame nearly killed them. She's really struggled to bring up her son, with no home, no money, no secure relationship. Only men who want to make money from her plight. The self-righteous, if they haven't passed by on the other side, have condemned her, told her she's contaminated, unclean, and that she's lost all hope of ever being accepted back into the fold. As for the hypocrites, she could tell you a tale or two.

The good shepherd

Miriam had been sitting in the shadows when she heard Jesus tell the story, heard him hint that the shepherds themselves were at fault. If they'd been doing their job properly, the sheep wouldn't have got lost in the first place. Then she heard him talk about a different sort of shepherd, one who went right down into the dark and dangerous places: into the back streets, the red-light districts, the no-go areas, the wilderness. One who went the distance – and at no little risk to himself. It cost him dear, that shepherd. Can God really be like that? And like a woman? Now there's a thought! Luke is using one of his favourite devices – parallel stories, male and female. God searches, as a woman would, for a lost coin; it's not especially valuable, but, nevertheless, she hunts high and low, because it matters. Perhaps she matters too, then.

The acceptance

So Miriam creeps slowly forward and sits at Jesus' feet, accepted. And smiles her 'yes' to the party in heaven where the angels will rejoice. What is more, Miriam finds to her complete astonishment that she will be the guest of honour.

The Pharisee

Ben was standing up front as Jesus spoke – and then wished he wasn't. He'd never been so insulted in his life. Which one of you, having 100 sheep . . .? How dare he? As if a Pharisee would ever demean himself by such a profession – thieves and sabbath-breakers, all of them. 'What is it about the lost and vulnerable that has God all of a flutter?' he asks himself. How can God actually like common people – sinners?

And whatever happened to repentance? It's not just about being lost and then found. There's the four-step plan of salvation, the detailed initiation preparation, the formula for faithful living, the duties of religion. No pain, no gain.

The invitation

Ben's invited to the party in heaven, too. But will he go? He's a religious man; faithful at worship every week, sincerely honours God and does his level best to lead a good life. He keeps well clear of the unruly elements of society and the usual temptations that might cross his path.

The rejection

So he thinks to himself that this party might not be up his street, the company not quite what he's used to. This time, apparently, the guest of honour is an unmarried mother and a prostitute. It could equally well be a thief or drug addict, or a hoodie with several ASBOs to his name. Once it was a leper, another time a tax collector, once even a murderer! The host might be above reproach, but his special guests certainly aren't. It's all very well for him to say, 'Come on, rejoice with me', he has no reputation to worry about!

Ben can't see that everyone is lost, including him. But there are the lost who want to be found, and the lost who don't even know they're lost.

Barbara Steele-Perkins

Hymn suggestions

I will sing the wondrous story; Amazing grace; The King of love my shepherd is; Hark, my soul, it is the Lord.

Thirteenth Sunday after Trinity (Proper 19)
15 September
Second Service **Gathered Together**
Ps. 124, 125; **Isa. 60**; John 6.51–69

There is something quite beautiful about the image of peoples and nations being gathered together. The whole idea of 'gathering' is something that can bring comfort in a world where people are more and more dispersed and atomized. More and more people live alone, families are scattered, community is often fractured, nations fragment. Is it possible then to build a new kind of community, a new kind of society, a new peaceable kingdom in which people are bound together and gathered together? If we were building a city, would the hope of building human community be an important part of the design brief? Does the Church have anything to contribute to this intention? These days, significant places of human 'gathering' might include football stadiums, concerts or protests, but the church is also still a place where communities gather in times of joy and sorrow, and day by day and week by week to worship almighty God and share bread and wine together. The universal Church at it's very best is still a place that gathers together people of all nations, people of all backgrounds, high and low, rich and poor, one with another.

The prophet Isaiah presents a vision of the ingathering of the dispersed. Peoples and nations shall come from far away; they will be drawn together by the light of the people of Israel and find their home in a new and generous city. There is a nod to Advent and Epiphany in this evocative reading, as sons and daughters come from afar and kings bear gifts of gold and frankincense to lay at the feet of the Holy One of Israel. They come to a new city that is built upon the promise of peace; the walls of this city are called Salvation, the gates are named Praise, and those gates will always be open. There will be no violence or destruction, and there will be no need of the sun or the moon or artificial lighting, for the Lord will be the one light, which gives light to all people. We are presented with a vision of human flourishing in a gathered community.

Reunited on this table

In the Gospel of John, Jesus reminds us of the most obvious way in which people are gathered together, when they eat. To eat together with others is a fundamental way of gathering, of becoming one body. We share food together to celebrate, to commiserate, to build community, to show affection and share love. Eating together can break down barriers and forge new relationships. Eating together can build community. It is therefore no surprise that the Church's life is focused on a shared meal, in which bread is taken, blessed, broken and given. Christ enters into this meal. He says, 'I am the living bread', and elsewhere in John's Gospel, 'I am the bread, of life.' Christ becomes the food that gathers all people together from the ends of the earth, bringing together those who are far away and those who are near. He commands his disciples to share a meal in remembrance of him and in anticipation of a new kind of kingdom. Through the simple act of eating and drinking, this meal has the power to draw all things together.

There is a prayer that puts this succinctly, based on the ancient liturgies of the Church. It is used as the table is prepared during the Eucharist:

> As the grain once scattered in the fields
> and the grapes once dispersed on the hillside
> are now reunited on this table in bread and wine,
> so, Lord, may your whole Church soon be gathered together
> from the corners of the earth
> into your kingdom.[23]

That is the vision we are all hoping and longing for – the ingathering of the dispersed into a generous and loving community where all are welcome, all are valued, all are loved.

Victoria Johnson

Hymn suggestions

Bind us together; Glorious things of thee are spoken; Jerusalem the golden; Come let us join our cheerful songs.

Fourteenth Sunday after Trinity   (Proper 20)
22 September
Principal Service   **Forgive as We Are Forgiven**
(*Continuous*): Jer. 8.18—9.1; Ps. 79.1–9; *or* (*Related*): Amos 8.4–7; Ps. 113; 1 Tim. 2.1–7; **Luke 16.1–13**

I have a strong sense that somewhere in the world the committee that put together the lectionary are chortling, as they think of all the preachers wrestling with the parable of the dishonest steward.

I imagine that the writers of commentaries have done well out of it, too, as puzzled preachers have gone in droves to the bookshops hoping that the latest commentary might have solved the riddle. Unfortunately, they will have wasted their money.

Confusion

No one really knows what this parable means. Was Jesus really applauding the behaviour of a dishonest, self-seeking rogue? Are we really supposed to use our money to win friends? Even the so-called experts are really stumped.

Of course, this parable is not literally about money or stewardship, just as the parable of the lost sheep is not about animal husbandry. It's a parable. If any of you first learnt the Lord's Prayer in the Scottish version you will have the advantage over the rest of us. You will know that 'debts' often mean something much more than money. A story about debts is likely to be a story about sin, forgiveness and grace.

The parable of the unmerciful servant

There's another parable known as the parable of the unmerciful servant, and it has a similar structure. An initial reckoning between master and servant gives way to the servant's own reckoning with other debtors, and then there's a further final reckoning between master and servant. In both parables, it's the servant in the middle who is the main character.

These two stories are almost the reverse of one another. In one, the first reckoning with the servant leads the master to be forgiving. The master forgives the debt. But then the servant goes off and is unforgiving with those who owe him. He does not connect at all the forgiveness he has received with the forgiveness he might give. In the final, final reckoning, at the end of the parable, he is condemned.

In complete contrast to that story, in the parable of the dishonest steward, in the first reckoning the master is unforgiving, and the steward is sacked without mercy. But this steward, in a kind of reverse of the other parable, goes and forgives the debts of his debtors. And in the final, final reckoning, the master does not condemn this servant, but actually praises him.

Forgiveness and grace

Both stories are profoundly symbolic. They are about God, about us and about forgiveness and grace. We learn that just as God forgives us, so we are to forgive others. And in today's parable we hear the heart-warming story of someone who in fact managed to be forgiving, even when he had not been forgiven himself.

I'm convinced that this is an important part of the gospel, because it finds a place within the Lord's Prayer. We say each day: 'Forgive us our debts, as we forgive our debtors.' We are not talking about our bank accounts, but about the way we have come to know the forgiveness and grace of God. We who have known grace can only live graciously towards others ourselves.

Generous in love and mercy

Sometimes I have seen people behaving more like the unmerciful servant, and I have done it myself. It is all too easy and a strong temptation. Sometimes I have seen dishonest rogues being bigger hearted than anyone would expect. These parables show us that God applauds grace of heart and longs for all God's people to be so transformed by holy love that they will be generous and forgiving to others. The God whose servants we truly are is generous in love, mercy and grace. As God's servants, we are called to echo this with our own lives.

I imagine that nowhere among all the thousands of sermons preached on this text will there have been one quite like this one. And perhaps somewhere in Christendom, someone will have found a truer reading or a more reasonable one. But if there is error in the reading, may there be truth in the message. And if there is gospel here, then hear it.

Susan Durber

Hymn suggestions

Before the throne of God above; Forgive our sins as we forgive; Take this moment, sign and space; Dear Lord and Father.

Fourteenth Sunday after Trinity   (Proper 20)
22 September
Second Service   **Where Is He?**
Ps. [128] 129; **Ezra 1**; John 7.14–36

There's a traditional story of a little ocean fish. He swims up to an older fish. 'Excuse me,' he says to the older one, 'but where is this ocean that everyone tells me about?' 'You're in it,' replied the older fish. 'Oh no, this is just *water*,' said the little fish. And he swam off to look for the ocean elsewhere.

It's all too easy to be unaware of precisely where we are, and where to look for God.

Where is Jesus?

Our Gospel reading often asks the question, 'Where?' First, it's the Jews. They are on the lookout for Jesus. It's a big festival, the Festival of Booths (or 'tents', a festival to recall the wilderness journeying of their ancestors after the Exodus from Egypt), and good Jews would normally go to Jerusalem to share this occasion together. Just before our reading today started, we have the bigwigs watching out for him. They've got their eye on him – or would certainly like to. And then, at the beginning of our passage, he crops up, really obviously, at the Temple itself, and he even puts himself on the podium and starts teaching people about God. This puts them on the back foot, and so their next question is, 'Where did he learn all this?'

Seeking

Jesus, talking about different teachers' authorities, contrasts the teacher who teaches simply by himself, who is only 'seeking' to gain honour for himself, with the teacher who teaches on the authority of the one who sent him, who is 'seeking' to gain honour precisely for that one who sent him. Jesus sees himself as this second kind of teacher, one sent by God.

There's a lot more 'seeking' in this passage. The Jewish authorities are 'seeking' Jesus. A few lines later, Jesus refers to them 'seeking', looking for an opportunity, to kill him. The crowd repeats his words, questioning who is 'seeking' to kill him. A little while later, they have been impressed by his teaching, and now they are questioning whether this really is the one the authorities are 'seeking' to kill.

It's when Jesus makes it very clear where he's from and where his teaching's from that the authorities really get fidgety. 'God', is his plain answer. 'You do not know him. I do know him; because I am from him, and he sent me.' Now they really do 'seek' to seize him. But Jesus claims the protection of his Father, the one who sent him. 'You will search for me (seek me), but you will not find me,' he declares, much to the puzzlement of everyone who's listening. Where's he off to now?

He's not talking about a geographical place, but about being in the presence of God.

Where is God?

One of the reasons they just can't see this is that for them God's presence was in the Temple. Which is precisely where Jesus was teaching at this moment, remember. So he would seem to them to be talking nonsense. He's claiming God has sent him. And he's claiming that he would go back to God. And that there they would not find him. The Jewish authorities' response would be, 'But God's in the Temple, isn't he, so obviously we can find you there, if you are who you claim to be?'

That God was present in the Jerusalem Temple had for centuries been an important idea in their faith. At the complete destruction of the Temple by the Babylonians back in 586 BC, it was a big challenge to work out how to understand the presence of God if he wasn't at 'home' in his Temple. But then it was rebuilt 50 years later. Ezra, chapter 1, introduces this story. Ezra tells how the Persian king Cyrus sent the Jews, with many treasures and resources, to rebuild the Temple, around 536 BC. God makes his home among his people once again. Again and again in these verses Ezra describes the Temple to be rebuilt as the 'house' or 'home' of 'the LORD (who is) in Jerusalem'. God has a house first and foremost: there's a different word for 'Temple', which is not used until chapter 3, but the word 'house' or 'home' is often used in Ezra 1. It's clear that *this building* is seen as God's dwelling place. And it's also clear that *Jerusalem* is the place where God lives: we're told that's what Cyrus understands, and that's what he keeps repeating in his edict.

So that's what the Temple means to the Jewish authorities in Jerusalem in Jesus' day. But in AD 70, not long after Jesus' time, and before John's Gospel was written, this great Second Temple was destroyed now by the Romans in response to a Jewish revolt. It remains in ruins today, with only one great and precious wall still standing.

Jesus' message was that you wouldn't necessarily find God in the Temple: you would find God in Jesus' own being. So Jesus for

Christians has begun to stand for the Temple. In Jesus, we meet God.

So the question, 'Where is God?' can be answered, for Christians, with 'in Jesus'.

Megan Daffern

Hymn suggestions

Jesus, restore to us again; Lord of all your love's creation; Be still, for the presence of the Lord; Dear Lord, we long to see your face.

Fifteenth Sunday after Trinity (Proper 21)
29 September
(For St Michael and All Angels, see p. 349.)
Principal Service **Don't Miss It!**
(*Continuous*): Jer. 32.1–3a, 6–15; Ps. 91.1–6, 14–end [*or* 91.11–end]; *or* (*Related*): Amos 6.1a, 4–7; Ps. 146; 1 Tim. 6.6–19;
Luke 16.19–end

I don't think it's going to be easy to figure out what Jesus wanted us to get out of the parable we've just heard – or any of the parables. Even in the strange world of parables, this one, of the rich man and Lazarus, is particularly odd. Most of the parables are at least about things we know something about. A farmer sows seed in a field; a woman mixes yeast with flour to make bread; a young man says to his father, 'Give me my share of the inheritance . . .'. But most of the action in this parable takes place not in this world, but in the next world. It's not an earthly story with a heavenly meaning, but a hellish story with an earthly meaning. There's no evidence that the rich man ever saw the poor man, ever noticed him, ever paid him any attention. They live only a few feet apart, but they are in different worlds. As so often with parables, there's a sudden reversal of fortune. The poor man dies, and, in the words of some translations, he's immediately 'carried to Abraham's bosom', an old Jewish phrase meaning 'right next to the heart of God'. The rich man also dies, but he moves to the bowels of Hades. Agonized in torment, he looks up and sees Lazarus, and calls up, 'Father

Abraham, please . . .'. To which Abraham says, 'O my child, no. You've had your good things in life, and what's more there's a great chasm . . . It's too late, too late, too late.'

Wrong choices?

Our parable is the story of a man who made the wrong choice. There are people in my neighbourhood who have lost their houses because of greed on the stockmarket, which has brought our economy to the brink of disaster. And the message of this riddle is that one day greedy people like that will stand before the bar of God's justice and hear the voice of God saying: 'All right, Buster, you've had all the good things in life you're ever going to have.' And I say 'Yeah!'

But two things keep me from stopping there. First is the chill of recognition. I'm not a rich man. But if you pull the camera back and look at me in relation to the population of the world, I'm near the top of the pyramid. Whatever this parable has to say to the rich, it has to say to me. The second thing that prevents me from stopping there is that Jesus doesn't stop there. Luke doesn't stop there. As soon as he's uttered this parable, Jesus gets back on the road to the cross, to Jerusalem. And on the road he encounters an honest-to-God rich man, Zacchaeus. And Jesus doesn't say, 'All right, Buster, you've had all the good things in life you're ever going to have.' He says, 'Come on down, Zacchaeus, I'm staying at your house today.' And before that day is over, Zacchaeus is jumping for joy. And Jesus is saying, in language very like our parable, 'Today salvation has come even to this house, because he too is a son of Abraham.' The trap door opens. We fall to a deeper level.

Too late

What is this story about? Wealth and poverty? Yes; but there's something deeper going on here. The key to it is in what Father Abraham says. 'Child . . . between you and us a great chasm has been fixed, so that those who might want to pass from here to you cannot do so.' Those are not the words of an angry judge. Those are the words of a heartbroken parent. What's going on here is what might be called the penultimate theology of the gospel, the next to last. The ultimate theology is: 'It's never too late; the table of grace is always waiting.' But that would be cheap grace if it were not for the penultimate. Every now and then, a window opens and there it is, the kingdom of God right before us, an opportunity to be a part of God's action in the world. There it is; it's open. And then it closes. And we miss it. And it's too late. There's a man in a nursing home. He's just lost his wife of 60 years. He's tormented by memories of failure in their marriage. The many, many times she asked him: 'Say you love me!' 'Honey, I don't like to talk about it; I just do it.' 'But I like to hear it.' 'Well, that isn't my way.' The last week of her life she went into a coma. He sat beside her bed, saying over and over again, 'I love you, I love you.' But it was too late. Some of us understand this very personally. I cannot believe that when I was a young father I got on a plane and flew somewhere to give a speech to people who no longer remember me or what I said, instead of going to a school event that my little girl Melanie begged me to go to. Now I'm older I know I made the wrong decision; and now I'm ready to go to that event. But my daughter would say, 'Oh, Dad, it's too late. I'm not that little girl any more who needed her father that night. You missed it.' The blessing of God in the form of a beggar on the outside of the door – the rich man needed Lazarus a lot more than Lazarus needed the rich man. Why did he miss him? He was too rich, too focused on himself, too suspicious, too numb to the possibility that the blessing of God could be there. Don't miss it. Don't miss it.

Tom Long

Hymn suggestions

Just for today; This is the day; God is love, let heav'n adore him; All my hope on God is founded.

Fifteenth Sunday after Trinity (Proper 21)
29 September
Second Service **Nehemiah's Night Ride**
Ps. 134, 135 [*or* 135.1–14]; **Neh. 2**; John 8.31–38, 48–end

The anonymous characters who compile the lectionary have set us a challenge. For this and the following three Sundays they have directed us to a political autobiography. Now, as it happens, I devour political autobiographies but this is not from the pen of a recent politician. It is, in fact, the only political autobiography to be found in the whole of Scripture. The writer is a man who took leave from a high-ranking post in the court of the King of Persia to build a city wall and restore some semblance of order and hope to his beleaguered fellow Jews in Judah.

It may be essential reading for historical purposes, and to fill out the antecedents of Christianity, but is it good news, a preach-worthy text? You'll be able to answer that question for yourselves in ten minutes. But the rationale is that in the humdrum, mundane, often squalid circumstances in which we live, God is to be seen and heard. He is both agent and actor in our historical drama, nudging his recalcitrant people to strive for liberation and healing.

The time and place

It's no later than 440 BC, 150 years since the fall of Jerusalem and the end of the nation of Israel. The hopes of the Jewish people didn't match the reality. True, the Temple had been rebuilt, 70 years before Nehemiah appears on the scene, but it was a pathetic replica of its former self; some of the deported Jews had returned to their homeland, but it was only a trickle, leaving Judah thinly populated. When Nehemiah's brother led a delegation from Jerusalem to expose the appalling conditions in the city, Nehemiah felt the call to act.

The 'sickness of the heart'

Nehemiah was, like Joseph and Daniel, a person who had reached the highest level in an alien nation, Persia, the greatest nation on earth at the time. He knew he would be putting himself at risk in requesting a leave of absence to travel the long and dangerous journey back to Jerusalem. But Nehemiah learnt always to curb his impulsive and hot-headed character by spending time in prayer and laying his plans before God. The king, himself a wise, humane and successful leader, gave him the opening. He could read the faces of his officers, and when he looked at Nehemiah's countenance he discerned a 'sickness of heart' and wanted to know the reason for his condition.

Once, in the course of conversation, a friend of mine mentioned that, after taking a service at the church where her husband was vicar, the bishop phoned her. He'd noticed at the communion rail that her face seemed troubled. That single gesture opened the way to a long friendship that sustained my friend years later when she faced a terminal illness.

Nehemiah secured permission from the king to return to his homeland with the promise of materials from the royal forest, and a retinue and letters of commendation to ensure his safe passage. What might have been a mere business arrangement was felt to have the nudge of the divine. Nehemiah could declare to his Jewish compatriots that 'the hand of my God was upon me'.

City walls

The most pressing problem Nehemiah faced was the security of the city. Walls have long been a vital strategic aspect of the great cities of the world, in places such as China, Croatia, Spain, Morocco, France, York. Built and rebuilt, they are the concrete expression of our insecure, threatened and conflictual natures. We need walls, it seems, to teach us how to be liberated from their confinement. If not physical walls, then at least mental boundaries are an intrinsic component in maintaining national and personal identity. The wall meant more than re-establishing security for Jerusalem and its citizens. It reflected the parlous state of the nation's faith and earned the reproach and mockery of the surrounding peoples. The rebuilding of the city wall became a necessary step in renewing faith in God.

Surveying the city

The rebuilding of the city wall was a demanding task. It had to be done with speed and stealth, otherwise the enemies within Judah would thwart the project before it had even begun. But Nehemiah was a determined and energetic man and wasted no time. Three days after he had arrived in the city he made a nocturnal inspection of the existing walls, before sharing his plans with the Jewish leaders. The plans were arrived at not simply by human considerations; Nehemiah attributes to them 'what my God had put in my heart to do for Jerusalem'. This divine mandate was important when Nehemiah shared his vision with the leaders of Judah. Nehemiah said, 'Come, let us rebuild the walls of Jerusalem', but he wisely left it for the leaders to give the go-ahead and set the timescale. 'Let us start building,' they replied.

Opposition

The erection or rebuilding of public walls and buildings is usually guaranteed to divide opinion and reveal the competing interests and aspirations on either side of the divide. This was evident in an extreme form in the reaction to Nehemiah's plans. The chief opponent was the governor of Samaria, Sanballat, who exerted authority over Judah. He it was who kept the subjugated Jews well and truly demoralized. So he viewed the rebuilding of the city walls with alarm, as a land grab, an attack on his territory, an attempt to curb his power. Others too enjoyed the religious and moral laxity that was widespread, and felt their position would be threatened.

Nehemiah didn't confront them with his royal authority. Instead he responded to their ridicule by declaring faith in the power of God to reward the project with success. This was the beginning of a 12-year struggle, but we can rejoice that God raised up a man of such energy, faith and determination, who still reminds us to attend to the spiritual dimension that lurks behind every commonplace, mundane activity.

Roger Spiller

Hymn suggestions

City of God, how broad and far; The Church's one foundation; Teach me, my God and King; Jerusalem the golden.

Sixteenth Sunday after Trinity (Proper 22)
6 October
Principal Service   Worthless Slave to Intimate Friend
(*Continuous*): Lam. 1.1–6; *Canticle*: Lam. 3.19–26, *or* Ps. 137 [*or* 137.1–6]; *or* (*Related*): Hab. 1.1–4; 2.1–4; Ps. 37.1–9; 2 Tim. 1.1–14; **Luke 17.5–10**

The blood-donor has gone down as one of the all-time great comedy sketches. Tony Hancock is giving blood, for the first time, and nervously awaits his turn in the waiting room. He's in a self-congratulatory mood and keen to enlist his fellow donors: 'Well, it's a grand job we're all doing. Yes, I think we can all be proud of ourselves. Some people, all they do is take, take, take out of life and never put anything back.' But then his mask slips: 'Do we get a badge for doing this?' 'No, I don't think so,' replies the stern male donor sitting next to him. 'Pity, we should have something for people to pick us out by . . . I mean, nothing grand, a little enamelled thing, with a little motto, nothing pretentious, like: "He gave it for others so that others may live".' When he discovers that his fellow donor has given blood 20 times before, Hancock feels shamed, and reprimands him: 'All right, no need to boast,' and proceeds to read out the list of all the donations he's ever made.

We can all recognize the need for recognition for the work we do, which is ludicrously exposed in the sketch. It's a need we can all recognize even if we keep it well under wraps, the yearning for recognition, acknowledgement, appreciation.

The thankless role of the servant

The servant who was introduced in our Gospel was expected to be a versatile chap, quick to adapt and switch roles, first on the farm, ploughing, before turning his hand to the sheep. And then after a long day's work, back into his master's house, doubtless in need of a rest, he reappears as a cook and butler. We can imagine him being treated like the Spanish waiter, Manuel, who is rushed off his feet by the owner of the Torquay boarding house, played by John Cleese, who keeps his long-suffering waiter up to the mark by delivering frequent slaps on his face. Did the master in the parable thank the servant. No! Why should he? He was only doing his duty for which he was paid.

The 'entitlement culture'

It's been said that ours is an 'entitlement culture', where the focus is on rights, rewards, recognition. Disinterested service, freely given, for its own sake, without any thought of reward, is belittled. Of course, we would also hope that the master, to whom service is due, would show pleasure and thanks, but he is not obliged to do so and nor should it be expected of him.

The verses that precede our Gospel reading are addressed to the apostles and so it's been suggested that the parable is meant to focus on the Christian community and its leadership. Has the entitlement culture also permeated our church community so that those who work and worship in this voluntary organization expect acknowledgement, recognition and rewards for their service?

Who are we serving?

Once the co-ordinator of the flower arrangers in the church where I was vicar, a delightful woman, Doris, unwittingly tried to put me in their debt, saying that her team were doing all this for me. 'No,' I gently reminded her, 'you and I are doing what we do for God.' 'Let's just say,' she replied, 'we're doing this for each other.' Her correction is significant. It makes a world of difference if we think we're simply serving each other, in a human transactional relationship. Or whether we see our primary service to God for all we do. It's only when our hearts are set on serving God that we are weaned off our entitlement culture; that we cannot make claims on God or build up credit before him. When we have done everything we are still undeserving servants.

Role reversal

So, if we expect that people are thanked for coming to church, the choir is thanked for its services and the young people are automatically given a 'round of applause', might we just be feeding our culture of entitlement? And does it also turn worship into a stage for performers rather than a body lost in 'wonder, love and praise'? What if the whole congregation were to see themselves as worship leaders, some speaking, some praying, some overseeing the details? And for what purpose is the worship offered? The worship is intentionally offered to God. God occupies the place now occupied by the congregation. And the minister or priest? They are the choreographers. This, at any rate, was the suggestion of the Danish theologian Søren Kierkegaard. The suggestion has been taken up in different ways. In some churches that have liturgical colours, members of the congregation are encouraged to dress in the appropriate colours; some go further, and the scarf-like stole worn by the priest is passed round to the different people who pray and read.

An apprenticeship in service

What matters is that within the church we are weaned off the entitlement culture that distorts our relationship with God, and, instead, that we serve an apprenticeship in offering ourselves to God, through service, work and worship. Yes, of course, we will be quick to affirm, thank and bless others for who they are, as well as what they do. But we won't deceive ourselves that we can win God's thanks and praise. And then the really good news can break into our lives. In and of ourselves we are unworthy servants, but through Christ we become his friends, honoured, blessed, served by him who though Lord and King emptied himself and became the servant of all.

Roger Spiller

Hymn suggestions

Ye servants of God; Brother, sister, let me serve you; Teach me my God and King; Meekness and majesty.

Sixteenth Sunday after Trinity (Proper 22)
6 October
Second Service **Decisive Redress for Social Distress**
Ps. 142; **Neh. 5.1–13**; John 9

We were introduced to Nehemiah in last Sunday's reading. He's on leave of absence from his high-ranking post in Persia and on a mission in his home country of Judah to rebuild the city wall so that the citizens can regain their security, self-respect and hope after years of neglect. But the project draws fierce opposition from large sections of the community whose ringleader was Sanballat. After attempts to pour scorn on the whole enterprise, opponents made threats of violence on the builders. With prayer, and declaring trust in God's protection, Nehemiah stationed people in strategic places behind the walls with swords and spears and bows, so that half of the workers were assigned to protection duties, leaving the other half to get on with building the wall. Even that was no guarantee of security, and the builders themselves had swords at the ready while they worked, so no one was off guard, not even to permit a change of clothing.

The seeds of social unrest

While engaged with rebuilding, Nehemiah was met with a protest, the threat of social unrest, the charge that Jews were exploiting fellow Jews. If there was a single cause of the unrest, we're told it was the result of famine. That meant that subsistence families were forced to take out loans, mortgage land and property, and even sell their older children into slavery to raise money for food. But the family budget included a land tax, a temple tax, and even a clergy tax to cover the cost of clergy who numbered 10 per cent of the population. The building of the wall may have made things worse. The menfolk were taken off the land and farms in rural areas, so we find 'wives' are explicitly associated with the outcry. Of course their oppressors were not merely 'fellow Jews', although it made sense to show that they were 'flesh of our flesh'. They appear to have been Jews from a privileged stratum of the population, probably the more affluent Jews who had returned from Babylon. It was galling, then, for the Jews who had eked out a subsidence living during the miserable years in Judah to be confronted by wealthy Jews returning to their homeland, now that the country showed signs of improving, only to be exploited by these latecomers.

A time to blush

Nehemiah himself was in a delicate and potentially compromised position. He too was one of these wealthy Jews who had been parachuted back into Judah. It's no surprise, then, that when he addressed them he deflected criticism on to 'the nobles and officials,' a rather ambiguous, ill-defined segment of the population. When the complaint was against the increased land tax, Nehemiah might have blushed. It was, after all, the role of the governor, such as himself, to collect the taxes on behalf of the King of Persia and to add his own expenses, including a generous food allowance to cover his household. Nehemiah was therefore quick to declare that he had himself declined these perks, choosing instead to bear the cost of a very large and culturally diverse household.

The complaint of the poor was addressed with characteristic immediacy and passion by Nehemiah after due time of reflection. The offence was quite simply that they had failed to observe the legal exemption for the poor, whose property and offspring could not be seized against debt.

Handling injustice

We see the deft way in which Nehemiah decided to handle this potentially inflammable discontent. He called a gathering, a cross section of the population, secured popular support, isolated and shamed the offenders, and compelled them to take immediate action. His case was that, while he and his people had bought back his own people who had been sold to other nations, they were doing the exact opposite: selling their own people who then had to be bought back by Nehemiah and his people. This was wrong and was a betrayal of their trust in God. As to lending money and grain, Nehemiah declared that he and his people were lending money and grain, presumably with no interest, to shame the abusers.

The abusers were cornered and it was time for decisive action. 'Let us stop this taking of interest,' says Nehemiah, and then clinches his argument: 'Restore to them, this very day, their fields, their vineyards, and their houses, and the interest on money, gain, wine, and oil that you have been exacting from them.'

'This very day'

Are there not echoes here of the scales that are always weighted against the poor? What of the poorer families living in rented accommodation in big cities who are being displaced from their homes and forced to find alternative accommodation, separate from family and friends, so that greedy landlords can re-let their properties to local government for larger rent? What of the young and poor individuals seeking to escape their intolerable circumstances, who are preyed upon by charlatans posing as saviours but who are slave traders? What of the loan sharks whose exorbitant interest repayments have sentenced families to a life of desperation and debt repayment?

Nehemiah's attack on abusers of the poor succeeded. Those in the wrong immediately and unreservedly agreed to recompense all who had been exploited. And, to be sure, a binding covenant was administered by the priests. It was concluded with a liturgical act of emptying the folds or pocket of a robe, which carried the veiled threat of excommunication if the pledges were not delivered.

Nehemiah, while not a priest or prophet, had found the voice of prophecy. He exposed injustice and called for reparation to be made. The call cannot await inquiries, investigations, commissions, reports, white papers. 'Restore to them this very day' . . . that from which they have been robbed!

Roger Spiller

Hymn suggestions

Sing we a song of high revolt; Make way, make way; How firm a foundation; Brother, sister, let me serve you.

Seventeenth Sunday after Trinity (Proper 23)
13 October
Principal Service   **An Ecology of Praise**
(*Continuous*): Jer. 29.1.4–7; Ps. 66.1–11; *or* (*Related*): 2 Kings
5.1–3, 7–15c; Ps. 111; 2 Tim. 2.8–15; **Luke 17.11–19**

What happened to the young woman who came to me for advice
because, having become a committed Christian, she had her first
serious prospect of marriage with a man who wanted her to convert
to Judaism like himself? I didn't hear from her again.

What happened to the socially inadequate man who contacted
me every day for eight months after his wife threw him out of his
home, who needed my help to furnish another home, resurrect his
television repair business and agree a way forward? I didn't hear
from him again.

And what happened to the colleague who sought my advice on
her future career, and needed references? I didn't hear from her
again.

Ingratitude

We might have expected that people who've sought our help would
come back, update us on what developed and offer their thanks.
But they never did. But then we might all recall with alarm and
shame the occasions when we've not returned to express our thanks
to those who've been there for us.

There were ten men whose condition was so repulsive, socially
isolating and condemnatory that they were prepared to swallow
all their racial, religious and social prejudices in order to grasp one
last straw, and called out to an alien religious guru for healing. And
when they did as he said, and showed themselves to a priest, they
were released from their disease and their lives were transformed.

When just one of them turned back, and came to Jesus, Jesus
said: 'Were not ten made clean? But the other nine, where are they?'

Thankfulness is in short supply, it's the victim of a short memory. When we get what we want, we move on to the next thing.
Are you among the nine who do not return or the one who does?
Thankfulness is more than the politeness that causes parents to nag
their children: 'Now don't forget to say thank you.' 'Have you written your thank you letters?' Thankfulness spreads life and healing

around us. It disarms the carping, negative, fault-finding Victor Meldrew outlook on life.

All ten lepers were healed. God's goodness is unconditional. You can't earn it, don't deserve it, can't make up for it. Nor is God willing to play along with our childish bargains that dare to reward God for answers to our prayers.

Praise and thankfulness

All ten lepers were healed. The leper who returned didn't get an extra reward. But, says Jesus, 'Your faith has made you well.' Did you notice the first thing the man did when he saw that he was healed? He turned back to *praise* God. And only after praising God did he *thank* Jesus. Why does the sequence matter? Don't the two words add up to the same thing? Not quite. 'Thanks' is a response to someone for a named benefit that we have received from them. It does no more than acknowledge our indebtedness. But praise is different. The man addressed God not just in thanks for a blessing received but in praise to God for God's very self. He was taken out of himself and his restricted, contractual world of tit for tat, rights and rewards, strict reciprocity, and transported into God's realm of gift and grace. His whole world was gloriously enlarged and he was in a relationship with God, no longer a self-serving suppliant, but a son in a grace-filled relationship with his heavenly Father.

Made whole by praise

Praise directs us outwards, to the vastness of God's life and love. It erodes our self-centred preoccupations that shrink the limits of our world. And it blesses us with a capacious, generous, joyful spirit. There's even scientific evidence that suggests those who have the capacity to bless live better and longer, and cope better with sicknesses. Praise blesses people for who they are, not what they do. It's infectious, seductive, irresistible, evangelistic. Praising God sums up our Christian vocation. Being a people of praise is precisely what we're called to be.

We don't have leprosy, but we're still not fully healed until, like George Herbert, our heart pulses with praise. So may the pulse of our heart beat regularly to the sound of God's praise.

Roger Spiller

Hymn suggestions

To God be the glory; I am a new creation; O for a heart to praise my God; Praise to the holiest in the height.

Seventeenth Sunday after Trinity (Proper 23)
13 October
Second Service **Defusing Intimidation**
Ps. 144; **Neh. 6.1–16**; John 15.12–end

Nehemiah is on leave from his court duties in Persia as governor of Judah. The first task he set himself was to rebuild the city walls. He made a swift start, but last week we heard that the rebuilding was interrupted by a protest by poor and exploited Jews that he had to resolve. Now, it's back to the wall, so to speak. The wall is complete, except the doors have still to be hung. His opponents, led by Sanballat, have Nehemiah in their sights and try to ensnare and kill him.

A plot foiled

The first ruse was to tempt Nehemiah to a meeting. The place proposed was outside Judea and may have even been close to Sanballat's home. Nehemiah is quick to smell dark purposes, and naturally refuses. But I expect he derived some pleasure in his reply. He excused himself on the grounds that it would mean taking time out from building the wall. As he puts it, 'I am doing a great work and I cannot come down . . .' That they persist four times to organize a meeting shows their desperation, but the answer is always the same.

Fake news

So another device was needed. Sanballat writes a formal, open letter to Nehemiah. He accuses Nehemiah that he's building the wall as part of his plan to rebel and to make himself king, and that he's arranged for prophets to declare in Jerusalem that 'There is a king in Judah'. Of course it's a fabrication, fake news. But if there's even the smallest hint that a claim could just be credible, we know that it will have legs and run and run. News that the city walls were being rebuilt would certainly have raised fresh hopes that a messianic figure would appear.

Nehemiah's adversaries realize that nothing can be more certain to alienate and activate the existing powers than to threaten their power. It will be true of King Herod, true also of Governor Pilate and Emperor Caesar Augustus. It's reminiscent of the trumped-up charges of the opponents of Jesus. They selectively used his language even though they distorted it for their own purposes. It's fake news, as we say, but once given air time it's impossible to remove. Social media, the lure of brief, spontaneous, ill-considered communication can injure, distort and transport us to a virtual reality where truth need have no reference to reality beyond itself, but becomes the instrument to dispense pain, grief and bewilderment. Of course, Nehemiah stood firm, unyielding, fortressed by his God.

An assassination plot rejected

One more, final, attempt is made to ensnare Nehemiah. A man purporting to be a prophet, Shemaiah, declared that he had a prophetic message for him. Shemaiah was supposed to be confined to his house, so it's strange that he proposed a meeting with Nehemiah elsewhere, in the Temple, a meeting behind locked doors where, he suggested, Nehemiah would be protected from a planned assassination. Of course, as was his practice, Nehemiah sought to discern God's will and realized that Shemaiah had been a henchman hired by the ubiquitous Sanballat. As the courageous Nehemiah said: 'Should a man like me run away? Would a man like me go into the temple to save his life? I will not go in!'

Success at last

And now we hear the news that the wall is finished. Begun in the middle of July it was completed early in September, before the grape and olive harvest. It took only 52 days and was constructed in the heat of summer. Nehemiah had spent 12 years as governor before resuming his role in Persia. The walls helped to deliver security, although a deft arrangement for house patrols was also initiated by Nehemiah. But the security of the wall made it possible to build homes and encourage people to live within the perimeter wall.

Walls tell God's story too

We know that Nehemiah was a strict observer of the ancestral faith. He was opposed to its dilution, and to religious and moral laxity, targeting the widespread practice of mixed marriages. This had probably been necessary during the years after the exile, but now it put at risk the identity of the faith of Israel. In the last visit we make to the book of Nehemiah, we will see how another great figure, Ezra, a figure like Moses, sets about renewing faith in God. Meanwhile, there's a tantalizing comment on the effect of the rebuilt wall in the eyes of all the enemies of Nehemiah and the neighbours of Israel: 'All the nations around us were afraid and fell greatly in their own esteem; for they perceived that this work had been accomplished with the help of our God.'

Roger Spiller

Hymn suggestions

Lights abode, celestial salem; Come build the church, not heaps of stone; The Church's one foundation; Ye that know the Lord is gracious.

Eighteenth Sunday after Trinity (Proper 24)
20 October
Principal Service **Persistent Petitioning**
(*Continuous*): Jer. 31.27–34; Ps. 119.97–104; *or* (*Related*): Gen. 32.22–31; Ps. 121; 2 Tim. 3.14—4.5; **Luke 18.1–8**

So we're a nation of complainers – and that's official. That should give us sympathy for the widow in today's Gospel. She has a grievance. She feels she's been wronged. And the judge can't be persuaded to take any interest; he's totally indifferent to her plight. But she has a secret weapon, the capacity for persistent complaining. She's obviously been hounding him day after day, month after month, perhaps even for years, and finally he's worn down and relents.

We think of people who are aggrieved and pursue their search for justice over decades. Consumer complaints programmes mushroom. There was an angry tenant who wanted an injustice rectified by Birmingham City Council. She mounted her own protest outside the Council House, year after year, each day erecting billboards setting out the nature of her dispute, placed strategically around the civic area, until she won.

Now, Jesus' parable is not a licence to pursue petty, questionable rights for ourselves, nor to join the tidal wave of litigation. It's to commend persistence in our relationship with God, especially when we risk losing heart. The dogged, aggressive pursuit with God of something that matters deeply to us is commended by Jesus.

We can, as the Old Testament scholar Walter Brueggemann put it, have an exaggerated sense of ourselves that doesn't give God access, believing instead that we have to face life alone. But if we're religious folk, we're more likely to have an exaggerated sense of God that leaves no significant space for us in any relationship with God. 'Can the creature question the creator?' So we can become restrained, polite, dishonest in our relationship with God. What, you may ask, is the point of exhorting us to persistent complaint, lament and brazen language towards God?

Redistributing power

First, it redistributes power – speech is the exercise of power. You know how people who speak most in a group are always deemed more powerful and influential, even if what they actually say is less valuable than the contribution of quieter members. People who speak come into the picture, become noticed and usually get nominated to serve on committees. And people who are persistent, troublesome, awkward have to be reckoned with.

Well, petitionary prayer redistributes power, because it takes the petitioner seriously and engages God. The woman in the parable is a widow, a person who has been rendered powerless in ancient – and modern – society. She faces a powerful man, a judge, a man who presides over life-and-death issues. She has no claim on him, she's easily dismissed as just another troublesome petitioner, especially since he's quite indifferent to how people perceive him. But speech redistributes the power; the judge is mobilized to act because of the new-found power that the woman has discovered in the power of speech. The parable is billed as the antidote to losing heart, and losing heart comes through a sense of powerlessness, of being out of control, helpless in the face of chaos and meaninglessness. And we can regain our purchase on our life when we get into lively conversation with God.

When we persist in criticism, perplexity, petition, we are able to take the initiative with God, to develop our ego strength over against God, which is necessary for responsible faith. God doesn't want yes-men and yes-women – supine, obsequious, over-respectful. A consenting silence is no match for the tragic, harsh realities of life.

Mobilizing God

Not only does persistent speech and prayer redistribute power, it also makes a difference. It's been said that the reason we're enjoined to persist in prayer is not so that God can know our needs but that we can know them more deeply. Well, that's OK as far as it goes. It does change us too, enabling us to relinquish our anger and move on. But what's being said is that speech changes both parties. The voice of human hurt and hope evokes the presence and response of God. Our rage, anger, alienation not only changes us, it changes both sides of the relationship. It draws God freshly into the question; it mobilizes God to notice and face it in God's own way. The persistence of the woman made a difference not only to her but to her situation. God is contrasted to the judge, not by being unresponsive but by being more responsive to our cries.

Recall the incident of blind Bartimaeus. He shrieks out. He will not be silenced, and Jesus hears and heals him. The man's capacity to cry out and persist brings healing. Had he not persisted, he would not have come to new life. And the harsh, desperate cries of lament in some of the psalms of Israel elicit from God a caring, transformative response. God who has been silent is called back into conversation. God is not offended by such speech, but welcomes it and is moved to new possibilities because of it. God is drawn into the pain and anguish and injustice through our persistent prayers and protests.

We're given permission to engage God as our conversation partner through abrasive, defiant, daring speech. We're invited to put passion and realism into our prayers, to voice the grievances and injustices to God, and to recall him to his covenant responsibilities. This renews our prayers, our jaded Christian lives. What it did for the psalmists and prophets, the blind and sick men and women who petitioned Jesus, it can do for us. It can turn our complaints into unfettered praise.

Roger Spiller

Hymn suggestions

Restore, O Lord, the honour of your name; Father, hear the prayer we offer; We bring you, Lord, our prayer and praise; For the healing of the nations.

Eighteenth Sunday after Trinity   (Proper 24)
20 October
Second Service   **At the Water Gate**
Ps. [146] 149; **Neh. 8.9–end**; John 16.1–11

A hunger for the word of God

After the rebuilding of the wall, we're told, on a month designated for feasting, 'all the people gathered together in the square before the Water Gate'. The people took the initiative to assemble. But this was not a worship service. We know this because it was deliberately held in the public square, the Water Gate and not the Temple area. It was the heartfelt response of the populace, after the walls had been rebuilt. This was a popular, lay-inspired event, and it was they who decided the programme. It was for all the people, men and women and those who had the ability to understand. They instructed a man, Ezra, a priest, newly arrived at the head of a large number of Jews from Persia, formerly Babylon, to bring with him the book of the law to read to the people. Ezra, we're told, stood above the people on a wooden platform serving like a pulpit, where he could be seen by all the people. But he didn't stand there alone, in splendid isolation as priests might do today. Some 13 assistants stood with him. This was no clerical takeover. The laity were in charge, and they knew what they wanted. They wanted to hear the Scriptures read and explained. This was arguably the first sermon recorded in the Bible. And what an encouraging event it proved to be.

Attentive listening

When Ezra opened the book, we're told 'all the people stood up'; they rose in adoration. We do the same for the Gospel, but this was more like a standing ovation at a concert. And just as we do before preaching, Ezra invoked God's presence and blessed the Lord. Again spontaneity reigned, and the people responded, 'Amen, Amen'. Then followed bodily movements reminiscent of a charismatic gathering.

259

People lifted up their hands, they bowed their heads and they worshipped with their faces to the ground. Muslims will tell you that when they prostrate themselves for worship, they use nearly all the bones in the body, and having done it, it feels like a heavy workout. But, then, the meaning of worship – liturgy – is *ergo*, work, a total engagement of mind and body. Ezra read 'from early morning until midday', but the assembly was undaunted, attentive, responsive. The timescale would not have been sufficient for reading the whole of the five books of Moses, so extracts were doubtless selected. Ezra doesn't merely read the Bible, he interprets it and renders it understandable, which is the twofold character of preaching. The law had long been neglected, and Judah had declined into religious and moral laxity, but now they came face to face with the demands of God. Not surprising, then, was the reaction of the people: 'All the people wept when they heard the words of the law.' And we discover that the preaching leads into Bible study groups. The people who have been looking pretty on the platform with Ezra are lay people who move down into the congregation and work in groups with the assembly so that they can be sure that the law is understood.

Go out with joy

Now, if you read the text, you'll see there's another group who appear alongside this lay-led gathering, called Levites. Scholars think the editor of the text, who represents the interests of priests, has inserted them into the text to give them recognition. But Ezra, Nehemiah and the Levites are at one in sending people away. The people are transfixed and shocked by what they have heard, but they are told that this is no time for mourning, 'for the joy of the LORD is your strength'. Instead they are instructed to go and 'eat the fat and drink sweet wine', and in their excitement they must not forget the poor, or even those who've not got round to cooking. The event challenges the view that Jewish law is heavy, burdensome, joyless, about as exciting as reading a dictionary. But this huge gathering went home 'to make great rejoicing, because they had understood the words that were declared to them'.

A second serving

Next day it was the turn of heads of ancestral houses, with the priests and Levites, to have their study day. The specialists, like the clergy, prefer to come to something that's specifically arranged for them. So this second sitting enabled leaders to forget their roles, titles and status and to open themselves afresh to the demands of the law. And what this group discovered was a law that called the people of Israel to play, to enact over the course of a week the conditions in the wilderness period when God dwelt in a tabernacle and the people in booths.

Enacting the faith

If you happen to be visiting Jerusalem on the days before this festival, you are struck by a remarkable sight. Male Jews in black sartorial attire are hastily scurrying around with long planks of wood and sizeable tree branches to their houses. They're building temporary outdoor extensions to their homes where they will camp out with their families for seven days once a year. They will relive, at this Festival of Booths or Tabernacles, those same conditions as their ancestors.

We've seen in these brief readings from Nehemiah how he was God's chosen agent to save the community, bringing it recognized political status, security and good administration. But it needed Ezra to reform its inner life, which, with the providential support of a foreign king, he was able to achieve. Israel was no longer a nation, her national institutions could not be revived, but under Nehemiah and Ezra she had recovered her faith, which has continued to secure her future through great adversity.

Roger Spiller

Hymn suggestions

Stand up and bless the Lord; God in his wisdom, for our learning; Lord, be thy word my rule; You shall go out with joy.

Last Sunday after Trinity (Proper 25) 27 October
Principal Service **The Pharisee and the Tax-Collector**
(*Continuous*): Joel 2.23–end; Ps. 65 [*or* 65.1–7]; *or* (*Related*): Ecclus. 35.12–17, *or* Jer. 14.7–10, 19–end; Ps. 84.1–7; 2 Tim. 4.6–8, 16–18; **Luke 18.9–14**

Hearing the parable afresh

They say familiarity breeds contempt. In relation to the parable of the Pharisee and the tax-collector, familiarity certainly creates a problem. We tend not to connect with the sharp intake of breath it would have caused. 'Two men went up to the temple to pray, one a Pharisee and the other a tax-collector . . .' There he is, the Pharisee, up in the chancel. What is he like? He's an impressive guy. You only had fast on the Day of Atonement. This guy fasts twice a week. Deuteronomy instructs tithing grain, wine, oil and the firstborn from the flocks. This guy tithes on everything. He stands up and prays aloud in the Temple, just as is expected of such a professional religious man. His prayer is reasonable: he is not an extortionist, an adulterer or a tax-collector. He doesn't screw over his neighbours. Here is a virtuous, religious man. He has a sound religious pedigree.

In 587 BC the Babylonians trashed Jerusalem: Temple destroyed, sacrificial system scuppered, exile beckoning. How were the people to sing the Lord's song in a strange land? But they did: the biblical faith was kept alive by the Scribes (like Ezra) and the Hasidim – the spiritual forebears of our man.

By Jesus' day, under Roman occupation, what were the Pharisees up to?

Did they start bloody insurrections like the Zealots? No, they did not.

Did they run off to the desert like the Essenes. No, they did not.

Did they collude with the system like the tax-collectors. No, they did not.

Under occupation, the Pharisee tried to teach and keep the faith alive. When we read of the Pharisee, picture the nun working on a tough estate. Respected, regarded, right-on religious type.

How would Jesus' hearers have regarded a tax-collector? There he is by the door. With the weight of Rome behind him, he can bump up our taxes in order to cream off a percentage for his back pocket.

The reason you don't have enough money for medicine for your daughter is because he robbed you. You couldn't pay the temple tax last year (which incidentally made you unholy) because he ripped you off. Your family is barely subsisting because of our friend the tax-collector. That low-life scumbag is hand in glove with the Romans. Treacherous dog. Don't go near him; he's ritual filth. He enters the houses of unclean people, touches unclean objects and unclean money. Pond life. A no-good, low-down, double-dealing, rotten, fork-tongued, con artist. We have to get this, if we are to get the parable. Tax-collector – think loan shark swimming through the waters of that tough estate.

Taking a closer look

The Pharisee does seem a bit full of himself. In the Greek, the implication is that he is praying to or about himself. Is he really engaging with God? He compares himself to others in order to establish his position.

I remember a very good piece of guidance the Warden of Cranmer Hall gave to my year group when we started ordination training. 'Don't compare your marks to others.' He was an astute man; so many of us wanted to know how we measured up against our colleagues. 'Where am I in the pecking order?' This need to place ourselves in relation to others isn't limited to academic life. I am reminded of that sketch with John Cleese, Ronnie Barker and Ronnie Corbett: 'I look down on him because I am upper class . . .' What is this need to rank ourselves against others, if not pride?

At root, the Pharisee expresses pride that closes his eyes to the humanity of others and his ears to God. Virtue, puffed up and polished, is lethal. A small dose can inoculate us against God; that way death lies.

Jesse Jackson said, 'Never look down on anybody unless you're helping them up.' Beware of looking down on the Pharisee. Rather, let's look at him and see ourselves reflected back. Can you see your reflection in his eyes? There I am a little too full of my own importance, a little too Pharisaical. Can you see yourself? Who do we look down on? Jesus said: 'Do not judge, so that you may not be judged.'

The parable stings us and offers us honey. It is the sting that the elder brother knew; the foot-stamping it's-not-fair of the labourers who came early in the day; the slap in the face to religious self-righteousness. The honey comes as a balm to those who have known the loneliness, pain and shame of that far-off country. Have you ever really stuffed up, perhaps once, perhaps many, many times? That dreary cycle of wilfulness and failure, greed and need. Welcome to the tax-collector's world. This parable points to the grace of God offered to all who know their need of him, whether they are pushing through an ethical business deal, or cutting uppers with cement; lap dancing or praying; selling their body or preaching on a parable. 'There is no distinction, since all have sinned and fall short of the glory of God.'

Moving towards mercy

We are called to make the journey from saying like the Pharisee, 'God, I thank you that I am not like other people: thieves, rogues, adulterers, or even like this tax-collector', to the place where we can say like the tax-collector, 'God, be merciful to me, a sinner.' Then we can really sing the Kyries with integrity: Lord, have mercy; Christ, have mercy. And the wonder of it all is – he does.

Kate Bruce

Hymn suggestions

Empty, broken, here I stand; Amazing grace; And can it be; Faithful one, so unchanging.

Last Sunday after Trinity   27 October
Second Service   Singlemindedness
Ps. 119.1–16; Eccles. 11 and 12; **2 Tim. 2.1–7**; *Gospel at Holy Communion*: Matt. 22.34–end

'I'm too busy being a vicar that I don't have time to be a priest.' So said a colleague of mine. The 'priest', we should make clear, denotes a way of being, being for God and being for people, whereas a 'vicar' is the name of a role in a structure. The priest has functions, to be sure, but they spring from the deeper sources of their calling, whereas the vicar, chaplain, padre carries multiple, revisable and often interminably open-ended expectations. The comment is no less shared by other ministers. It is also a frequent complaint echoed by many 'professional' people who had a vocation for, say, teaching or medicine and find that other tasks have displaced their first love.

First things first

Some years ago, feeling the heat of remorseless diocesan responsibilities crossing a wide area, a verse from our Epistle reading hit me between the eyes: 'No one serving in the army gets entangled in everyday affairs.' In the image of a soldier, it's a warning against becoming distracted by home and business concerns. The context of Paul's letter makes clear that this reference is primarily to ministers. But this is not an attempt to stray into managerial advice. Instead, it makes a theological point concerned with singlemindedness to the service of Jesus Christ. Singlemindedness is, of course, a theme aired in Jesus' teaching – 'Seek first the kingdom of God' – and pours scorn on otherwise legitimate family duties that would usurp wholehearted commitment to his call to discipleship.

St Paul, for one, formulated and left no one in doubt about the purpose and priority of his divine commission. His missionary strategy has been shown to be realistic and coherent, while always open to revision at the dictate of the Holy Spirit. He could then have the satisfaction of recording that he had preached the gospel over an extensive area.

Temptation to diversify

Ministers and priests can find themselves deflected from their primary calling by the competing demands of different constituencies with whom they work. At a time of institutional decline the prospects for new diversifying and creative ministerial initiatives piles on additional pressure, and the popularist temptation to be showing our humanity and our relevance can lead to media-savvy but secondary and displacement activities.

Ministerial priorities

In a society that is fast losing its corporate memory of the Christian story, and where the need for Christian literacy is urgent and overdue, our text invites a reassessment by the local church community of the shape and core commitments of our ministers and priests. The local church has to be more concerned at the spread of the gospel than the safeguarding of its physical survival into the future.

In clarifying our core commitment, do we not need a greater emphasis on faith than on religion, and a greater attention to God than to the Church? One prescient thinker, F. D. Maurice, concluded: 'We have been dosing people on religion, when what they need is the living God.'

If we are to recover that singlemindedness required of us by our reading, this will involve space and acceptance for nurturing the hidden life of the priest or minister. If we are defined more by our interior life, we can be more secure in declining the external pressures that can displace our primary calling.

Redistributing responsibilities

Eugene Peterson, who has published some of the best books on ministry, describes how in the church of which he was a leader, he concluded that he was so locked into administration and 'running errands', as he called it, that he 'didn't have time to be a pastor'. So he decided to notify his church committee that he was leaving. As he explained: 'I want to preach, I want to lead the worship, I want to spend time with people in their homes. That's what I came here to do. I want to be your spiritual leader. I don't want to run your church.' The committee thought for a moment and then said, 'Let us run the church, and you be our pastor.'

Make room for the stones

A philosophy professor stood before his class with a big, empty bowl and proceeded to fill it with large stones. He asked the students if the bowl was full. They agreed that it was. He then picked up a box of pebbles and added them into the bowl, and they rolled into the spaces between the stones. 'Is the bowl full now?' 'Yes,' said the students. He picked up a bag of sand and poured it into the bowl. The sand slipped into the spaces between the rocks and the pebbles. Once more, he asked if it was full, and they said that it was. The professor then emptied two cans of beer into the bowl. The professor explained: 'I want you to recognize that this bowl represents your life. The stones are the important things in your life and the pebbles are the other things that matter. If you put the sand into the bowl first, there is no room for the pebbles or the stones. The same goes for your life. If you spend all your time and energy on the small stuff, you will never have room for the things that are important to you. Take care of the stones first – the things that really matter. The rest is just sand.'[24]

Roger Spiller

Hymn suggestions

Seek ye first the Kingdom of God; Teach me, my God and King; Fill thou my life, O Lord, my God; I the Lord of sea and sky.

Bible Sunday   27 October
Principal Service   **The Book that Reads Us**
Isa. 45.22–end; Ps. 119.129–136; Rom. 15.1–6; **Luke 4.16–24**

Mirror

The German sculptor Ernst Barlack produced a life-size wooden carving of Moses. He holds in front of him a large open Bible. You might expect it to depict Hebrew writing representing the Ten Commandments. But, instead, there is a plain, flat, bright, shiny surface. That tells us something crucial about the purpose of the Bible and the way we should use it. The Bible is there to help us to see ourselves. As the great Reformer John Calvin said, it is a mirror in which we see ourselves.

We read a book, listen to a concert or see a play to be entertained and perhaps, also, to be informed. But when the book, concert or play is a masterly work, we find that it becomes self-referential. We find ourselves being drawn in. We simply have to make connections with ourselves in order to appreciate it. And when we do, we find that our lives are being questioned, refreshed, changed, seen differently. It may affect our ideas, our mood, our hopes, and the aspirations we set for our lives.

A typical view of the Bible is that it is instruction for living: rules, teaching, advice. That's why we might have expected the sculpture of Moses to be holding out a page marking the Ten Commandments. That is true. St Paul says as much near the end of his letter to the Romans. But any 'instruction' can only be on the basis of the glorious, storied good news that occupies most of the letter. And, if it is instruction, its purpose is not to ensnare us into legalism. Its purpose, as Paul said, is to give us hope. 'Turn to me and be saved' – that's 'instruction' and command from Isaiah, our Old Testament reading.

Story

Barlack's depiction of the Bible as a mirror is surely correct. Most of the Bible is in the form of story, up to 87 per cent or more. And story, whether a play, book or even a concert, does its work by involving its hearers, drawing them into the characters and the plot so that we are able to see ourselves in a new light, inhabit different characters and make connections between the plot and the story-lines of our own lives.

It helps that a lot of stories are binary: Abraham and Isaac, Jacob and Esau, David and Goliath, rich man and Lazarus, Martha and Mary, Pharisee and publican, priest and Samaritan, prodigal son and elder brother. We can't sit on the fence. We simply have to make a choice, and often to switch from one to the other. And when we do, and feel irritated and hostile to the rich man, Martha, the Pharisee, the penny drops and we suddenly realize that we have inadvertently stepped into their shoes. Coming face to face with the story of our own lives can be too painful to see. But seeing ourselves in the narratives of Scripture, reading but also being read by the sacred text, can pierce our defences. The purpose of Scripture is not primarily information, but formation.

'Today'

In the account of Jesus' reading in the synagogue, Jesus chooses a portion of the Old Testament to interpret and identify his own vocation. The purpose of the Bible is, then, to direct us to Jesus and to let him address us. 'Today', he said, 'this scripture has been fulfilled in your hearing.' When we hear Jesus address us, it is always 'today', no matter how many times we have heard him before. The reading gathers up all our human hopes for peace, freedom, healing, liberation, and for hearing God's favour and love towards us. As poetry it activates the primary religious faculty, the imagination, through which we see God's alternative world of the kingdom breaking in among us. The purpose of the Bible is not information, or even formation, but transformation. And that begins 'today', when we let the Bible read us.

Those looking to the Bible for a neat and tidy presentation will have their work cut out. There are clashing images, Semitic exaggerations, competing and varied accounts of the same event. When we try to find sense and meaning, we encounter ambiguity; when we want clarity and closure, we find we have instead to live with a disturbing open-endedness. When we want to still the voice of Scripture that has wormed it's way into our minds, it keeps confronting us afresh.

The Bible you open will open you. Read the Bible, it will read you. 'My relationship to the Bible', says Barbara Brown Taylor, 'is not a romance, but a marriage. The Bible is my conversation partner, and it can and will answer us back.' Today, let it be yours.

Roger Spiller

Hymn suggestions

Break thou the bread of life; God has spoken – by his prophets; Come, Lord, to our souls come down; O for a thousand tongues to sing.

Fourth Sunday before Advent   3 November
Principal Service   **Where Am I in the Story?**
Isa. 1.10–18; Ps. 32.1–8; 2 Thess. 1; **Luke 19.1–10**

Where am I in the story? Am I the outsider, a senior tax-collector who is despised for being disloyal, greedy, extortionate, rich and – and this is not my fault, for being small – they call me 'Shorthouse'. Or am I one of the respectable people in the crowd, true to my faith and to my nation, moderate in my appetites, fair to others, no richer than I deserve to be and as tall as I want to be?

Jesus' call: welcomed or resented?

Jesus picks me out for special favour. He stops, looks up and calls me by name. He announces that he is coming to stay at my house. I climb down the tree and welcome him with tremendous joy. Or am I outraged? Jesus picks an outsider for special favour . . . someone who is rightly despised for being disloyal, greedy, extortionate, rich and short. I am not the only one who complains at the unfairness of it all.

'He has gone to stay at a sinner's house,' they said. We have all heard about other unfair things that he has said and done about respectable people: preferring lepers, tax-collectors, Samaritans, women – even immoral women – over people who deserve special honour for their religious and moral qualities, bringing shame on the honourable and honour on the shameful. And when he points out that he is going in to the house of a sinner, the man makes a great show of being a reformed character: 'I am going to give half my property to the poor, and if I have cheated anybody I will pay back four times the amount.' Jesus: 'Today salvation has come to this house, because he too is a son of Abraham. For the Son of Man has come to seek out and to save was lost.'

Outsider or insider?

If I am the outsider, the sinner, then the good news is that salvation has come to my house. I am accepted just as I am, simply because I longed for the salvation only he could bring. He has come into my house, shares my table and makes me, an outsider, into an insider to his grace and love. I am enabled to be a new person with a new relationship to others. Perhaps Paul was talking about people like me: 'God will make you worthy of his call, and will fulfil by his power every good resolve and work of faith.'

Or perhaps I am one of the objectors in the crowd, one of the respectable folk who habitually doubt the sincerity of the repentant sinner. One of the people who enjoys being on the inside nearly as much as I enjoy knowing that other people are on the outside.

I am both!

So, which am I? Of course I am both: older brother and a prodigal son, Pharisee and tax-collector, rich man and Lazarus, Zacchaeus and one of the despisers in the crowd. But whoever I am, Jesus can turn things around for me. The only difference between hypocrites and sinners in the gospel is that sinners know they are sinners and know they need salvation. If I want to be accepted, then I am accepted; he stops and looks at me and invites himself into my life. The Son of Man has come to seek and to save me when I was lost. But now I must be someone who recompenses others, a builder of justice in an unjust world. I am invited to share a meal with the Lord. He is coming to my house; he accepts me as the person I am, but does not leave me to remain the same. He gives me undeserved mercy and he enables me to act justly to others. Today, salvation has come to my house!

Duncan Macpherson

Hymn suggestions

The Spirit lives to set us free; I heard the voice of Jesus say; I come with joy, a child of God; O for a thousand tongues.

Fourth Sunday before Advent 3 November
Second Service **Searching for Lazarus**
Psalm 145 [*or* 145.1–9]; Lam. 3.22–33; **John 11.[1–31] 32–44**

It doesn't help that there are two characters called Lazarus in the Gospels. In Luke's Gospel, 'Lazarus' is the name of the beggar 'covered with sores' who lay at the gate of the rich man. Later in Christian history his name was adopted for leprosy hospitals, frequently called Lazar Houses.

Then there is Lazarus the brother of Mary and Martha. This Lazarus appears only in John's Gospel, but legends soon grew up around him. One legend states that because of persecutions he was forced to flee to Cyprus and there was made the first Bishop of Larnaca. Another legend says that he, Mary Magdalene and Martha were pushed on to a boat without sails or oars and set adrift in the Mediterranean. The boat miraculously made its way to Marseille where Lazarus became the first bishop. A variant of this legend has the boat landing in Provence on the beach of Saintes-Maries-de-la-Mer. And to add to the confusion, the legend of Lazarus features in a procession in a nearby town, Tarascon. Here, the Tarasque, a large and fearsome dragon, is hauled through the streets, the original having been tamed, it is said, by Martha. Even more confusion follows, because the procession now incorporates a jolly, corpulent man called Tartarin of Tarascon, the hero of a nineteenth-century French novel. It is all great fun.

All we can safely say, I guess, is that Lazarus was seen by the early founders of Christianity as an important figure because he was brought back from the dead by Jesus. It's not entirely surprising therefore that he was claimed as a patron saint by different communities around the Mediterranean.

A multi-layered story

But what can we, in our generation, make of the gospel account of Lazarus? It is a dense and multi-layered story. It interweaves a

271

series of sub-themes. For example, it features Jesus' strong emotions: he wept, he was deeply moved. It features the disciples in dialogue with Jesus, including Thomas who, thinking that Jesus' return to Jerusalem might well result in his violent death, urged the other disciples to follow him: 'Let us also go, that we may die with him.' It features a flash-back to the woman who had anointed Jesus and wiped his feet with her hair; it refers to the symbolism of light; it rehearses the motif of the disciples not understanding Jesus. It includes a brief exposition of the nature of resurrection, which provides the context for Jesus proclaiming, 'I am the resurrection and the life.' It reprises the complex relationship between Jesus and the Jews; it offers a description of the physical processes of bodily decay after death; it places the concept of the glory of God in the middle of the account and it concludes with Jesus' ringing shout: '"Lazarus, come out!" The dead man came out, his hands and feet bound with strips of cloth, and his face wrapped in a cloth. Jesus said to them, "Unbind him, and let him go."'

In such a many-layered story there is not one single message we can take from it. It requires us to reflect upon it, to think about it slowly; it is more like the condensed truths that we find in poetry than the truths we discover in prose.

Of course, there is a place for careful analysis of the story, but its power resides not in each detail but in the way the details reflect light on each other. It is like a brilliant, cut diamond whose facets illuminate all the other faces of the jewel.

Try another analogy: this time from painting. Imagine standing in front of a Rembrandt self-portrait. If we believe we can understand the power of that painting by analysing each individual brushstroke we shall fail to understand the painting as a whole. It is only as we allow each element in the painting to play upon all the other elements, and only as we allow the painting to play upon our minds and to enter our souls, that we can begin to glimpse what it is about.

It is exactly the same with John's story of Lazarus. The complex beauty of the story requires from us a thoughtful, time-enriched response. It cannot be rushed; it is not susceptible to instant understanding. It gently demands our attention – which it then repays.

The legends that our forebears created around the saints, and especially around Lazarus, for the most part do not have the complex beauty of a Rembrandt painting or a story by St John, but they may have a kernel of spiritual wisdom at their heart. But if we insist on analysing the legends without allowing our imaginations to play their part, we shall find ourselves disappointed. It is highly unlikely, of course, that Lazarus and his sisters actually drifted across the Mediterranean and landed in Provence, but if we are willing to be open-hearted and humble we may find that those legends point us, often with a humorous smile, to the rich and complex underlying truths of our faith. We recall the words of Christ: Jesus said to them, 'Unbind him, and let him go.'

Perhaps in our generation we need to learn that if we are to discover some of the rich and complex beauty of our faith and of God, our minds and hearts need to be liberated from our cultural shackles.

Christopher Herbert

Hymn suggestions

The Spirit lives to set us free; I come with joy, a child of God; Breathe on me, breath of God; And can it be.

Third Sunday before Advent   10 November
(For Remembrance Sunday, see p. 275.)
Principal Service   **A Happy Return?**
Job 19.23–27a; Ps. 17.1–9 [*or* 71.1–8]; 2 Thess. 2.1–5, 13–end;
Luke 20.27–38

He looked rather forlorn. It had been raining and mine was obviously not the first door on which he had knocked. With a damp smile meant to suggest both friendliness and conviction, he said: 'Don't you agree these are the last days?' Without pausing for reply, he went on to detail the terrible things going on in our world: wars, rumours of wars, destruction, pestilence and despair. Yes, indeed, all the signs are that God is about to roll up the map of human history.

He had, perhaps, been doing some revision at the Signs of His Coming website, which helpfully lists the 45 definitive indicators of Christ's imminent return. It concludes: 'I suggest you quickly enter into a relationship with Jesus Christ if you haven't already done so! He is coming soon! What must you do to be saved? Click here and find out!' Google tells me there are at least 12 million other websites dealing with the same topic.

Is Christ about to come back? A question asked by more people now than for many centuries. Perhaps you haven't thought about it? Perhaps it's not part of your working faith, as it were? Yet even us staid Anglicans say at almost every Eucharist, 'Christ has died: Christ is risen: Christ will come again.' Though some have told me that they can't say those words with much conviction, and they wonder what the declaration does to the uniqueness of Christ's incarnation.

Our reading from Second Thessalonians is just the kind of scriptural passage so many of those excited by the prospect of Christ's imminent return look to. Its instruction not to be deceived fits the idea of the generality of people fooling themselves. Its reference to the power of lawlessness seems to confirm people's sense of things being out of hand. And its declaration of annihilation from the mouth of the Lord Jesus reinforces the expectation of a coming fearful conflict. And yet its assertion of eternal hope and comfort is rooted in an already certain salvation. The Thessalonians are themselves the first fruits for salvation. Not that the day of the Lord is already here. But neither that nor what they already experience is entirely divorced from the end. So what are we to make of this sense of salvation present yet also expected?

Four thoughts: first, that much teaching about the return of Jesus comes across as profoundly selfish. The believer is portrayed as one snatched from the jaws of chaos with little thought for others, whereas the Thessalonians are encouraged to express their hope 'in every good work and word'. As first fruits they strive to live their hope socially.

Second, the Thessalonians are urged to recognize 'the mystery of lawlessness . . . already at work'. Whatever else these thoughts of the end are about, they are not about literal or proscriptive description. We do well not to be overly eager to use such passages as a straightforward account of reality. Truth and glory require of us more discernment than that.

Third, where's the incentive for action for righteousness if everything has already been decided? Again and again, Jesus tells his followers to be active in the cause of his kingdom. Isn't that the opposite of a resigned acceptance that on such and such a day everything is to end? We are urged not to be those who take pleasure in unrighteousness.

And fourth, Jesus clearly said that no one knows the time of his return. Haven't there been wars and rumours of wars in every age? Might not the feeling that everything is worse than before be simply a matter of perspective?

274

Does that mean we dispense with the idea of Christ's return? Certainly not! Two great and abiding truths are guarded by the doctrine. History, it says, has a meaning and direction that has its source and ultimate goal in Jesus. This isn't just about our own destiny as individuals. We are to lift our eyes to the vision of the whole of humanity having its end in Christ. Glory indeed! And second, it assures us of what that journey towards glory looks like. We look to Christ's way of being and doing as the shape of the way we should do and be. If Christ's first coming shows us what life can be in its wholeness, then the second coming assures us that in the end Christ's way of being and doing prevails.

So yes, there is something hanging over us, but it is the cross of a God of infinite love, not a mushroom cloud of annihilation. Stand firm; hold fast – away with despair, cynicism and fatalism. Live for today in the confidence of where history is going, and leave the determination of time and end to God, who alone knows. Stand firm in hope; live righteousness; be the first fruits of salvation here and now. That gives a whole new meaning to looking forward.

Christopher Burkett

Hymn suggestions

O God of Bethel, by whose hand; God is love, his the care; Now let us from this table rise; At the name of Jesus.

Remembrance Sunday   10 November
Remembering

(The readings for the day, or for 'In Time of Trouble', or those for 'The Peace of the World' can be used. The readings for the Second Service of the Day are used here.)
Ps. 40; 1 Kings 3.1–15; Rom. 8.31–end; *Gospel at Holy Communion*: Matt. 22.15–22

Conflict[25]

I tried to imagine what I'd feel like if my son Patrick were called up to fight in a war. Those would be dark days for me. I know I'd be afraid – afraid that he wouldn't come back, or that he would come back, but permanently maimed in either body or spirit. I know I'd be afraid for the future as well as for him – for the sort of a life there will be for all of us if the world goes on like this, and if the world keeps forgetting. But the burning question is, 'What will I do with my fear?' I know, too, that I'd be angry; angry that my son's whole life is rearranged against his will; angry that he could be gun fodder; angry that grown men and women can't make peace round a table; angry that ideologies take precedence over human lives; angry when I hear the violence of war glorified. I'd be very angry! But what will I do with my anger?

Complication

And why aren't I angry now? Since 1945, British servicemen and -women have been engaged in 80-odd mini-wars, and there are dark days now somewhere in the world – civil war in Somalia, religious war in Afghanistan, tribal war in Darfur. At this very minute, perhaps, someone else's son or daughter is being killed or maimed in one of the armed conflicts happening somewhere, right now. The young British or American woman stationed in Iraq; the Iraqi bystander caught up in the crossfire; the Israeli and the Palestinian young men who throw stones or grenades at each other on dark street corners; the youngster who ties a bomb to his waist and blows up 15 people – including himself; the extremist who shoots the abortion clinic doctor in cold blood. These are dark days indeed, and spine-chillingly so, when people believe their actions carry the stamp of divine approval.

But violence is not only on the fields of war; it's everywhere. In a house not too far away there's an abused child; further down the street a battered woman; round the corner a mugger waiting to pounce on the old man shuffling home. In a place not too far away, in these days of instant news, there's a persecuted minority; in this place it's women; in that place it's Jews or Muslims, somewhere else it's Christians; and elsewhere again it's gay people.

These are dark days. What are the children of light doing – the followers of the Light of the World? How are we letting our light shine? I'm fearful when it's my son, when it's my back yard. I'm angry when it's my son. And, if I'm not careful, the darkness deepens, and the light remains under the bushel basket. So what do I do with my fear and my anger? In my better moments, of course, I do find that deep within myself I am also fearful – I am also angry – on behalf of others and their mothers. But the question remains: as a child of the light, as a follower of Jesus Christ, what do I do with them?

Martin Niemöller was a Lutheran pastor who stood up to Hitler. In the 1930s, he went with a delegation to meet Hitler and, being a young man, he stayed at the back of the room and watched and listened. When he got home, his wife said, 'What did you learn today?' He said, 'I learnt that Herr Hitler is a very frightened man.' That fear led to war, oppression and genocide.

Sudden shift/reversal

Brother Roger of Taizé was murdered a few years ago. He feared for the future – not for himself, but for the world. During the Second World War, he hid Jews and helped them to reach safety. But after the war, he gave house room to Germans and offered them a part in a future where peace and reconciliation could triumph. Brother Roger's fear led to peace-making efforts and reconciliation.

Sadako was afraid, too. She lived near Hiroshima and was badly burned. In the hospital, she was taught how to make origami figures, and her favourite was the crane. An old Japanese legend said that anyone who faithfully made 1,000 cranes would have their wish fulfilled. So Sadako began folding. Her wish? To get better. Then she realized that wasn't going to happen, so she changed her wish and began to pray for peace between nations. As she finished each crane, she whispered to it: 'I write peace on your wings; fly all over the world.' Sadako only completed between 600 and 700 cranes, before she died. But other children learnt of her wish, and if you visit the Hiroshima Peace Park any year on 6 August, thousands of paper cranes are suspended from the tower. Sadako's fear for the future became an initiative for peace. A drop in the ocean perhaps, but meaningful nonetheless. Which is important for us.

Unfolding – so what?

Today we remember the past – we give thanks for our freedom and for those who paid the price with their lives, or their physical or mental health. But all that remembering is mere sentiment, unless – unless, as children of light, as followers of the Light of the World, we let our light shine: we let our fear and our anger be channelled; we work and pray for peace and for justice; we support the peace-keepers and the peace-makers. The sort of peace that includes the absence of war, but is far more than that – the peace of God that goes way beyond our understanding. I know that my fear and my anger won't amount to many drops in the ocean. But I can be responsible for making sure that they do go in the ocean, and that they're contributing towards a just world at peace.

Barbara Steele-Perkins

Hymn suggestions

For the healing of the nations; Jesus Christ is waiting, waiting in the streets; O God, our help in ages past; Lord of lords and King eternal.

Second Sunday before Advent   17 November
Principal Service   **Digging for Truth**
Mal. 4.1–2a; Ps. 98; 2 Thess. 3.6–13; **Luke 21.5–19**

In 1864 a young British officer in the Royal Engineers called Charles Wilson undertook work with the Ordnance Survey in Jerusalem. He discovered a large stone structure, now known as Wilson's Arch, which he believed had carried a road from the Old City directly on to the Temple Mount. Just three years later in 1867 he was followed by another officer from the Royal Engineers, Charles Warren, who continued to survey Jerusalem and began a series of exploratory archaeological digs under the Western Wall of the Temple.

In 1867 Warren crawled along some tunnels near the Gihon spring and discovered a large vertical shaft, now known as Warren's Shaft. It was another breakthrough in understanding the construction of the Temple Mount.

Since those mid-Victorian times the work of excavation under the Western Wall has continued on and off over the decades, depending on local political circumstances. But now it is possible for visitors to go into the tunnels and excavations, and literally walk down through the layers of Jerusalem's history.

Among the most astonishing discoveries made by archaeologists was the Master Course. It consists of four huge blocks of stone, the largest of which is 44.6 feet long, approximately 11.5 feet deep and 11 feet high, and is estimated to weigh about 628 tons. It was put in place by the builders of the Temple working under the authority of Herod the Great, and was constructed with such precision that no mortar was used to cement one block of stone to another. The Master Course was designed to act as a stabilizing countervailing thrust for a vault underneath the Temple Mount.

But in AD 70 the stones on top of the Master Course were toppled from their original positions by Roman soldiers under the leadership of Titus. They besieged Jerusalem and destroyed the Temple. Some of those stones still litter the ground nearby. The destruction was in response to a Jewish revolt, and the destruction of the Temple was the Roman equivalent of 'shock and awe'. Thousands of Jews were killed, and many thousands were carried into captivity. It was the end of the Temple – and, symbolically, the end of the Promised Land.

The magnificence of the Temple

Which brings us to today's Gospel reading. You will recall that someone had pointed out to Jesus the magnificence of Herod the Great's Temple. It was indeed a remarkable sight, but Jesus prophesied that it would be destroyed and that not one stone would be left upon another.

But this leaves biblical commentators with a problem. Did Jesus actually prophesy the destruction of Jerusalem, or might Luke, as he was writing his Gospel, having heard about that destruction by Titus, put the words into the mouth of Jesus? The answer, of course, depends upon the date attributed to the actual writing of the Gospel, and that is disputed.

The imagery that Jesus was using in this chapter could well have been drawn from other sources, from the long tradition of highly coloured apocalyptic writing that was, unsurprisingly, in vogue at the time. After all, if the country you believe has been promised to you by God is under military occupation by a foreign power, you have to try to make theological sense of it. Strong and vivid theological language about God's overarching sovereignty and his ultimate control of history had a strong appeal. The disciples were aware of this, hence their question to Jesus about when God would show his divine hand and restore Israel. Were they living, they wondered, in what were called the endtimes? Would the universe be rolled up like a scroll and the new reign of God begin?

Well, we know that the entry of God into history as had been long imagined did not happen. Certainly the Temple was destroyed, and certainly there were wars and rumours of wars, but the promised denouement couched in technicolour terms did not occur. Instead, a man was killed by crucifixion on a hill outside Jerusalem.

Recovering from the blow

It was a shattering blow to the thought-world of the apostles. Having grown up on stories and prophecies about the moon turning to blood, stars falling from the skies, and the sea surging uncontrollably, when none of this happened and when their beloved teacher had been killed, what were they to make of the way things had turned out?

They went through a change in their thinking the scale of which we find almost unimaginable. Their whole mental universe had come crashing down and they were left to pick up the pieces. Everything had to be reconstructed.

But what they discovered with fear and trembling and head-over-heels joy was that Jesus had risen from the dead. His presence with them and the prodigal gift of the Holy Spirit took them on an entirely new and totally unexpected journey. It was as radical and as wonderful as being born again. They learnt a new theological language. They created new forms of communal relationships. They saw the world in an entirely new way, a world that could never be the same again.

We are the heirs of that immense mental and spiritual shift . . . and we are truly blessed in being so.

Christopher Herbert

Hymn suggestions

Sing to God new songs of worship; You are the King of Glory; For the healing of the nations; Ye that know the Lord is gracious.

Second Sunday before Advent   17 November
Second Service   **Steadfast in the Faith**
Ps. [93] 97; **Dan. 6**; Matt. 13.1–9, 18–23

> 'Be sober, be vigilant, because your adversary the devil, as a roaring lion, walketh about, seeking whom he may devour: whom resist, steadfast in the faith.'

This sentence from the first letter of Peter, in traditional language, is often used at the evening office of Compline. It forms a prayer of protection that keeps prowling lions at bay during the night. It encourages each one of us to resist them and stay steadfast in the faith even as we sleep. It's appropriate to relate these words to the incredible reading from the book of Daniel. The tale of Daniel and the lions is one of those biblical stories that is memorable and dramatic, often told to wide-eyed children anxious to hear whether Daniel will be eaten alive or protected by God.

It's a story about a hero whose faith overcomes all things, even protecting him from the jaws of a hungry predator. It's easy to be dazzled by the drama of the unfolding narrative, but at its heart there is a simple message. This is a story about what faith can do.

Daniel is good and honest. He is a God-fearing man, but he is beset by the corruption and hatred of those around him. They are seeking to trick him and destroy his life. Daniel is described as 'faithful', and the evil desires of those who are jealous of him come to nothing at first, so they have to raise their game. The only way they can unsettle Daniel is to undermine his faith in God; indeed, they try to make his faith a criminal offence in the kingdom. Daniel resists his adversaries prowling around and clawing at him, and he ends up in the middle of the lions' den, putting his life in God's hands. Will Daniel survive the night?

What can faith do?

In his teaching, Jesus often talks about the power of faith. Your faith has made you well, he says to those who come to him for healing. He also describes how faith the size of a mustard seed can move mountains. In the parable of the sower, Jesus speaks of how faith can bear much fruit. Once again, we are given an image of an 'evil one' prowling around and snatching away the seed that is planted in the heart. There are other temptations, too, that devour the seeds of the kingdom. The cares of the world, times of trouble and persecution, the lure of wealth – these things are like roaring lions seeking their prey, ready to gobble up the first green shoots of faith that emerge from the earth.

Only those seeds planted in good soil, or in a steadfast heart, are able to flourish. Daniel is one such person in whom faith is strong, whose faith has the power to move mountains and shut the mouth of lions. Daniel is described in the Letter to the Hebrews as one of the heroes of the faith. The writer goes on to say that we have been given an even greater promise in Jesus Christ, which will make us all more than conquerors. Christ is the sign of God's faithfulness to each one of us. In him we find the strength to nurture our faith and let it grow and blossom and shine; in him alone we are protected from the evil one and from vicious predators without and within.

We can also be encouraged by those whose faith in Christ has made them strong enough to resist evil, and to do what is good;

witnessing to the glory and might of the Lord of heaven and earth just as Daniel did. We are surrounded by a great cloud of witnesses whose faith provides encouragement for our own.

We are all sometimes challenged by things that beset and besiege us. These things might not take the form of a prowling lion, but there is plenty in our world today to undermine and threaten our faith – hatred, malice, gossip, persecution, corruption, scepticism, apathy, to give a few examples. It is also sobering to remember that Christians are still persecuted for their faith. As they are steadfast in their faith and witness to the living God, we must honour them by being steadfast in our prayers and confident in what faith can do.

Great is his faithfulness

The word 'steadfast' is not a fashionable word, but it is one that Christians must hold on to. It reminds us that we need strength to live out our faith. It takes courage to be a Christian in the world today wherever we are. We can, though, also be reassured that God is steadfast in his promises to us.

At the end of the story, after a worrying night, King Darius awakes in the morning to find that Daniel is alive and has been spared. King Darius makes a proclamation to the whole world about the God whose steadfast love endures for ever and saved Daniel from the mouth of the lions. 'For he is the living God, enduring for ever. His kingdom shall never be destroyed, and his dominion has no end. He delivers and rescues, he works signs and wonders in heaven and on earth.'

Thanks be to God for his faithfulness and his steadfast love for us, which are new every morning and endure for ever and ever.

Victoria Johnson

Hymn suggestions

Great is thy faithfulness; Have faith in God, my heart; Before the ending of the day; O Jesus, I have promised.

Christ the King   24 November
(Sunday next before Advent)
Principal Service   **Jesus, Remember Me!**
Jer. 23.1–6; Ps. 46; Col. 1.11–20; **Luke 23.33–43**

We're in the kingdom season – the season filled with 'remembering' – and today we celebrate the feast of Christ the King. On this, the last Sunday of the Church's year, just before we plunge into the watching and waiting of Advent, into the extraordinary mysteries of the incarnation at Christmas, into the splendours of Epiphany, we take a deep breath and celebrate Christ as King over time and eternity. We remind ourselves, before we begin the Christian story again, that Christ is Sovereign Lord in all things. Christ, who is, and was, and is to come.

The promised king

The Old Testament prophets, like Jeremiah, spoke out against the leaders of Israel in their day – particularly King Zedekiah, but others too. Instead of shepherding the people, these leaders were driving the people away from faith. Instead of leading with integrity they caused fear and mayhem. Through Jeremiah, God declares that he will step in and lead the flock himself. Jeremiah prophesies that a new king will arise – one who will exercise wisdom, justice and righteousness. Israel will live in safety. Judah will be saved. That is the shape of the leadership to come. Jeremiah sees this as a new and mighty King David – remembering a hero of old.

God's radical response

But God never does things quite as we expect. Yes, he steps in to lead his people in the person of Jesus Christ in whom all the fullness of God was pleased to dwell. Jesus exercises wisdom and justice and righteousness – but there are some surprises in this new king. Not least that he ends up crucified as a common criminal – an unthinkable event for Israel. What sort of king is this King of the Jews? A sick joke, surely! God's idea of kingship turns our human understanding upside down. Jesus is a king in a new mould, who champions the lowest and the least, who spends quality time with the dregs of society, who has nowhere to lay his head, who sits light to the trappings of the Temple, who teaches and heals, breaks down barriers and gives away power. This is a king who saves his people by sacrificing himself. This is radical kingship.

Different reactions

Faced with this new idea of kingship, people react in different ways. Take the two criminals crucified with Jesus. One looks at the crucified Christ and derides and mocks him: 'Are you not the Messiah? Save yourself and us!' He embodies the angry and cynical approach to Jesus that we meet so often in our society – 'If there's a God, why is there all this suffering; why doesn't he do something about it?' The other criminal, faced with the suffering Christ, is overcome with a huge sense of guilt and asks for forgiveness and a place in Jesus' realm – 'Jesus, remember me when you come into your kingdom.' *'Re-member me'* – put me back together again, make me whole, make me one with you. In Christ all things hold together.

As the body of Christ in this place we should be on the look out for those reactions as people come to seek for Jesus – and be prepared to work with them. To help people express their anger with God and introduce them to some of the mystery. We don't have all the answers – we never will in this life – but we have hope and we believe. And then for those who feel guilt that they have moved away from God, we can make them welcome, make them realize that Jesus longs to bring them home, and that we long for the body here to be 're-membered'.

Wisdom, justice and righteousness

If we are a community who lives under the kingship of Christ, and has a part within that kingship, then we too need to exercise wisdom and justice and righteousness.

- Wisdom that realizes that faith is not black and white, that people are complex and that God is full of surprises and calls us to grow and to change.
- Justice that all may be equal in the sight of God irrespective of age, gender, ability, sexual orientation, race. We are to be a just community that champions the oppressed and fights for the least.
- Righteousness – a community of integrity and truth, whose behaviour is transparent and filled with the Holy Spirit, those who long for God to make peace and reconcile all things.

Wisdom, justice and righteousness – and there's more. Those of the kingdom who see Christ as their King must be prepared to sacrifice themselves so that others may be saved by Christ: to stand back and let others come forward; to go out of their way to welcome

284

strangers; to speak of Jesus, however risky; to go the extra mile for those in need.

In the next few weeks during the Christmas season we will receive many visitors and guests into our fellowship, and it's very important that as the members of the body of Christ we are welcoming and hospitable, inclusive and open to the outsider and stranger making their way to see something of Jesus. Let's not get in the way or mislead those who tentatively try to reconnect with God and are hoping that Jesus will remember them.

So let's keep on encouraging people to seek for God. Let's demonstrate that this is a community that believes Christ is King deeply and takes his kingship seriously, and let's go out of our way in the coming season to help people say: 'Jesus, remember me when you come into your kingdom.'

Catherine Williams

Hymn suggestions

Christ is the King, O friends rejoice; Crown him with many crowns; Christ reigns triumphant; Lord enthroned in heavenly splendour.

Christ the King Sunday   24 November
(Sunday next before Advent)
Second Service   **The Leadership of God**
Ps. 72 [*or* 72.1–7]; **1 Sam. 8.4–20**; John 18.33–37

Throughout the Old Testament we are confronted with the people of God's insistent and feverish desire to be like other nations. They hanker after their gods and their customs. They easily abandon their own ways. Most of all, they want a king to reign over them.

At the same time, we also see God's steadfast desire for them to be different. Their vocation isn't to be *like* the nations, but *a light* to the nations.

This determination to have a king reaches its climax in our reading from 1 Samuel. The reasons given are small-minded and graceless. 'You are old,' they say to Samuel, 'and your sons do not follow in your ways; appoint for us, then, a king to govern us, like other nations.' That, of course, is the crux of the matter.

Not that the period of the judges had been such a huge success. But it was part of that distinctive pattern of life and leadership that set Israel apart.

Samuel is crestfallen. He is indeed an old man. But he is rich in wisdom and he has served them faithfully. He feels rejected.

God speaks to him, making the true duplicity of the people's insistence plain: 'They have not rejected you', says God, 'but they have rejected me from being king over them.'

This is the point: it isn't that Israel had no king; Yahweh, the Lord, was king. But they want another.

Moses and Joshua and the judges that followed them were not kings over Israel, but emissaries, charged with the great responsibility of leadership, but called to exercise that leadership in a way that was radically different from the practice of other nations, who gathered pomp and power to themselves and made everyone else their subject.

God tells Samuel to allow their request. It is as it has always been and probably always will be. The people of God turn their backs on the ways of God. 'From the day I brought them up out of Egypt to this day,' says God, they forsake me.

But God asks Samuel to give them one last warning: tell them how the kings of the nations actually dispose their duties. The king will take for himself what is yours, says Samuel. Your sons he will enlist in his armies; your daughters will serve him. He will make himself powerful. He will tax your grain and your wine. The best of your vineyards and olive orchards will be his; so, too, your cattle and your donkeys, your flocks and your slaves. In short, he will be a despot. This is what you are choosing.

But the people refuse to listen to the voice of Samuel. 'No,' they say, 'give us a king.'

Blessed are the meek

It is a desperately sad passage of Scripture. We witness not just Samuel's despair, but God's. It is not that kings are by definition corrupt. But it remains the case today, that any person who is given unchecked power can easily become very dangerous. The best leadership is always exercised by those who know how to be led and who are obedient to an agenda higher than their own. Isn't this what Jesus means when he says, 'Blessed are the meek'? A meek person is one whose leadership – be it a nation, a football team, a business or a family – is governed by the disciplines of service and duty, and who is more aware of the responsibilities of their office than the perks and powers that may also be available and are always waiting to seduce and corrupt. Meekness – the meekness we see in Jesus and Moses (incidentally, the only people in the Bible to be described this way) – is a leadership and lifestyle that God says could be a light to the world. By rejecting these high ideals, that light is dimmed.

It will go wrong, warns Samuel. Then you will cry out to God and God will not answer you.

Though here, perhaps, choked by disappointment, Samuel goes a little too far.

The story of Israel does go from bad to worse. Good kings fail. Often bad kings replace them. The kingdom itself is divided and then conquered. Jerusalem falls, and the people are taken into exile. They were indeed like other nations: badly governed; at war with themselves; unable to do what they knew was right; condemned to repeating the mistakes of the past; and sinking in the quicksand of their own stubborn failings.

But God did answer them. He did reassert his own kingship over them – but in the most surprising way.

Christ our King

Today the Church celebrates the feast of Christ the King. It is the last day of the Christian year. We end it by declaring that God has acted in our world to establish his rule of justice and peace by making his Son, our Saviour Jesus Christ, Lord and King. He does this by entering into the quicksand of our failures himself and raising us up. At the same time he shows us that kings – and the kingship of God – is not at all as we thought it.

Pilate asks Jesus, 'Are you a king?' Jesus answers, 'Is that your idea? My kingdom is not of this world.'

But Jesus could equally have said, my kingship is not like the kingship of this world. Just as Jesus shows us what humanity is supposed to look like, so he shows us what leadership should be. For a throne, Jesus the King has a wooden cross. For a crown, Jesus the King has twisted thorn. For a royal sceptre, Jesus the King has a sword piercing his side.

Through his cross and resurrection, Jesus saves us from the consequences of aping the world and thinking we know best. He shows us the true nature and extent of God's love for us. And in becoming king, demonstrates a way of servant leadership from which both Church and world still have much to learn.

Stephen Cottrell

Hymn suggestions

Rejoice, the Lord is King; The King of Love my Shepherd is; Servant King; Lead us, heavenly Father, lead us.

Sermons for Saints' Days and Special Occasions

St Stephen, Deacon, First Martyr   26 December
Hello God, Are You There?
2 Chron. 24.20–22, *or* **Acts 7.51–end**; Ps. 119.161–168; (*if the Acts reading is used instead of the Old Testament reading, the New Testament reading is* Gal. 2.16b–20); Matt. 10.17–22

Do you ever find yourself looking at life's troubles and wondering where God is? South Sudan, Syria, Afghanistan, your own personal civil wars. Is God there? Perhaps our readings today can renew our faith in the transforming presence of God in all circumstances. The passage from Acts is full of contrasts – the hideous and the hopeful, the demonic and the divine, ferocity meets forgiveness. In the blue corner we have Stephen, handling himself with striking grace, and lurking near the red corner, doing the metaphorical equivalent of holding the spit bucket, we find Saul. This reading opens a window on to the sheer nastiness of which humanity is capable, and at the same time the clouds part and we see the transformative power of God enabling Stephen to endure. God is right there – in the midst of darkness, bringing transformative possibilities.

Is God at work here?

Quick flashback. In Acts 6, Stephen is described as being of good standing, full of the Spirit and of wisdom and faith. Like Jesus, Stephen performs wonders and signs. Like Jesus, he gets under the skin of his opponents and bests them in debate. Like Jesus, Stephen is a man who provokes violent response from some. Stephen's enemies despise him with a venomous passion. They scheme against him with false accusations of blasphemy. Throughout Acts 6 and 7, the clouds are massing and darkness thickens. Suddenly, Stephen is confronted, bounced before a kangaroo court, falsely accused as a blasphemer. The situation is dire. 'O God . . . are you there?' And yet at the end of Acts 6 we read that Stephen's face 'was like that of an angel'. God is at work here.

There may be trouble ahead

The camera zooms in on Stephen just as he has finished his powerful speech before the religious leaders. His final note, full of prophetic ire, accuses his hearers of being stiff necked, in opposition to the Holy Spirit, betrayers and murderers of God's chosen one. Not subtle! There may be trouble ahead. The hearers are enraged, and the storm breaks. The seething cauldron bubbles over. More contrast. We see the people grinding their teeth in fury, and Stephen full of the Spirit gazing into heaven. In the midst of terrible trouble God comes and opens Stephen's eyes to the great backdrop against which all our lives are played out. Stephen sees the Son of Man standing at God's right hand. He points to Jesus as judge and ruler over all. His hearers plug their ears and howl in fury at this. But Stephen, supported by God's vision, keeps on treading in his Master's footprints. There may be trouble ahead, but God is present.

Hope meets the hideous

The people, boiling with a hideous red-hot indignation, drag Stephen out of the city, echoing Jesus' journey to Golgotha. They pick up stones and hurl them at Stephen. Hear the sounds: 'whump', 'crack', 'smack', as the missiles hit Stephen's head and body. Brutal. Horrible. Violent. Human nastiness at its worst. However, far from being a cowering wreck, Stephen is presented as a picture of calm. While they are stoning him, he prays, following the footprints of his Master, handing over his spirit to Jesus and asking that his murderers might be forgiven. The demonic will not have the last word. Stephen, in his death, communicates something powerful: God is the God of transformative, empowering hope.

Human life can be taxing and tough, but the story doesn't end there. Human death can be violent and horrific, but the story doesn't end there. A young Saul holds the coats and nods approvingly . . . but the story doesn't end there. Jesus will be a stone that makes Saul stumble in his righteous certitude. The bully-boy bystander will become a key person in the creation of God's holy nation. A staggering reversal.

What a picture of hope in the face of the hideous. With God there is always tomorrow – even a tomorrow that awakens us on a different shore.

With God there is always tomorrow

For those who know illness, despair, opposition, violence, loss, our readings call us to look for the transformative presence of God. In South Sudan, Syria, Afghanistan, in our own personal civil wars, we can hold on to hope. God is present in all circumstances. When we tread the way of Jesus we see beyond the immediate. OK, we are not Stephen. We are just ordinary, fallible, not so eloquent, not so strong as Stephen, lacking his faith and courage. Like Thomas we question and doubt, like Phillip we fail to fully grasp who Christ is and what he shows us. But to their followers, Jesus offers his words of assurance, as he does to us: 'I am the way, the truth and the life.' With him, whatever we face, it is never the end of the story. With God there is always tomorrow.

Kate Bruce

Hymn suggestions

Stephen, first of Christian martyrs; Jesus the Lord said, I am the way; For all thy saints, O Lord; Morning glory, starlit sky.

St John, Apostle and Evangelist   27 December
The Beloved Disciple
Ex. 33.7–11a; Ps. 117; 1 John 1; **John 21.19b–end**

Today we commemorate the work of St John the Evangelist, this self-effacing figure about whom we have little reliable knowledge except for his legacy of the Gospel, Epistles and the Apocalypse. Matthew and Luke give us the wonderful Christmas stories with all their myth, legend, wonder and mystery – the angelic messenger, a pure virgin, a return to an ancestral city, no room at the inn, birth in a stable, shepherds in the fields, a chorus of angels, a mysterious star, wise men from the East, a jealous king and the massacre of the innocents. Yet it is St John who, writing much later than the other evangelists, interprets the significance of Jesus in more philosophical terms.

It's St John's Prologue that is taken to be the concluding reading and the last word on the wonder of the incarnation. Its rich cadences perfectly capture the sense of awe and breathless wonder of the incarnation. You can sense that the writer is participating in a mystery that is too great for him. He's bowled over. 'The word became flesh and lived among us' – literally 'pitched his tent among us'. And in speaking of Jesus Christ as the Word, he links him with creation itself. Jesus is God's perfect self-expression, the Word that called the world and all creation into being. But look also at the first chapter of his first epistle.

Undermining the Gnostic sect

We owe it to St John to reformulate the Christian faith at a time when it was at risk of being hijacked by misguided sects. Both the Gospel and the epistles were deliberately written in the white heat of argument and opposition to the teaching of Jesus. The opponents were Gnostics, people who wanted to annex Christianity as a form of science fiction, an esoteric way of believing that had well and truly lost touch with reality. This group abhorred the flesh, and sought salvation in an escape from it. They would have been irritated by St John's insistence that the Word had become flesh. John roots us in the history of the person of Jesus. The test of orthodox faith is quite simply: 'Do you believe that God has come in the flesh of Jesus?'

But St John is also a canny person – and, while he contradicts the views of his opponents, he also steals their language and ideas. So the great themes of light and life, water and bread, used by his adversaries, are enlisted by John in the service of the gospel – these great archetypal themes speak to us all, and so John offers us a vocabulary with which to understand our deepest needs and experiences. Light, life, water, bread – these concern us all, speak to all of us, and he takes all the great themes and shows how Christ fulfils them, for Christ is himself life, light, bread and water.

Light of the world

In the Prologue to his Gospel John tells us that the life of the Word was 'the light of all people'. Light has come into the world, the light that enables us to see things truly, as they really are, the light of revelation, the light that enables us to see our way in this world, the light that enables us to see God: 'No one has ever seen God. It is

God the only Son . . . who has made him known.' And this light is not a light for some, for the rather select band of John's followers, or even for Christians alone. This light 'enlightens everyone', even those who eventually lapse into darkness. And the darkness cannot comprehend, extinguish, overcome it. That's the heart of the Christian faith that will sustain us in all the dark clouds of a new year. We don't deny the darkness, we simply affirm that light overcomes it.

So we celebrate St John – who with St Paul established the philosophical foundations of Christianity. He enlisted the intuitive, sensory, artistic in the service of Christian faith. And his majestic words gladden our hearts with the good news that light has come into the world, and that nothing in your life and mine can overcome the light that is the life of all people.

Roger Spiller

Hymn suggestions

Word supreme, before creation; Longing for light (Christ, be our light); Lord, the light of your love is shining; Thou whose almighty word.

Holy Innocents   28 December
Children on the Cross
Jer. 31.15–17; Ps. 124; 1 Cor. 1.26–29; **Matt. 2.13–18**

The day before yesterday we honoured Stephen as a 'deacon' and a 'martyr'. Yesterday, we gave thanks for John, an 'apostle' and 'evangelist'. We have some understanding of what these terms mean, but what, please, is a 'holy innocent'? We have enveloped the infant victims of Herod in so much incense that we can no longer see them. Do we suppose that the tiny tots skewered by Herod's soldiers were holier or more innocent, whatever those words mean, than the kids up the road who escaped the carnage?

The plight of vulnerable children

Here are the first children we meet in the story of Jesus, and already we sense the hesitancy and equivocation about the status of children that has always beclouded Christian thinking about them and

293

that continues to bemire its ministry to them. Hard heads soften. Augustine witters. These little ones, he says, are 'buds, killed by the frost of persecution the moment they showed themselves'. One steadier voice speaks, that of Pope Leo the Great (400–461):

> They were able to die for him whom they could not yet confess. Thus Christ, so that no period of his life should be without miracle, silently exercised the power of the Word before the use of speech . . . Christ crowned infants with a new glory, and consecrated the first days of these little ones by his own beginnings, in order to teach us that no member of the human race is incapable of the divine mystery, since even this age was capable of the glory of martyrdom.[26]

Not that there was anything particularly glorious in the 'sordid particulars' of being butchered by one of those soldiers. But we take Pope Leo's point. Bethlehem's slaughtered children are martyrs, a title and status that has nothing to do with their 'innocence' or 'holiness', still less with any precocious piety we suppose they displayed. Theirs is the 'graced vulnerability' that both makes them helpless before Herod and sets little children at the centre of the Christian Church.[27]

We used to say, before the law was belatedly changed, that those old enough to die for their country should be allowed the vote. By the same token, those old enough to die for Christ – even if not yet three – should surely be allowed the sacrament of his love for them.

A universal story of child abuse

Matthew understands the massacre of Bethlehem's children as answering to Jeremiah's haunting description of Rachel weeping inconsolably for her children, slaughtered when Jerusalem fell to the Babylonians. Matthew's method is to take Old Testament texts and to make up stories that can then be interpreted as their fulfilment, as if those texts were predictions of what would happen centuries later. So we have the stories of the journey of the magi and of the flight into Egypt. But Matthew must not be supposed to be misleading us by such a method of storytelling. If we are misled, it is not by Matthew but by our mistaken assumption that what a story teaches depends on whether it happened.

In truth, the story of what Herod did to Bethlehem's under-3s is anchored in history. Whether or not Herod indiscriminately murdered all Bethlehem's under-3s in the hope of thereby eliminating the threat posed by one child in particular – and he was butcher enough to have done so – what he allegedly did is what countless tyrants certainly have done. The voice of Rachel, weeping for her children, is heard throughout history.

At the Feast of the Holy Innocents we contemplate the suffering of children. We think of children who are victims of cruelty or neglect. We think of children who suffer lingering painful illness. We think of children dying of hunger. We think of children caught up in natural disasters.

Focus on particular children

Because it is too easy to think in such generalities, we hold in mind – if we dare – the single image. So I think of a nameless newborn baby girl, dumped in a Delhi station toilet, discarded simply because she's female. I think of Pintu working in a tannery, surrounded by piles of stinking cattle flesh, and not paid a penny – a twenty-first-century slave. I think of the Jewish baby, impaled on a Nazi bayonet. I think of the Haitian child, surviving for days under the rubble of his fallen home in Port-au-Prince until he finally succumbs to his thirst.

Each such child is the child on the cross. The Feast of the Holy Innocents and Good Friday are the same day. The spear of Herod's soldier and the Nazi bayonet are both thrust into Christ's side. The whimpering, unheard cry from the child beneath the rubble – 'I'm thirsty' – is the dying word of Jesus. And so we pray, in John Masefield's words,

> Lord, give to men who are old and rougher,
> The things that little children suffer.

John Pridmore

Hymn suggestions

When Christ was born in Bethlehem; Unto us a boy is born; Why, impious Herod, shouldst thou fear; From the eastern mountains.

Naming and Circumcision of Jesus 1 January
What's in a Name?
Num. 6.22–end; Ps. 8; Gal. 4.4–7; **Luke 2.15–21**

We can deduce quite a lot from a name. Names can indicate the background, pedigree, social standing in which their bearer has been born. We know someone with the name of Portal or de Pfeffel wasn't born in the East End of London. Or what do you infer from the names of a former Dean of Lincoln some years ago – Oliver William Twisleton-Wykeham-Fiennes? Other names link with famous figures past and present. Naming can be a canny way of investing the child with the hopes and expectations of its parents. It can be a heavy burden, just as the name of a famous parent can be a handicap for a son or daughter wishing to strike out on a different course. It was fortunate that the child named Martin Luther King turned out all right and didn't let down the reputation of the illustrious man after whom he was named. Jacob Rees-Mogg, known affectionately as the MP for the Eighteenth Century, attracted comment recently when he named his latest son Sixtus Dominic Boniface. It was thought he was simply calling each child numerically, in Latin, of course. But it transpired that he called his latest child, and earlier children too, after the names of favourite popes and saints. If that leaves large shoes for his sons to fill, at least it sets out before them a glorious vocation and gives them something to emulate.

Names that embody divine messages

This gets us closer to the way in which in biblical times names were chosen with care, for what they meant and wanted to pass on to their children. The name of a child embodied a promise or vocation, sometimes made by God. The birth of the child would be evidence of the message given by God in the choice of name. Each of the children of the prophet Isaiah, for example, signified the future that lay before the nation: the names were a living embodiment of the promise God was making through them to the nation or king. One was a real tongue twister because it packed in a big message: Maher-shalal-hash-baz! It was a sign to Ahaz that God was coming to get him.

Sometimes the birth name is changed. It was customary during slavery, for example, when a slave had a new owner. Names are still given at the point of baptism to signal the transition to new life in Christ. In the biblical period a name change was made at the command of a divine messenger, or by Jesus. It marked a significant change that had or was to happen, or a prospective new vocation to be entered into. So Abram becomes Abraham, Jacob becomes

Israel, Simon becomes Peter, and Saul becomes Paul. All these biblical names hark back to glory days of the patriarchs, the time of the Exodus and the entry into the Promised Land.

The name of Jesus

This sets the scene for the naming of Mary and Joseph's firstborn son. Luke mentions his circumcision and naming in just one verse. 'He was called Jesus, the name given by the angel before he was conceived in the womb.' It has the shorter form, Y'shu, we call Jesus, and the longer form, Yehoshua, Joshua. The meaning of both is identical: 'God saves'.

Luke shows us that a major transition from Israel to Jesus is underway. Characters like Zechariah and Elizabeth, Simeon and Anna, represent the piety of Israel and stand on the edge of the new era beginning with Jesus. Behind them stand Hannah and Miriam. They form a chorus that hails the advent of John and Jesus. And Mary's song, the Magnificat, expresses the aspirations of the poor people who are also part of Israel and look for deliverance. They have been waiting long for deliverance, and now it comes. Jesus' name identifies its deliverer. The message to the shepherds sounds formal to our ears. Luke deliberately casts it in the form of an imperial proclamation: 'I am bringing you good news of great joy . . . to you is born this day in the city of David a Saviour, who is the Messiah, the Lord.' What is Luke up to? What is he intending that we should hear by this proclamation? The chapter began with another proclamation, this time by the Emperor to all descendants of the house of David. This second proclamation to shepherds acts as a counter charge to that imperial decree. An act of challenge and defiance. And it echoes and picks up the language Isaiah himself used in his own announcement of the birth of the heir to the throne of David. And now the long period of waiting is over. Luke goes out of his way to mention that the Saviour is born 'this day'. And shortly another prophet, Simeon, will confirm it. 'Master, *now* you are dismissing your servant in peace . . . for my eyes *have seen* your salvation.' Jesus is named 'God saves'; his name invokes power and blessing, 'Jesus! The name that charms our fears, that bids our sorrows cease, 'tis music in the sinner's ears, 'tis life and health and peace.'

Roger Spiller

Hymn suggestions

How sweet the name of Jesus sounds; To the name of our salvation; Jesus, the name high over all; O for a thousand tongues to sing.

Week of Prayer for Christian Unity   18–25 January
Finding Christ in the Stranger – Why We Need Each Other
Jer. 33.6–9a; Ps. 100; **Col. 3.9–17**; Matt. 18.19–22

Christ in the stranger

Once, when I was going through a particularly difficult time in my life, a time of loss, I was walking through the city where I lived hardly caring where I went. Suddenly a man I had never met before, rather scruffy in appearance, and smelling slightly of drink, stumbled into my path and said into my face, 'Get through it girl.' And I did get through it.

A Lutheran pastor I once knew was visiting a McDonalds, having just taken a very difficult funeral service. As he started on his fries, a very large man came and sat at his table. My friend was nervous. 'How are you doing, Father?' the man said. (The clerical collar of course . . .) 'You look like you've had a bad day. Would you like to talk about it?' Something made my friend tell the story of how the day had been, how he'd driven at first to the wrong cemetery and then not felt he'd done a good job for the family. Then, this unknown man reached across the table and asked whether he believed all that stuff about Jesus rising from the dead. My friend mumbled that he did believe it, but that there were days when it was hard to believe it. 'I thought so,' said the stranger, and then left. Years later my friend read the story of the journey to Emmaus, and suddenly realized who the stranger was in McDonalds all that time ago. It is firmly in the tradition of our faith that Christ comes to us in the company of strangers.

We cling to our friends and fear the stranger

But we cling very hard instead to our friends, and to Christians of our own kind, in the hope that we will find Christ there. This can't be good for us and it can't be good for church unity, not for the mission of the Church, not for interfaith dialogue, or for the peace of the world, or for human flourishing. The Bible tells us, and experience tells us, that it is often through the stranger that God speaks. And so it is that through meeting other Christians, praying with them, getting to know them, that we shall hear God speaking and see the face of Christ.

Biblical hospitality

Wherever you look in the Bible you find stories of God's people being hospitable, being welcoming, open and receptive to the world and its people. And you find stories of people receiving the hospitality of others, believing that they will in doing so meet God himself. Hospitality is often thought of as being welcoming to our friends, to neighbours, or to business associates. But the biblical understanding of hospitality is about welcoming the stranger. The Greek word for hospitality is a word that means literally 'love of the stranger' – *philoxenia*.

The other important thing about biblical hospitality is that it's as important to receive it as to give it. We can readily think of the Church as 'host'. But in all those stories about Jesus sharing meals with disciples, with Pharisees, with tax-collectors, with whoever it was, he was not the host, but pretty much always the guest. Jesus was the stranger who was welcomed. He did not invite people to enter his space on *his* terms – he willingly entered *their* homes, their space, their communities, and laid himself open to them. And when he asked the disciples to follow him, he sent them out in such a vulnerable condition that they would have to rely on the hospitality of others. To be a disciple is to be open to receive hospitality and vulnerable enough to need it.

Hospitality seems to be everywhere in the gospel story. There is the call to love the stranger. There is the mission to go out with nothing in order to be dependent on the kindness of strangers. But also, and perhaps most importantly, there is the story of Jesus the stranger; the one who was born away from home, the one who had no home to call his own, the one who appeared as a stranger on the Emmaus road. And there is that powerful tradition that Jesus said, 'I was a stranger and you visited me . . .', and, 'If you did it for one of the least of these you did it for me.' When we welcome the stranger, we are welcoming Christ himself. When we seek fellowship with Christians who seem strange to us, we will find Christ there.

Making friends out of strangers

Jesus prayed that this disciples would be one, and would call themselves friends. But we have become strangers to one another. The call
to Christian unity is not so much a call to debate ideas or doctrines,
but a call to meet those who are strangers to us, but who are also our
sisters and our brothers. And in whose strange faces we may yet see
the face of Christ. It's as important, and as wonderful, as that.

Susan Durber

Hymn suggestions

*Eternal Ruler of the ceaseless round; Like the murmour of the
dove's song; Affirm anew the threefold name; Let us build a house
where love can dwell.*

Conversion of St Paul   25 January
Theology for Mission

Jer. 1.4–10; Ps. 67; Acts 9.1–22 (*if the Acts reading is used
instead of the Old Testament reading, the New Testament reading
is* **Gal. 1.11–16a**); Matt. 19.27–end

There is no one for whose conversion millions of Christians down
the centuries can be more thankful than that of Paul of Tarsus.
Without a person of his formidable brilliance, vision and energy,
and above all his single-minded commitment to the gospel, it is
impossible, in human terms, to see how the Christian Church could
have got off the ground and become a worldwide movement.

Questions

St Paul had become a Christian only a few years after the resurrection, when he encountered the risen Lord. He was and remained
a Jew, but what did it mean for him and fellow Jews to embrace
Christ? Was the Jew still subject to the law, to Jewish rites and traditions? Or was he or she discharged from them altogether? What
of the Gentiles? Should there be a mission to those outside the house
of Israel? Might a mission to the Gentiles be attempted only after
the mission to Jews had been completed, as many argued?

Theology

There was no body of teaching on which to provide answers to all the unforeseeable issues that were springing up. No ready-made theology by which to steer the infant church. No agreed creeds or teaching that could define truth from heresy, still less rule against the tide of new-fangled teachings that were attracting even Christian converts away from the gospel that had brought them to embrace Christ. It was to Paul that we owe a coherent theology that has proved definitive. Paul inherited formulas and pithy credal statements, such as that 'Christ died for our sins', but that could hardly satisfy the questions as to how Christ's death actually dealt with our sins. It would take an inspired and masterly thinker to set out a coherent compendium of Christian life, beliefs and practices.

Paul was the first and great theologian, comparable only to the later, unknown and mystical writer we call St John. His theology was written in the white heat of fierce disputes and often acrimonious and underhand attempts by opponents to traduce new converts. They sought to return Jewish converts to Christianity back to their Jewish religion and to tempt Gentile Christians to form an accommodation with Greek philosophical thought. Paul's account of Christianity among all other expressions we have is 'truest in the form it took with Paul', so said the eminent New Testament scholar C. K. (Kingsley) Barrett. During the intervening years since the time of Paul, his writings have impacted afresh on outstanding figures, often leading to seismic change, figures such as St Augustine, Martin Luther and the theologian Karl Barth.

Missionary

If his theological reflections drove Paul to preach the gospel to others and to be a pioneer missionary, then, conversely, his call to be a missionary to the Gentiles impelled him, in turn, to write his letters to the churches in which he laboured. Busy clergy and lay workers can be tempted to discount 'theology' as a luxury or distraction that gets in the way of pressing pastoral duties. But without the rigorous thought and reflection modelled to us by Paul, we can easily lose our focus, and find little that is fresh and compelling to say when we are meeting with people. On the other hand, those who find it natural to be immersed in study have Paul to remind them that, if theology is not put to work and allowed to inform and inspire preaching, pastoring and discipleship itself, it becomes an intellectual indulgence.

Cost

As a missionary, Paul spent himself for the sake of the gospel, as he was not shy to declare. Then there was the toll on his body as a result of punishments and the interminable travel and dangerous sea voyages. Then he had to come to terms with his own unnamed bodily affliction. More telling was fierce and widespread hostility, ridicule and rejection that he encountered, even from the churches he himself had founded. Others, too, questioned his authority and apostleship, and formed factions and divisions that seriously undermined his ministry. But it led him to reveal in his letters a warm, sensitive figure who could boast about his credentials that excelled all those of his critics, but who knew he could boast only in Christ crucified, and in his own weakness made strong by his Lord.

Grace

No one did more to analyse and explain the gospel than Paul. No other New Testament writer does more to expose the futility of thinking we can secure a relationship with God through virtue, goodness, service and religious practices than St Paul. And none is more eloquent in showing us the unconditional, limitless super-abundance of grace that alone can secure our relationship with God through Christ. Says Paul: 'It is no longer I who live, but it is Christ, who lives in me.' Thanks be to God for his inexpressible gift.

Roger Spiller

Hymn suggestions

To God be the glory; Tell all the world of Jesus; And can it be; In Christ there is no east or west.

Presentation of Christ in the Temple (Candlemas)   2 February
Hope Realized in Jesus
Mal. 3.1–5; Ps. 24.[1–6] 7–end; Heb. 2.14–end; **Luke 2.22–40**

They were just doing what was expected, it was an ordinary ritual, not all that different from the ritual around any new baby. Mary and Joseph with their family and friends were taking their firstborn son Jesus into the Temple, to be presented to God, given to God, and then bought back, on a temporary loan, as it were, from God by means of a sacrificial offering. It was a predictable ritual.

The extraordinary

But then something extraordinary happened, which causes the Church around the world to celebrate today. The parents Mary and Joseph were to have a disclosure that would change everything, and reach down even to us. And the means by which this would be brought about would be two separate, unlikely, elderly characters. And for a few moments their lives would coincide with that of Jesus and his parents.

After living for so many years, Simeon and Anna had seen it all – and like a generation among us that still remembers the horrors of the Second World War, they were old enough to recall the days when the invading Romans conquered Jerusalem and their lives were changed for ever. Since their late teens or early twenties, they had lived under oppression, like so many in Europe in our day.

Anna was once married, expecting like all young woman to have a baby. Instead, she saw her hopes for a child evaporate when after seven agonizing years her husband died. And being barren, she would have forfeited any chance of being remarried and be condemned to live out her days on the margins of a society that had little use for her. We can disparage or patronize the elderly.

Surprise fulfilment

Both Simeon and Anna are witnesses to the fact that all the hopes and yearnings for salvation come to fruition now, as God reveals his son in the Temple. This brief encounter with Mary and her baby lasts only a moment. When it's over, they move on and we never see them again. But the moment is unforgettable.

The birth of a child is one of the most amazing of human experiences. Roman Catholic priest and writer Timothy Radcliffe tells of being in Rwanda during the genocide, together with a brother in his religious community who had given 25 years of his life to the country. Everything was destroyed, most of his friends had been killed. They wept together. But that Christmas, Timothy received a photograph of the brother with two big Rwandan babies in his arms On the photograph, the brother had written, 'Africa has a future'.

What Simeon and Anna witness to is the audacious claim that the hope of the world is found not in human initiative, in strategy and programmes and policies, but in the activity of God through his Son Jesus. He is, says Simeon, 'a light for revelation to the Gentiles'. He is, says St John, 'the light of the world'. But it doesn't happen without cost. Simeon's final, fateful words speak of resistance and suffering, and so move us from Christmas towards Lent and Christ's suffering.

Healing and hope for Anna and Simeon

Anna and Simeon waited and prayed, and God revealed to them that this was the child they had waited for all their lives. They understood that their private hopes and the hopes of the world were answered in the baby cradled in his mother's arms. In Rembrandt's painting of Simeon, there is absolute calm. No one moves or speaks, but everyone looks. Simeon holds the child, in amazement and veneration. He knows he has seen salvation, and that is enough.

The hurt in Anna's heart, the shattered dreams, the long years spent on the fringes of society, are the reason Jesus came. The reign of fear in today's world, the hunger, pain and suffering we see on faces around us and in the news, the abuse of power, the erosion of honesty in public life, the rise of tyrants and rampant injustice, are the reasons Jesus came. Jesus is at work reconnecting this broken world with the God who created it, giving us the reason for living and hoping.

Simeon didn't live to see how it all turned out, but he died in peace knowing that darkness was defeated and light had broken through. And Anna, a woman of sorrows, makes her final appearance in a burst of joy. She may have been disqualified from a woman's role in her culture, but God gave her a starring role in his story. God places the woman who never got to welcome a baby of her own, first in line to welcome this one. She is the first evangelist, the first to proclaim the good news that Jesus is the deliverer.

And we are invited to lay aside our false hopes and disappointments and bear witness to the hope and light that Jesus has brought into our own lives. Our vocation is to be the successors of Simeon and Anna, bearers of the hope and light and glory that is to be found fully in Jesus Christ. We're to declare and to demonstrate in our church life and our individual witness that the one whom Mary presented in the Temple is none other than the light of the world.

Roger Spiller

Hail to the Lord who comes; Faithful vigil ended; When candles are lighted on Candlemas Day; Lord, the light of your love is shining.

St Joseph of Nazareth 19 March
Keep Him in the Crib
2 Sam. 7.4–16; Ps. 89.26–36; Rom. 4.13–18; **Matt. 1.18–end**

Where's Joseph?

A survey of nativity sets in a well-known Oxford Street store revealed an absence of anyone resembling Joseph who was married to Mary, who gave birth to Jesus. Approached by a customer bemused by this anomaly, a sales assistant was equally baffled: 'Joseph', he said, 'has done a runner.'

The attempt to write out Joseph from the nativity scene and show Mary as a single parent ignores the rock-like support that Joseph gave to Mary and the infant Jesus through dangerous and turbulent months. We glimpse this in Luke's Gospel, although it is written from Mary's perspective. But St Matthew gives us the picture from Joseph's perspective and allows us a glimpse into his inner world.

Joseph's dilemma

We're to imagine the young Joseph and Mary falling in love and becoming engaged and living in their own homes according to the strict custom operative in their home region of Galilee. The excitement and joy soon evaporate as Joseph learns that Mary is pregnant. Matthew tells us his readers that the birth is 'from the Holy Spirit', but Joseph doesn't know this, and since the idea of a miraculous birth was unknown in Judaism, it would not have removed his scepticism if he did.

In his BBC mini-series, *The Nativity*, *EastEnders* scriptwriter Tony Jordan depicts Joseph refusing to accept Mary's account of her pregnancy given in Luke.

It's fine for people in big hats to say the angel did this and that, but blokes like me, sitting in pubs, will say, 'So, your missus comes to you and says that she's pregnant – but, don't worry, it's

God's. And then you have a dream and it's all OK?' They won't believe it. So, in my version, Joseph loves Mary but he can't come to terms with it. And when he has the dream, he thinks it's just his brain telling him what he wants to be true – even when Mary tells him what the dream was about.

The messenger's answer

That was surely a likely reaction by a responsible and righteous man. Confusion turns to fear as Joseph seeks the way to protect his wife from scandal and to maintain his blameless and upright reputation in the situation in which he found himself. He decides this is best achieved by terminating the engagement by stealth, while maintaining his care and support for his wife. But it's now Joseph's turn to hear the angelic command in a dream: 'Do not be afraid to take Mary your wife into your home.' By doing this rather than divorcing Mary as he had proposed, Joseph is assuming public responsibility for the mother and child. And he is instructed to exercise a father's right to name the child and thus to acknowledge Jesus as the legal father of the child.

Parental grief and confusion

The personal anguish was matched by physical upheaval. We have yet to find evidence that a general registration occurred at the time of Jesus' birth that required a mother in labour to travel, as we have it in Luke's Gospel. Nevertheless, in Matthew's Gospel, the holy family aren't spared a horrendous journey with the infant Jesus, as they become fugitives in their own country and refugees in Egypt in order to escape the infant genocide by one king of the Jews. And up to two years later when they learn that it's safe to do so, they uproot again to return to their own country. In this dangerous, barbaric and unpredictable world Jesus is born, and Joseph cherishes the young child and his mother Mary.

When they come to the Temple to fulfil the legal requirements, they hear from Anna and Simeon the poignant vocation that will be thrust upon their son, and the heart-breaking consequences that Mary will be expected to face. They must have been bewildered and disturbed by the news. Joseph resurfaces again when Jesus is 12 years old and they take him to the Temple for the festival. As the firstborn son, he will have received particular attention and home learning from Joseph. The confidence and linguistic skills, intimated by his engagement in the Temple, will have reflected well on Joseph's careful nurture and tuition. He had other sons who, we might infer from their later negative response to Jesus, might have placed additional strains on the head of the family. And when Jesus finally took his leave of the builders' yard, there was more parental anguish as Jesus seemed to renounce his natural family: 'Who is my mother, and who are my brothers?'

Joseph roots our faith

Today we rejoice and give thanks for Joseph, the just, kind and selfless man who stood by Mary and provided a secure home for Jesus. He did more. He provided a link to the ancestral line of David. Without evidence that Jesus was of royal lineage, the claim that Jesus was the Messiah, of the house of David, would not have been taken seriously. For us, too, even the little that we know of Joseph may be sufficient to rid us of the idea that Jesus was an isolated religious guru, detached from ordinary human life. And we can find a place for Joseph in our hearts. Let's insist that he always has his rightful place in our cribs.

Roger Spiller

Hymn suggestions

O blessed St Joseph, how great is your worth?; Let saints on earth in concert sing; Soldiers who are Christ's below; We love the place, O God.

Annunciation of Our Lord to the Blessed Virgin Mary 25 March
Good News for Ordinary People
Isa. 7.10–14; Ps. 40.5–11; Heb. 10.4–10; **Luke 1.26–38**

Mary represents little people, poor people, marginalized people, insignificant, ordinary people in Luke's Gospel. His account of the visit of the divine messenger contrasts with Matthew's. In Matthew, the angel Gabriel directs his message to Joseph, the legal father of Jesus, a man of Davidic descent. Luke's account is written from a woman's point of view, from the perspective of the world's little people. In honouring Mary, God honours them too.

Why Mary?

We can wonder at the choice of Mary as the bearer of Jesus the Christ. We see how God narrows down his choice of a mother to bear his Son. The messenger is sent to Galilee, then more particularly to the city of Nazareth, then more particularly still to a virgin betrothed to a man called Joseph, and finally – wait for it – to a virgin 'whose name was Mary'.

In human affairs it's not reckoned to be wise to consider what might have been. But at least here, if we're not to take God's ways of working for granted, it may be valuable to go on asking, 'Why Mary?' Why not Hannah or some other person? Why Nazareth and not one of the more prestigious towns about which/whom no one could every say, 'Can anything good come out of Nazareth?' And why this young woman who was emphatically not from David's line?

Little people

God's choice could always have been very different. There are no constraints on God. And the fact that he freely chooses Mary for his great vocation speaks volumes about God's disposition towards us. We can affirm that God does not shun the ordinary members of society; he shows a preference for the poor. The world is full of little people, people who lack a voice, who rely on others to speak for them, who need encouragement to find their own voice. Yet God chose one of them to be the bearer of the Saviour of the world.

The angel addresses her with an opening greeting. It's often been translated 'Hail', which sounds more special than it is, since hail is close to, and comes from, the same root as 'hello'. It could also mean 'Rejoice', but 'Greetings, favoured one' is now the more accepted translation. And it may surprise us that God's angels are such good linguists! They speak the language of the people. 'Hello,' says Gabriel.

Of course, Mary is as 'much perplexed', and fearful, by the visitation of the angel as by the astounding contents of the message itself. God's word always surprises, always stretches credulity, always brings the challenge of disturbance and dislocation; it is blessing and demand at the same time.

Favour with God

The words of the angel explain God's choice of Mary. 'You have found favour with God.' Other familiar words were 'Mary full of grace'. There was sharp disagreement when these words were taken to mean that God's calling of Mary was a recognition of her intrinsic grace, grace as a personal possession such that she could also dispense grace to others. There is an exuberance in Luke's word, a fulsomeness in the grace and favour, but it is because it is bestowed on Mary, and not a recognition of Mary's inherent grace or the basis of God's call. God has graciously blessed Mary. It's God's gift, not Mary's reward. Mary has been elected, of all the women on earth, to conceive the Messiah and to give birth to the Son of God. Gabriel's words that follow aren't original.

Perplexity

Mary's reaction turns now from fear to perplexity. So far Gabriel's message can be applicable to any normal birth. The only problem for Mary is that she isn't living with her betrothed and hasn't consummated the marriage with Joseph. The angel's reply to Mary shows God's provision exceeded what Mary could imagine: 'The Holy Spirit will come upon you, and the power of the Most High will overshadow you.' These are close to the words that will be spoken at Jesus' baptism, close, too, to the words that will be spoken at the transfiguration, and they echo the overshadowing mode of God's presence with his people in their journey to the Promised Land. God is the creative power in the birth of Jesus through human procreation. And for those finding difficulty with a virgin birth, the angel says that 'Nothing will be impossible with God'.

It's not impossible for God to act. If there is such a God it would be surprising if God never acted in particular and surprising ways to accomplish his purposes. It would be very odd if the resurrection were the only incomprehensible, miraculous event. If Jesus' end was extraordinary, as it was, might not also his beginning be extraordinary? And if God does act in history, as the Hebrew Scriptures witness, what more obvious time to act than at the first moments of Jesus' human existence?

Mary's response is the perfect expression of discipleship. 'Here am I, the servant of the Lord; let it be with me according to your word.' For Mary, God's word is enough. She is the first person to hear the gospel. And for Luke she is the first Christian disciple.

'We have turned Jesus into an abstraction and . . . abstractions haven't got mothers.' So said the Roman Catholic theologian Karl Rahner. Jesus can be an abstraction for us. Attending to Mary assists us to root Jesus in our human history with all the stress, pain and relief of human procreation. That assists us in making Jesus part of our story, and makes his story the clue to our own. And Mary's story of the surprising, unconditional grace of God amd her response is the model for the discipleship to which God is calling us.

Roger Spiller

Hymn suggestions

The Angel Gabriel from heaven came; For Mary, Mother of our Lord; With Mary let my soul rejoice; Sing we of the blessed Mother.

St Mark the Evangelist   30 April
The Pioneer Evangelist
Prov. 15.28–end, *or* Acts 15.35–end; Ps. 119.9–16; Eph. 4.7–16; **Mark 13.5–13**

Today, St Mark's Day, we celebrate the largely unknown author of the earliest Gospel. We could profitably focus on any event narrated in his Gospel, his prologue, or his dramatic, abrupt ending bereft of a resurrection appearance, or the dark, sober, tragic presentation of Jesus' crucifixion. But let's today look more broadly at his Gospel as a whole. For no other book in the New Testament has been more influential than the one that bears Mark's name.

Why a Gospel?

We take the four Gospels for granted, but it was by no means inevitable that there would be a Gospel at all, a written account purporting to tell the pre-Easter account of Jesus' public ministry. The expectation that Jesus would return within the lifetime of his hearers ruled out any need for an account to be written in his lifetime. It was four decades after Easter that Mark took up his pen. But what literary form would serve the unique life, death and resurrection of Jesus? If he knew the current secular forms of writing, he didn't follow them. Instead, he created a wholly new literary genre he called 'gospel', a word that he was the first to introduce into the New Testament. The gospel is 'good news', but it also describes Mark's new literary form, 'the Gospel of Mark'. The Gospel as a whole is appropriately called 'gospel' because, for Mark, it's purpose is evangelistic: to be the vehicle of the good news, and to set out the story of salvation through Jesus Christ so that its hearers may believe Jesus is the Lord.

Mark as theologian

The Gospel of Mark is a pacy, direct, urgent, brief, dramatic narrative that can be read in 60 minutes. It's a concrete, eye-witness, on-the-spot style of writing, but it's combined with a wider, truly cosmic and future perspective. It gives us the content of missionary preaching as well as a progress report on the responses made to the gospel by fishermen, tax-collectors, women, the poor, the Gentiles, and the disciples themselves.

The primitive, simple and often crude style of Mark's Gospel led scholars to think of its author as a scissors-and-paste editor who was heavily dependent upon his oral and eye-witness sources, notably St Peter. But now we know that could not have been further from the truth. Mark, we now recognize, is a theologian in his own right, with a perspective he wants to share with us. And he's writing not simply to describe the brief public ministry of Jesus, but to show how his life and teaching could interpret the new circumstances in which the church found itself. By the time Mark was writing, the church was facing persecution from Roman authorities and hostility from Judaism. Mark's focus on the cost of discipleship and the inevitability of suffering, and his hostility to Jewish authorities and to Judaism, serves to act as an encouragement to the challenges to the church in the time he was writing. But in his plain, unvarnished, unromantic account, Mark has preserved something of the early years of Jesus and his ministry in Galilee. He sees Jesus 'after the flesh'. The Jesus of Mark's Gospel is human and weak, revealing limitations, showing the range of human emotions: tears, anger and frustration. The disciples are not spared the exposure of their dullness, stupidity, lack of faith and slowness to understand the gospel.

Come inside

Jesus is human and yet Mark shows that he is also surrounded by an aura of mystery. His true identity is veiled in secrecy, hidden from sight. The 'insiders' like the disciples, who are expected to 'see', fail to do so, and become 'outsiders'. And the self-styled 'outsiders' – a Gentile, a Roman centurion, a few women – are surprised to find themselves as 'insiders'. They, together with the disciples, will proceed to Galilee and point to the community that God will call into life. As 'outsiders' ourselves we are invited to become 'insiders'. If St Paul compels us to think, Mark invites us to visualize, to see. We are told about those who 'see and yet do not see'. But not only told. We are given the opportunity to experience this for ourselves. As we read Mark's Gospel, characterized by twists and turns, by surprises and reversals, the Gospel performs this reversal on us too. If it casts us into darkness, it also brings us into the light. Outsiders, we are beckoned to become insiders.

Today we recognize St Mark's great literary achievement and its huge and continuing significance for the future of the Christian faith. It's a Gospel of the amazing, incomprehensible condescension and love of God, which is even now addressing all who will open their hearts and enter his kingdom. 'Open my eyes, so that I may behold wondrous things out of your law.'

Roger Spiller

Hymn suggestions

We have a gospel to proclaim; God in his wisdom, for our learning; Break thou the bread of life; Come, Lord, to our souls come down.

SS Philip and James, Apostles   1 May
Many Ways of Following the Way
Isa. 30.15–21; Ps. 119.1–8; Eph. 1.3–10; **John 14.1–14**

That Philip and James should be remembered on the same day could perhaps be considered a happy accident that came about after the church that was home to their relics was dedicated to both their names in sixth-century Rome. They were two of the 12 apostles but, other than being brothers in Christ, there is not believed to be any familial connection.

Philip is a little better known than James, who is sometimes called the 'less' to distinguish him from a more prominent man of the same name, James, Son of Zebedee. Why our James was considered 'lesser' we will not know. Perhaps he was younger or quieter than the other James, who was one of the 'Sons of Thunder' and may have had a temper.

Philip

We know Philip came from Bethsaida, and was called by Jesus to follow him, bringing others along with him too, namely Nathanael. Philip also engages in various dialogues, which usually exasperate Jesus and prompt him to question whether his disciples really understand what is going on. In John's Gospel, Jesus reveals to his disciples that he is the way, the truth and the life, and that through him all people can come to know the Father. Philip responds in a rather dull-minded way: 'Lord, show us the Father, and we will be satisfied.' One can almost imagine Jesus rolling his eyes, and then gently smiling down upon him as he says, 'Have I been with you all this time, Philip, and you still do not know me?'

It is easy for the smug disciples of today to look on with incredulity at Philip's questioning and James' relative anonymity, but both apostles help us respond to Christ in our own unique way, just as they did. Philip's questioning, and the way in which James quietly follows, tell us something about discipleship.

James

James, in his way, is able to witness to the quiet perseverance we all need to follow Christ. As Christians we are called to be persistent, and as the prophet Isaiah says, 'in quietness and in trust shall be your strength.' There is no such thing as a celebrity Christian, but those who walk in the way of the Lord, as James did, are still destined to be saints. Much of the life of faith is simply about getting on with it and living it out in all that we are and all that we are called to do. We can thank James for the fact that he did just that, and, as one of the apostles, gives us confidence that sometimes we are called to do the same.

Philip's vocation

Philip's vocation was to ask what we might call the stupid question. Christ has indeed made to be known to us the mystery of the

Father's will, but sometimes we cannot understand clearly what that means; we are faced with a divine reality that is beyond our understanding. That might be a daunting thought, but Philip's human curiosity and unfeigned heart show us that, like the apostles, our questions and clouded vision do not prevent Christ from calling us to follow him. Philip's very human response also gives us confidence to ask God the obvious questions that sometimes perplex us on our journey of faith.

Brothers in Christ

Was it, after all, such an accident that Philip and James are remembered together? Between them, these brothers in Christ give us a glimpse of the multifaceted discipleship to which we are all called. Though there is no one particular way of being a disciple, and no one way of being a Christian, we are all called to follow the way, the truth and the life of Jesus Christ.

How that manifests itself in our lives, our worship, our churches, may vary hugely between us, depending on our circumstances, our context, our personality and so on, but regardless of these differences we are all gathered up into Christ as his family, as his disciples in this age. As it says in the Letter to the Ephesians, however our calling is made manifest in our lives, we were chosen in Christ before the foundation of the world, to be holy and blameless before him in love.

Victoria Johnson

Hymn suggestions

O Jesus, I have promised; Give me the wings of faith to rise; How beauteous are their feet; Will you come and follow me?

St Matthias the Apostle   14 May
Earth-Shattering Events
Isa. 22.15–end; Ps. 15; Acts 1.15–end (*if the Acts reading is used instead of the Old Testament reading, the New Testament reading is* 1 Cor. 4.1–7); **John 15.9–17**

Two devastating earthquakes in Nepal in a month a few years back reminded us that, in some parts of the world, even the ground beneath

314

our feet can't be guaranteed to provide us with solid support. An earthquake is at one terrifying end of the scale of those experiences that come to everyone at points of dislocation, confusion, unsettledness or abandonment. It's not only the literal tectonic plates that shift. Sweeping changes in society give many that 'left-behind' feel. Modern technology seems to pass us by. And the major life changes of moving house, childbirth, divorce, bereavement, unemployment or the 'empty nest' can leave us profoundly disoriented.

The disciples' world shattered

Jesus' friends had experienced a literal earthquake, just after he died. But that had been minor, as far as we know, compared to the emotional earthquake caused by his death itself. And though they soon found themselves caught up in the astonishing whirlwind of joy brought about by his rising again, there remained a nagging sense of pain and incompleteness. What about the fact that they were now just 11, not 12? What about the one who had betrayed their master and then been so eaten up with self-loathing that he had gone and killed himself? I don't think the pain and shock and sorrow of Judas' death would have gone away soon.

But in this emotional situation, overwhelming joy at Jesus' rising combined with that aching twang over Judas' death, Peter was given strength to step forward and point the company of Jesus' friends to solid ground on which they and all who joined them could rely: solid ground made up of two elements.

Solid ground: the purpose of God

First, the purpose of God. Peter's first words were these: 'Friends, the scripture had to be fulfilled.' Somehow, even the treachery, failure and loss of Judas was held within the larger purpose of God. We should not misunderstand this in a crude sense. It was not that Judas was cruelly pre-programmed to do what he did. It was rather that he exemplified a sad and ancient truth about human deceitfulness, and the fragility even of close bonds. And that it was inevitable that Jesus, the one truly obedient human, should suffer from this weakness in others. Jesus was never either willing or able to *compel* the loyalty of anyone.

So within the seismic shock of all that had happened to them, God remained sovereign.

Solid ground: the apostles' witness

The second element of this 'solid ground' that Peter pointed to was the continuing witness of the 12 apostles. This is where Matthias comes in. There were, of course, plenty of witnesses to Jesus. The gathering of disciples after Jesus' ascension numbered around 120, and it would start to multiply exponentially very soon. But Jesus had appointed 12 to be with him and to be sent out as his uniquely authorized representatives. And Peter knew that after Judas' death it was important for that number to be made up again.

Why? Well, 12 was a significant symbolic number, the number of Israel's tribes: in choosing 12, Jesus had surely wanted to signal that he was re-forming Israel from the inside out. And I think that Peter would have understood that appointing a new number 12 would send out a signal: despite the tragedy of Judas, the purpose of Jesus was not going to be thwarted.

It's important to look at what the qualification was for this role of the new twelfth apostle:

> One of the men who have accompanied us throughout the time that the Lord Jesus went in and out among us, beginning from the baptism of John until the day when he was taken up from us – one of these must become a witness with us to his resurrection.

In the days before printing and before recording, it was vital to have eyewitnesses who could guarantee the reliability of a message or a tradition or a story that you wanted to pass on. What they needed was not just someone who had had visions of Jesus or encounters with him after his death. They needed someone who had known Jesus all along – from the time when he was baptized, through the months of their travelling between villages and towns, often hungry, tired, sweaty, showing the outcast types that they had a place in God's kingdom, bringing new beginnings to those who thought they would never get better or become accepted, listening, sharing, weeping, laughing – witnesses who could testify that it was this same Jesus who had now been raised from death by God and proclaimed King over all through his ascension to heaven.

After the emotional earthquake they had experienced, and in the midst of the ongoing nagging pain over Judas, this was the solid ground on which the followers of Jesus could and would continue: the simple, honestly shared memories and understanding of Jesus that the 11, now 12 again, had gained through those precious years in his company. The role of Matthias, the new apostle, was anything but an honorary one. It wasn't just to fill an empty chair at a members-only club. It was to be a vital piece of the solid foundation on which the Church would find its security.

Strange as it may seem, this apparently fragile thing, the memories and eyewitness testimony of these 12 friends of Jesus, would become a rock on which the Church could remain secure for indefinite generations, in the midst of many upheavals. Because the testimony of the apostles and those associated with them in due course took written form and became what we know as the New Testament, the reliable account of Jesus, who he was, what he did, who he is now, and what he would always mean for his followers and for the world. Trusting in Jesus as the New Testament bears witness to him, we find a place of security in an uncertain world.

Solid ground: the gift of Jesus

There is no promise of insulation here from earthquakes of any kind. Just an assurance that, in their midst, we have the rock of an unchanging Saviour who is always on our side.

Stephen Wright

Hymn suggestions

Restore, O Lord, the honour of your name; Blest are the pure in heart; I, the Lord of sky and sea; All my hope on God is founded.

Visit of the Blessed Virgin Mary to Elizabeth
31 May
A Narrative Sermon
Zeph. 3.14–18; Ps. 113; Rom. 12.9–16; **Luke 1.39–49 [50–56]**

Tonight, I am going to put myself in the place of the two women in the Gospel reading we heard. I invite you to be transported back in your imagination as both Elizabeth and Mary are each awaiting their firstborn child.

Mary speaks first about Elizabeth

She is getting quite old now, I suppose, my cousin Elizabeth, but oh! how radiant and fulfilled she seems. It must have been an incredible shock and surprise when Zechariah came home and said he had seen an angel, as he prepared the incense offering in the Temple. The message had so astounded him that he questioned the angel when told his elderly wife would conceive. At that, the angel struck him dumb until such time as God fulfilled his promise. And the angel went on to name the child – 'John', 'Gift of God' – how appropriate is that. After so many faithful years of service, her husband as a priest of the Lord and herself, too, upright and blameless. But what a reward for such faithfulness.

Yet she looks a little tired – not surprising, though, six months pregnant at her age. So much to cope with. Yet tonight, when I walked in the door, what an amazing experience, her child leaping in her womb, recognizing his even younger cousin in my womb.

Perhaps she has many questions to ask: why now, how did God do this, what will be the outcome for her son?

And yet, I do understand. She feels she is blessed by God, through the words of the angel, the messenger from God. This is her time, a time of healing from the past pain in her life. She was scorned, now she is blessed, she knows God's mercy. Yet she speaks of me, and my child, as the one of whom the prophets spoke. She says I am the one who has been chosen to fulfil God's promise. And she has spoken of this with me, as if I, a young girl compared to herself, would understand, yet in a deep way I do. We share so much.

And now, Elizabeth speaks about Mary

She is so young, my cousin Mary. And yet was the first person to hear this amazing news, that our God is to be incarnate in a small child. And she responded in joyful song: my soul glorifies the Lord, and my spirit rejoices in God my saviour; his mercy extends to those who fear him from generation to generation; he has performed mighty deeds with his arm; he has brought down rulers from their thrones, but has lifted up the humble; he has filled the hungry with good things, but has sent the rich away empty.

I suppose it would be easy to hear Mary's joyful response here and take it for granted, as though there were no other way she might have responded to the angel's message. After all, many people are joyful when they find out they're pregnant, especially me, and if that baby also fulfils God's promise, well, why wouldn't she be happy, we might ask. But no one was expecting Mary to be pregnant yet, least of all her fiancé, Joseph, since they aren't yet married. She must have known immediately that this had all the makings of a scandal that could see her ostracized and destitute. And second, while being the mother of the long-awaited Messiah is obviously an incredible privilege, it's also an awesome responsibility. I don't know about you, but if an angel came to me and said that I was to be responsible for raising God's only son, my first response would be: 'Err, are you sure you've got the right person here? Isn't there anyone else who could do it better?' And it's not as though Mary is an experienced, accomplished mother, either, confident in her child-raising abilities – she is young, and this is to be her first.

Yet she said yes, and responded with joy. Why? Because she harboured an undeservedly high opinion of her own abilities? Hardly. Rather, because she had a heart that instinctively trusted God and obeyed him. 'I am the Lord's servant,' she said. 'May it be to me as you have said.' It is this heart, and not any special skills she has, that makes her qualified for this most special of tasks. Mary was ready and willing to be a vessel for God's power, and wasn't planning to rely on her own strengths and abilities.

I know how she feels, I also place myself in God's hands and trust him with my life.

God is looking for the same kind of response from us. He isn't calling us to give birth to the Messiah, of course. But, spiritually speaking, Jesus lives inside each of us, and we are all being formed into his likeness. If we allow it to, this amazing reality of which we have been made a part can instil in us the same joyful response that Mary had, and the same desire to go and share that joy with others.

Diana Jones

Hymn suggestions

For Mary, mother of the Lord; Lord Jesus Christ; Lord of the home, your only Son; Tell out my soul, the greatness of the Lord.

St Barnabas the Apostle   11 June
Big-Hearted Barnabas

Job 29.11–16; Ps.112; **Acts 11.19–end** (*if the Acts reading is used instead of the Old Testament reading, the New Testament reading is* Gal. 2.1–10); John 15.12–17

'The man with the biggest heart in the church' is how William Barclay described Barnabas. That makes Barnabas one of the greatest 'mirrors' of God – for our God has the biggest heart in the whole universe!

Barnabas is the sort of person you love having in a church – or anywhere. Perhaps his Christian friends paid him the greatest compliment by giving him a new name. Instead of Joseph, which is what his mother called him, they surnamed him Barnabas, 'son of encouragement'.

I love Barnabas and the Barnabases of today – people who encourage others rather than criticize. It is tragic that Christians can often be dispensers of acid rather than love. So how did the 'man with the biggest heart in the church' encourage?

Giving

When he saw need, he acted, generously. When St Luke tells us in Acts of the way the early believers shared their goods, it is Barnabas who gets a special mention. Why? Did he give with the greatest warmth and joy? We are told that he sold a field and brought the money and laid it at the feet of the apostles. As a Cypriot, that would mean he was giving away the income that came from growing vines and figs. His open generosity is contrasted immediately with the calculating attitude of Ananias and Sapphira, who 'keep some back' and 'lie to the Holy Spirit'. Giving is either generous or stingy – either cheerful or grudging. The graph of Christian giving jumps from the minimum to the maximum – there is little in between. The reason is that true giving springs from the heart. If the heart is not open towards God, there is resentment and a parting with the least that can respectably be given. When the heart has opened there is no shortage of money. So it is for the work of the Church and the relief of the needy when Barnabas is entrusted to carry the collection to Judaea for their famine relief. His encouragement was practical.

Doing

Barnabas was ready to act. He was called to engage in missionary service and to work with Paul with the Gentiles. It meant strategic thinking, and work and effective action for the gospel. In today's Church he would be equally concerned to spread the gospel and contend for the truth. He would be ready to go across the street or even across the world with the gospel of Christ. But you would also see him caring for the elderly, painting the gutters, and no doubt with a New Testament in his hip pocket. He was a 'doer of the word' and not just a hearer.

Being

Barnabas was concerned for people. After Saul was converted, the leading apostles in Jerusalem were suspicious of him, as St Luke records: 'They were all afraid of him, for they did not believe that he was a disciple.' It was Barnabas no less who took Saul in hand, vouched for his changed life and introduced him to the apostles. Through the mediation that Barnabas offered, Saul was accepted as an evangelist. I think of an elderly woman who found herself in an evening service next to a man who was obviously unfamiliar with the worship and new to Christianity. He had been a militant atheist all his life, but God had found a chink in his armour and that evening he came along to church. She sensed that he was someone who needed her attention, although she felt she couldn't cope. She warmly encouraged him to stay for coffee. Once he had a hot cup of coffee in his hands she found help from others. The result was dynamic in that man's life. She was a Barnabas.

Challenges

When Greeks began to turn to Christ in Antioch there was some consternation in Jerusalem as to how they should respond. So they sent Barnabas to visit Antioch as their representative, to find out what was going on and to take any action that was necessary. It was the right choice, because he didn't work to the church's rule book. With his large heart, he looked through the traditions and saw the grace of God at work in the lives of Greeks. As a fellow Cypriot, Luke explains that Barnabas was 'a good man, full of the Holy Spirit and of faith'. Barnabas rapidly realized that there was a big job to be done in Antioch that required the assistance of an effective evangelist. So he went off to Tarsus, where Saul was staying, and brought him back to Antioch, where they both worked together to great effect. Saul grows in leaps and bounds, and before long we read not 'Barnabas and Saul' but 'Saul and Barnabas'. Such was the influence of the ministry in Antioch that it was here that the followers of Jesus were first called 'Christians'.

Friendship endures conflict

Later, when Paul planned to revisit the churches that he had established, Barnabas put forward Mark, his protégé, as a travelling companion. But Paul had found that Mark had proved somewhat unreliable when he pulled out of an earlier missionary journey with him, and was no longer willing to work with him. This precipitated a sharp disagreement between Barnabas and Paul, but Barnabas was more than willing to give Mark a second chance and to accept him as his travelling companion. Towards the end of his life, Paul writes, 'Get Mark and bring him with you, for he is useful in my ministry.'

There was a more serious disagreement with Paul. Barnabas had supported Paul in resisting the Jewish requirement that Jewish Christians should not share table fellowship with Gentile Christians. Peter had originally sided with Paul too, and had shared hospitality with Gentile Christians. When James let it be known that this meant that Jews were ceasing to be Jews, and that they must withdraw from communion with Gentile Christians, Barnabas followed and Peter fell into line behind James. From that point on, Barnabas separated from Paul, but such was the warmth of Barnabas that he could still think of him as a kind of colleague.

Is there someone who would grow if we wrote off their past mistakes and trusted them afresh? We all respond more to encouragement than to criticism. Would others call us an encourager? If not, is our experience of God and his love deficient? For the more we love God, and know his love for us, the more we will have 'big hearts' and will also be a mirror of God, like Barnabas, who had 'the biggest heart in the church'.

Michael Baughen

Hymn suggestions

Lord, you give the great commission; Make me a channel of your peace; God, we praise you! God, we bless you; God, whose city's sure foundation.

Day of Thanksgiving for the Institution of Holy Communion (Corpus Christi) 20 June
A Living Presence

Gen. 14.18–20; Ps. 116.10–17; **1 Cor. 11.23–26**; John 6.51–58

One of the most important words that you will ever use in church is 'Amen'. It means that you give your wholehearted agreement. When you say 'Amen' you mean, 'Yes, it is so. Indeed. Yessssss.' So think of one of the most important times when you say 'Amen'. It is when the priest or the minister of communion says to you, 'The body of Christ' or 'The blood of Christ'. You reply, 'Amen'. Amen, you say. Yes, you say, indeed, this is so, this is the body of Christ, this is the blood of Christ. This is his living presence among us, and I am taking it gratefully into my life, into my heart, into my soul. All this you mean when you say 'Amen'. So do not say thank you, as some people now do. There is a growing trend for people to say thank you, but that is not right. Of course we are grateful for this great gift to us, but save your thank you for your private prayers back in your pew. You do kneel down and thank God for this great gift, don't you? This is what we remember today, Corpus Christi, which means 'the body of Christ' in Latin. It is the feast when we thank God for the mystery of Christ's living presence among us, every Eucharist, under the humble forms of bread and wine. Through these humble elements he can touch our lives and bless and guide us and be there as we return to the busy world outside with all our commitments. It means that he is with us. Think of our second reading today. We hear, 'Do this in remembrance of me' – the words of Jesus conveyed to us by St Paul. But the word 'remembrance' is an inadequate translation. What is really meant here is a vivid recollection of the one of whom we speak, a bringing of past and present together in one living memory.

Jesus Christ here with us

St Paul goes on to tell us that every Eucharist we are proclaiming Christ's death. But this does not mean that we are proclaiming a dead Christ. For Paul, as for us, the life, teaching, death on the cross and resurrection of Jesus are all one seamless event. In proclaiming his death we recall his sacrifice on the cross, and the power of the resurrection. This sacrifice sets us free. The resurrection means that, as the risen Lord, he is no longer bound by the constraints of a particular time and can thus be present when his disciples gather to pray, to proclaim the gospel, to forgive sins, to suffer for his sake, to bring help to others in his name. Above all, Jesus is present when they assemble to do once more what he did at the Last Supper with his disciples. This is why we speak of the 'real presence', that sense we have of Jesus Christ here with us, knowing us, relating to us, reaching out to us, coming into our lives, going with us out into the world.

How can this be possible? Well, I have to ask you to wrestle a little with philosophy. Don't despair. It really is powerful stuff. Here is the philosophy: time does not apply to God. It doesn't make sense, does it, to speak of God as past, present or future. God always is. God is always now. With God there is quite simply eternity. And so when we celebrate the Eucharist, when we stretch out our hands to the bread of life and the cup of salvation, time falls away, because we are entering into the eternal realm. The Last Supper took place 2,000 years ago, but it is not a past event, rather it is a single reality that we enter into again and again. Here ends the philosophy. But think of it. It does make sense. It gives us a grasp of this great mystery of the Mass, with our sense of the real presence. Jesus Christ is not a past event but an ever-living reality, and at the Eucharist we realize that in the most profound way.

Enough for us

Finally here is a simpler thought, but one equally moving. You will remember that in the story of the feeding of the 5,000 we hear about food that did not run out. There was enough for everybody. There is enough here for us and there will be enough at every Eucharist. Christ will always come to his people, and draw them deeper into his life and his love, when they receive him under the form of bread and wine, his sacred body and precious blood. So take time when you come up for communion today. This is the feast of the Eucharist itself, this is a time when we recall more than ever that the Lord is here. Even with us. Even in busy, bustling, ambitious London. In the grandest cathedrals of Europe, in grass-hut chapels of Africa, in shanty towns in Brazil: he comes to his people. Thanks be to God.

Terry Tastard

Hymn suggestions

Now my tongue the mystery telling; Soul of my Saviour, sanctify my breast; All for Jesus, all for Jesus; The bread we break and share.

Birth of John the Baptist   24 June
An Unforgettable Birth

Isa. 40.1–11; Ps. 85.7–end; Acts 13.14b–26, *or* Gal. 3.23–end;
Luke 1.57–66, 80

Help, we need a birth story

Nobody thinks of writing an account of a birth unless the child becomes famous, by which time it is likely that their sources have died, disappeared or been stricken by acute memory loss. When, however, the resurrection of Jesus cast its great light on the preceding life of Jesus, and the first Christians were no longer around, Luke and Matthew doubtless felt constrained to tell the story as they saw it. With a tradition of assiduous, trained memories, and aided by eyewitness reports, it was not difficult to set down the gospel record of Jesus' public ministry. But what was to be done to produce birth stories for Jesus, and for John? It's thought that Mary the mother of Jesus might still have been alive when Luke picked up his pen, but we can't assume that she was used by Luke. There are hints of material that might have been used. But then there is Luke's marvellous capacity for storytelling, so that we have to credit him with a measure of artistic creativity in the service of the gospel.

The sentence for unbelief

Luke introduces us to an elderly, childless couple, Zechariah and Elizabeth. Zechariah is a priest, one of a large number, estimated to be about 18,000, living in Palestine at the time of Jesus. He's on a rota for light duties at the Temple, which involves one week every six months. We find him on duty in good spirits. Zechariah has won the ballot for a once-in-a-lifetime privilege. He has the opportunity to burn the incense; this serves as a call to worship.

On this of all days there comes to him an angel of the Lord, who overawes him with terror and fear. The secret prayers of the couple will be answered, he tells them, their feelings of shame will evaporate. Moreover, the child to be born will 'be filled with the Holy Spirit'. And he will 'make ready a people prepared for the Lord'. When Zechariah dares to question the veracity of the message – and who could blame him? – the angel rises to his full splendour and says in a commanding voice: 'I am Gabriel. I stand in the presence of God.' The good news incurs a penalty. For Zechariah's unbelief, he will be mute until the promise comes true. There follows the comical scene where the crowd are kept waiting for the Aaronic blessing, and when Zechariah finally appears he can only point and gesticulate and leave them to imagine what had occurred to him in the sanctuary. When he goes back to his home in the hill country, you can imagine what the neighbours will make of an elderly woman now secluded and a strong and vocal priest who can no longer speak. Our storyteller now takes his leave of Zechariah and takes us to Nazareth. Gabriel is back in action, this time to face Mary with his own brand of perplexing, overpowering news. Not only that – he serves as the messenger to tell her that Elizabeth has also conceived and is in the sixth month of her pregnancy.

Disagreement over the child's name

But now we skip back to the home of Zechariah and Elizabeth where there is a gathering for the circumcision and naming of the child, now eight days old. There is a disagreement as to what he shall be called. Custom suggested he would be given his father's name, or perhaps his grandfather's. His mother knows that the angel specified that he should be called 'John', meaning 'God has given grace'. But it's the role of the father to choose the name, and the comedy has returned as Zechariah still can't speak to settle the issue, until somebody produces a writing tablet. The amazement that follows seems related to the choice of name. But there was fear among the neighbours, and heightened expectation over a large area as to what the child would become.

John was called to prepare the way of the Lord. But was it clear that it was the Messiah whose way he would be preparing? And there are signs that John too had disciples, not all of whom converted to Jesus, and that the transfer from John to Jesus was not without cost to John. Why did the Prologue of St John's Gospel need to insist that John was not that light, not the Messiah, not Elijah.

Reliving the Old Testament forebears

Luke shows how Zechariah and Elizabeth, Mary and Joseph relive the careers of their Old Testament forebears, Elkanah and Hannah, parents of Samuel, and, more obviously, Abraham and Sarah. In this way Jesus himself is continuous with the whole history of Israel. John the Baptist's birth signals the return of the voice of prophecy after many years where the word of God has been scarce. He is regarded as the last prophet of the old covenant. He is the man full of the Holy Spirit, who is to identify Jesus the Messiah. And without the stern, declamatory sounds of this wild wilderness man, how could we ever hope to be prepared to encounter and receive Jesus into our hearts and lives?

Roger Spiller

Hymn suggestions

The angel Gabriel from heaven came; On Jordan's bank the Baptist's cry; Bless the Lord, the God of Israel; Sing we the praises of the great forerunner.

SS Peter and Paul, Apostles   29 June
Two Challenging Saints

Zech. 4.1–6a, 10b–end; Ps. 125; Acts 12.1–11 (*if the Acts reading is used instead of the Old Testament reading, the New Testament reading is* 2 Tim. 4.6–8, 17–18); **Matt. 16.13–19**

Today we celebrate the two great leaders who steered the Christian Church from its origins to the point when it reached out to the known world. We know more about each of them than we do about any of their contemporaries.

Peter

St Peter was with Jesus from the beginning of Jesus' public ministry, when Jesus called him to forsake his fishing and to become his disciple. We know him as the spokesperson for the disciples, and as Jesus' chosen member of his inner circle. As an eye witness of

Jesus in the intimate and critical moments of his life, there is strong reason to believe that he handed on a unique and incomparable legacy to the writer of the first Gospel, Mark, and through him to the other Synoptic Gospel writers. Quicker to rush to speech than to weigh situations, and led more by heart than head, Peter was, nevertheless, designated the 'rock' whom Jesus appointed to be the foundation of his Church.

Paul

Paul, by contrast, appeared after his conversion, with a commission to lead the embryonic Christian community as it was beginning to reach out beyond its Jewish frontiers. He was convinced by his call to be the pioneer missionary to the Gentiles. In doing so he would also be fulfilling the expectation of the prophets, and perhaps also of Jesus to bring the Gentiles to worship the God of Israel. The expansion of the Jewish movement among Gentiles raised unforeseen and far-reaching questions. These concerned the fundamental nature and message of the gospel itself. It is to Paul's brilliant theological mind and luminous and incomparable letters that the early Church was steered through some dangerous shoals and was able to preserve and pass down the centuries a revolutionary and gracious gospel.

Difference

Peter, together with his brother Andrew, were the first disciples Jesus called to follow him. Being an eyewitness from the very beginning was a key criterion for being an apostle, at least in Luke's eyes. Paul, by contrast, was converted after Jesus had ascended, and his authority and apostleship were open to question. Peter himself was regarded as one of the 'pillars', along with James and John, in the Jerusalem headquarters. Paul begins his ministry as something of a free agent, priding himself on the fact that he did not consult the apostles in Jerusalem, and relied instead on a commission that came direct from the Lord Jesus. It's possible to see, but also to exaggerate, the more centralist, controlling role of Peter with the centrifugal and free and revolutionary style of Paul. After a period of three years, Paul did go to Jerusalem, staying with Peter and seeing James. They approved of the division of labour, that Peter would be the apostle to the Jews and Paul the apostle to the Gentiles. This dramatic carving up of most of the known ancient world would surely give these two Christian giants sufficient breathing space to exercise their respective areas of responsibility.

Shared responsibility

Of course they overlapped, notably in Antioch. Would Peter and Paul work well together with their respective responsibilities for Jewish and Christian converts? Yes, it appears they did. Paul took a broad, revolutionary position with regard to Gentile converts. They were the descendants of Abraham no less than the Jews, through faith and not works of the law. Peter, too, was content to reject the requirement on Jews to abstain from table fellowship with Gentile Christians. New converts, both Jews and Gentiles, thus enjoyed Christian table fellowship together, and that was likely also to include the Lord's Supper or Eucharist.

Disruption and resolution

The situation was soon to change. When James heard from inter-lopers in the church, sent, according to St Paul, to spy out their free-dom, he reacted with horror. This meant that Jews were ceasing to be Jews, he argued. Peter's response, if true to form, seems predict-able. Acting, as Paul said, through 'fear', the absence of James was apparently more powerful than the presence of Paul, Peter switched and sided with James, withdrawing from communion with Gentile Christians.

This was a new situation that couldn't have been foreseen. St Paul suggested a meeting in Jerusalem to thrash out a way forward. The timing of the 'council' is not certain. Paul takes with him Titus, an uncircumcised Greek, and Barnabas, a Jewish Christian. The radi-cal mix is hardly accidental. It suggests that Paul is in a provocative mood in order to force a conclusion. He knows that James is likely to insist not only on separate table fellowship but also on circumci-sion. Paul recorded what he claims to have said to Peter's face, in his letter to the Galatians. He uses his trump card to win his case: 'If you, though a Jew, live like a Gentile and not like a Jew, how can you compel the Gentiles to live like Jews?' For Paul this was hypocrisy, which also ensnared Barnabas. In the event, there was a compromise. Jews were permitted to eat with Gentile Christians, and it was accepted that the circumcised and uncircumcised would exist together in one body. We don't know whether James accepted the compromise.

We cannot be sure whether Peter and Paul were reconciled, although church tradition suggests that Peter and Paul taught together in Rome and founded Christianity in that city. Eusebius cites Dionysius, Bishop of Corinth, as saying, 'They taught together in like manner in Italy, and suffered martyrdom at the same time.' Each of them gave their whole lives in service to the gospel and the Church, and for their inestimable contribution we rejoice and give thanks today.

Roger Spiller

Hymn suggestions

The Church's one foundation; Come, build the Church – not heaps of stone; The Church of God a kingdom is; For all the saints.

St Thomas the Apostle   3 July
The Faith to Doubt
Hab. 2.1–4; Ps. 31.1–6; Eph. 2.19–end; **John 20.24–29**

Faith or doubt?

Poor Thomas Didymus, to give him his full name. He's paid a heavy price for refusing to believe, without evidence, that a man was alive and well two days after his execution and burial. And so this sanest of men, this independent-minded individual, this pseudo-scientist, has for ever been cast as the patron saint of doubt and scepticism. But that's not surely how the Gospel writer saw him. He's not so much the last, slowest and most doubtful of the disciples as the final and definitive eyewitness of the Church's good news for every generation: that Jesus, born in flesh, crucified and buried in godlessness, has been raised by God the Father to new, indestructible life. The Gospel writer intended to bring his Gospel to a glorious conclusion with the most exalted testimony in the New Testament, given by Thomas: 'My Lord and my God.' In doing so, John is underlining the place of doubt and questioning in the development of faith. And when the risen Christ returned, Jesus didn't belittle him for his doubts. Rather, he met Thomas' demands and helped him to reach an exalted faith.

330

Facing doubts

We've been hard on Thomas and this has led many of us to grow up thinking that it is not acceptable to doubt or question. Doubts are then concealed, swept under the carpet, left unaddressed, where they can gnaw away at the foundations, in the basement of our lives. And because we feel we're not given permission to express them, they cannot be engaged with, and we miss the opportunity that doubts give us to deepen and enrich our grasp of God.

Of course there's a wilful disbelief, minds as closed and bolted as the doors of the room where the disciples were sitting – a Richard Dawkins kind of refusal to entertain the evidence on which the experiment of faith can be determined. It's not doubt but indifference that is the opposite of faith, a refusal to engage with the evidence.

The resurrection of Jesus strains credulity. It is, after all, God's act of recreation, no less, brought forward from its expected timescale at the end of the age. It's God's vindication of the way of suffering, self-giving love shown perfectly in Jesus against all the brutal, coercive forces that were pitted against it. It's God in the frail, fleshly creature whose final agonies and injuries had emptied him of life and reduced him to a corpse. And it's the surprising action of God that reconciles the world through the murder of his dear Son, confounding human logic, wisdom and calculation. How then can it really be received without a struggle, and without doubt and questioning? How can our faith be responsible, first hand, personal, if it doesn't result from passionate exploration of the truth?

Faith's place for doubt

Doubt, then, is a sister to faith. Without it, we may take too much for granted; faith may be inherited rather than owned and appropriated for ourselves. So Thomas is the one who can give us courage to face our doubts and help the Church to show to a sceptical generation that you don't have to leave your brain behind when you come to church, or take everything on trust, unquestioningly – as if the Church is fearful that a few honest questions will bring the whole Christian edifice down like a tower of playing cards. If you don't have doubts, says one Christian writer, you're either kidding yourself or asleep.

But what of those of us who come after, who can no longer access Jesus through the senses? Don't tell me, show me, says our generation. People who are tired of the institutional church, despairing of religion, impatient with doctrine and dogma, still ask like the men who come to Philip, 'Sir, we want to see Jesus.' This is why we come here: we want to see Jesus. We want to be like Thomas and see for ourselves. The world wants to see Jesus. And it looks to us, his body, for the telltale marks that enable people to respond, 'My Lord and my God.'

Where can Jesus be seen?

People will see Jesus through his body when it expends itself, surrenders its own life for others. When it dies to the need to ape the successful, managerial, deterministic lifestyle that it is meant to subvert. People will see Jesus through his body when it lives and identifies with the people with whom Jesus kept company: the poor, the marginalized, the sick, the wounded. People will see Jesus when we're concerned not merely for our own survival or the survival of our churches but for the transformation of all society and the restoration of hope in our hope-starved world. People will see Jesus, and we will discover more of Jesus, when we accept his commission to live his risen life; to die daily to self so as to live from the resources of his invisible life. So we, his people, become ourselves part of the evidence of the resurrection. We bear his wounds so that his life can the more clearly, visibly, tangibly be seen in us.

We come seeking Jesus. When we reach out our hands to take his body, and hold his broken body in our hands, we begin to see him. And when we hear his word, the word of the cross, we know that he is here, and we join with Thomas in proclaiming, 'My Lord and my God'. And then we are sent out so others might see him too.

Roger Spiller

Hymn suggestions

Blessed Thomas, doubt no longer; Firmly I believe and truly; Dear Lord, we long to see your face; Come, living God, when least expected.

St Mary Magdalene   22 July
A Flawed Human Encourages Saintliness
Song of Sol. 3.1–4; Ps. 42.1–10; 2 Cor. 5.14–17; **John 20.1–2, 11–18**

It is a great joy to preach on Mary Magdalene. I have a special affection for her because, among all the female saints, she is one of the few who seems human enough to be a role model for women today. Even if Mary Magdalene is not the same person as the 'woman who lived a sinful life' mentioned in Luke's Gospel, as modern scholarship affirms, she clearly was very different from the 'virgin', 'mystic' or 'wife and mother' who has usually been seen as a suitable female candidate for canonization. So her story offers hope and encouragement to those who have experienced the darker side of life, and yet whose lives have been transformed by the experience of the love of God. She is truly 'a sister in Christ'.

An inspiration

Mary Magdalene is also an inspiration to women ministers such as myself, because in her we have the strongest evidence that Jesus accepted and used the ministry of women. Indeed, if the qualifications for the title of 'apostle' are that you were a companion of Jesus in his earthly life, an eyewitness of the resurrection, and were sent by Jesus to proclaim the good news to a specific group of people, then Mary Magdalene can claim to be the first apostle.

By virtue of our baptism, we are all sent to proclaim the gospel – and the story of Mary Magdalene has important things to teach us about how we do that.

The unlikely called

First, it shows us who Jesus called to be his agents in proclaiming the kingdom of heaven. He did not call the clever, the good, the rich and influential; he called the poor, the broken, the outcast. He turned upside down the world's standards.

Mary Magdalene may not have been a prostitute. But the New Testament tells us that Jesus cured her of seven devils. Since, in biblical language, seven is the number of totality, this says that she was regarded as completely possessed, completely in the power of Satan, completely excluded from normal society.

Jesus ignored this. He touched, he kept company with, he used as his agents, the sinful, the sick, the outcast. And his total loving acceptance of them, while they were still sick, sinful and outcast, transformed them into saints. And we are called to do the same. But do we?

333

Who do we accept?

It is so easy for us to fall back into the attitude of the scribes and Pharisees described in the Gospels, to seek to ensure that only the pure and the perfect are admitted to our fellowship and given authority in the Church. If we find in our congregation a woman who is high up in business or education, and another who shouts out during the service and eats up all the food at parish breakfast, which one do we welcome in ~ and whom do we try to persuade to worship elsewhere? But which is the Magdalene?

Second, Mary Magdalene's story teaches us what our response to the love of God in Christ should be. Jesus gave Mary freedom – from possession by devils and enslavement to Satan – and her response was to give back that freedom and become his devoted slave. Luke tells us that Mary, and other women who had been healed by Christ, used their own resources to support him.

The exorcism of the demons in her would have allowed Mary to return to normal life. Becoming a camp follower of Jesus put her straight back into the category of the excluded again. But the total commitment that she showed is what God in Christ demands of us. Again and again, in his teaching and his parables, Jesus says that the only proper response to the call to build the kingdom is unconditional obedience: 'Go sell all that you have and follow me.' Mary Magdalene gives us a pattern of devoted discipleship that endured to death and beyond. She called Jesus 'my Lord', even when she believed him to be in the grave. Is it an example we are prepared to follow?

Don't cling – go and tell

The third lesson we can learn from Mary's story is perhaps the hardest for us to accept, as it was for her. Mary gave her life totally to Jesus. Even after his death, that devotion continued. We can imagine the extravagance of her joy when she found he was no longer in the tomb; all she wanted to do was to hold on to him, to keep him safer. But then came apparent rejection: 'Don't touch me. Don't hold on – go and tell . . .'

Many people find in the Church that peace, that security, that Mary knew in the physical presence of Jesus. But Christ says to us, as he said to her, 'Don't cling on to me – go and tell . . .'

Before we can take the good news to others, we may have to stop clinging to things that will prevent us from getting the message across – perhaps traditional words, styles of music, buildings, institutional structures. Jesus' words to Mary Magdalene warn us of the danger of holding on to what is peripheral. We are to let go, and find him where he is already, alive and at work, in the world around us.

Welcome the unacceptable, respond with all you have, and don't cling to what limits God's mission – a pattern for discipleship that Mary Magdalene gives us today.

Anne Peat

Hymn suggestions

Mary, weep not, weep no longer; Walking in a garden; Good Joseph had a garden; Christ is alive! Let Christians sing.

St James the Apostle   25 July
The Woman with No Name
Jer. 45.1–5 *or* Acts 11.27—12.2; Ps. 126 (*if the Acts reading is used instead of the Old Testament reading, the New Testament reading is* 2 Cor. 4.7–15); **Matt. 20.20–28**

It was one of Clint Eastwood's iconic films, *The Good, the Bad and the Ugly*. Clint played the hero who wore a poncho, a brown hat and brown boots, and smoked cigarillos. He was never named and thus, a touch obviously, was known as 'The Man with No Name'. It enhanced his image of toughness and rugged self-reliance, and increased the air of mystery that surrounded him.

Well. It's a huge leap from that Clint Eastwood character to today's Gospel, but when you look carefully at the reading you will notice that the heroine shares Clint Eastwood's fate: she is similarly not named. She is simply described as 'the mother of Zebedee's sons'. Does she not have a name? Some commentators claim that she was called Salome, and they cite Matthew 27.56 in their evidence. The verse refers to the women who were present at the crucifixion, looking on from a distance – 'Among them were Mary Magdalene, and Mary the mother of James and Joseph, and the mother of the sons of Zebedee . . .', which, it hardly needs pointing out, does not mention the name 'Salome'; but the commentators add 'Look at Mark 15.40'. This is what that verse states: 'There were also women looking on from a distance; among them were Mary Magdalene, and Mary the mother of James the younger and of Joses, and Salome.'

So, say the commentators, she is not named in Matthew's version of the crucifixion event, where she is simply described as the mother of the sons of Zebedee, but in Mark's Gospel a woman called Salome *is* mentioned at the crucifixion (without any mention of 'the sons of Zebedee'), therefore Salome must be the mother of James and John. You can see how the commentators ingeniously reached their conclusion, but it is not entirely convincing, is it? Better to stick with the text as it is, not least because it points up something rather striking.

The encounter

Consider again the encounter between the mother of the sons of Zebedee and Jesus. She has no name; she is, as it were, therefore of no importance, she has no power in her own right. But she wants the very best for her sons. So, accompanied by them (was this a set-up job?), she kneels at Jesus' feet (note how beseeching that gesture is) and asks Jesus that her sons should be given the most honoured places in the forthcoming kingdom. Jesus does not reply to her question, but, perhaps guessing that this really is a set-up, a pre-arranged job, turns not to the mother but to James and John and explains that the awarding of special places is not in his gift; that belongs solely to God. But he adds a sharp and frightening rider within his answer:

> 'You do not know what you are asking. Are you able to drink the cup that I am about to drink?' They said to him, 'We are able.' He said to them, 'You will indeed drink my cup . . .'

Remember that this exchange happened in the context of Jesus telling his disciples that they were about to go up to Jerusalem, where he would suffer torture and be killed. The 'cup' to which Jesus referred in his answer is obviously the cup of suffering.

We know that James did indeed drink that 'cup', but more than ten years later. According to the Acts of the Apostles (12.2), James was beheaded by Herod. That grisly event is normally dated to AD 44.

Deepening insight

But let's get back to the story. As a result of the mother's question and Jesus' response, the other disciples round on James and John. There was an altercation. But what helps to make the story so intriguing is that it is such typical human behaviour. Faced with the terrible, unpalatable situation that Jesus has foretold his own death, the disciples take their anger and fear out not on James and John's mother, nor on Jesus, but on their colleagues. It's classic displacement activity.

Jesus is forced to intervene again, and reminds them that the desire for status and power should not be part of their thinking. Instead, he tells them:

'Whoever wishes to be great among you must be your servant, and whoever wishes to be first among you must be your slave; just as the Son of Man came not to be served but to serve, and to give his life a ransom for many.'

So an episode that began with the beseeching question from the mother of the sons of Zebedee ends with a sharp reminder to all of us about our own hunger for power and status. Like the mother of Zebedee's sons, we are not named in the story, but the implication for all of us is painfully obvious.

Following Christ as a disciple is about humility, about not seeking power, about being willing to go wherever he leads, even to suffering and death.

It really is a hugely demanding task we have been given. And all we can do is to pray that, as we follow Jesus in our various situations, we might have the courage and the strength to do as he says.

James did indeed drink from the cup. Are we capable of doing the same?

Christopher Herbert

Hymn suggestions

Great God, your love has called us here; For all thy saints, O Lord; Love divine, all loves excelling; Father of heaven, whose love profound.

Transfiguration of Our Lord   6 August
Excited on the Mountain, but Living on the Plain
Dan. 7.9–10, 13–14; Ps. 97; 2 Pet. 1.16–19; **Luke 9.28–36**

Mount Tabor

Towering over the fertile plains, dominant, isolated and unmissable, is Mount Tabor.

It's no surprise that mountains have always been places of holiness. In the days when people believed we had a triple-decker universe (hell, earth, heaven), a mountain top was the obvious place for having an experience of God. It was, after all, much closer to where God dwells.

Mountains can be inspiring places. On a clear day, the views can astound us. From up here, the world looks different, proportions are altered, perspectives need adjusting.

But mountains are also hazardous places. The wind howls more strongly, the cold bites more sharply, blinding fog can sweep in with no warning and suddenly a beautiful vista disappears, obscured by cloudy cataracts.

When Peter, James and John witnessed Jesus' transfiguration, there was a powerful mix of inspiration and hazard. They were caught up in one of the most mysterious visions of the gospel, and although it only made sense after the resurrection, it felt wonderful. But also terrifying. This mystical experience was a combination of compelling fascination and repelling fear.

And as quickly as the clouds blow in and melt away again, the vision ends and the disciples are left wondering what happens now. The answer is that there is work to be done, so they need to make their way back down the narrow, precipitous mountain path to the plains.

But this is no ordinary valley floor. Green, lush and productive it is, but it's a plain with a past. Indeed, it's a plain with a future that already echoes through the present.

The plain of Jezreel

Here, at the base of Mount Tabor, sprawling across southern Galilee, is the plain of Jezreel. Throughout history, this plain has been a place of great battles. Fourteen hundred years before Christ, the Israelite judge Deborah commanded her army into bloody

338

battle, wiping out the native Canaanites. Not long after Jesus, the first Jewish–Roman war was waged here. There were battles in the Arab period, battles during the Crusades. Napoleon waged war on this same plain, and even in the 1940s battles were still being fought on it. Beautiful the plains are, but there's a great deal of blood in their fertile soil.

But this plain has another name too. It's also known as the plain of Armageddon. If you happen to have a literalist approach to the book of Revelation, then this plain is the place where the final battle between good and evil will be played out. And so will begin the end of the world.

This is the place that awaited Jesus and the three disciples after experiencing his transfiguration on the mountain top. They'd had a glorious vision. The two great figures of the law and prophets had appeared with Jesus. They'd heard the divine voice confirm him as God's chosen son.

On top of Mount Tabor, and on the plain stretched out below, past and future were woven together into a mysterious present. Luke tells us they kept silent and 'in those days told no one any of the things they had seen'.

This was something they needed time to process. It takes time for our hearts and minds to reflect, to question, to come to understanding after an experience like that. The event comes first; comprehension follows, although often in a trickle rather than a rush. In the disciples' case, it wasn't until the pain of Holy Week was past that they realized they had been given a preview of Jesus' Easter glory. Past and future had been woven into their present.

Peter offered to build some dwellings, to contain the experience. But despite the light-filled wonder of what had happened on the mountain top, life couldn't be lived there. They had to descend again. Wonderful experiences enrich our lives, but they enrich them so that we can more creatively live in the ordinary.

The valley floor is the place of daily life. It's a place that is often beautiful and fertile, but it's also a place where you and I encounter our battles.

Equipped not protected

The life of faith isn't about being protected; it's about being equipped. The battles we wage in the plains of daily life are many.

They include war with our own weaknesses; struggling with famine, poverty and natural disaster; persevering through persecution; finding hope in illness and personal tragedy.

But alongside the challenges, life on the plain brings the joys that warm our hearts and the relationships that help make us whole.

Just as Jesus calls us to the mountain top for a new perspective on life on the plain, so he calls us to carry his transfigured glory – and all that it promises – back to the everyday.

Time past and time future weave into a challenging present. That's because it's in battle as well as in laughter, in darkness as well as in light, that the power of his resurrection transfigures us and makes us agents of transfiguration in his world.

Brett Ward

Hymn suggestions

Christ, upon the mountain peak; O vision blest of heavenly light; 'Tis good Lord, to be here; From glory to glory.'

The Blessed Virgin Mary   15 August
Calling and Response
Isa. 61.10–end, *or* Rev. 11.19—12.6, 10; Ps. 45.10–end; Gal. 4.4–7; **Luke 1.46–55**

Today we are remembering the Blessed Virgin Mary – the mother of our Lord. Mary's calling and response, life and witness has much to teach us about our own discipleship and vocation as we follow Christ.

A dangerous 'Yes'

God is full of surprises. God does the unexpected and calls his followers to journey with him on adventures into the unknown. God chooses and commissions Mary to bear his son – an incredible honour, but not without real risk. Being pregnant and unmarried was not just a scandal in first-century Jewish society, it was punishable by death. And so Mary's 'Yes' to God is fraught with danger – well beyond her comfort zone, and open to misunderstanding from every side. What an extraordinary way for God to bring about the salvation of the world – through a teenage, unmarried mum. Mary's obedience to God requires courage, recklessness and deep faith.

So when God calls us as individuals and as a church to follow him, it is a call to costly, surprising, risky, adventurous living – which may be open to misunderstanding and ridicule. Where we've grown comfortable in our faith, and God seems cosy and undemanding, we may have stopped listening to God's surprises, and just pleasing ourselves. Obedience to God's call requires courage. Being a disciple of Jesus Christ should be costly. Obedience does not mean slavishly following a set of rules, but being in tune with the living Spirit of God who will not be pinned down by the smallness of our imaginations.

Carrying Christ

Carrying the Christ child within her, Mary sings her song, the Magnificat. Carrying the Word incarnate, she sings words that can be traced back through the Scriptures – the words of Hannah, and of the prophets Isaiah, Zephaniah and others. Mary declares that her whole being praises God. She is confident that God will restore order, will save the poor, will act with strength and mercy, and will keep his promises. Mary is the new daughter of Zion, clothed with the robe of righteousness and called to rejoice. She proclaims salvation for her people Israel. She declares the good news of God, and models a new way of living.

When we were baptized each of us became part of the body of Christ – we too carry Christ within us, and as a church we proclaim and model Christ for others. St Paul, writing to the churches in Rome, showed what that looks like. The Church must show genuine love, hate evil, hold on tightly to goodness. Christians are to love one another, to honour each other, to serve God with passion, courage and energy. Don't be half-hearted in your faith, don't be lukewarm – let others see how Christ makes a real difference in your life.

So often the national and international church is portrayed in the media as at war with itself and the world. Church synods, assemblies and conferences are made to look like battlegrounds. The world looks in and sees God portrayed as small-minded, tight, repressive, mean and angry. But as Christians living in our local communities, working at grass-roots level, we can show something different. We can be alongside people in their everyday lives – to rejoice and weep and bless and promote harmony. And what is done at grass-roots level is what makes the real difference. When people see the Holy Spirit at work in ordinary everyday ways they will be drawn in and want to know more of the real Christ, who is very attractive.

Bringing God into focus

Bearing Christ didn't just change Mary – didn't just make her 'full of grace' – it also changed the people around her. Mary's soul magnified the Lord – her whole life, the person she was, brought God into focus for others, showed others the glory and majesty of the Lord. Christ within Mary gave Joseph a generosity of spirit. Christ within Mary made John the Baptist in Elizabeth's womb jump for joy. Christ within Mary brought a Pentecost experience for Elizabeth – she was filled with the Holy Spirit and spoke prophetically about Mary as the mother of the Lord. Christ in us should bring God into focus for others. That's easy in church, when we worship, pray, sing and serve. But we should also be doing it at work, at school, at home, in the pub, in the supermarket – wherever we are. Our lives, souls, actions, words should magnify the Lord, should bring God into focus for others. We should help others have a bigger vision of what God can and will do for and with people – all of whom he loves without beginning or end. Christ within us makes a difference to us and to others.

May Mary model for us obedience in the face of God's challenges and mysteries. May she remind us to be people of good news, and hope – who carry Christ within us and who look for and long for the best that can be. May Mary challenge us as the Church to bring God into focus for everyone, whoever they are. May Mary teach us to be people who fight against local injustice, who interact with local people in their joys and sorrows, who take risks and do surprising and courageous things to make the world more aware of the living God. Give thanks for Mary: may she be for us an example and inspiration as we exercise our calling as disciples of Jesus Christ.

Mary said: 'My soul magnifies the Lord, and my spirit rejoices in God my Saviour.'

Catherine Williams

Hymn suggestions

Tell out my soul; Ye who own the faith of Jesus; For Mary, mother of the Lord; Virgin born, we bow before thee.

St Bartholomew the Apostle   24 August
A Saint with an Uncertain Identity

Isa. 43.8–13; Ps. 145.1–7; Acts 5.12–16 (*if the Acts reading is used instead of the Old Testament reading, the New Testament reading is* 1 Cor. 4.9–15); **Luke 22.24–30**

It's St Bartholomew's Day. But unless your mind was fully on the job when we prayed the Collect, you could be forgiven for not having noticed. When we came to the readings there was no memorable gospel incident to bring Bartholomew to mind: nothing on a par with Thomas in his doubts, or Peter affirming Jesus as the Christ, or Judas in his treachery.

Mistaken identity?

The Bible scholars tell us that the person whom Matthew, Mark and Luke call Bartholomew is the same person to whom John gives the name Nathanael – but no lectionary compiler appears ever to have backed that particular horse and dared to include the appropriate verses from the first chapter of John's Gospel among the readings for St Bartholomew's Day. (The Synoptics put it the other way round and pair Bartholomew with Philip.) But it's worth remembering what John has to say. He tells us that Philip went and told Nathanael he had found the Messiah and that he brought Nathanael to Jesus, which would put Nathanael/Bartholomew among the earliest of the Twelve to be chosen.

And having gone that far with John's account, let's go a step further. John tells us that Jesus, seeing Nathanael coming, described him even from afar as 'an Israelite in whom there is no guile'. Perhaps it was precisely that transparent honesty that earned him foundation membership in the Lord's team.

Finding a reading

And now it's time to stretch the imagination. Just picture a group of four people sitting round a table. It's the lectionary committee in session. Bibles in countless versions, concordance, dictionaries litter the room. Says one: 'Has anybody got a bright idea about a New Testament reading for St Bartholomew's Day?' Another voices what all are thinking: 'Difficult to find something appropriate for a person we know so little about.' The third – perhaps a man from the pew rather than a scholar, amazed at his own cheek – says: 'The first thing that comes into my mind at the mention of Bartholomew is a London hospital.' 'Perfect,' says the fourth. 'Let's go for that passage in Acts that tells of our risen Lord's healing ministry functioning freely through his faithful apostles.' And we are told of how the people bring out their sick – the sick in mind and body – 'and they were all cured'.

We thank God for Bart's, past and present, and pray his blessing on its future. And so to the Gospel. One of the continuing encouragements of Christianity – perhaps its greatest – is the way in which it lays down almost as a ground rule the fact that God uses men and women still, in all their frailty, as his ministers. That human frailty is never far away – and never has been. So Luke tells us of a dispute among the disciples – not among the half-hearted hangers-on, but among the chosen Twelve, the leadership itself. And the dispute? About status, of all things. It sounds inconceivable that those first followers of Jesus should be concerned about who was the greatest – until we remember our own weaknesses in that direction.

And then Bartholomew comes to our rescue – this man of uncertain identity with no strong strings to his bow, no deeds or words adjudged worthy of being noted by the Evangelists. Yet Jesus chose him. Amazingly, he chooses us too.

Michael McAdam

Hymn suggestions

Saints of God! Lo, Jesu's people; Give us the wings of faith to rise; How beauteous are the feet; Lo, round the throne, a glorious band.

Holy Cross Day   14 September
The Power of Place
Num. 21.4–9; Ps. 22.23–28; Phil. 2.6–11; **John 3.13–17**

Today is Holy Cross Day. It's a feast with a complicated history that we needn't go into in detail now. What we need to know is that it goes back to the fourth century when the Emperor Constantine had embraced Christianity. His mother Helena undertook a programme of removing the pagan shrines from Jerusalem. During excavations in the city, she is said to have uncovered the three crosses of Golgotha, of which the cross of Jesus was identified by a miracle. The basilica of the Holy Sepulchre was built on the site and dedicated on this day in the year 335.

The ambiguity of place

If you have been to Jerusalem you may well have rather mixed memories of the Holy Sepulchre. The standard archaeological guide to the Holy Land says:

> One expects the central shrine of Christendom to stand out in majestic isolation, but anonymous buildings cling to it like barnacles. One looks for numinous light, but it is dark and cramped. One hopes for peace, but the ear is assailed by a cacophony of warring chants. One desires holiness, only to encounter a jealous possessiveness: the six groups of occupants – Latin Catholics, Greek Orthodox, Armenians, Syrians, Copts, Ethiopians – watch one another suspiciously for any infringement of rights. The frailty of humanity is nowhere more apparent than here.[28]

The author might have added that for the last two centuries, the only person trusted to be a key-holder of the church has been a Muslim.

The power of place

Huge crowds of tourists make it impossible to enjoy the church during the daytime. However, at 4 o'clock in the morning, when it opens, it is one of the most moving places in the world, with shafts of dawn light piercing the incense-laden gloom, and Copts and Armenians beginning their morning office in chants as old as Christianity. And then you begin to see why, as the guide goes on, 'those who permit the church to question them may begin to understand why hundreds of thousands thought it worthwhile to risk death or slavery in order to pray here'. The belief that Jesus died and was buried here is among the very earliest memories of the Christian Church in Jerusalem. We can safely trust it.

Human instinct is always to trace the story of faith in this world's landscapes. Christianity tells of incarnation in a specific place at a specific time among a specific people. Sacred geography, preserving memory at holy places and shrines, praying and making pilgrimage towards them, is to recognize the footprints of the divine in the stones and soil of this good earth. The Church of the Holy Sepulchre is a baffling, untidy and not an especially beautiful place. Yet paradoxically this is precisely why it speaks so eloquently of the cross. The mess, confusion and pain of human life belong inescapably to Golgotha. Its holiness is true to the world as we know it. If it were a cleaned-up, sanitized place in which to etherealize and indulge in beautiful thoughts we wouldn't altogether believe in it.

Places that point beyond

But this basilica is a shrine that draws all sorts and conditions to itself. Its reach is as wide as the earth. Out of the particular comes the universal. For, while Christianity inhabits and suffuses place and space, it goes beyond them. This 'particularity' matters for the universal invitation of the gospel. St John's Gospel is of a piece in proclaiming that as Christ came for that people at that time, so he comes for this people at this time and for all people for all time. Whatever precious meanings attach to the shrines of our faith, Christianity doesn't impose obligations to pilgrimage in the way that Muslims are obliged to make Haj to Mecca, for Christ crucified and risen transcends all the limitations of geography. The Desert Fathers told of a man who had saved all his life to make a lifetime's pilgrimage to Jerusalem and walk seven times round the Church of the Holy Sepulchre. Just as he set out on his journey, he met a poor man clothed in rags who begged the pilgrim for alms. So the pilgrim gave him all he had, walked round the beggar seven times and said: I have accomplished my pilgrimage. I have visited Jerusalem and honoured the place where Christ died. That is Christianity.

Today's Gospel gives us St John's timeless statement of divine love poured out for the salvation of our race: 'God so loved the world that he gave his only Son, so that everyone who believes in him may not perish but may have eternal life.' It is pure gift. There are no works for us to perform, no tasks to accomplish, for Christ has finished the work he came to do. On this feast of the Exaltation of the Holy Cross we look on him whom we have pierced, who is exalted in triumph on the Tree, our King crowned on his throne of Golgotha. We look – and live.

Michael Sadgrove

In the cross of Christ I glory; Were you there when they crucified my Lord?; When I survey the wondrous cross; Lift high the cross.

St Matthew, Apostle and Evangelist   21 September
An Unlikely Apostle
Prov. 3.13–18; Ps. 119.65–72; 2 Cor. 4.1–6; **Matt. 9.9–13**

Evangelist?

It's been said that a saint is a person whose life has not been scrutinized too closely. This would certainly be true of St Matthew, the saint the Church commemorates today. After all, what do we know, really know, about Matthew? Tradition has it that he was the writer of a Gospel. Tradition yes, but most New Testament scholars think it's extremely unlikely that he ever wrote a Gospel. For one thing, Matthew's Gospel copies a staggering 90 per cent of Mark's Gospel. Now, since Matthew was an eyewitness of Jesus, why would he be so dependent upon a writer who didn't see and know Jesus for himself? He would surely have his own stories to tell. And then, from the dating of the Gospel, it's unlikely that Matthew would have been around to have completed the Gospel himself. Tradition might mean only that Matthew collected together some sayings of Jesus, which, as a tax-collector with literacy skills, would be plausible; not that he himself wrote the Gospel in anything like the form we have it today.

Apostle?

But if he wasn't the writer of a Gospel, his other claim to fame was as an apostle. Well, in St Mark's list of apostles, Matthew is certainly included. But that doesn't quite settle the issue, because by the time of Mark's Gospel, some 35 years after Jesus called his disciples, there was evidently some confusion over the exact composition of the Twelve. So, Mark seems to think that Levi was an apostle, even though Levi was not in Mark's own list of apostles. Some think that Levi's name was originally in the list but was subsequently changed to Matthew because Matthew had become more well known. Or perhaps Levi and Matthew were names of one and the same person. Even the brief story of the call of a tax-gatherer, which in today's Gospel concerns Matthew, is attributed to Levi in the Gospels of Mark and Luke.

Now, this little excursion into scholarly opinion is not to tell us that we have no business thinking of saints like Matthew, about whom little is known. It's to remind us that God makes saints; saints are not self-made. And so even in the story of Matthew's call it is Jesus, not Matthew, who takes centre-stage.

You can never explain, or account for, God's call. So Jesus calls Matthew, a tax-collector. He even goes out of his way to enter the tax office and confront him over the counter.

We know what devout Jews thought about tax-collectors – doing the dirty work of the Romans, and so collaborators, extortionists, taking a slice of the money on the side; and so also sinners, members of one of the despised trades, and that included a surprising group, sailors, shopkeepers, doctors, bath attendants and butchers.

Sinner

Matthew acts out of self-interest, he's the prototype sinner. His lifestyle takes its toll, it's become a way of life, habitual, addictive. He's marginalized. All societies have people whose jobs put them in the social line of fire: traffic wardens, VAT inspectors, and tabloid journalists. And there are those whose duties lay them more open to corruption and abuse than others. We're not to excuse them, but it's pretty impossible for them to dig themselves out of the pit they've fallen into. So what prospect for Matthew and for others who are dissatisfied with themselves? None but for an amazing call from one who woos and beckons us with love.

Jesus

'Follow me,' said Jesus, and where do you think Jesus might have led him – to an Alpha course, to confirmation preparation, to an intensive training in Christian discipleship? Instead he took him for a meal, gave him hospitality, probably in his own temporary home, at which the door was always kept open – for he was soon besieged by 'many tax collectors and sinners'. There is no threat, no intimidation, no menace in Jesus' house. Those accustomed to living on the fringes of society are accepted. His door is always open, there are no closing hours. There's room for those who want to come.

This unconditional generosity can offend our religious sensibilities, as it did the Pharisees. They lived by rules, drew tight boundaries against 'outsiders'. We seem to need to create outsiders as the ones on whom we can project the dark, sinister bits we see in ourselves.

Jesus threatens such a world, blurs the lines and uncovers grace, so amazing that people who are snug in their religious identities are left unsettled. There's only one condition, one thing necessary. It's to know you're sick. There isn't a category called 'the sick', any more than there is a category called 'the disabled', or 'the blind', or 'the dying'. We are all sick, disabled, blind, dying, and that's the basis of Christian hope and healing. As T. S. Eliot put it, 'Our only health is the disease' and 'to be restored, our sickness must grow worse'.[29]

So the saints aren't people who intimidate us by their holiness. They encourage us by the grace of God, which transforms the unlikely, hopeless and marginal people, whom both religion and society have written off, into men and women who embody the healing and restorative grace of Jesus Christ.

Roger Spiller

Hymn suggestions

Christ is the one who calls; Amazing grace, how sweet the sound; We turn to Christ anew; And can it be.

St Michael and All Angels   29 September
The Elusiveness of Angels
Gen. 28.10–17, *or* Rev. 12.7–12; Ps. 103.19–end; **Rev. 12.7–12**, *or* Heb. 1.5–end; John 1.47–end

Over 40 years ago a book was published entitled *Mister God, This is Anna'*.[30] Its author was a man who went under the pseudonym of 'Fynn'. The book immediately entered the best-seller lists, and many of those who read it were very moved by the story. It tells of a little girl in the 1930s called Anna who had run away from her unhappy and abusive home. She was found seated on a grating somewhere in the East End of London by a gentle giant of a teenager called Fynn who took Anna home where she was looked after by his mother. Anna, according to the book, was a wise and questioning little girl much given to theological and philosophical musings.

Until relatively recently the identity of the author was not known, but a careful bit of sleuthing by a number of people seems to have established that Fynn's real name was Sydney Hopkins. He had been born in the East End, and as a young man had entered an educational and therapeutic community called Finchden Manor in Kent. After some years of work as a research chemist, he returned to Finchden as a teacher. If you are interested to find out more, take a look at Wikipedia.

Sharp insights

The curiously whimsical and even slightly unsettling nature of the book is that it is not clear how far it is autobiographical. It is not clear either whether Anna was real or whether she was a character created by the author. In the book, she died in an accident when she was 7 years old, and Fynn was devastated.

The question of reality can be left to one side, for what the book undoubtedly captures is that sharp insight that some children have about life, and the even sharper questions that they can bring to questions of meaning.

When Anna was musing one day, she said to Fynn: 'The diffrense [*sic*] from a person and an angel is easy. Most of an angel is in the inside and most of a person is on the outside.'

It's worth pondering, not least because it chimes with our experience. We have all met people who have an inner quality that seems angelic: they are good through and through, deeply loving and wise, and have about them a hint of eternity. You feel better for being in their presence. They bring life to life.

It's all too easy for these qualities to be sentimentalized, but 'angelic' people could not be more real. They have an inner laughter, a profound sense of joy. Which is not to say that they have not experienced real difficulties in their lives; usually they have. They have often been through deep suffering, and yet have come through that suffering in a way that has left them wounded yet healed. They seem to radiate an inner truth. They have poise. They have grace.

Elusive angels

Describing angelic people is really difficult; the right words are incredibly elusive. Yet you and I know, in ways that are beyond words, who such people are and what they are like.

But perhaps we shouldn't be too surprised by the difficulties of discovering the right words. Elusiveness seems to be one of the characteristics of angels. Look at biblical descriptions of them and you'll soon realize that angels come and go. They don't stay for tea or to have lengthy conversations. No sooner have they made their announcements than they have gone. They fly, it would seem, between heaven and earth with ease, yet never even shed a feather to indicate that they have been present. All that they leave behind is an announcement.

But now consider this. Let me take an example, by analogy, from music.

You may have been to a concert where the music has been performed with such flair and skill that at the end you have found yourself unable to describe the effect that it's had on you. The wonder you experienced was beyond words. In such circumstances, words feel heavy, awkward and entirely inadequate. A joy-filled silence is the only response possible. Or think of that moment when you fell in love. You may remember that the joy of being with the beloved was beyond expression. Or remember the time when you went for a walk in the hills and a view took your breath away.

All those experiences might be said to have the characteristics of an epiphany. No words, yet the experience was in reality a kind of announcement, for you knew that your life had been deepened, changed and transformed by the experience.

The experience is then taken down into our souls. We continue to reflect upon it, often many years later – and it continues to feed us, to shape us and to form us.

Is it any wonder that Anna, whoever she might have been, described angels as 'more in the inside'?

It should be our prayer (shouldn't it?) that we may always remain open to the signals from eternity, so that our inner lives become filled with the healing love of God, and that through his grace we may be brought to that vision of heaven where with angels and archangels we join in singing: Holy, Holy, Holy . . .

Christopher Herbert

Hymn suggestions

Come, let us join our cheerful songs; Stars of the morning; Sons of the Holy One; How great thou art.

St Luke the Evangelist   18 October
Kingdom Agents

Isa. 35.3–6, *or* Acts 16.6–12a; Ps. 147.1–7; 2 Tim. 4.5–17;
Luke 10.1–9

Note on delivery – this is a sermon that traces out a theme through the Gospel of Luke. If space allows, the sermon can be delivered through the space, as though the scroll of the Gospel was rolled out and we were moving to different parts of it.

Kingdom agents

Our Gospel focuses in on the 70 who go ahead of Jesus, representing him in attitude, action and proclamation. They are sent as kingdom agents with a clear preaching programme: 'the kingdom of God has come near.'

Buckle up – on this St Luke's Day we are going on a zip through Luke's Gospel, to see what we can learn about being a kingdom agent.

Luke's tips for kingdom agents: urgency and poverty

Luke 4.43 – Jesus describes how he must proclaim the good news of the kingdom of God to other cities, not just Capernaum. Kingdom agents are called to follow the Master. We *must* proclaim the kingdom in words and works. Urgency here.

The kingdom pops up in Luke 6.20: 'Blessed are you who are poor, for yours is the kingdom of God.' Another lesson here: kingdom agents need a sharp awareness of our own poverty.

Countercultural clowns

In chapter 8.1, Jesus hammers home his message of the good news of the kingdom of God. The 12 disciples are with him, and some women who finance the work. Kingdom agents are men and women collaborating often in countercultural ways. Look how the women support the work financially. Not the norm in the context. Kingdom agents are not bound by convention.

Trace the thread again: Luke 9.2, Jesus sends the 12 to proclaim the kingdom, giving them authority over demons and disease. Jesus' workers step out of the comfortable, responding as the situation requires, trusting that Jesus is the healer and restorer, acting in his name. Sometimes this is scary, and you may feel you are wearing shoes that are way too big. Clowns wear big shoes; kingdom agents may look like fools.

There may be trouble ahead – keep steady

Just a few verses later, in Luke 9.11, Jesus speaks in Bethsaida about the kingdom of God, and people are healed. This power is not going to make Jesus popular. People are either for the kingdom and enter it, or they sense it and despise it. Kingdom agents can expect trouble.

Again, the thread of the kingdom stands out from the tapestry of Luke. 9.62. 'No one who puts hand to the plough and looks back is fit for the kingdom of God.' Kingdom agents need a steady focus on the task in hand.

A kingdom of subtle potential

Skimming on in Luke, the kingdom recurs in chapter 13, in two parables. Jesus compares the kingdom to a mustard seed growing into a tree sheltering many birds. The kingdom may look tiny, but see what it becomes. Kingdom agents need imaginative vision, to see potential, and patience in the process of growth.

Jesus speaks of the kingdom as leavening yeast. The kingdom might look insignificant but it affects everything it comes into contact with. Trust that a little of the kingdom goes a long way.

In chapter 17 Jesus states that 'the kingdom of God is among you'. Kingdom agents need to recognize that the kingdom doesn't come with fanfares and fireworks. It is subtle; a reality closer than our heartbeat.

With childlike freedom

A chapter later, Jesus states: 'whoever does not receive the kingdom of God as a little child will never enter it.' Do you ever feel too small to do this kingdom stuff? Take courage. Agents of the kingdom bear hallmarks of the child: trust, curiosity, humility, playfulness, joy, the willingness to look daft, and to belly laugh. Kingdom agents are not pompous, proud or posturing – they are like little children. Which comes as a mighty relief.

The kingdom theme pulses on – chapter 18 – 'it is easier for a camel to go through the eye of a needle than for someone who is rich to enter the kingdom of God.' Kingdom agents need to be free of baggage and fleet of foot, unencumbered by material concerns.

There's always more, so think big and pray bigger

In chapter 19, Jesus tells a parable about the kingdom near and now, but also not yet. Kingdom agents handle such complexity with simplicity. There is always more to hope for, to work for and to expect. Kingdom agents think *big*, roll up their sleeves and pray and act with an outward focus. Crying out on behalf of the dispossessed: refugees so desperate they pile into unsuitable boats; those trapped in war whose houses are rubble, whose future is bleak; communities of intergenerational unemployment, where hopelessness is part of the way of life. Kingdom agents hold out healing hands to the cancer sufferer, the bereaved, the disturbed, the lonely, the abused, asylum seekers, homeless people, those in the grip of ravaging, narcotic hunger.

Agents of the kingdom foster feral prayers, randomly praying for the old fella on the bench in town, the child at the bus stop, the soldier in the picture.

Don't forget the criminal's plea from his cross to be remembered in the kingdom, and Jesus' promise that he would join him in paradise that day. The kingdom stretches into the unknown territory beyond death; a cause for profound hope.

Therefore

Agents of the kingdom, tell them all: 'The kingdom of God has come near to you.' Show this in prayer, works of healing, and random acts of kindness and hope. If the shoes feel too big, and you feel like a clown, that's fine. Just be a faithful clown; a faithful kingdom agent.

Kate Bruce

Hymn suggestions

Forth in thy name, O Lord, I go; Take my life and let it be; Make me a channel of your peace; Seek ye first the kingdom of God.

SS Simon and Jude, Apostles   28 October
Known to God
Isa. 28.14–16; Ps. 119.89–96; Eph. 2.19–end; **John 15.17–end**

In the middle of the thirteenth century a man called Jacopo, who came from a town called Varazze, about 19 miles from Genoa, created a book; a book that was to have a huge influence on the Church in the following centuries. The book became known as the *Golden Legend* and contained stories about the saints. Jacopo had collected and compiled the stories and legends from a large number of sources. There are stories about famous saints like St Peter, as well as stories about slightly more obscure saints, such as St Lupus, Archbishop of Sens, who, it was claimed, witnessed a jewel falling from heaven into a chalice on an altar. The lives of over 180 saints were recorded by Jacopo, and so popular did his book become that there are still over 1,000 handwritten copies of it in existence. The *Golden Legend*, by the way, is now available in a two-volume English edition that runs to almost 800 pages.

If you look in the *Golden Legend* for stories of Simon and Jude there are plenty, including one rather exotic one, which said that through their charismatic holiness they tamed two man-eating tigers; the tigers apparently became 'as meek as lambs'. The other stories involved them travelling to Persia, preaching the gospel there and engaging in feats of rhetoric that confounded many of the magicians they encountered on their travels.

Who were Simon and Jude?

But the problem about Simon and Jude is that, apart from the legends that grew up around them, we know very little about them; even their origins and their names are contested. For example, in Luke's Gospel Jude is called 'son of James', which some in the Western Church have interpreted to mean 'brother of'. They cite the fact that in Mark's Gospel a person called Jude appears in a list of the children of Mary: Jude is a version of Judas. 'Is not this the carpenter, the son of Mary and brother of James and Joses and Judas and Simon, and are not his sisters here with us?' But if that person was one of the disciples and also Jesus' brother, why did Luke not say so? And as for Simon, he too emerges out of obscurity. In Mark and Matthew he is called 'the Canaanean', whereas in Luke he is called 'the Zealot', perhaps an understandable confusion because the root word can be translated either way.

So, those are about the only 'facts' we have about two of the Twelve. But there is one tiny and important detail that might explain the origin of the legends about Simon and Jude and their travels in Asia Minor and Persia.

Thaddaeus and Jude

The Armenian Orthodox Church claims that it was originally founded by Thaddaeus, and Thaddaeus (another name for Jude) was, of course, one of the original 12 apostles. In these circumstances, where Simon and Jude are otherwise lost in the mists of time, it is striking that Armenia, which in the fourth century was the first country in the world to adopt Christianity as its official religion, should claim such a strong association with Thaddaeus. If Thaddaeus was not their founder, why didn't they choose a better-known saint instead? The fact that they claimed Thaddaeus/Jude as their founder, it seems to me, might be significant.

It's no more than a hint, but a hint nevertheless, that the legends about Simon and Jude going to Persia might have a tiny grain of truth in them. Otherwise, the very mistiness of the historical whereabouts of these two saints might also explain why Jude, in particular, has been invoked as the patron saint of lost causes.

Is being known by God the key?

Is being known by God the key?

But there is another element about these two apostles that bears thinking about. Let's be clear: they were indeed members of the Twelve. In other words, they had been called by Jesus; they had witnessed his miracles, had heard his teaching, and witnessed his death and resurrection. They were of immense significance, and yet, to all intents and purposes, they have disappeared off the map. They came from obscurity and, apart from briefly appearing in the limelight as apostles, they have returned to obscurity.

But is this not a comfort? How many of us can claim any degree of public fame? And even if we can, will it not be the case that after 100 years we too shall be forgotten?

Let's put it like this: if God be God, and if he is our creator and redeemer, then are we not held within the mind and love of God this side of the grave and beyond? We are part of God's creation, we are his children, we are his offspring, and so it is not our own so-called importance or status that matter; what matters is that we are bound up in the life of God now and always. And for that gracious and abundant gift, created for us by and through Jesus Christ, we should offer our heartfelt thanks and praise.

Maybe, therefore, Simon and Jude, those elusive, unknowable saints, have a message for us, after all.

Christopher Herbert

Hymn suggestions

All for Jesus, all for Jesus; We sing for all the unsung saints; For all thy saints, O Lord; Blessed are the pure in heart.

All Saints' Day   1 November
Letting the Light Through
Dan. 7.1–3, 15–18; Ps. 149; Eph. 1.11–end; **Luke 6.20–31**

Saints aren't cool. Except those that give their name to football clubs. They can remind us of remote and intimidating figures, unctuous, interfering, killjoys. Piety isn't respected any more. The idea of the saint lacks street cred.

Today's Gospel, the opening words of the Sermon on the Mount, are some of the most well-known words of Jesus. Comfortable words for the poor, for mourners, the hungry, those who are reviled, but deeply threatening to the rest of us. They are a set of snapshots of an alternative lifestyle – a way of life that is unfashionable, countercultural, at odds with the self-centred lifestyle.

That's the prospectus for saints. They're not people who feature in *The Sunday Times* list of wealthy. A rich businessman remarked to Mother Teresa, 'I wouldn't do your job for a million dollars.' 'Neither would I,' she quipped.

But saints aren't just special people, remembered in church calendars. They're not necessarily pious, they haven't allowed their religion to take over their humanity.

Like a clear-glass window

A mother was pointing out to her little daughter the names of the saints depicted in the windows in their church. 'I see,' said, the little girl. 'Saints are people who let the light through.' Saints are like a window, not even a glorious stained-glass window, but a clear-glass window. You don't even notice it at first. You only know the light. It's the very transparency that enables it to let the light through. Those glossy, heavily adorned personalities are artificial light. They switch on and off at will. But saints are people who are rounded, consistent, whole. They are attractive, they communicate by their life, they cross all barriers. And through the saints, as the hymn 'Rejoice in God's saints' puts it, we learn how to praise. They are the evidence, the really unanswerable evidence that God's radical alternative is possible in the messiness of the world. If they're too complete in themselves, invincible in their own giftedness, self-sustaining so that they have no need of God, they only illuminate themselves.

Feeling good and bad

'Good people make us feel bad; saints make us feel good.' One bishop who had met Mother Teresa said that she made you feel big and small at the same time. Small, yes, challenged, disturbed, a little shamed. But made you feel big as well, showing you what you can become. We're not asked to be heroic, but to let God's light and love through. But saints are not just people in stained glass – they are often ordinary people, acting in extraordinary ways. The ones that speak most clearly to us are the ones who in themselves are weak and vulnerable, beset by temptation, softened by sin and with a background that, if they were famous, would give any gossip columnist a field day.

We're to celebrate saints, but also to be saints ourselves, windows that let in the light. Pope John Paul said:

We need heralds of the gospel who are experts in humanity, who know the depth of the human heart, who can share the joys and hopes, the agonies and distress of the people, but who are at the same time contemplatives who have fallen in love with God. For this we need saints today.

And we, with all the saints, are called to live out the alternative reality we have in Christ. Not to conform, but 'to be transformed by the renewing of our minds'. Called with all the saints to make real and evident and visible the alternative life in Christ that will defeat the expiring, predictable, prevailing world order.

Roger Spiller

Hymn suggestions

Blest are the pure in heart; For all the saints; Rejoice in God's saints today and all days! Ye watchers and ye holy ones.

Commemoration of the Faithful Departed (All Souls' Day)   2 November
Letting Go
Lam. 3.17–26, 31–33, *or* Wisd. 3.1–9; Ps. 23, *or* 27.1–6, 16–end; **Rom. 5.5–11**, *or* 1 Pet. 1.3–9; John 5.19–25, *or* John 6.37–40

The experience of bereavement touches nearly every single one of us. We know that death is an inevitable part of the human condition. But nothing can prepare us for the depth of our pain and loss. We feel alone, isolated, devastated, as if like an amputation part of ourselves has been torn away leaving us crippled, drained and empty. Every loss brings its own unique kind of grieving: the loss of a baby or child with a life that had barely had a chance to unfold; the dissolution of a lifelong marriage partnership, where everything was done together; the loss of someone on the threshold of an exciting new path; the death of a mother with a young family who will not see her children grow up, and whose children will be deprived of her love and perhaps, in time, even of any memory of her; the loss of one's elderly parent that signals the end of an era and reminds us of our own mortality; the death to older parents of a son or daughter who could have expected to outlive them; sudden death that leaves us shocked and numb; the long, harrowing, slow wait for an expected death.

When we have invested so much of ourselves, our love, our hopes, our dreams, in a relationship, then the shattering of that relationship removes the foundations of our world. That's why the Bible calls death the enemy. For it outrages and cheats and deprives us of our most treasured relationships. And in calling death the enemy, we are given permission to acknowledge how deeply we've been hurt and how much we have lost – to project our rage and anger and lament at God that such devastation should be visited upon us.

Letting go

Loss will leave permanent scar tissue in our hearts, but we have finally to let go. Denial or evasion will be deeply damaging. We have to let go even though every opportunity to move on and rebuild lives will seem unwelcome, premature, and the chance of new friendships, new pleasures will seem like a betrayal of the one whose life was wedded inseparably to our own. But after a time, we begin to find healing; the ragged, dismembered half of our life that seemed brutally torn away from us will be healed, and can lead to a bigger, richer self. It will be hard for some of you who are in the early weeks and months of loss ever to believe that you will find healing and happiness. Others of you will have felt you've begun to rebuild your lives, only to find how, after months and years, that sense of loss will steal up upon you like a great ocean wave and overwhelm you. An anniversary, some news we long to share, a piece of music, the striking of Big Ben on New Year's night that puts our loved one for ever in the past – anything can show the rawness of the wound we thought was beginning to be healed. But we do have to let them go, in the words of the poet May Sarton:

If I can let you go as trees let go
Their leaves, so casually, one by one;
If I can come to know what they do know,
That fall is the release, the consummation,
Then fear of time and the uncertain fruit
Would not distemper the great lucid skies
This strangest autumn, mellow and acute . . .
Love will endure – if I can let you go.[31]

Hope through Christ

This is also the time when the Church celebrates the communion of saints, known and unknown, ordinary and extraordinary – men and women and children and young people who experience God's cherishing and live in the light of his presence; whose lives radiate light and hope upon all who live in this twilight world. It declares to us that nothing is lost. Our loved ones live on in our hearts, and we give thanks to God for every remembrance of them.

If there's any reason to embrace the future with hope, it can only be because of what happened on one Friday afternoon, when, from the sixth hour to the ninth, 'there was darkness over all the land', for in that impenetrable darkness Jesus let go and handed himself over to his Father, and God met him on the other side of death and raised him to new life. And so the heart of darkness, of loss and bereavement, has become for us too, as for Jesus, the very place where life and hope are born.

This is the ground of hope – that nothing can separate us from God's love, and that loss is the prelude to gain and life. That emboldens us to hand over not only our loved ones but to begin to let go of our own selves. For, those who have learnt best how to die are those who have learnt to let go, in the course of their life, a thousand small attachments; each letting go is a small rehearsal of the time when we must let go of everything and hand ourselves over finally to God.

Nothing can separate us from the love of God, neither death nor life . . . nor anything else in all creation.

John Knox expressed it thus:

> The Spirit has created a relationship between us and God which makes itself felt as having no temporary terminus at all. We know that we shall always be loved of God. We know this, not because of anything about us, but because it is God who loves us. We know he will hold us forever in his hand. We know this, not because it is we who are held, but because it is his hand which holds us. We know that we cannot drift beyond his care, not because we see an end to how far we can wander or be carried, but because we know his care can be subject to no limits whatsoever. Nothing can separate us from the love of God, neither life nor death.[32]

Thanks be to God.

Roger Spiller

Hymn suggestions

O love that wilt not let me go; Lord, if faith is disenchanted; The Lord's my shepherd; Thine be the glory.

St Andrew the Apostle   30 November
A Great Networker

Isa. 52.7–10; Ps. 19.1–6; Rom. 10.12–18; **Matt. 4.18–22**

Any Scottish people in? Andrew is not just the patron saint of Scotland, but also of Georgia, the Ukraine, Russia, Greece and Cyprus – as well as fishermen and fishmongers.

Andrew was, of course, the brother of Simon Peter, and, as we just heard, one of the first disciples to be called by Jesus to follow him.

In fact, that's one of his names – 'First-Called'. They were from a place called Bethsaida in Galilee, but at the time of Jesus' ministry they were living at a house in Capernaum.

The call of Andrew

There he was, with his brother, on the shore of the Sea of Galilee, casting their nets into the water, when along walks this young man, who says 'Come, follow me!' It seems so simple. What was it, we might wonder, that compelled them to immediately leave their nets and follow Jesus?

In John's Gospel we get a slightly different account, and a bit more information. Here we are told that Andrew was one of two disciples of John the Baptist – when Jesus passes by, and John says, 'Look, the lamb of God!' And they begin to follow Jesus, and Jesus turns round to them and says, 'What do you want?' And they end up spending the day with Jesus. And then Andrew goes and tells his brother Peter, 'We've found the messiah!', and he brought Peter to Jesus.

It's not entirely obvious how these two accounts fit together. I think they're both true. I tend to think that John's account gives the earlier events. So that when Jesus calls Andrew and Peter by the Sea of Galilee, Andrew at least has already met him and spent a bit of time with him. The way had been prepared. Who prepared the way for us? Whose call might we play a part in?

Why give up?

But nevertheless we might ask, 'Why do people give up things?' What would make someone give up what they know, their jobs, their security? What makes someone leave behind a career in order to become a vicar? What makes someone give up their time in order to serve? What could have that effect? And the answer can only be the person of Jesus – the astonishing magnetism of his presence and personality.

This can be known and felt today, as we read stories about him in the Gospels, as we pray to know him better. Sometimes the call to follow comes slowly, sometimes dramatically. We won't all be called to change jobs or give up careers, but eventually, whether suddenly or slowly, we become aware of his call to follow him.

We won't necessarily know where that will lead. 'You'll be catching people!' Jesus said to Andrew and Peter. I wonder what they thought he meant? How would the people in question feel about this?

Did Andrew and his brother Simon Peter have any inkling that they would end up crucified like the person who was asking them to follow him (Peter upside down, and Andrew on a diagonal cross)? No, of course not. God, in his mercy, only reveals things little by little. Could Peter have guessed that there would be a great church in Rome dedicated to his memory? Could Andrew have supposed that whole countries – Scotland, of course, but also Greece, Russia, and so on – would take him as their patron saint? No, of course not. They couldn't have seen the glory or the pain. They only saw him, and that was enough.

And for Andrew especially, this call, this call to catch people, right away, causes him to want to bring others to Jesus. This is what we see when he spends the day with Jesus and then he can't wait to tell his brother Peter, and to bring him to Jesus too. Andrew is the one who finds the small boy with his five loaves and two fishes – and brings him to Jesus. And later on, when there are some Greeks at a festival who hear about Jesus, and they come to Philip and say, 'We want to see Jesus', and Philip tells Andrew and they tell Jesus. So Andrew brought people to Jesus. And that's what he spent his life doing.

And we might ask ourselves – who are we going to bring to Jesus? Who are we going to bring to Jesus in prayer? Who might we invite to church this Christmas time? Whose story might we play a small part in? It might be the beginning of something life-changing?

John Taylor

Jesus calls us o'er the tumult; Will you come and follow me?; Dear Lord and Father of mankind; Let our choirs new anthems raise.

Harvest Festival
The Anonymous Giver
Deut. 26.1–11; Ps. 100; Phil. 4.4–9, *or* Rev. 14.14–18;
John 6.25–35

No place for thanks in the food chain

All good gifts around us are sent from heaven above. Really, do you believe that? Do you thank God, when you're at the checkout? I know I don't. And even if you do, we can be sure that most people don't. We simply don't see ourselves as beneficiaries of gifts, but as purchasers of commodities. Not sent from heaven but delivered to our supermarket. Farmers and agriculturalists are more directly dependent on the elemental forces of nature, the weather, seasonal variations and the natural world than the rest of us. That close connection with nature can lead to wonder and even to gratitude. But it exposes the unpredictable character of nature and the natural order. The Gospel tells us not to be concerned with food, drink, clothing. Try telling that to the larger numbers of people having to rely on food banks.

Of course, harvest festival is a warm and nostalgic fixture, recalling memories of an idyllic past. But is that all that's to be said about harvest? Must we jettison once and for all the idea that God is the 'maker of all things bright and good'?

God's place

We can't think of God as being one cog in the food chain. God, the concept of God, implies a being who is more than another cause or force within the universe alongside others. God is that supreme agency who sustains all the processes of nature, without master-minding every one. God isn't a control freak. God makes the world make itself. Not that the world is left to run on its own. The world is not just running its course, winding down like some cosmic clock, left to itself. Creation didn't just happen once, but God goes on creating. He's like the composer, or playwright in residence – reworking, re-creating as we go. The world is being held in being, day by day, minute by minute. In the words of Gerard Manley Hopkins, 'There lives the dearest freshness deep down things.'[33] And believers claim that great, climactic events like the Exodus, the life of Jesus, the resurrection are the unmistakable clues that reveal him.

The anonymous Giver

But there's nothing to compel us to recognize God as the Giver. Like the Jews who disputed with Jesus in our Gospel, it was more natural for them to credit Moses for procuring bread in the desert to give the gratitude to God where it properly belonged. Why didn't God tie his gifts more closely to himself, so we couldn't receive the gift without recognizing the Giver? When I was on the staff of a large church, returning home after the midnight service, my clergy colleagues and I would find an envelope through our letterboxes with bank notes as a gift. We tried to speculate as to who this anonymous giver might be, but we had no idea and would never know who the giver might be.

But think, had we have known, it would have completely changed our relationship with the person. The balance of power relations would have shifted, even if we tried not to treat them differently. We would have felt a sense of indebtedness to the person; our freedom would have been restricted. Instead, the experience suggested that we should treat everybody we met as special, as a giver, as indeed they are.

God is the anonymous Giver, who stands behind and with and under his creation, but he doesn't leave poster notes reminding us to thank him, just hints and glimpses, tell-tale signs of his character for those with eyes to see. His love means that he also gives us freedom, freedom even to doubt his goodness or reality. And God doesn't deprive us of his gifts when we fail to give him thanks and treat them as our right.

There is a story about a man who wanted to see and hear God. So he went out to a hilltop and yelled and pleaded with God: 'Speak to me!' And a bird sang. But he missed the answer, and he again begged God to speak to him, and all he heard was the sound of children playing in the distance. 'Please, God, touch me!' he cried, and the wind blew across his cheek. And discouraged at not having his plea answered, the man prayed, 'God, show yourself to me!' And a butterfly flew across his path. And when he got home, convinced that God had forsaken him, his daughter ran out to greet him, but he still felt abandoned by God. Seen aright, anything can be a gift from God.

When we take out a packet of beans, a tin of soup, or smell the smell of 'mellow fruitfulness', as we do in church this morning, we may not immediately think of God. But the inherent fruitfulness of the earth, the variations of the seasons and the weather, the labours of farmers, distributors, retailers, the fact that there is a world at all rather than nothing, and the fact that we, of all people, are alive and blessed, and that this is a new day, is cause for living thankfully.

God's supply chain

God's gifts flow to us but they shouldn't stop there. They must be passed on. Ghandi said, 'To those without food, bread is the only form in which God dares to appear.' The hungry have a double deprivation – they are deprived of food, and they are deprived of the chances that we have to rejoice in God's provision. Food is political, and our giving will take the form of political choices and actions.

Harvest, then, invites us to see life not just as a given but as a *gift*. If we see all of life as gift, free, unconditional, undeserved, our life and our view of life will change for ever. The whole of life will be lived in a vital, new relationship. We'll recognize the Giver behind his gifts, and love the Giver for the sake of Godself. And we will be channels of his gifts to others.

Roger Spiller

Hymn suggestions

Come, ye thankful people, come; Praise and thanksgiving; For the fruits of all creation; O Lord my God, when I in awesome wonder.

All-Age Talks

Nativity or Crib Service

Preparation

You will need: a selection of nativity scenes (Christmas card images are fine, though you might want to include the odd 3D nativity set too, and you may also want to refer to your church's crib scene).

If you choose to extend the talk with the optional activity at the end, you will also need enough paper cut-out people and pens for your congregation to have one each.

Delivering the talk

If your service includes a nativity play, it can work well if your talk takes place while the participants are still 'in situ' as a tableau at the front of the church.

Begin with a crib scene. Depending on what kind of crib scene you are using as your main focus, you might say something like one of the following:

- *If you have just completed a nativity play*:
  What a wonderful play! Well done everyone! We've told the Christmas story, and we've ended up with a 'live' crib scene here at the front just like the ones we see on our Christmas cards.
- *If you are using a large crib scene in church*:
  I want you to gather around if you can, and have a good look at the crib scene here by the lectern (or wherever it is – most churches have one somewhere).
- *If you're primarily focusing on the nativity scenes on Christmas cards*:
  I'm going to pass around some Christmas pictures – crib scenes from Christmas cards that I've received. Have a good look at them.

You can have more than one focus – it's fine to pass around Christmas cards as well as look at the church crib scene or the 'live' tableau at the end of a play. How you decide to do it will probably be determined by how large your congregation is, and the layout of your church, as well as what has happened earlier in the service.

Whatever nativity scene you use as your focus, encourage people to have a good look, get them to engage with what they are seeing, identify the characters, wonder who is there and whether anyone is missing. If you have people with visual impairments you might like to make sure they get a 3D set to touch or hold. Younger children might enjoy interacting with a knitted nativity set. Make it as interactive as possible.

Then, as you start to interact with people, talking about what they're seeing, you can start to weave in the following points:

- In some traditions, nativity scenes always have extra characters in them – there's often a boy and a dog, and a man carrying a string of onions! I wonder who they are? They're not in the Bible, but somehow they've found the baby Jesus and have come to worship him too. *If you can get hold of a picture that includes these figures, you might like to circulate it.*

- Look carefully at the nativity scenes. Everyone is gathered around the manger with the baby Jesus, but there's always a gap in the crowd, there's always room for one more person to go and kneel before Jesus and worship him. *Do make sure this is true for the images you're using – it is almost invariably true, but I'm sure there are exceptions that prove the rule.*

- There's room for the donkey, for the wise men's camels, and probably a few sheep too. There's room for the man with the onions, the boy and the dog if they were to turn up. There's room for the innkeeper and his family. There's room for anyone who wants to come and find a place here with Jesus.

- There's room for us, too, because Jesus came for all of us. We can be part of the world welcoming Jesus, just as we can respond to Jesus' invitation to us. That's why we can sing, 'Be near me, Lord Jesus, I ask thee to stay close by me for ever and love me, I pray.'

You might like to end the talk by gathering around whatever crib scene you choose, inviting people to imagine being there, that first Christmas, and singing 'Away in a manger'. Or you can do the following extension activity, and then sing the song.

Extension activity

Give out the paper cut-out people and the pens – if you still have children at the front of the church, you can get them to pass round the pens and cut-out people as they return to their seats.

Invite everyone to decorate their paper people as themselves. While they do so, encourage them to talk among themselves about what it might be like to go to the stable and be there with Jesus and the shepherds, wise men, and Mary and Joseph. How would it feel? What would they bring as a gift?

When they're ready, encourage them to bring their paper people to the church's main crib scene, and find a place to add themselves to the gathered figures. Depending on the congregation size, you might want to get creative with where you put people, and make strategic use of Blu-Tak!

You can also have some smaller paper people available for people to take home with them to add to their home crib scenes.

Ally Barrett

Christingle Service

Preparation

You will need: A Christingle for yourself, the means to light it, and a small vial of iron powder (not filings), which can be bought online. You may also need someone to hold the Christingle for you. You will also need to practise beforehand!

Health and safety: Christingles are never risk-free, so it's sensible to set a good example when it comes to health and safety. If you ask someone to hold the Christingle for you, make sure it's an older child or an adult, rather than a younger child, and it's not a bad idea for them to wear some basic safety gear – goggles and gloves – if for no other reason than this will remind the congregation to be careful if they try to replicate the talk at home.

Do they need to have any previous knowledge? This talk outline assumes that the basic symbolism of the Christingle has already been explained earlier in the service. You can find user-friendly explanations on the Children's Society's website.

Will this work anywhere? This talk works best when you are able to move among the congregation, or in a small to medium-sized church. When it has been used successfully in cathedrals and very large churches, the actions have been carried out synchronously by a small team of people in different parts of the building.

And finally: Don't try to use this as an exact script – read it through so you understand how it goes, then make it your own, adapting it to your own style so that you are comfortable speaking without notes, leaving your hands free to do the actions.

Delivering the talk

Start with your vial of iron powder – show it, sprinkle some between your fingers, back into the container. You might like to invite people to wonder with you what it is. Then explain what it is:

> It looks just like dust, doesn't it? In fact, it's what the earth's core is made of. It's iron, the most common element in our planet. It's earth-dust, nothing more; we might remember that the Bible tells of God making the first human being from the dust on the ground – and we have iron in our blood. You can't get anything more earthy than this. It's grey and dull, really – common as muck. It doesn't look like anything special – it's not even brightly coloured like the orange that represents the world in the Christingle. It doesn't look like it's going to do anything amazing. Not on its own, anyway.

Remind everyone that the candle on the Christingle represents Jesus, the Light of the World, who came to shine in all the dark places of the earth. Light your own Christingle, and dim the lights. Wonder aloud:

> What will happen if we introduce the dust of the earth to the light of the world?

Carefully sprinkle some of the iron powder into the flame so that everyone can see – the iron should turn to bright orange sparks, clearly visible in a dark church. Demonstrate this several times, in different parts of the church, so that everyone has had a chance to see it. Delight in the sparkles, along with your congregation.

The dust of the earth seems to come alive when it touches the light of Christ – Jesus came into the world to bring it to life, to bring energy and joy to places that were grey and lifeless. When Jesus said 'I am the light of the world', he meant that he was bringing the light of heaven right into the earth's darkness. When he said 'You are the light of the world', he meant that he could transform our dull dustiness into bright shining sparks of God's love in the world! Reminding us that although we're sort of made of dust, it's actually stardust; reminding us that the God who made us made the universe – all the stars and planets and the space between – and that there's a special place in that universe for each of us.

At this service, we turn from dust to sparkles! The light of Jesus is with us, and is bringing us to life all the time, so that we can bring his light and life to the dark places of this world. That's our life's work, and we do it in the transforming love and power of Jesus. So today and every day, let's shine as lights in the world!

As an added bonus, here's an extra verse you can add if you are singing 'This little light of mine', that reflects the message of the talk:

When I am feeling dull and grey,
and sunshine seems so far away,
when I don't know quite where to start,
I remember the stardust in my heart:
all it needs is a tiny spark
to get me shining in the dark.
So Jesus, give me your fire divine
to let my little light shine!

If the collection in your service is in aid of the Children's Society, you may wish to include something about the work of the charity in the service, either as a separate talk or as part of the talk above. The most natural way to do this is to reflect on how the charity brings the light and love of Christ to children in trouble, whose lives are impoverished, troubled, or in danger, enabling them to 'come to life' and fulfil their potential.

Ally Barrett

Notes

1 P. T. Forsyth, *Positive Preaching and the Modern Mind*, London: Independent Press, 1907, p. 37.
2 Second Helvetic Confession (1562, revised 1564).
3 C. K. Barrett, *A Commentary on the First Epistle to the Corinthians*, 2nd edn, London: A & C Black, 1971.
4 Simone Weil, *Gravity and Grace*, Abingdon: Routledge, 2002.
5 T. S. Eliot, *The Rock*, Chorus I.
6 I am indebted for this concept to Dietrich Bonhoeffer, *Creation and Fall*, New York: Macmillan, 1959.
7 C. S. Lewis, *Surprised by Joy*, London: Collins, 2012, p. 266.
8 Annie Dillard, *Pilgrim at Tinker Creek*, London: Picador, 1976, p. 182.
9 R. S. Thomas, 'Mediations', in *Collected Poems: 1945–1990*, London: Phoenix Press, 2001, p. 275.
10 T. S. Eliot, *Four Quartets: Burnt Norton*, I, London: Faber and Faber, 1944.
11 Henri Nouwen, *The Return of the Prodigal Son*, London: Darton, Longman & Todd, 1994, p. 122.
12 Cited by Kenneth E. Bailey, *Jesus Through Middle Eastern Eyes*, London: SPCK, 2008, p. 418.
13 Elizabeth Rooney, 'Hurting', *A Widening Light: Poems of the Incarnation*, Wheaton, IL: Harold Shaw, 1984, p. 99.
14 From the hymn 'The Royal Banners forward go'.
15 Sydney Evans, 'Christian Ministry to the Dying', *Expository Times* 78:2 (October 1966), p. 8.
16 E. V. Rieu, *The Four Gospels*, Harmondsworth: Penguin Books, 1952.
17 Albert Schweitzer, *Quest of the Historical Jesus*, trans. I. H. Hoover, New York: Dover Publications, 2005.
18 John Calvin, *Institutes of Religion*, II.16.16.
19 John Calvin, *Corpus Reformatorum*, 37.48.
20 John Henry Newman, *Parochial and Plain Sermons*, Vol. 6, London: Rivingtons, 1870, p. 214.
21 I am indebted for this image to Ronald Rolheiser, *Seeking Spirituality*, London: Hodder & Stoughton, 1998.
22 Hymn by John L. Bell, 'Will you come and follow me' (1987).

23 *Common Worship: Services and Prayers for the Church of England*, London: Church House Publishing, 2000, p. 292. © The Archbishops' Council 2000.

24 Cited in James Lawrence, *Growing Leaders: Reflections on Leadership, Life and Jesus*, Oxford: Bible Reading Fellowship, 2004.

25 The subdivisions are the names Eugene Lowry gives to his narrative sermon structure, known as 'Lowry's Loop'.

26 Sermon on the Solemnity of the Epiphany.

27 David H. Jensen, *Graced Vulnerability: A Theology of Childhood*, Cleveland, OH: Pilgrim Press, 2005.

28 Jerome Murphy-O'Connor, *Oxford Archaeological Guide to the Holy Land*, Oxford: Oxford University Press, 1998, p. 45.

29 T. S. Eliot, *Four Quartets: East Coker*, London: Faber and Faber, 1944.

30 Fynn (Sydney Hopkins), *Mister God, This is Anna*, London: William Collins & Sons, 1974.

31 May Sarton, 'The Autumn Sonnets', I, in *Collected Poems 1930–1973*, New York: W. W. Norton & Co., 1974.

32 John Knox, *Christ and the Hope of Glory*, Nashville, TN: Abingdon Press, 1960, pp. 43f.

33 From Gerard Manley Hopkins, 'God's Grandeur'.

373

Acknowledgement of Sources

The author and publisher acknowledge with thanks permission to us the following text under copyright:

'Autumn Sonnet' by May Sarton (Copyright May Sarton). Reproduced by permission of A.M. Heath & Co. Ltd.

Quote from the poem 'Hurting' by Elizabeth B. Rooney. Used by permission of the Elizabeth B. Rooney Family Trust.

'Ann Griffith' by R.S. Thomas in *Collected Poems: 1945–1990*, Bloodaxe Books, 1993. Used by permission of the Estate of R.S. Thomas.

Four Quartets: East Coker, T.S. Eliot, Faber and Faber, 1944. Permission applied for.

Four Quartets: Burnt Norton, T.S. Eliot, Faber and Faber, 1944. Permission applied for.

Index of Names and Subjects

 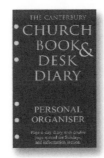 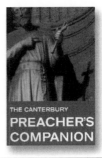

Advance order for the 2020 editions *(available May 2019)*

quantity

Prices are subject to confirmation and may be changed without notice

CANTERBURY CHURCH BOOK & DESK DIARY 2020 *Hardback* £19.99 + p&p* ....

CANTERBURY CHURCH BOOK & DESK DIARY 2020 *Personal Organiser* (A5) £19.99 + p&p* ....

CANTERBURY PREACHER'S COMPANION 2020 *Paperback* £19.99 + p&p* ....

For details of special discounted prices for purchasing the above in any combinations
or in bulk, please contact the publisher's Norwich office as shown below.

Order additional copies of the 2019 editions

Subject to stock availability

Hardback Diary **£19.99*** .... Organiser **£19.99*** ....

Preacher's Companion **£19.99*** .... A5 Personal Organiser **£19.99*** ....

Ask for details of discounted prices for bulk orders of 6+ copies of any individual title when ordered direct from the Publisher.

Sub-total £................

*Plus **£2.50** per order to cover post and packing (UK only): £................

All orders over £50 are sent POST FREE to any UK address.
Contact the Publishers office for details of overseas carriage.

TOTAL AMOUNT TO PAY: £................

I wish to pay by ...

... **CHEQUE** for £ .... made payable to **Hymns Ancient and Modern Ltd**

... **CREDIT CARD** All leading credit and debit cards accepted *(not American Express or Diners Club)*
Your credit card will not be debited until the books are despatched.

Card number: .... Expiry: ____ /____

Issue No: ____ Valid from: ____ /____

Switch or Maestro only

Signature of
cardholder: .... Security code:_____

Last three digits on signature panel

Please PRINT all details below.

Title: .... Name: ....

Delivery address: ....

....

....

.... Post Code: ....

Telephone or e-mail: .... Date: ....

Please ensure you have ordered the edition you require for the correct year. No liability will be accepted for incorrect orders

Return this order form or a photocopy – with details of payment – to

Norwich Books and Music, 13A Hellesdon Park Road, Norwich NR6 5DR

Telephone: 01603 785900 Fax: 01603 785915 Website: www.canterburypress.co.uk